MicroPython for the Internet of Things

A Beginner's Guide to Programming with Python on Microcontrollers

Second Edition

Charles Bell

Apress®

MicroPython for the Internet of Things: A Beginner's Guide to Programming with Python on Microcontrollers, Second Edition

Charles Bell
Warsaw, VA, USA

ISBN-13 (pbk): 978-1-4842-9860-2   ISBN-13 (electronic): 978-1-4842-9861-9
https://doi.org/10.1007/978-1-4842-9861-9

Managing Director, Apress Media LLC: Welmoed Spahr
Acquisitions Editor: Mark Powers
Development Editor: James Markham
Coordinating Editor: Jessica Vakili

Cover designed by eStudioCalamar

Cover image by bert b@Unsplash.com

Distributed to the book trade worldwide by Apress Media, LLC, 1 New York Plaza, New York, NY 10004, U.S.A. Phone 1-800-SPRINGER, fax (201) 348-4505, e-mail orders-ny@springer-sbm.com, or visit www. springeronline.com. Apress Media, LLC is a California LLC and the sole member (owner) is Springer Science + Business Media Finance Inc (SSBM Finance Inc). SSBM Finance Inc is a **Delaware** corporation.

For information on translations, please e-mail booktranslations@springernature.com; for reprint, paperback, or audio rights, please e-mail bookpermissions@springernature.com.

Apress titles may be purchased in bulk for academic, corporate, or promotional use. eBook versions and licenses are also available for most titles. For more information, reference our Print and eBook Bulk Sales web page at http://www.apress.com/bulk-sales.

Any source code or other supplementary material referenced by the author in this book is available to readers on GitHub (https://github.com/Apress). For more detailed information, please visit https://www.apress.com/gp/services/source-code.

Paper in this product is recyclable

I dedicate this book to my big sister for instilling in me the thirst for knowledge by teaching me to read the dictionary at an early age.

Table of Contents

About the Author

Charles Bell conducts research in emerging technologies. He is a member of the Oracle MySQL Development team for the Oracle Cloud Infrastructure as a principal developer assisting in the development of high availability and backup solutions for the MySQL HeatWave Service in OCI. He lives in a small town in rural Virginia with his loving wife. Dr. Bell received his doctorate degree in engineering from Virginia Commonwealth University in 2005. His research interests include database systems, software engineering, sensor networks, and 3D printing. He spends his limited free time as a practicing maker, focusing on microcontroller and 3D printers and printing projects.

About the Technical Reviewer

Sai Yamanoor is an embedded engineer based in Oakland, CA. He has over ten years of experience as an embedded systems expert, working on hardware and software design and implementations. He is a coauthor of three books on using Raspberry Pi to execute DIY projects, and he has also presented a Personal Health Dashboard at Maker Faires across the country. Sai is also working on projects to improve quality of life (QoL) for people with chronic health conditions. Check out his projects at https://saiyamanoor.com.

Acknowledgments

I would like to thank all of the many talented and energetic professionals at Apress. I appreciate the understanding and patience of my editor, Mark Powers, and production editor, Nirmal Selvaraj. They were instrumental in the success of this project. I would also like to thank the army of publishing professionals at Apress for making me look so good in print with a special thank you to the reviewers for their wise counsel and gentle nudges in the right direction. Thank you all very much!

Most importantly, I want to thank my wife, Annette, for her unending patience and understanding while I spent so much time with my laptop.

Introduction

Internet of Things (IoT) solutions are not nearly as complicated as the name may seem to indicate. Indeed, the IoT is largely another name for what we have already been doing. You may have heard of "connected devices" or "Internet-ready" or even "cloud-enabled." All of these refer to the same thing – be it a single device such as a toaster or a plant monitor or a complex, multidevice product like home automation solutions. They all share one thing in common: they can be accessed via the Internet to either display data or interact with the devices directly. The trick is applying knowledge of technologies to leverage them to the best advantages for your IoT solution. In this book, we explore how to build IoT solutions using an easy-to-understand programming language named MicroPython running on small, dedicated microcontroller boards.

Intended Audience

I wrote this book to share my passion for Python and IoT solutions. I especially wanted to show how anyone can program their own IoT solutions in Python using MicroPython on small microcontroller boards, such as the Raspberry Pi Pico and Arduino Nano RP2040 Connect. The intended audience therefore includes anyone interested in learning how to build IoT solutions, hobbyists, and enthusiasts who don't want to spend a lot of time learning a complicated programming language to control hardware through software in IoT solutions.

How This Book Is Structured

The book was written to guide the reader from a general knowledge of microcontrollers and MicroPython to expertise in developing MicroPython solutions for the IoT. The first several chapters cover general topics including a short introduction to the Internet of Things, what microcontroller boards are available, as well as how MicroPython works. Later chapters present a tutorial on programming in MicroPython as well as an introduction to electronics. This is followed by four projects that you can implement to learn how to build basic MicroPython IoT solutions. We move on from there to learn how to use cloud systems to make our IoT solutions useful. Throughout the book are examples of how to implement many of the concepts presented. The following is a brief overview of each chapter included in this book:

- *Chapter 1, "What Is the Internet of Things?"*: This chapter presents and answers the questions of what the IoT is and how IoT solutions are constructed. You are introduced to some terminology to describe the architecture of IoT solutions as well as some examples of well-known IoT solutions. The chapter concludes with a demonstration of MicroPython.

- *Chapter 2, "Introducing MicroPython"*: This chapter presents an overview of what MicroPython is and how you can get started using MicroPython boards.

- *Chapter 3, "MicroPython Hardware"*: This chapter discusses some of the hardware available for MicroPython, including the Raspberry Pi Pico, Arduino Nano RP2040 Connect, and several other alternative boards. The chapter also presents some of the accessories available for each board.

- *Chapter 4, "How to Program in MicroPython"*: This chapter presents a tutorial on learning to program in MicroPython. It covers all of the basics of the language you need to get started writing your own MicroPython scripts.

- *Chapter 5, "MicroPython Libraries"*: This chapter presents an overview of the various MicroPython libraries available for use in your scripts. It includes many examples of how to get started using the libraries to interface with hardware.

- *Chapter 6, "Low-Level Hardware Support"*: This chapter presents an overview of the low-level hardware abstractions available for the Pyboard and WiPy ports of MicroPython. The differences of the libraries are presented along with several complete examples to demonstrate the functionality.

- *Chapter 7, "Electronics for Beginners"*: This chapter presents a short introduction to electronics including the types of components you will be using in the book along with a list of recommended tools. The chapter concludes with a survey of the types of sensors available for IoT solutions.

- *Chapter 8, "Project: Hello, World! MicroPython Style"*: This chapter presents a hands-on project to help get you started programming hardware and building MicroPython solutions. The project is a clock programmed in MicroPython using a real-time clock (RTC) module.

- *Chapter 9, "Project: Pedestrian Crossing"*: This chapter presents another hands-on project that interfaces with LEDs and buttons to build a pedestrian stoplight simulation. The project also demonstrates how to control your hardware remotely via a web page.

- *Chapter 10, "Project: Plant Monitoring"*: This chapter presents a more complex hands-on project that demonstrates how to generate sensor data and view it over the Internet. The project is a plant monitoring solution that you can expand from one to many plants.

- *Chapter 11, "Project: Using Weather Sensors"*: This chapter presents the last hands-on project that combines all that you have learned in the book to build a working IoT solution. The project is a small weather sensor node that uses the new Adafruit IO cloud services to store and visualize the data.

- *Chapter 12, "Cloud Computing"*: This chapter introduces cloud computing, including a brief description of the major cloud computing vendors and their services as well as which services you may want to consider for use in your IoT projects.

- *Chapter 13, "Arduino IoT Cloud"*: This chapter presents a tutorial on how to start writing your projects to use two of the major cloud computing services; one is free to use and the other is a paid subscription service. You will see how to get started with each service.

- *Chapter 14, "MQTT with Adafruit IO"*: This chapter takes the project from Chapter 10 and demonstrates how to turn this general project into one you can use the cloud to display results to anyone on the Internet.

- *Chapter 15, "ThingSpeak"*: This chapter expands the project from Chapter 10 to show how you can make use of cloud computing to create impressive visuals and connect the results to other cloud computing services for additional analysis.

- *Chapter 16, "Where to Go from Here"*: This chapter concludes the tour of MicroPython IoT solutions with suggestions for more projects to explore and where to go to find new project ideas including where to look to find answers to questions or problems you may encounter when developing your own MicroPython IoT projects. The chapter also discusses how you can join the community of IoT, MicroPython, and electronics enthusiasts by becoming a Maker.

How to Use This Book

This book is designed to guide you through learning more about what the Internet of Things is, discovering the power of MicroPython, and seeing how to build your own IoT solutions.

If you already have your own Raspberry Pi Pico or Arduino Nano RP2040 Connect board and are familiar with some of the topics early in the book, I recommend you skim them so that you are familiar with the context presented so that the later chapters, especially the examples, are easy to understand and implement on your own. You may also want to read some of the chapters out of order so that you can get your project moving, but I recommend going back to the chapters you skip to ensure you get all of the data presented.

If you are just getting started with MicroPython and microcontrollers, I recommend reading the book in its entirety before developing your own IoT solutions. That said, many of the examples presented in the early chapters are building blocks for what follows in the project chapters.

Downloading the Code

The code for the examples shown in this book is available on the Apress website, `www.apress.com`. You can find a link on the book's information page on the Source Code/Downloads tab. This tab is located in the Related Titles section of the page.

Contacting the Author

Should you have any questions or comments – or even spot a mistake you think I should know about – you can contact me at drcharlesbell@gmail.com.

CHAPTER 1

What Is the Internet of Things?

If you've been watching the technology world lately, chances are you have encountered numerous mentions of the term Internet of Things (IoT). Most media references and company advertisements label this or that as the Internet of Things but with little or no explanation about what it means. Even when you find some depth of what it means, the text tends to focus on the problems and challenges or the promise of making our lives better. Some claim that the Internet of Things will bring about the inevitable evolution of our society as we become more connected to the world around us every day.

However, you can avoid diving into such heady concepts or reciting rhetoric to get started with the Internet of Things. In fact, through the efforts of many open source developers and vendors, you can explore the Internet of Things without intensive training or expensive hardware and software. Best of all, you can explore the Internet of Things without learning much about programming or spending months learning how to code!

This book is intended to be a guide to help you understand the Internet of Things and to begin building solutions that you can use to learn more about the Internet of Things. Since this is a beginner's book, we will examine the programming language and environment, followed by a detailed look at the hardware. We will also learn the basic knowledge of electronics and then explore several projects to help us understand how to work with the software. The final project will bring all the aspects together to help understand the Internet of Things and even how to write custom software for building solutions for the Internet of Things using cloud solutions. Best of all, we do so using one of the easiest programming languages and easy-to-use open source microcontroller boards.

© Charles Bell 2024
C. Bell, *MicroPython for the Internet of Things*, https://doi.org/10.1007/978-1-4842-9861-9_1

So, what is the Internet of Things, hence IoT?[1] Let us begin by explaining what it isn't. The IoT is not a new device, proprietary software, or some new piece of hardware, nor is it a new marketing scheme to sell you more of what you already have by renaming it and pronouncing it "new and improved."[2] While it is true that the IoT employs technology and techniques that already exist, the way they are used and the ability to access the solution from anywhere in the world makes the IoT an exciting concept to explore. Now let's discuss what the IoT is.

The essence of the IoT is interconnected devices that generate and exchange data from observations, facts, and other data, making it available to anyone. While there seem to be some marketing efforts attempting to make anything connected to the Internet an IoT solution or device – not unlike the shameless labeling of everything "cloud" – IoT solutions are designed to make our knowledge of the world around us more timely and relevant by making it possible to get data about anything from anywhere at any time.

As you can imagine, if we were to connect every device around us to the Internet and make sensory data available for those devices, it is clear there is potential for the number of IoT devices to exceed the human population of the planet and for the data generated to rapidly exceed the capabilities of all but the most sophisticated database systems. These concepts are commonly known as addressability and big data and are two of the most active and debated topics in IoT.

However, the IoT is all about understanding the world around us. That is, we can leverage the data to make our world and our understanding of it better.

The Internet of Things and You

How do we observe the world around us? The human body is a marvel of ingenious sensory apparatus that allows us to see, hear, taste, and even feel through touch anything we encounter. Even our brains can store visual and auditory events recalling them at will. IoT solutions mimic many of these sensory capabilities and therefore can become an extension of our own abilities. While that may sound a bit grandiose (and it is), IoT solutions can record observations in the form of data from one or more sensors and make them available for viewing by anyone anywhere via the Internet.

---

[1] https://en.wikipedia.org/wiki/Internet_of_Things
[2] For example, everything seems to be cloud-this, cloud-that when nothing was changed.

Sensors are devices that produce either analog or digital values. We can then use the data collected to draw conclusions about the subject matter. This could be as simple as a sensor to detect when a door, window, or mailbox is opened. In the case of a switch on a mailbox, the knowledge we gain from a simple switch opening or closing (depending on how it is implemented and interpreted) may be used to predict when incoming mail has arrived or when outgoing mail has been picked up. I use the term predict because the sensor (switch) only tells us the door was opened or closed, not that anything was placed in or removed from the mailbox itself – that would require additional sensors.

A more sophisticated example is using a series of sensors to record atmospheric data such as temperature, humidity, barometric pressure, wind speed, ambient light, rainfall, etc., to monitor the weather that allows us to perform analysis on the data to predict trends in weather. That is, we can predict within a reasonable certainty that precipitation is in the area.

Now, add the ability to see this data not only in real time (as it occurs) but also remotely from anywhere in the world, and the solution becomes more than a simple weather station. It becomes a way to observe the weather about one place from anywhere in the world. This example may seem to be a bit commonplace since you can tune into any number of television, web, and radio broadcasts to hear the weather from anywhere in the world. But consider the implications of building such a solution in your home. Now you can see data about the weather in your own home!

In the same way, but perhaps on a smaller scale, we can build solutions to monitor plants to help us understand how often they need water and other nutrients. Or perhaps we can monitor our pets while we are away at work. Further, we can record data about wildlife in our area to better understand our effect on nature.

IoT Is More Than Just Connected to the Internet

If a device is connected to the Internet, does that make it an IoT solution? That depends on whom you ask. Some believe the answer is yes. However, others (such as myself) contend that the answer is not unless there is some benefit from doing so. For example, if you connected your toaster to the Internet, what could be the benefit of doing so? It would be pointless (or at least extremely eccentric) to get a text on your phone from your toaster stating that your toast is ready. So, in this case, the answer is no.

However, if you have persons such as responsible teenagers or perhaps older adults whom you would like to monitor, it may be helpful to be able to check to see how often they use their toaster and when. That is, you can use the data to help you make decisions about their care and safety.

To me, if there is no use for the data, whether it is something that is viewed in real time or is stored for later processing, then simply connecting it to the Internet does not make it an IoT solution. There must be some gain in the use of the device. Thus, being connected to the Internet doesn't make something IoT. Rather, IoT solutions must be those things that provide some meaning – however small that has benefit to someone or some other device or service.

More importantly, whatever we build IoT solutions to do, they allow us to sense the world around us and learn from those observations. The real tricky part is in how the data is collected, stored, and presented. We will see these in practice through examples in later chapters. See the sidebar for an example of a controversial IoT device – a common household appliance.

However, IoT solutions can often take advantage of companies that provide services that can help enhance or provide features you can use in your IoT solutions. These features are commonly called IoT services and range from storage and presentation to the infrastructure services such as hosting.

INTERNET-ENABLED APPLIANCES: MARKETING HYPE?

One of the ideas or concepts that seems to be becoming popular is the connecting of major household appliances to the Internet. While manufacturers may want you to believe this is a new and exciting IoT device, the truth is it is neither a new idea nor is it a world changing IoT solution.

I was fortunate to participate in a design workshop held on the Microsoft campus in the late 1990s. During our tour of the campus, we were introduced to the world's first Internet-enabled refrigerator (also called a smart refrigerator or simply Internet refrigerator).[3] There were sensors in the shelves to detect the weight of food. It was suggested that, with a little ingenuity, one could use the sensors to notify your grocer when your milk supply ran low, which would enable people to have their grocery shopping not only online but also automatic.

---

[3] https://en.wikipedia.org/wiki/Internet_refrigerator

Now, nearly 25 years later, we're seeing manufacturers building refrigerators that connect to the Internet. However, unlike the first smart refrigerator, these new devices are positioned to be a social media focal point for the household. Many don't provide any meaningful data about the contents of the refrigerator outside of the gadget-like ability to see a video image of the contents without opening the door, which could have been solved by installing a glass door.

Suffice to say, IoT enthusiasts like me scratch their heads at how something like this could possibly be useful, much less sell well. Sadly, these new Internet refrigerators do indeed seem to be selling well, but I wonder if consumers have been sucked into the hype. For an interesting commentary on why the Internet refrigerator isn't for you, do a Google search and you'll find a lot of opinions – most negative (and yet, people still buy these things).[4]

Let's judge the Internet refrigerator with my definition of IoT: Does it enhance your life by providing you information about the world around you? Well, if you need to check to see how much milk you have while 3000 miles away from home, then I guess it may be beneficial, but for the multitude of us who prefer to just open the door and look before we go to the store, it may not be an IoT device.

IoT Services

Sadly, there are companies that tout having IoT products and services that are nothing more than marketing hype – much like what some companies have done by prepending "cloud" or appending "for the cloud" to the name. Fortunately, there are some good products and services being built especially for IoT. These range from data storage and hosting to specialized hardware.

Indeed, businesses are adding IoT services to their product offerings faster than anyone can keep up with the latest. And it isn't the usual suspects such as the Internet giants. I have seen IoT solutions and services being offered by Cisco, AT&T, HP, and countless startups and smaller businesses. I use the term IoT vendor to describe those businesses that provide services for IoT solutions.

You may be wondering what these services and products are and why one would consider using them. That is, what is an IoT service and why would you decide to buy it? The biggest reason you may decide to buy a service concerns cost and time to market.

---

[4] www.howtogeek.com/260896/why-buying-a-smart-fridge-is-a-dumb-idea/

If your developers do not have the resources or expertise and obtaining them will require more than the cost of the service, it may be more economical to purchase the service. However, you should also consider any additional software or hardware changes (sometimes called retooling) necessary in the decision. I once encountered a well-meaning and well-documented contracted service that permitted a product to go to market sooner than projected at a massive savings. Sadly, while the champions of that contract won awards for technical achievement, they failed to consider the fact that the systems had to be retooled to use the new service. More specifically, it took longer to adopt the new service than it would have to write one from scratch. So instead of saving money, the organization spent nearly triple and were late to market. Clearly, one must consider all factors.

Similarly, if your time is short or you have hard deadlines to make your solution production ready, it may be quicker to purchase an IoT service rather than create or adapt your own. This may require spending a bit more, but in this case the motivation is time and not (necessarily) cost. Of course, it is a mixture of both cost and time.

So, what are some of the IoT services available? The following lists a few that have emerged in the last few years. It is likely more will be offered as IoT solutions and services mature.

- *Enterprise IoT data hosting and presentation*: Services that allow your users to develop enterprise IoT solutions from connecting to, managing, and customizing data presentation in a friendly form such as graphs, charts, etc.

- *IoT data storage*: Services that permit you to store your IoT data and get simple reports.

- *Networking*: Services that provide networking and similar communication protocols or platforms for IoT. Most specialize in machine-to-machine (M2M) services.

- *IoT hardware platforms*: Vendors that permit you to rapidly develop and prototype IoT devices using a hardware platform and a host of supported modules and tools for building devices ranging from a simple component to a complete device.

Now that we know more about what IoT is, let's look at a few examples of IoT solutions to get a better idea of what IoT solutions can do and how they are employed.

A Brief Look at IoT Solutions

An IoT solution is simply a set of devices designed to produce, consume, or present data about some event or series of events or observations. This can include devices that generate data such as a sensor, devices that combine data to deduce something, devices or services designed to tabulate and store the data, and devices or systems designed to present the data. Any of these may be connected to the Internet.

IoT solutions may include several of these qualities whether they are combined into a single device such as a web camera, into a sensor package and monitoring unit such as a weather station, or into a complex system of dedicated sensors, aggregators, data storage, and presentation such as a complete home automation system. Figure 1-1 shows a futuristic picture of all devices everywhere connected to the Internet either to databases, data collectors or integrators, display services, and even other devices.

Figure 1-1. *OnStar App Key Fob Feature[5]*

Let's look at some example IoT solutions. The IoT solutions described in this section are a mix of solutions that should give you an idea of the ranges of sizes and complexities of IoT solutions. I also point out how some of these solutions leverage services from IoT vendors.

---

[5] https://pixabay.com/en/network-IoT-internet-of-things-782707/

Sensor Networks

Sensor networks are one of the most common forms of IoT solutions. Simply stated, sensor networks allow you to observe the world around you and make sense of it. Sensor networks could take the form of a pond monitoring system that alerts you to water level, water purity (contamination), or water temperature, detects predators, or even turns on features automatically such as lighting or feeding the fish in your garden pond.

If you or someone you know has spent any time in a medical facility, chances are a sensor network was employed to monitor body functions such as your body temperature, heart rate, respiratory capacity, or even movement range of your limbs. Modern automobiles also contain sensor networks dedicated to monitoring the engine, climate, and even in some cars road conditions. For example, the lane-warning feature uses sensors (typically a camera, microprocessor, and software) to detect when you drift too far toward lane or road demarcations. Manufacturing plants also employ sensor networks in monitoring and controlling the machines, conveyors, and more. Shipping clearinghouses also employ sensor networks to help route packages to the correct bins and ultimately to the correct trucks or planes for transport.

Thus, sensor networks employ one or more sensors that take measurements (observations) about an event or state and communicate that data to another component or node in the network, which is then presented in some form or another for analysis. Let's look at an example of an important medical IoT solution.

Medical Applications

Medical applications including health monitoring and fitness are gaining a lot of attention as consumer products. These solutions cover a wide range of capabilities such as the fitness features built into the new Apple Watch to Fitness bands that keep track of your workout and even medical applications that help you control life-threatening conditions. For example, there are solutions that can help you manage diabetes.

Diabetes is a disease that affects millions of people worldwide (diabetes.org/). There are several forms: type 1 and type 2. The most serious is type 1 (diabetes.org/diabetes-basics/type-1/?loc=db-slabnav), but type 2 can also be serious if not managed properly. Those afflicted with type 1 diabetes do not produce enough (or any) insulin due to genetic deficiencies, birth defects, or injuries to the pancreas. Insulin is a hormone the body uses to extract a simple sugar called glucose, which is created from sugars and starches, from blood for use in cells. Failure to monitor your blood sugar can result in dangerously low or high blood sugar levels, both of which can be life threatening and if not controlled can cause long-term damage to internal organs, nerves, and other areas. It is a most serious condition.

Type 1 diabetics must monitor their blood glucose to ensure they are using their medications (primarily insulin) properly and balanced with a healthy lifestyle and diet. If their blood glucose levels drop too low or too high, they can suffer from a host of symptoms. Worse, extremely low blood glucose levels are very dangerous and can be fatal.

One of the newest versions of a blood glucose tester consists of a small sensor that is left in the body for as much as a week along with a monitor that connects to the sensor via Bluetooth. You wear the monitor on your body (or keep it within 20 feet at all times). The solution is marketed by Dexcom (dexcom.com/) and is called a continuous glucose monitor (CGM) that permits the patient to share their data to others via their phone. Thus, the patient pairs their CGM with their phone and then shares the data over the Internet to others. This could be loved ones, those that help with their care, or even medical professionals.

Figure 1-2 shows an example of the Dexcom CGM monitor and sensor. The monitor is on the left and the sensor and transmitter are on the right. The sensor is the size of a small syringe needle and remains inserted in the body for up to a week.

Figure 1-2. *Dexcom Continuous Glucose Monitor with Sensor*

A feature called Dexcom Share permits the patient to make their data available to others via an app on their phone. That is, the patient's phone transmits data to the Dexcom cloud servers, which is then sent to anyone who has the Dexcom Share app and has been given permission to see the data. Figure 1-3 shows an example of the Dexcom Share CGM report from the Dexcom Share iOS app, which allows you to easily and quickly check the blood glucose of a friend or loved one.

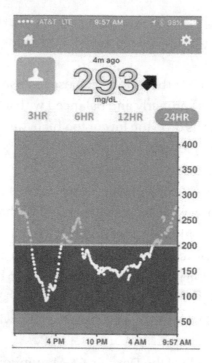

Figure 1-3. *Dexcom Share App Report*

Not only does the app allow the visualization of the data, it can also relay alerts for low or high blood glucose levels, which has profound implications for patients who suffer from additional ailments or complications from diabetes. For example, if the patient's blood glucose level drops while they are alone, incapacitated, or unable to get treatment, loved ones with the Dexcom Share app can respond by checking on the patient and potentially avoiding a critical diabetic event.

While this solution is a single sensor connected to the Internet via a proprietary application, it is an excellent example of a medical IoT device that can enhance the lives of not only the patient but everyone who cares for them.

Dexcom also provides a free Windows application called Dexcom Studio (`http://dexcom.com/dexcom-studio`) to allow patients to see the data their monitors collect and generate a host of reports they can use to see their glucose levels over time. Reports include averages, patterns, daily trends, and more. They can even share their data with their doctor. Figure 1-4 shows an example of the Dexcom Studio with typical data loaded.

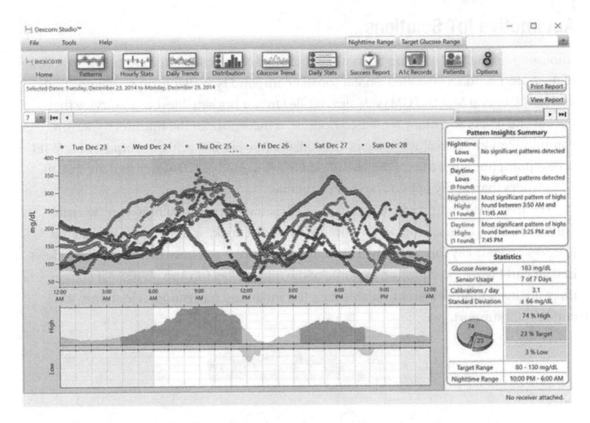

Figure 1-4. *Dexcom Studio*

WHAT ABOUT BLOOD GLUCOSE TESTERS – GLUCOMETERS?

Until solutions like the Dexcom CGM came about, diabetics had to use a manual tester. Traditional blood glucose testers are single-use events that require the patient to prick their finger or arm and draw a small amount of blood onto a test strip. While this device has been used for many years, it is only recently that manufacturers have started making blood glucose testers with memory features and even connectivity to other devices such as laptops or phones. The ultimate evolution of these devices is a solution like Dexcom, which has become a medical IoT device that improves the quality of life for diabetics.

Combined with the programmable alerts, you and your loved ones can help manage the effects of diabetes. If you have a loved one who suffers with diabetes, a CGM is worth every penny for peace of mind alone. This is the true power of IoT materialized in a potentially lifesaving solution.

Automotive IoT Solutions

Another personal IoT solution is the use of Internet-connected automotive features. One of the oldest products is called OnStar (onstar.com) and is available on most late-model and new General Motors (GM) vehicles. While OnStar is a satellite-based service that has several levels and many fee-based options, it incorporates the Internet to permit communication with vehicle owners. Indeed, the newest GM vehicles come with a WiFi access point built into the car! Better still, there are some basic features that are free to GM owners that, in my opinion, are very valuable.

The free, basic features include regular maintenance reports sent to you via email and the ability to use an app on your phone to unlock, lock, and remote start – all the features on your key fob remotely. This is a cool feature if you have ever locked your keys in your car! Figure 1-5 shows an example of the remote key fob app on iOS. Of course, there are even more features available for a fee, including navigation, telephone, WiFi, and on-call support.

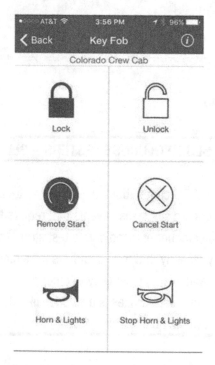

Figure 1-5. *OnStar App Key Fob Feature*

The OnStar app works by connecting to the OnStar services in the cloud, requesting the feature (e.g., unlock) that is sent to the vehicle via the OnStar satellite network. So, it is an excellent example of how IoT solutions use multiple communication protocols.

The feature I like most is the maintenance reports. You will receive an email with an overview of the maintenance status of your vehicle. The report includes such things as oil life, tire pressure, engine and transmission warnings, emissions, air bag, and more. Figure 1-6 shows an excerpt of a typical email you would receive.

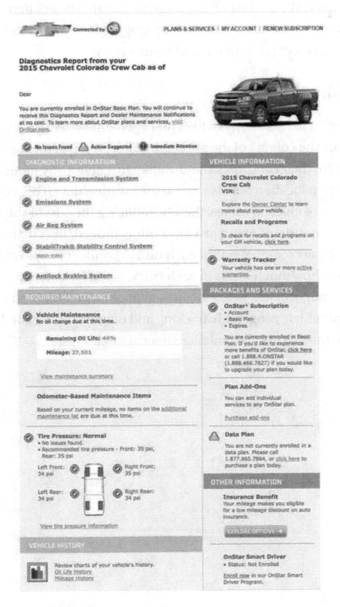

Figure 1-6. *OnStar Maintenance Report*

Notice the information displayed. Actual data is transmitted to OnStar from your vehicle. For example, the odometer reading and tire pressure data are taken directly from the vehicle's onboard data storage. That is, data from the sensors is read and interpreted, and the report is generated for you. This feature demonstrates how automatic compilation of data in an IoT solution can help us keep our vehicles in good mechanical condition with early warning of needed maintenance. This serves us best by helping us keep our vehicles in prime condition and thus in a state of high resell value.

I should note that GM isn't the only automotive manufacturer offering such services. Many others are working on their own solutions ranging from an OnStar-like feature set to solutions that focus on entertainment and connectivity.

Fleet Management

Another example of an IoT solution is a fleet management system. While developed and deployed well before the coining of the phrase, IoT, fleet management systems allow businesses to monitor their cars, trucks, and ships – just about any mobile unit – to not only track their current location but also to use the location data (GPS coordinates taken over time) to plan more efficient routes, thereby reducing the cost of shipment.

Fleet management systems aren't just for routing. Indeed, fleet management systems also allow businesses to monitor each unit to conduct diagnostics. For example, it is possible to know how much fuel is in each truck, when its last maintenance was performed or, more importantly, when the next maintenance is due, and much more. The combination of vehicle geographic tracking and diagnostics is called telematics. Figure 1-7 shows a drawing of a fleet management system.

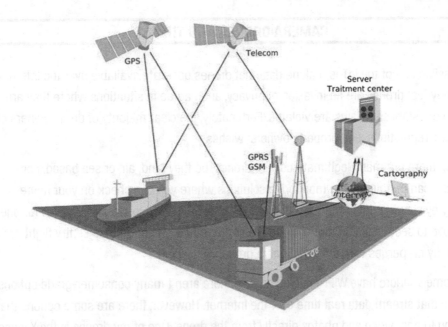

Figure 1-7. *Fleet Management Example*

In the figure, you will see the application of GPS systems to track location as well as satellite communication to transmit additional data such as diagnostics, payload states, and more. All of these ultimately traverse the Internet, and the data becomes accessible by the business analysts.

You may think fleet management systems are only for large shipping companies, but with the proliferation of GPS modules and even the microcontroller market, anyone can create a fleet management system. That is, they don't cost millions of dollars to develop.

For example, if you owned a bicycle delivery company, you could easily incorporate GPS modules with either cellular or wireless connectivity on each delivery person to track their location, average travel time, and more. More specifically, you can use such a solution to minimize delivery times by allowing packages to be handed off from one delivery person to another rather than having them return to the depot each time they complete a set of deliveries.

CAMERA DRONES AND THE IOT

One possible use of the IoT is making data that drones generate available over the Internet. Some may feel drones are an invasion of privacy, and I agree in situations where they are misused or established laws are violated. Fortunately, the clear majority of drone owners obey local laws, regulations, and property owners' wishes.

However, there are many legitimate uses of drones, be they land, air, or sea based. For example, I can imagine home monitoring solutions where you can check on your home remotely by viewing data from fixed cameras as well as data from mobile drones. I for one would love to see a solution that allowed me to program a predetermined sentry flight path to monitor my properties with a flying camera drone.

While some vendors have WiFi-enabled drones, there aren't many consumer-grade options available that stream data real time over the Internet. However, there are some options that allow you to post video and photos directly from the drone. One of my drones is the Yuneec Breeze (`www.yuneec.com/en_US/products/breeze/overview.html`), which allows me to post photos and video collected from the drone to social media. Interestingly, these drones are being called "selfie drones" since they have features that allow autonomous modes, including a mode where the drone follows you filming your antics or circling your position and other interesting features.

While these new drones require a manual action to post data, it is just a matter of time before we see real-time IoT solutions that include drones. Of course, the current controversy and indeed the movement of the US government to register and track drones along with increasing restrictions on their use may limit the expansion of drones and IoT solutions that include drone-acquired data.

IoT and Security

The recent rash of massive data breaches proves that basic security simply wasn't good enough. We've seen everything from outright theft to exploitation of the data stolen from very well-known businesses like Target (over 40 million credit card numbers may have been compromised) and government agencies like the US Office of Personnel Management (over 20 million social security numbers compromised).

IoT solutions are not immune to security threats. Indeed, as IoT solutions become more and more integrated into our lives, so too will our personal data. Thus, security must be taken extremely seriously and built into the solution from the start.

This includes solutions we develop ourselves. More specifically, if you design a weather station for your own use, you should take reasonable steps to ensure the data is protected from both accidental and deliberate exploitation. You may think weather data isn't a high risk but consider the case where you include GPS coordinates for your sensors (a reasonable feature) so that people can see where this weather is being observed. If someone could see that information and determine the solution uses an Internet connection, it is possible they could gain physical access to the Internet device and possibly use it to further penetrate and exploit your systems. Thus, security isn't just about the data; it should encompass all aspects of the solution from data to software to hardware to physical access.

There are four areas where you may want to consider spending extra care ensuring your IoT solution is protected with good security. As you will see, this includes several things you should consider for your existing infrastructure, computers, and even safe computing habits. By leveraging these areas, you will be building a layered approach to security: often called a defense-in-depth method.

DO I REALLY NEED TO WORRY ABOUT SECURITY?

If you're wondering why I've included this section in a beginner's book on the IoT and Python, consider for a moment what you ultimately want to do with the knowledge you gain from this book. If you are only interested in learning how to work with your new MicroPython board and have no aspirations for developing anything more, then you may want to skim these sections. However, if your goals include making MicroPython IoT solutions that you deploy – especially if you plan to connect it to the Internet – you will want to consider security in your solution. Either way, I strongly recommend reading and adhering to these tips for securing your IoT solutions.

Security Begins at Home

Before introducing an IoT solution to your home network, you should consider taking precautions to ensure the machines on your home network are protected. This is important because if someone gets access to your home network, they can achieve all manner of nefarious activities.

The most common mistake made is not securing a home WiFi network. Not only does this mean your neighbors can jump onto your network and hog your bandwidth, it also means they may be able to get to the systems on your home network leaving your IoT devices, computers, appliances, etc., vulnerable to attack.

Fortunately, there are some best practices for securing your home networking to help reduce these risks. These include the following:

- *Use passwords*: This may seem like a simple thing, but always make sure you use passwords on all your computers and devices. Also, adopt good password habits such as requiring longer strings, mixed case, numbers, and symbols to ensure the passwords are not easily guessed.

- *Secure your WiFi*: If you have a WiFi network, make sure you add a password and use the latest security protocols such as WPA2 or, even better, the built-in secure setup features of some wireless routers.

- *Use a firewall*: You should also use a firewall to block all unused ports (TCP or UDP). For example, lock down all ports except those your solution uses such as port 80 for html.

- *Restrict physical access*: Lock your doors! Just because your network has a great password and your computers use super world espionage spy encrypted biometric access, these things are meaningless if someone can gain access to your networking hardware directly. For IoT solutions, this means any external components should be installed in tamper-proof enclosures or locked away so they cannot be discovered. This also includes any network wiring.

Some of these you may know how to do it, but others may require help from a friend who knows more about the devices and networking. For example, if you don't know what a firewall is, ask someone to help you. A little extra security is worth the effort to learn the basics of how to set up a firewall.

Secure Your Devices

As mentioned earlier, your IoT devices also need to be secured. Some practices to consider include the following:

- *Use passwords*: Always add passwords to the user accounts on any device that has an operating system. This includes making sure you rename any default passwords. For example, you may be tempted to consider a wee Raspberry Pi too small of a device to be a security concern, but if you consider these devices run one of the most powerful operating systems available (forms of Linux), a Raspberry Pi can be a very powerful hacking tool.

- *Keep your software up to date*: You should try to use the latest versions of any software you use. This includes the operating system as well as any firmware or programming tools you may be running. Newer versions often have improved security or fewer security vulnerabilities.

- *If your software offers security features, use them*: If you have servers or services running on your devices, and they offer features such as automatic lockout for missed passwords, turn them on. Not all software has these features, but if they are available, they can be a great way to defeat repeated attacks.

Use Encryption

This is one area that is often overlooked. While it is an option normally used only by solutions that transmit confidential data such as commercial IoT devices, if you plan to send data you feel is sensitive, you can further protect yourself and your data if you encrypt both your data as it is stored and the communication mechanism as it is being transmitted. If you encrypt your data, even if someone were to gain physical access to the storage device, the data is useless because they cannot easily decipher the encryption. Use the same care with your encryption keys and passcodes as you do your computer passwords.

Security Doesn't End at the Cloud

There are many considerations for connecting IoT devices to cloud services. Indeed, Microsoft and others have made it very easy to use cloud services with your IoT solutions. However, there are two important considerations for security and your IoT data:

- *Do you need the cloud?*: The first thing you should consider is whether you need to put any of your data in the cloud. It is often the case that cloud services make it very easy to store and view your data, but is it necessary to do so? For example, you may be very concerned and quite keenly eager to view logistical data for where your dog spends his time while you are at work, but who else would care to view this data? In this case, storing the data in the cloud to make it available to everyone is not necessary.

- *Don't relax!*: Many people seem to let their guard down when working with cloud services. For whatever reason, they consider the cloud more secure. The fact is, it isn't! In fact, you must apply the very same security best practices when working in the cloud that you do for your own network, computers, and security policies. Indeed, if anything, you need to be even more vigilant because cloud services are not in your control with respect to protecting against physical access (however remote and unlikely) nor are you guaranteed your data isn't on the same devices as tens, hundreds, or even thousands of other users' data.

Now that we have an idea of how we should include security in our projects, let's take a brief look at the programming language we will use in this book – Python.

Python and the IoT

Python is a high-level, interpreted, object-oriented scripting language. One of the biggest tenants of Python is to have a clear, easy-to-understand syntax that reads as close to English as possible. That is, you should be able to read a Python script and understand it even if you haven't learned Python. Python also has less punctuation (special symbols) and fewer syntactical machinations than other languages.

Here are a few of the key features of Python:

- An interpreter processes Python at runtime. No compiler is used.

- Python supports object-oriented programming constructs by way of classes and methods.

- Python is a great language for the beginner-level programmers and supports the development of a wide range of applications.

- Python is a scripting language but can be used for a wide range of applications.

- Python is very popular and used throughout the world giving it a huge support base.

- Python has few keywords, simple structure, and a clearly defined syntax. This allows the student to pick up the language quickly.

Origins

Python was developed by Guido van Rossum from the late 1980s to the early 1990s at the National Research Institute for Mathematics and Computer Science in the Netherlands and maintained by a core development team at the institute. It was derived from and influenced by many languages, including Modula-3, C, C++, and even Unix shell scripting languages.

A fascinating fact about Python is it was named after the BBC show *Monty Python's Flying Circus* and has nothing to do with the reptile by the same name. Quoting Monty Python in source code documentation (and even a humorous diversion for error messages) is very common, and while some professional developers may cringe at the insinuation, it's considered by Pythonistas as showing your Python street cred. If you like Monty Python, I encourage you to use snippets from the shows in your code. One place I like to have fun with is printing messages. My favorite goes something like this:

```
> DUPLICATE FILE ERROR: He says they've already got one!
```

Some may wonder how a language like Python could possibly be helpful in writing IoT solutions. The answer to that is a cool product called MicroPython. In short, MicroPython is a condensed, optimized code of Python 3 that has been loaded in hardware. This means rather than having to have an interpreter run on an operating system to execute the Python code, the MicroPython chip can run the Python code directly on the hardware. No operating system is needed. In fact, MicroPython has basic file I/O built in.

We'll learn more about MicroPython in the next chapter. It's an exciting new option for those who want to explore IoT but don't want to learn a complex programming language or spend a lot of time learning new operating systems, tools, and hardware. But first, let's look at how easy it is to use MicroPython.

Online MicroPython Simulator

For those of you who are eager to get a taste of what it is like to use MicroPython to control hardware, the good folks over at Wokwi have an online (`https://wokwi.com/`), interactive IoT project simulator complete with simulated electronics such as sensors and output devices connected to one of the popular IoT platforms including a MicroPython simulator using one of the most popular MicroPython boards, the Raspberry Pi Pico (`www.raspberrypi.com/products/raspberry-pi-pico/`).

When you visit the site, you will find a long list of IoT simulators that use a variety of boards. If you scroll down, you will see a set of MicroPython IoT project simulations as shown in Figure 1-8. If you click the *More MicroPython Projects* button, you will see the current list of available MicroPython projects.

Figure 1-8. *MicroPython IoT Project Simulations (Wokwi)*

There is also a MicroPython simulator for the Raspberry Pi Pico. If you scroll down the page to the IoT section, you will see a button named + *New Project* that allows you to create a new project as shown in Figure 1-9.

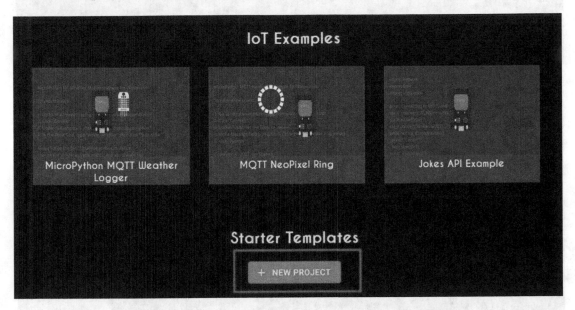

Figure 1-9. *Creating a New MicroPython Simulation Project (Wokwi)*

When you click the + *New Project* button, you will be prompted to choose a board to use in the simulator. If you are following along with this example, choose either the Raspberry Pi or Raspberry Pi Pico W (either will work in the following example).

The simulator will open with a new, blank project that shows a code window to the left and a simple graphic depicting the Raspberry Pi Pico board on the right. When you run code, the MicroPython console will appear on the right side below the board demonstration. For example, if you click the + *New Project* button and choose Raspberry Pi Pico, you will see a blank project as shown in Figure 1-10.

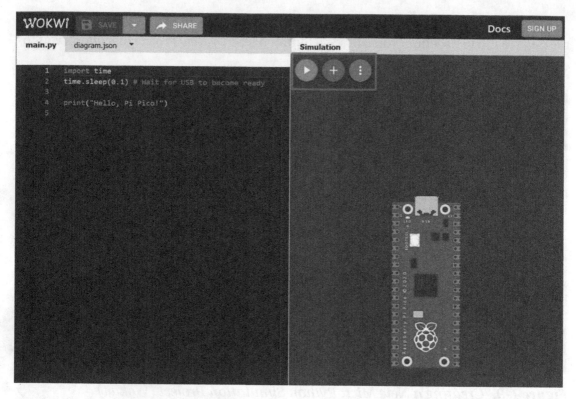

Figure 1-10. *Blank MicroPython Simulation Project (Wokwi)*

Notice at the top of the right side in the demonstration window, you will see three buttons. The first is a green circle with a white arrow. Clicking this button will run the code shown in the code window on the left. The blue circle with the plus sign allows you to add a new part (electronic component), and there is a feature that permits you to create connections to the board in the form of simulated wiring.

There are many components to choose from, and you are encouraged to try them out, but for this simple example, we do not need any components. Finally, the gray circle with the three dots opens a menu that permits you to zoom in or out and similar configuration functions.

The example we are going to see first uses only the Raspberry Pi Pico. More specifically, there is a user-controllable light-emitting diode (LED) on the board that we can use to turn on and off using MicroPython. The code for the example is shown in Listing 1-1.

Listing 1-1. MicroPython Blinky Example

```
from machine import Pin
from utime import sleep

print("MicroPython for the IoT: Blinky Example")
led = Pin(25, Pin.OUT)
while True:
  led.on()
  sleep(0.5)
  led.off()
  sleep(0.5)
```

The example is a variant of a classic "Hello, World!"[6] IoT project, but it is not important to know what the code does or how at this point. However, if you look at the code, most of it is easy enough to discern. The challenge in learning MicroPython is learning the syntax and special commands like those shown on the first two lines.

Now that we have some sample code, let's run the simulation! You can simply type the lines of code into the code editor on the left. When ready, click the green circle with the arrow. If you typed the code in without errors, you should see a new subwindow appear on the right that shows the MicroPython console window and our greeting message, and you should see the LED located on the Raspberry Pi Pico flash as shown in Figure 1-11. You will see the LED turn on and off twice per second.

---

[6]https://en.wikipedia.org/wiki/%22Hello,_World!%22_program

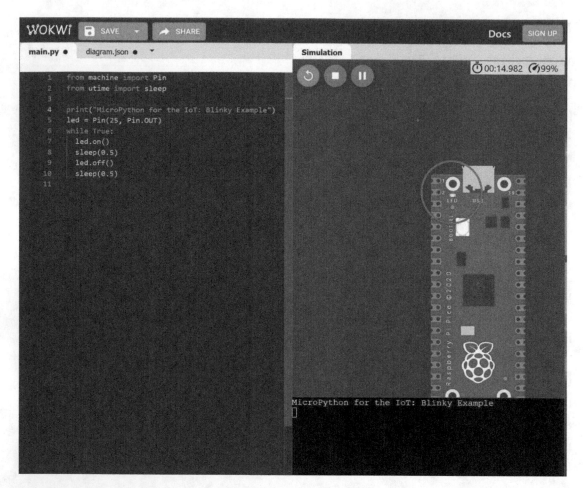

Figure 1-11. Blinky Code Simulation (Wokwi)

While you may not fully understand the Python code in the example, I suggest you take a few moments to try it so you can see how much fun it is (and how little code it requires) to control hardware with MicroPython. If nothing else, the simulator should give you an appetite to learn more about MicroPython.

Tip   Use https://wokwi.com/projects/new/micropython-pi-pico to navigate directly to the MicroPython simulator for the Raspberry Pi Pico.

You can also return to this simulator to try out your own code and simpler projects without the need to buy expensive hardware. If you would like to create and store your projects in the Wokwi platform, you can click the Sign Up button in the top right and follow the prompts to create your account. Once you have an account, you can create and save your projects on Wokwi, permitting you to explore all of the features on the Wokwi online simulators. Nice!

Summary

The Internet of Things is an exciting new world for us all. Those of us young in heart but old enough to remember *The Jetsons* TV series recall seeing a taste of what is possible in make-believe land. Talking toasters, flying cars that spring from briefcases, and robots with attitude notwithstanding, television fantasy of decades ago is coming true. We have wristwatches that double as phones and video players; we can unlock our cars from around the world, find out if our dog has gone outside, and even answer the door from across the city. All of this is possible and working today with the advent of the IoT.

In this chapter, we discovered what the IoT is and saw some examples of well-known IoT solutions. We also discovered how Microsoft is opening doors for Windows users by expanding its Windows 10 operating system to the IoT via the Raspberry Pi hardware. This is a very exciting opportunity for people who do not want to learn the nuances of a Linux-based operating system to explore the world of hardware and IoT from a familiar and well-understood platform.

In the next chapter, we will discover more about MicroPython, including how to program in MicroPython. As you will see, it is not difficult. We will then explore the hardware we will use to run MicroPython in more detail in Chapter 3 to complete our tour of getting started with MicroPython for the IoT.

CHAPTER 2

Introducing MicroPython

Now that we have learned more about the Internet of Things and saw a demonstration of MicroPython, it is time to learn more about MicroPython – how we can get started, how it works, and examples of what you can do with your own MicroPython board.

Learning MicroPython is very easy even for those who have not had any programming experience. Indeed, all you need to learn MicroPython is a bit of patience and a little time to get used to the syntax and the mechanisms unique to working with MicroPython, the boards, and the electronics. As we will see, there is a lot you can do with just a little knowledge.

In this chapter, we will learn more about MicroPython, including an overview of how to get started with one of the most popular boards. Don't worry if you don't have a board yet; the examples in this chapter are intended to give you a taste of what you can do rather than a detailed tutorial. That being said, we will see a detailed tutorial for the board used in this chapter as well as other boards in Chapter 3. We will also explore programming Python in more detail in Chapter 4.

Tip   I refer to the microcontroller boards that run MicroPython natively or can be loaded with MicroPython binaries as "MicroPython-compatible boards," or "MicroPython boards."

Let's start with a look at what MicroPython is, including why it was created and how to get started.

© Charles Bell 2024
C. Bell, *MicroPython for the Internet of Things*, https://doi.org/10.1007/978-1-4842-9861-9_2

Getting Started

The use of the Python language for controlling hardware has been around for some time. Users of the Raspberry Pi, pcDuino, and other low-cost computers and similar boards have had the advantage of using Python for controlling hardware. In this case, they used full versions of the Python programming language on the native Linux-based operating system.

However, this required special libraries built to communicate with the hardware. These libraries were designed to interface with the general-purpose input/output (GPIO) pins. The GPIO pins normally appear on the board in one or more rows of male pins on the board. Some boards used female header pins.

While these boards made it possible for those who wanted to develop electronics projects, it required users to buy the board as well as peripherals like a keyboard, mouse, and monitor. Not only that, but users also had to learn the operating system. For those not used to Linux, this can be a challenge in and of itself.

You may be wondering about microcontrollers such as the wildly popular Arduino (arduino.cc) or Espressif, also known as ESP boards (espressif.com). For those boards, you must use a C-like language[1] to program them, which may be more than some are willing to learn.

The vision for MicroPython was to combine the simplicity of learning Python with the low cost and ease of use of microcontroller boards, which would permit a lot more people to work with electronics for art and science projects. Beginners would not have to learn a new operating system or learn one of the more complex programming languages. MicroPython was the answer. Figure 2-1 shows the MicroPython logo in the form of a skill badge (an iron-on patch)[2] from Adafruit.

---

[1] Some may say C++, and I suppose there is some truth in that, but they're more like C for general, basic use.

[2] Yes, I have one.

Figure 2-1. *MicroPython Logo Skill Badge (Courtesy of adafruit.com)*

That's pretty cool, isn't it? It's a snake (a python) on an integrated circuit (chip). If you don't have anything to attach the patch to, Adafruit also stocks a nifty MicroPython sticker (`www.adafruit.com/products/3270`). I recommend getting one of these and displaying it proudly when you finish the book.

Origins

MicroPython[3] was created and is maintained by Damien P. George, Paul Sokolovsky, and other contributors. It was designed to be a lean, efficient version of the Python 3 language and installed on a small microcontroller. Since Python is an interpreted language and thus slower (in general) than compiled languages, MicroPython was designed to be as efficient as possible so that it can run on microcontrollers that normally are slower and have much less memory than a typical personal computer.

---

[3] Copyright 2014–2023, Damien P. George, Paul Sokolovsky, and contributors.

COMPILED VS. INTERPRETED

Compiled languages use a program, called a compiler, to convert the source code from a human-readable form to a binary executable form. There are a few steps involved in this conversion, but in general, we take the source code and compile it into a binary form. Since it is in binary form, the processor can execute the statements generated directly without any additional steps (again, in general).

Interpreted languages, on the other hand, are not compiled but instead are converted to binary form (or an intermediate binary form) on the fly with a program called an interpreter. Python 3 provides a Python executable that is both an interpreter as well as a console that allows you to run your code as you type it in. Python programs run one line of code at a time, starting at the top of the file.

Thus, compiled languages are faster than interpreted languages because the code is prepared for execution and does not require an intermediate, real-time step to process the code before execution.

Another aspect is that microcontroller boards like the Arduino require a compilation step that you must perform on your computer and load the binary executable onto the board first. In contrast, since MicroPython has its interpreter running directly on the hardware, we do not need the intermediate step to prepare the code; we can run the interpreted language directly on the hardware!

This permits hardware manufacturers to build small, inexpensive boards that include MicroPython on the same chip as the microprocessor (typically). This gives you the ability to connect to the board, write the code, and execute it without any extra work.

You may be thinking that to reduce Python 3 to a size that fits on a small chip with limited memory, the language is stripped down and lacking features. That can't be further than the truth. In fact, MicroPython is a complete implementation of the core features of Python 3, including a compact runtime and interactive interpreter. There is support for reading and writing files, loading modules, interacting with hardware such as GPIO pins, error handling, and much more. Best of all, the optimization of Python 3 code allows it to be compiled into a binary requiring about 256K of memory to store the binary and runs with as little as 16K of RAM.

However, there are a few things that MicroPython doesn't implement from the Python 3 language. The following sections give you an idea of what you can do with MicroPython and what you cannot do with MicroPython.

MicroPython Features

The biggest feature of MicroPython is, of course, it runs Python. This permits you to create simple, efficiently specified, and easy-to-understand programs. That alone, I think, is its best advantage over other boards like the Arduino. The following lists a few of the features that MicroPython supports. We will see these features in greater detail throughout this book:

- *Interactive interpreter*: MicroPython boards have built in a special interactive console that you can access by connecting to the board with a USB cable (or in some cases over WiFi). This console is called a read-evaluate-print loop (REPL) that allows you to type in your code and execute it one line at a time. It is a wonderful way to prototype your code or just run a project as you develop it.

- *Python standard libraries*: MicroPython also supports many of the standard Python libraries. In general, you can expect to find MicroPython supports more than 80% of the most commonly used libraries. These include parsing JavaScript Object Notation (JSON),[4] socket programming, string manipulation, file input/output, and even regular expression support.

- *Hardware-level libraries*: MicroPython has libraries built in that allow you to access hardware directly either to turn on or off analog pins, read analog data, read digital data, and even control hardware with pulse-width modulation (PWM) – a way to limit power to a device by rapidly modulating the power to the device, for example, making a fan spin slower than if it had full power.

---

[4] www.json.org/

- *Extensible*: MicroPython is also extensible. This is an excellent feature for advanced users who need to implement some complex library at a low level (in C or C++) and include the new library in MicroPython. Yes, this means you can build in your own unique code and make it part of the MicroPython feature set.

To answer your question, "What can I do with MicroPython?," the answer is quite a lot! You can control hardware connected to the MicroPython board, write code modules to expand the features of your program storing them on an SD card for later retrieval (just like you can in Python on a PC), and much more. The hardware you can connect to include turning LEDs on and off, drive servos, read sensors, and even display text on LCDs. Some boards also have networking support in the form of WiFi radios. Just about anything you can do with the other microcontroller boards, you can do with a MicroPython board.

However, there are a few limitations to running MicroPython on the chip.

MicroPython Limitations

The biggest limitation of MicroPython is its ease of use. The ease of using Python means the code is interpreted on the fly. And while MicroPython is highly optimized, there is still a penalty for the interpreter. This means that projects that require a high degree of precision such as sampling data at a high rate or communicating over a connection (USB, hardware interface, etc.) may not run fast enough. For these areas, we can overcome the problem by extending the MicroPython language with optimized libraries for handling low-level communication.

MicroPython also uses a bit more memory than other microcontroller platforms such as Arduino. Normally, this isn't a problem but something you should consider if your program starts to get large. Larger programs that use a lot of libraries could consume more memory than you may expect. Once again, this is related to the ease of use of Python – another price to pay.

Finally, as mentioned previously, MicroPython doesn't implement all the features of all the Python 3 libraries. However, you should find it has everything you need to build IoT projects (and more).

ARE MY PYTHON SKILLS APPLICABLE TO MICROPYTHON?

If you've already learned how to program with Python, you may be expecting to see something that stands out as different or even odd about MicroPython. The good news is your Python skills are all you need to work with MicroPython. Indeed, MicroPython and Python use the same syntax; there isn't anything new to learn. As you will see in the next few chapters, MicroPython implements a subset of Python libraries but still is very much Python.

What Does MicroPython Run On?

Due to the increasing popularity of MicroPython, there are more options for boards to run MicroPython being added regularly. Part of this is from developers building processor- and platform-specific compiled versions of MicroPython that you can download and install on the board. This is the fastest growing category.

There are two categories of boards you can use to run MicroPython. First are the boards that have MicroPython loaded from the factory and run only MicroPython. These include the Raspberry Pi Pico and Pico W, the Arduino Nano RP2040 Connect, Pyboard (the original MicroPython board), and similar boards that use the RP2040 chip from Raspberry Pi. Next are the boards that have available firmware options to install MicroPython on the board, including the ESP8266, Teensy, and more. We will see more about these boards in the next chapter.

Next, let's explore Python from our PC in the next section to give you an idea what the language is like and an opportunity to try it out yourself without needing a MicroPython board.

Experimenting with Python on Your PC

Since MicroPython is Python (just a bit scaled down for optimization purposes), you can run Python on your PC and experiment with the language. I recommend loading Python on your PC even if you already have a MicroPython board. You may find it more convenient to try out things with your PC since you can control the environment better. However, your PC won't be able to communicate with electronic components or hardware like the MicroPython boards, so while you can do a lot more on the PC, you can't test your code that communicates with hardware. But you can test the basic constructs, such as function calls, printing messages, and more.

So, why bother? Simply, using your PC to debug your Python code will allow you to get much of your project complete and working before trying it on the MicroPython board. More specifically, by developing the mundane things on your PC, you eliminate a lot of potential problems debugging your code on the MicroPython board. This is the number one mistake novice programmers make – writing an entire solution without testing smaller parts. It is always better to start small and test a small part of the code at a time, adding only those parts that have been tested and shown to work correctly.

All you need to get started is to download and install Python 3 (e.g., Python 3.11 is the latest, but new versions become available periodically). The following sections briefly describe how to install Python on various platforms. For specific information about platforms not listed here, see the Python wiki at https://wiki.python.org/moin/BeginnersGuide/Download.

Caution   There are two versions of Python available – Python 2 and Python 3. Since MicroPython is based on Python 3, you will need to install Python version 3, not Python version 2.

But first, check your system to see if Python is already installed. Open a terminal window (command prompt) and type the following command:

```
python --version
```

If Python is installed, you should see something like the following:

```
$ python --version
Python 3.11.4
```

If you saw a version like Python 2.X.Y, there is still a chance you have Python 3 on your machine. Some systems have both Python 2 and Python 3 installed. To run Python 3, use the following command:

```
python3
```

If Python 3 is not installed or it is an older version, use the following sections to install Python on your system. You should always install the latest version. You can download Python 3 from www.python.org/downloads/.

Installing Python 3 on Windows 11

Most Windows machines do not include Python, and you must install it. You can download Python 3 for Windows from the official Python website (`www.python.org/downloads/windows/`). You will find the usual Windows installer options for 32-bit and 64-bit versions as well as a web-based installer and a `.zip` format. Most people will use the Windows installer option, but if you must install Python manually, you can use the other options.

Once you download Python, you can launch the installer. For example, on my Windows 11 machine, I downloaded the file under the link named Latest Python 3 Release – Python 3.11.4. If you scroll down, you can find the installer you want. For example, I clicked the installer for Windows 64-bit machines. This downloaded a file named `python-3.11.4-amd64.exe`, which I located in my `Downloads` folder and executed by double-clicking the file.

Tip   Be sure to check the box to add the python executable to the command line so that you can run `python.exe` without specifying a path.

Like most Windows installer installs, you can step through the various screens agreeing to the license, specifying where you want to install it and finally initiating the install. Figure 2-2 shows an example of the installer running.

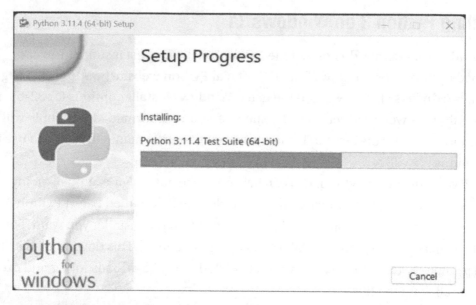

Figure 2-2. *Installing Python on Windows 11*

Tip   If you get stuck or need more detailed instructions, see the excellent article at How-To Geek: www.howtogeek.com/197947/how-to-install-python-on-windows/.

Once the installation is complete, you can try the test in the previous section to verify the installation. If you do not modify your PATH variable, you may need to use the Python console shortcut on the start menu to launch the console.

Installing Python 3 on macOS

If you are using macOS, you probably have Python installed since most releases of macOS install Python by default. However, if you were not able to run the preceding Python version command or it wasn't the correct version, you can still download the latest Python 3 from the Python website (www.python.org/downloads/mac-osx/). You will find several versions, but you should download the latest version available.

Once you download Python, you can launch the installer. For example, on my M1-based MacBook Pro, I downloaded the latest Python 3 file under the link named *macOS 64-bit universal2 installer*. If you scroll down, you can find the installer you want. For example, I clicked the installer for 64-bit machines. This downloaded a file named python-3.11.4-macosx11.pkg, which I located in my Downloads folder and executed.

Like most installers, you can step through the various screens agreeing to the license, specifying where you want to install it, and finally initiating the install. Figure 2-3 shows an example of the installer running.

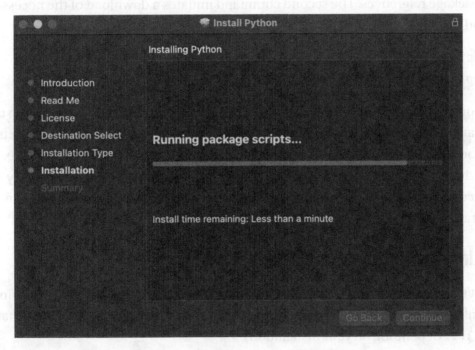

Figure 2-3. *Installing Python on macOS*

___

Note   Depending on which version of macOS you are running, and how your security settings are set, you may need to change them to run the installer since an identified developer does not sign it. See the *Security & Privacy* panel in your *System Preferences*.

___

Once the installation is complete, you can try the test in the previous section to verify the installation.

Installing Python 3 on Linux

If you are using Linux, the way you install Python will vary based on the platform. For instance, Ubuntu, Debian, Raspbian, etc., use `apt-get` commands, while other distributions have different package managers. Use the default package manager for your platform to install Python 3.11 (or later).

For example, on Debian or Ubuntu, we install the Python 3.6 package using the following commands. The first command updates the packages to ensure we have the latest package references. The second command initiates a download of the necessary files and installs Python.

```
sudo apt-get update
sudo apt-get install python3.11
```

If you are using a Raspberry Pi, you're likely running the Raspberry Pi OS (also called Raspbian). The base image includes Python 3.9 and that is sufficient for the projects in this book. However, if you want to install Python 3.11 or later, you can follow the instructions at `https://raspberrytips.com/install-latest-python-raspberry-pi/`.

Once the installation is complete, you can try the test in the previous section to verify the installation.

Running the Python Console

Now let's run some tests on our PC. Recall we can open a Python console by opening a terminal window (command prompt) and entering the command `python` (or `python3` or `python3.11` depending on your installation).

Once you see the prompt, enter the following code at the prompt (>>>). This code will print a message to the screen. The \n at the end is a special, nonprinting character that issues a carriage return (like pressing *Enter*) to move to a new line.

```
>>> print ("Hello, World!")
```

When you enter this code, you will see the result right away. Recall the interpreter works by executing one line of code at a time – each time you press Enter. However, unlike running a program stored in a file, the code you enter in the console is not saved. Listing 2-1 shows an example of running a simple Python program using the Python console. Notice I typed in a simple program – the quintessential "Hello, World!" example.

Listing 2-1. Hello, World! (Python Console)

```
C:\Users\chuck> python
Python 3.11.4 (tags/v3.11.4:d2340ef, Jun  7 2023, 05:45:37) [MSC v.1934 64
bit (AMD64)] on win32
Type "help", "copyright", "credits" or "license" for more information.
>>> print("Hello, World!")
Hello, World!
>>> quit()

C:\Users\chuck>
```

To quit the console, enter the code quit() as shown in Listing 2-1.

While that demonstrates running Python from your PC, it is not that interesting. Let's see something a bit more complicated.

Running Python Programs with the Interpreter

Suppose your project required you to save data to a file or possibly read data from a file. Rather than try and figure out how to do this on your MicroPython board, we can experiment with files on our PC!

In the next example, I write data to a file and then read the data and print it out. Don't worry too much about understanding the code – just read it – it's very intuitive. Listing 2-2 shows the code for this example. I used a text editor and saved the file as file_io.py.

Listing 2-2. File IO Example

```
# Example code to demonstrate writing and reading data to/from files
# Step 1: Create a file and write some data
new_file = open("log.txt", "w")    # use "write" mode
new_file.write("1,apples,2.5\n")   # write some data
new_file.write("2,oranges,1\n")    # write some data
new_file.write("3,peaches,3\n")    # write some data
new_file.write("4,grapes,21\n")    # write some data
new_file.close()  # close the file
# Step 2: Open a file and read data
old_file = open("log.txt", "r")  # use "read" mode
```

```
# Use a loop to read all rows in the file
for row in old_file.readlines():
    columns = row.strip("\n").split(",") # split row by commas
    print(" : ".join(columns))  # print the row with colon separator
    old_file.close()
```

I saved the code to a file to show you how you can execute your Python scripts using the Python interpreter using the following command. If you use Windows, you may need to modify the command to use the correct Python version such as "python3.exe file_io.py."

```
python ./file_io.py
```

Listing 2-3 shows the results of running the script.

Listing 2-3. Output for the File IO Example

```
C:\Users\chuck\Source\Ch02> python ./file_io.py
1 : apples : 2.5
2 : oranges : 1
3 : peaches : 3
4 : grapes : 21

C:\Users\chuck\Source\Ch02>
```

Notice the code changes the separator in the data by exchanging the comma as originally written to a space, colon, and another space. The code does this by splitting the line (string) read into parts by comma. Hence, the column data contains three parts, and we use the join() method to rejoin the string and print it. Take a moment to read the code, and you will see these aspects. As you can see, Python is easy to read.

Now that we've experimented with Python on our PC, let's see how to use MicroPython on a typical MicroPython board.

How MicroPython Works

Recall that MicroPython is designed to work on small microcontroller platforms. Some of these microcontroller platforms use a special chip that contains the MicroPython binaries (libraries, basic disk IO, bootstrapping, etc.) as well as the microcontroller, memory, and supporting components.

When you use a MicroPython board – like most microcontrollers – you must first write your code and load it onto the board. Most MicroPython boards have an embedded USB flash drive that mounts when you connect it to your computer using a USB cable. This flash drive stores a couple of files you can modify to change its behavior. You can also copy your program (script file) to this drive for execution at boot time. We will see how to do this in a later chapter.

You can also use the MicroPython console, which is very much like the Python console we saw in the last section. The MicroPython console is called the run-evaluate-print loop or REPL console. The console makes it very easy to get started and to debug (remove errors from) your program before loading it on the board for execution every time the board is powered on.

The Run-Evaluate-Print Loop (REPL Console)

If you have used another microcontroller board like the Arduino, you are likely familiar with some of the following. But if you haven't used such or have not used a terminal program, I provide all the steps you will need for each of the three major platforms: Windows, macOS, and Linux. The following sections walk you through connecting to the board for the first time.

I am using the Raspberry Pi Pico for these examples. You can use any other board that has MicroPython loaded by default, but be sure to check the vendor's documentation before starting to use the board for the first time. Some boards may require loading firmware before first use.

Connect the Board

To get started using the REPL console, connect the board to your computer using a USB to micro USB cable (typically), which provides power over the USB as well as connectivity for the console. Once the board boots (some boards can take up to one to two minutes to boot the first time), you can connect to the board using a terminal program. From there, we can use the REPL console in the same way we used the Python console.

Tip Some boards can take a few moments to boot, so if you don't get a connection, wait a few moments, and try again.

When the board finishes booting, you can browse the drive on the board using your computer. The best way to work with MicroPython boards is using an interactive development environment such as Thonny, which we will see in more detail in the next chapter. Using Thonny, you can use the file explorer feature to view the files on the board. Figure 2-4 shows an example of the files on the Raspberry Pi Pico I will be using in this chapter.

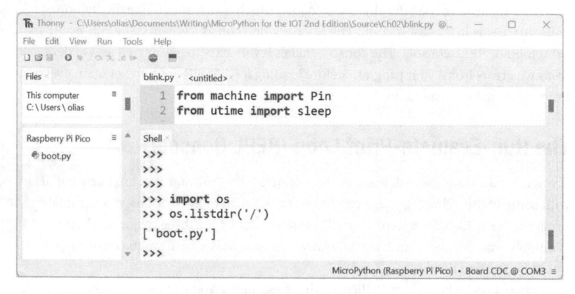

Figure 2-4. *USB Drive (Raspberry Pi Pico)*

Notice there is one file with a `.py` file extension, `boot.py`, which is executed on boot (hence the name). You can also create a file named `main.py`, which you can use to store your own program if you want to use the board independently (main runs on boot). Again, we will see this in action in later chapters.

Starting the REPL Console (Windows)

If you do not want to use Thonny, you can connect to the REPL console. For example, using Windows, you will need a terminal program like PuTTY, which was originally developed by Simon Tatham (`www.chiark.greenend.org.uk/~sgtatham/putty/latest.html`). PuTTY is a simple terminal program that is very easy to use and made for the Windows platform.

To install PuTTY, select the appropriate .msi file (32- or 64-bit), download it, then double-click the file to launch the installer. Follow the prompts to complete the installation. For example, I downloaded the file named putty-64bit-0.68-installer.msi.

Now that you have PuTTY installed, you must know the correct port to use. Open the *Device Manager* and navigate down the tree until you find the Ports (COM & LPT) entry and click to open it. Note that the board must be connected for this to work. You should see one or more entries in the subtree that indicate the COM ports (and printer ports) connected to your PC. The MicroPython board will be listed as simply *USB Serial Device (COMn)*, where n is a number like COM1, COM2, etc. For example, on my PC, it was listed as *COM3*. Figure 2-5 shows an example from my PC.

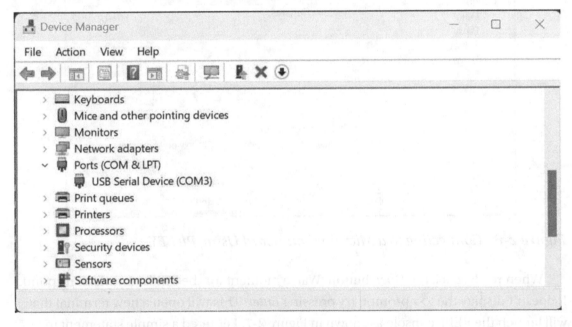

Figure 2-5. *Finding the COM Port on Windows 11*

Now we can open PuTTY and connect to the board. Use the shortcut on your Start menu to launch PuTTY or type PuTTY into the search box and click the entry when Cortana finds it. When PuTTY opens, you will see a dialog that you can use to connect via a terminal over the network. Since the board is connected via the COM port, we must click the small radio button marked *Serial*. We can then enter the COM port in the Serial line text box and set the speed to 9600. Figure 2-6 shows a properly configured PuTTY for connecting to the board on COM3 (as shown in the *Device Manager*).

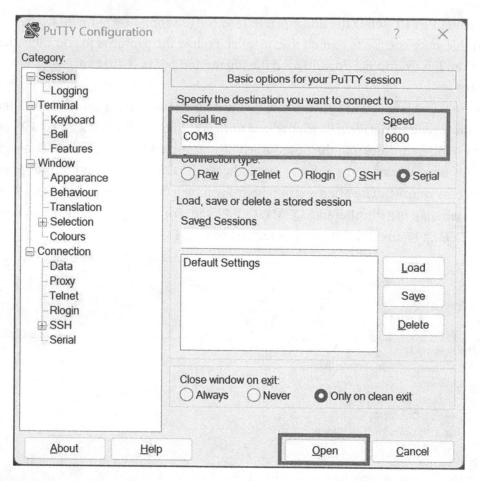

Figure 2-6. *Connecting to a MicroPython Board Using PuTTY*

When ready, click the *Open* button. Wait a moment for the REPL console to respond. It doesn't display the >>> prompt; try pressing *Enter*. This will open a new terminal that will launch the REPL console as shown in Figure 2-7. I entered a simple statement to demonstrate that the console is working.

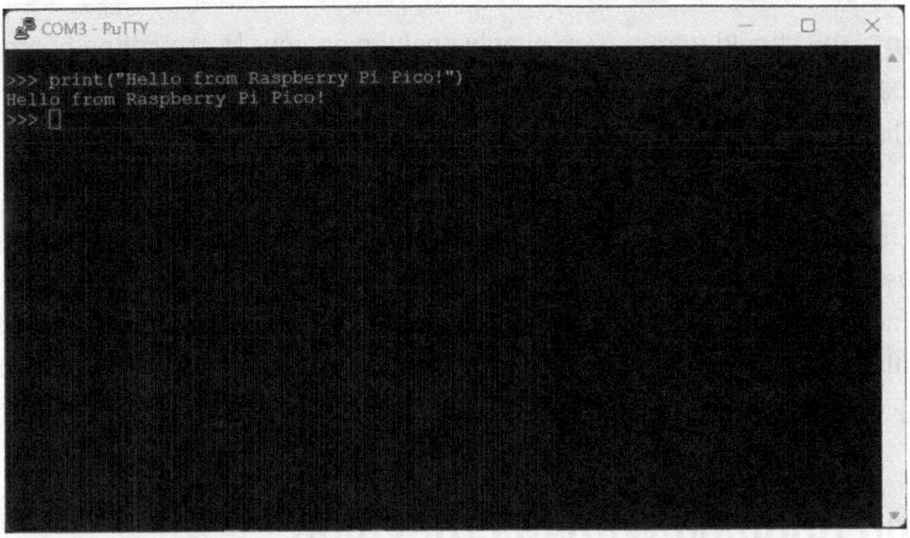

Figure 2-7. *The REPL Console (Windows 11)*

Tip   If you don't like the white (gray) on black color scheme, you can change them by clicking *Colours* in the tree control. Tread lightly as you must set the values separately (there is no scheme concept).

Starting the REPL Console (macOS and Linux)

To connect using macOS or Linux, you can use the following command. The only thing you may need to do is locate the correct device. I demonstrate this with the first command that lists the devices on my macOS system. Do this after you've connected to the MicroPython board.

```
$ ls /dev/tty.usb*
/dev/tty.usbmodem1422
$ screen /dev/tty.usbmodem1422
```

There is one oddity with the REPL console. The quit() doesn't work. To exit the console for some boards, you will need to reset the board or kill the connection. While this seems odd, I am certain it will be improved in the future, and recall we don't normally use the REPL console for running our projects; rather, we use it to test code, so a little hiccup on quitting isn't a big issue.

Caution   You should refrain from simply unplugging your MicroPython board. Some boards, like the Pyboard, present their base file system as a mountable USB drive. Disconnecting without ejecting the board can lead to loss of data.

Now it's time to take a tour of what we can do with MicroPython. The following section uses several example projects to show you what you can do with a MicroPython board. Once more, I will introduce the examples with a minimal amount of explanation and details about the hardware. We will learn much more about the hardware in the next chapter.

Off and Running with MicroPython

If you're like me when encountering innovative technologies, you most likely want to get started as soon as you can. If you already have a Raspberry Pi Pico or Pico W, you can follow along with the examples in this section and see a few more examples of what you can do with MicroPython.

The examples use some basic electronic components such as resistors, light-emitting diodes (LEDs), a momentary button, and jumper wires. If you have these components and want to replicate the examples, feel free to do so. Do not worry if this seems strange to you. We will examine each of these components, including how to use a breadboard to wire circuits in later chapters. Figure 2-8 shows the wiring diagram for the circuits that support all three examples.

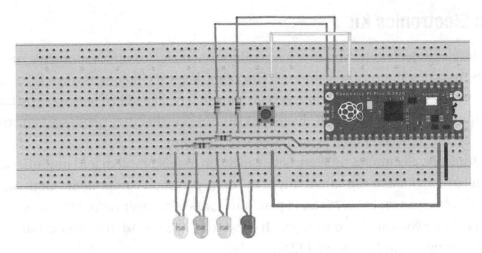

Figure 2-8. *Wiring Diagram for Examples*

Notice that we have the Raspberry Pi Pico mounted on a breadboard with four LEDs each with one leg (the ground or cathode pin) plugged into the ground rail with a jumper to one of the ground pins on the Pico. The positive pin (or anode) of each LED is connected to a 470 ohm resistor, which is connected to the GPIO header on the Pico (GPIO 14, 15, 16, and 17). Finally, we have a momentary button connected across the channel with one side connected to 3.3V on the Pico and the other to GPIO 13.

However, don't worry if you don't have a board yet. Again, I am including this section to help you learn more about what is possible through examples. Once we've discussed the details of the popular boards and how to program in MicroPython, we will dive into more complex projects that you can experiment with as you learn.

Additional Hardware

Before diving into the examples, I would like to introduce several key components that you will need later in this book. If you do not have these components, it is a clever idea to order them now so that when you get to the example projects, you will have what you need.

In addition to a MicroPython board, I consider these components as must-have items for anyone wanting to learn how to work with electronics and MicroPython. These include a basic electronics kit that contains the most common components you will need when learning electronics, a breadboard, and jumper wires. I will describe each of these in the following sections.

Basic Electronics Kit

The example projects in this book use several common electronic components, such as LEDs, switches, buttons, resistors, etc. One of the biggest challenges when learning to work with electronics at the hobby level is what to buy. I've talked to some who have made numerous trips to the local electronics store to get what they need, seeming to never have the right components no matter what they buy.

Fortunately, electronics retailers have caught on to this problem and now offer a basic electronics kit that contains many of the more common components. Both Adafruit (adafruit.com/products/2975) and SparkFun (sparkfun.com/products/13973) offer such kits. While you cannot go wrong with either kit, I like the Adafruit kit best since it has more components (e.g., more LEDs).

The Adafruit Parts Pal comes packaged in a small plastic case with a host of electronic components. Figure 2-9 shows the Parts Pal kit.

Figure 2-9. *Adafruit Parts Pal (Courtesy of adafruit.com)*

The kit includes the following components: prototyping tools, LEDs, capacitors, resistors, some basic sensors, and more. In fact, there are more components in this kit than you will need for many experiments. Better still, the kit costs only $19.95, making it a good deal (and the case is a great bonus).

- 1x – Storage box with latch

- 1x – Half-sized breadboard

- 20x – Male/male jumper wires – 3" (75mm)

- 10x – Male/male jumper wires – 6" (150mm)

- 5x – 5mm diffused green LEDs

- 5x – 5mm diffused red LEDs

- 1x – 10mm diffused common-anode RGB LED

- 10x – 1.0uF ceramic capacitors

- 10x – 0.1uF ceramic capacitors

- 10x – 0.01uF ceramic capacitors

- 5x – 10uF 50V electrolytic capacitors

- 5x – 100uF 16V electrolytic capacitors

- 10x – 560 ohm 5% axial resistors

- 10x – 1K ohm 5% axial resistors

- 10x – 10K ohm 5% axial resistors

- 10x – 47K ohm 5% axial resistors

- 5x – 1N4001 diodes

- 5x – 1N4148 signal diodes

- 5x – NPN Transistor PN2222 TO-92

- 5x – PNP Transistor PN2907 TO-92

- 2x – 5V 1.5A linear voltage regulator – 7805 TO-220

- 1x – 3.3V 800mA linear voltage regulator – LD1117-3.3 TO-220

- 1x – TLC555 wide-voltage range, low-power 555 timer

- 1x – Photocell

- 1x – Thermistor (breadboard version)

- 1x – Vibration sensor switch

- 1x – 10K breadboard trim potentiometer

- 1x – 1K breadboard trim potentiometer

- 1x – Piezo buzzer

- 5x – 6mm tactile switches

- 3x – SPDT slide switches

- 1x – 40-pin breakaway male header strip

- 1x – 40-pin female header strip

Breadboard and Jumper Wires

A breadboard is a special tool designed to allow you to plug in your electrical components and provide interconnectivity in columns so that you can plug the leads of two components into the same column and therefore make a connection. The board is split into two rows, making it easy to use IC in the center of the board. Wires (called jumper wires or simply jumpers) can be used to connect the circuit on the breadboard to the MicroPython board. You will see an example of this later in this chapter.

Fortunately, the Adafruit Parts Pal comes with a breadboard like the one shown in Figure 2-10. This shows a half-sized breadboard from Adafruit. This breadboard is called half since it is one-half the normal length of a standard breadboard. Best of all, it fits in the Parts Pal box.

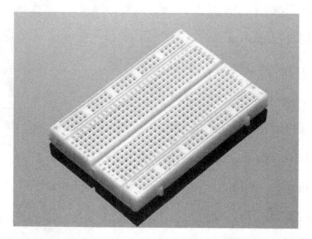

Figure 2-10. *Half-Sized Breadboard (Courtesy of adafruit.com)*

If you already have some components or decide to buy a different basic electronics kit that doesn't come with a breadboard, you can buy a breadboard separately from Adafruit (adafruit.com/products/64).

If your MicroPython board has male header pins instead of female header pins, you will need to get a separate set of jumper wires. Once again, Adafruit has what you need. If you need male/female jumper wires, order the Premium Female/Male Extension Jumper Wires – 20 × 6 (`adafruit.com/products/1954`). Figure 2-11 shows a set of male/female jumper wires.

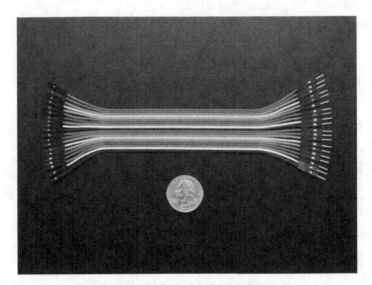

Figure 2-11. *Male/Female Jumper Wires (Courtesy of adafruit.com)*

Now, let's see some hardware in action!

Example 1: Blink an LED

In this example, we will demonstrate how to write code to turn on one of the LEDs. It's OK if you do not have your board set up (we will do this in Chapter 3), but if you do have your board ready, you can follow along. Again, this is for demonstration purposes, so you can see what is possible and how easy it is to work with hardware.

If you orient the board with the components added as shown in Figure 2-8, the four LEDs are a distinct color arranged left to right as yellow, blue, green, and red. If you're right-handed like me, you will probably orient the board so that the USB connector is on the left. In that case, the red LED is on the far left.

Let's write some code to turn the red LED on. Rather than simply turning it on, let's use a construct called a loop to turn it on and off every 250 milliseconds. Thus, it will flash rather quickly. Before I explain the code, let's look at the completed code. Listing 2-4 shows how the code would look. Don't worry; I'll explain each of the lines of code after the listing.

Listing 2-4.   Blink an LED

```
#
# MicroPython for the IoT Second Edition
#
# Example 1 - Blink LED
#
# Dr. Charles Bell
#
from machine import Pin # Get the machine Pin class
from utime import sleep # Import the sleep method

led = Pin(14, Pin.OUT)  # Get the GPIO 14 pin as output
led.off()               # Make sure it's off first

for i in range(0, 40):  # Run the indented code 40 times
    led.on()            # Turn LED on
    sleep(0.25)         # Wait for 250 milliseconds
    led.off()           # Turn LED off
    sleep(0.25)         # Wait for 250 milliseconds
led.off()               # Turn the LED off at the end
print("Done!")          # Goodbye!
```

The first lines of code are comment lines. These are ignored by MicroPython and are a way to communicate to others what your program is doing. Feel free to skip the comment lines when entering the code into the REPL console.

Next is a line of code that is used to import the Pin class from the machine library followed by importing the sleep() method from the utime library. The next two lines of code initialize a variable (led) connected to GPIO 14 setup as output (write), then we immediately turn the LED off by calling led.off().

Next is the main portion of the code – a loop! In this case, it is a for loop designed to run the block of code below it as indicated by the indentation 40 times. The for loop uses a counter, i, and the values 0 through 19 as returned by the range(0, 40) function. Within the body of the loop (the indented portion), we first turn the LED on with led. on(), wait 250 milliseconds using the sleep() method, which takes a variable expressed in seconds (hence, we use 0.25 for 250 milliseconds), then turn the LED off again and wait another 250 milliseconds. Finally, we turn the LED off and print a message that we're done.

You can enter this code line by line into the REPL console. You can skip those that start with #. Once you enter the for loop statement, you will be given a row without the >>> prompt. This is normal. Type in the next line using two spaces (for indentation, which establishes the block for the loop). After the second sleep() call, press Enter on a blank line to end the indentation block. Take a look at the board now. It should be blinking the red LED. Remember, the REPL console, like the Python console, runs the code as you enter it. If you want to blink the LED slower, just adjust the sleep() calls to increase the value to 0.50 or even 1.0. When the code ends, you should see the "Done" message as follows:

```
Done!
>>>
```

Note   On some platforms, such as macOS and Linux, you can use a text editor to enter the code, then copy and paste it into the REPL console. However, this does not work for all platforms or terminal programs. Try it yourself.

Example 2: Blink LEDs in Series

Now, let's turn the LEDs on and off in sequence using a counting variable inside a different loop (a while loop). In this case, we must cycle through the LEDs one at a time, turning each on then off after a short delay. So, it is like the previous example but, as you will see, demonstrates a bit more complexity. For example, we store the LED instances (from the Pin class) in an array.

This example uses two loops. First, we loop through the LEDs, turning them all off. The following shows how to do this. Notice I use a counting variable in the range of one to four. Inside the body of the loop, I get the LED from the array using the counting variable, then turn it off with `led.off()`. Turning the LEDs off at the start is a good habit and will take care of any events where you leave code running or interrupt code running so that one or more of the LEDs remain on. You can also fix this by resetting the board, but this method is preferred (and good practice).

```
for i in range(0,4):      # Turn off all of the LEDs
    leds[i].off()         # Turn the LED off
```

Next, we use another loop that will run ten times. Inside the body of the loop, I do something similar to the last loop by getting the LED from the array, turn it on, wait 250 milliseconds, turn it off, and wait another 250 milliseconds. Check the following code to see these elements:

```
for i in range(0, 10):    # Run the indented code 10 times
    for j in range(0,4):  # For each LED...
        leds[j].on()      # Turn LED on
        sleep(0.25)       # Sleep
        leds[j].off()     # Turn LED off
        sleep(0.25)       # Sleep
```

Listing 2-5 shows the completed code. Read it a few times until you're convinced it will work.

Listing 2-5. Example 2: Blinking the LEDs

```
#
# MicroPython for the IoT Second Edition
#
# Example 2 - Blink LEDs
#
# Dr. Charles Bell
#
from machine import Pin  # Get the machine Pin class
from utime import sleep  # Import the sleep method

# Create an array for the LEDs
```

```
leds = [Pin(14, Pin.OUT), Pin(15, Pin.OUT),
        Pin(16, Pin.OUT), Pin(17, Pin.OUT)]

for i in range(0,4):      # Turn off all of the LEDs
    leds[i].off()         # Turn the LED off

for i in range(0, 10):    # Run the indented code 10 times
    for j in range(0,4):  # For each LED...
        leds[j].on()      # Turn LED on
        sleep(0.25)       # Sleep
        leds[j].off()     # Turn LED off
        sleep(0.25)       # Sleep

print("Done!")            # Goodbye!
```

When you run the code, you will see the LEDs turn on in sequence starting with the red, then green, blue, yellow, and blue. Take some time to explore the code and, if you have programmed with Python before, consider making the first loop into a method and call it at the end to ensure all LEDs are turned off.

Example 3: Using a Button

This example demonstrates how to use the button with the board. It also demonstrates how to use an interrupt (called a callback function). That is, we create a function in our code, then tell MicroPython to execute that function when an interrupt occurs – in this case, when the button is pressed. Since this example is also complex, I will walk you through the code.

First, we import the hardware libraries and methods we want to use and set a variable for the green LED and turn it off. We also created a button class instance from the Pin library:

```
from machine import Pin    # Get the machine Pin class
from utime import sleep    # Import the sleep method
# Green LED
led = Pin(15, Pin.OUT)
# Button
button = Pin(13, Pin.IN, Pin.PULL_DOWN)

led.off()                  # Turn off LED
```

Next, we define a function. It's rather easy. We just use the def directive and give the function a name. Let's call it flash_led. The interrupt will pass a variable to the method but will not need it (named not_used). Inside this function, we flash the LED quickly (100-millisecond delay) five times. We've already seen the code to do this in the previous examples.

```
def flash_led(not_used):
    for i in range(0, 5):
        led.on()
        sleep(0.1)
        led.off()
        sleep(0.1)
```

Next, we create another variable by getting the user button. We then use the method irq() and pass in the trigger (when the callback is called) and the name of the function we created. This will establish the connection to run the flash_led() function when the button is pressed.

```
# Register the callback (ISR)
button.irq(trigger=Pin.IRQ_FALLING, handler=flash_led)
```

Listing 2-6 shows the completed code.

Listing 2-6. Example 3: Using a Button

```
#
# MicroPython for the IoT Second Edition
#
# Example 3 - Button with interrupt
#
# Dr. Charles Bell
#
from machine import Pin     # Get the machine Pin class
from utime import sleep     # Import the sleep method
```

```
# Green LED
led = Pin(15, Pin.OUT)
# Button
button = Pin(13, Pin.IN, Pin.PULL_DOWN)

led.off()                    # Turn off LED

# Setup a callback function to handle button pressed
# using an interrupt service routine
def flash_led(not_used):
    for i in range(0, 5):
        led.on()
        sleep(0.1)
        led.off()
        sleep(0.1)

# Register the callback (ISR)
button.irq(trigger=Pin.IRQ_FALLING, handler=flash_led)

print("Ready for testing!")
while True:
    sleep(0.25)
```

Once you see Ready for testing! in the REPL console, you can test it out. If you're timid or have an unusually high propensity for static electricity, use a nonconductive probe and press the button and observe the green LED flashes and then stops. Try it a few times until you're satisfied it works.

Summary

MicroPython is a very exciting addition to the microcontroller world. For the first time, beginners do not need to learn a new operating system or a complex programming language like C or C++ to program the microcontroller. MicroPython permits people with some or even no programming experience to experiment with electronics and build interesting projects. Thus, MicroPython provides opportunities for more hobbyists and enthusiasts who just want to get their projects working without a steep learning curve.

In this chapter, we discovered the major features of MicroPython. We also discovered that MicroPython is based on the Python that we find on our PCs. We even tested Python on the PC to show the similarities. Best of all, we saw firsthand how MicroPython works on a microcontroller board. In this case, we used the Raspberry Pi Pico to demonstrate three examples of Python code written to exercise discrete components connected to the board.

In the next chapter, we will discover a host of hardware we can use to run MicroPython and build our IoT projects. As you will see, there are many options ranging from boards that have MicroPython already loaded, allowing you to build your projects without extra setup, to common boards where you can load MicroPython yourself.

CHAPTER 3

MicroPython Hardware

Now that we've had a quick look at how MicroPython boards can be used, including a presentation on several forms of MicroPython projects, it's time to take a tour of the available boards and related hardware. As we will see, there are several boards that you can choose from, including those that have MicroPython already loaded so that they are ready to use out of the box; those that allow you to load MicroPython on the board; and those existing boards that, with a bit of work, can be worth investigating.

This chapter also includes how to get started using each of the boards discussed, including how to connect the board, load firmware, and more. You should read the entire chapter because while many of the concepts are the same, the procedures may be slightly different from one board to the next. Also, the focus of the chapter is the MicroPython-ready boards. While I briefly discuss alternative boards that you can use, the information in those sections can be useful for using boards not listed in this chapter.

Before we jump into looking at the available boards, let's discuss a few best practices and other practical advice for using MicroPython boards. These apply to all the boards in this chapter and likely any emerging board, and thus you should have these in mind when choosing your board.

Getting Started with MicroPython Boards

While you could just buy one of these boards and jump right into your IoT project, there are some things you should consider and keep in mind when working with your board. Specifically, some boards may require updates, some may require assembling hardware (soldering), and others may have limitations to consider. I will discuss these and more in this section. I also include some tips for using the boards on your PC.

© Charles Bell 2024
C. Bell, *MicroPython for the Internet of Things*, https://doi.org/10.1007/978-1-4842-9861-9_3

Firmware Updates

Those boards that include MicroPython on the chip may require firmware updates. Firmware[1] is the term used to describe software on a chip. Most boards have special chips that allow you to update MicroPython (and other aspects) on your own, allowing you to keep up with changes by the vendor, MicroPython, and more.

You should consider updating the firmware when you first receive the board or at any time you find you cannot access some library function, the operation fails, or when new hardware (add-on boards) are released. However, you should avoid updating your firmware too frequently.

My philosophy is simple: I only update firmware once when the board is new and only when something no longer works. If your project is working and you've not encountered any problems, there's no need to update it. One risk to updating the firmware too often is you could render your project useless if something changes in the firmware, such as old libraries or hardware no longer supported, changes to the library that breaks your code, and other annoying issues. My only exception to this rule is if the vendor has fixed a bug or improved the user experience, in which case I would update the firmware. The bottom line is, if it works, don't mess with it!

Tip   Update your firmware when your board is new and only when needed later.

A special mention is of those boards where you must load MicroPython yourself. Some of these boards may require you to update other parts of the system, such as a bootstrap mechanism, loading MicroPython in nonvolatile memory, etc. If you choose to use a board where you must load MicroPython, be sure to check the vendor's documentation for recommendations regarding updating the software on the board (may not be limited to just the firmware). Finally, some boards are new, so their firmware may not be in beta or a release candidate and not production quality. In these cases, I like to update the firmware more frequently until the production version is released.

---

[1]https://en.wikipedia.org/wiki/Firmware

Networking Issues

If your board has networking capabilities, you should take extra care when learning how to use the board. Specifically, take your time to follow the vendor's instructions for setting up networking and connecting your board to your network. For example, some boards have a very specific mechanism for connecting to WiFi networks. Failure to correctly configure your network connection will lead to a lot of frustration, especially if your project is intended to produce data that is accessed over the network.

If your board has networking capabilities, I recommend reading the documentation and running any examples that show you how to connect the board to your network. The time spent learning how to do this (and repeating it) will eliminate a lot of wasted time. Indeed, the number one mistake beginners make is hooking up their board, writing their code to send data to another system on the network only to discover it doesn't work. In this case, they've failed to ensure the networking portion works before using it for the first time.

This also applies to connecting the board to your PC. For those boards that allow you to access the onboard memory as a file system, this may not be an issue, but for other boards that require connecting over USB via special software, you should ensure you can connect to the board before trying to write your first Python program.

One Step at a Time!

Another very common mistake beginners make is sitting down and writing all their code in one pass without testing anything ahead of time. This creates a situation where if something doesn't work, a host of problems can mask it. For example, if there is some logic error or data produced is incorrect, it may cause other parts of the project to fail or produce incorrect results. This is made worse when the project doesn't work at all – there are too many parts to try and diagnose what went wrong. This often places beginners in a desperate situation of confusion and frustration. You students out there know exactly what I am talking about.

This can be avoided easily by building your project one step at a time. That is, build your project one aspect at a time. For example, if you're working with LEDs to signal something, get that part working first. Similarly, if you're reading data from a sensor, ensure you can do that correctly in isolation before wiring it all together and hoping it all works. Even the very experienced can make this mistake, but they are more equipped to fix it if something goes wrong (and they know better but it's a do as I say not as I do situation). We will build the examples in this book one step at a time. Some are small enough that there may be only one step, but the practice is one you should heed for any project you undertake.

Programming Tools

Some microcontroller vendors offer software development (programming) tools. Arguably, one of the most successful is the Arduino integrated development environment (IDE). The Arduino IDE provides all the tools you need to work (program) the Arduino – from writing your code to compiling to installing it on the board. However, the best IDE for working with MicroPython is Thonny.

If you have worked with the Raspberry Pi and Python, chances are you've run across a nice, small Python integrated development environment (IDE) named Thonny. Thonny is available for most platforms, including Linux, Windows, and macOS at `https://thonny.org/`. Simply download the installer for your platform and install it.

After you have installed Thonny and start it for the first time, on some platforms, you will be asked to choose a *language* and *initial settings*. The choices for settings include *Standard* and *Raspberry Pi*. The *Raspberry Pi* settings are simplistic, and you won't see the menu (but you can turn it on by switching the mode). So, you should select the *Standard* option as shown in Figure 3-1.

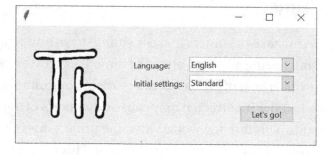

Figure 3-1. *Choose Initial Settings (Thonny)*

Caution   To perform this process, your Pico should not be connected to your PC. If it is, disconnect it before you continue.

Using Thonny, you can develop Python and MicroPython code and even run the code to test it. The editor is tailored for writing Python code and has many useful tools to help you with your coding. Better still, it does all of this using a simple, uncluttered user interface that is elegant in its simplicity.

Figure 3-2 shows an example of using Thonny to connect to and run MicroPython scripts on a MicroPython board. Notice there is a file explorer, editor, and REPL console window. Cool!

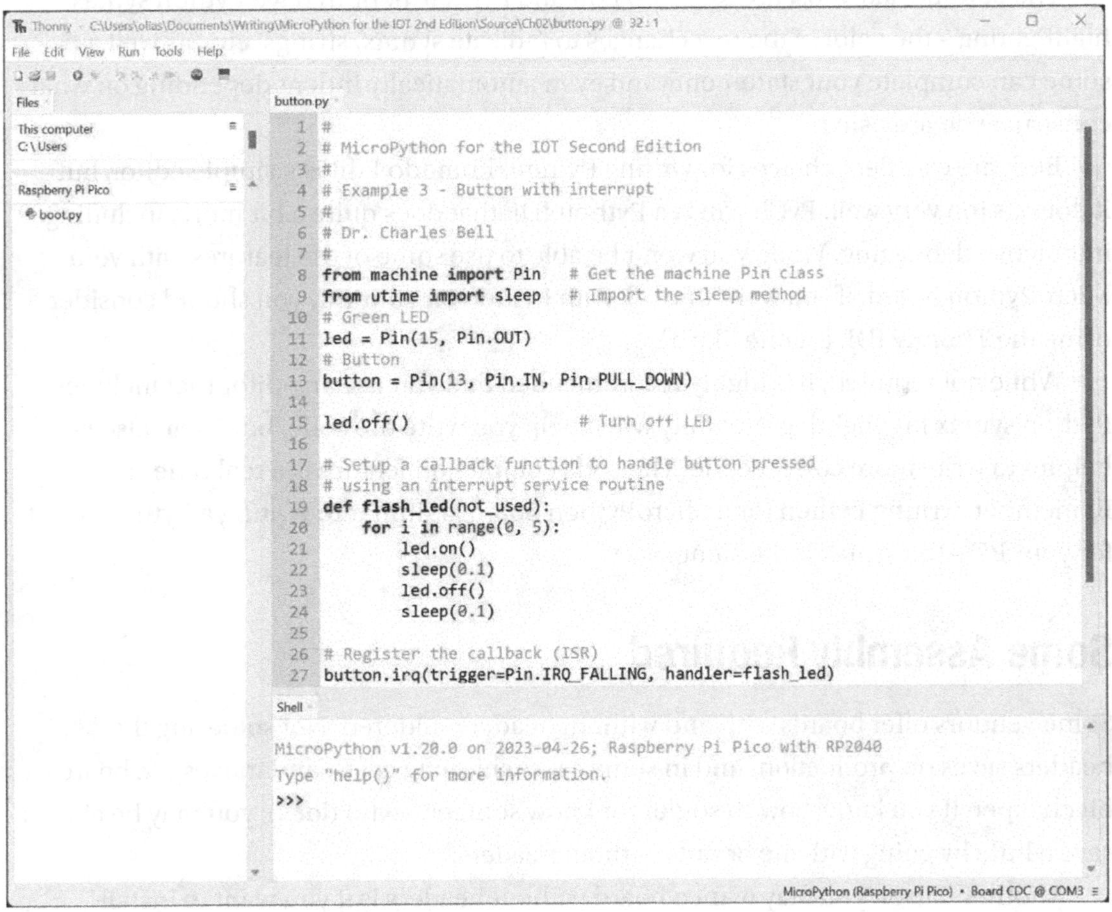

```
#
# MicroPython for the IOT Second Edition
#
# Example 3 - Button with interrupt
#
# Dr. Charles Bell
#
from machine import Pin    # Get the machine Pin class
from utime import sleep    # Import the sleep method
# Green LED
led = Pin(15, Pin.OUT)
# Button
button = Pin(13, Pin.IN, Pin.PULL_DOWN)

led.off()                  # Turn off LED

# Setup a callback function to handle button pressed
# using an interrupt service routine
def flash_led(not_used):
    for i in range(0, 5):
        led.on()
        sleep(0.1)
        led.off()
        sleep(0.1)

# Register the callback (ISR)
button.irq(trigger=Pin.IRQ_FALLING, handler=flash_led)
```

```
MicroPython v1.20.0 on 2023-04-26; Raspberry Pi Pico with RP2040
Type "help()" for more information.
>>>
```

Figure 3-2. *The Thonny IDE*

However, if you do not want to use an IDE, most of what you will need to do for writing Python scripts can be done without special software. In fact, there are several programming editors that support Python, including Komodo Edit (available from `www.activestate.com/komodo-ide/downloads/edit`), PyCharm (`www.jetbrains.com/pycharm/`), and the PyDev IDE plug-in for Eclipse (`www.pydev.org/`). The PyCharm IDE is offered as a community editor (free) as well as a paid application. Komodo Edit is also a free version of the more powerful, paid Komodo Edit IDE.

The editors I like most are Komodo Edit and PyCharm. Both have Python syntax highlighting – the color of the text changes to indicate syntax, strings, etc., as well as some can complete your statements and even automatically indent depending on what construct you are using.

Both are excellent choices for writing Python. Komodo Edit is a simple editor, but it does its job very well. PyCharm is a Python IDE that does quite a bit more, including interactive debugging. While you won't be able to use some of the features with your MicroPython board, if you want to work with Python on your PC, you should consider using the Thonny IDE (or one like it).

While not required, it is highly recommended that you use an editor that includes Python syntax highlighting. Not only will it help you write the code, but it can also be helpful to write more correct code. The code completion feature is a real time saver. Remember, writing Python for a MicroPython board is similar to writing a Python script for your PC – the syntax is the same.

Some Assembly Required

Some vendors offer boards with and without headers soldered. Not soldering the headers saves on production, and in some cases shipping costs, and makes the boards a bit cheaper. If you know how to solder (or know someone who does), you may be able to save a little by going with the boards without headers.

Another reason you may want a board without headers is if you want to install your board in a project enclosure or some other form of embedded installation. In this case, having the headers soldered may take up more space than you have or make the completed project a bit bulkier.

You may also encounter some add-on boards, breakout boards, or other discrete components that are not soldered with headers (or connectors). If you want to use these, you may have to solder the header or connector yourself. For example, most of the breakout boards from Adafruit (`adafruit.com`) and SparkFun (`sparkfun.com`) do not come with the headers soldered.

GPIO Pins

We learned a bit about general-purpose input/output (GPIO) pins in the last chapter. One of the things that differentiates the various boards is how the GPIO pins are arranged and even how many pins are provided. While most boards support a list of pins including analog and digital pins, some boards provide fewer pins than others.

If your project requires several pins – analog or digital – you should plan to choose a board that can support the number of pins you will need. Fortunately, most will; however, some of the newer boards that you can load MicroPython may not. For example, some versions of the ubiquitous ESP8266[2] (a low-cost WiFi chip) may support only a few pins, making it less than ideal for projects that have many components.

Figure 3-3 shows a drawing that illustrates the GPIO pins available on the Raspberry Pi Pico. You can find similar drawings (also called datasheets, mappings, or pinouts) from the manufacturer or vendor of your board.

---

[2]https://en.wikipedia.org/wiki/ESP8266

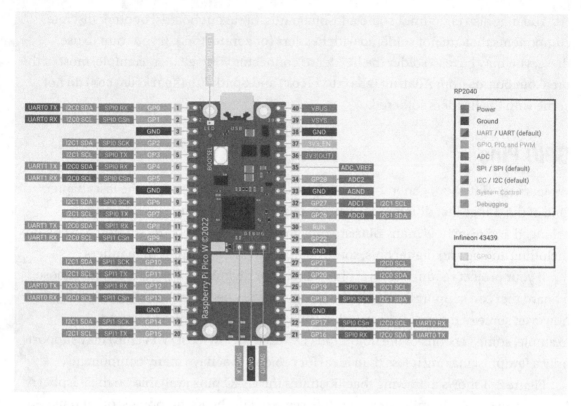

Figure 3-3. *Raspberry Pi Pico GPIO Pins (Courtesy of raspberrypi.com)*

Other Tips

This section includes several tips for things you may encounter when working with your MicroPython board. Consider these tips as things you should do before or during your experiments. Let's begin with the basics.

Visit the Community Forums

The very first thing you should do (even before buying a board) is to visit the community forums for the board(s) of your choice. Many of the vendors host and manage an online message forum for people to ask questions and for people in the community to provide their insights, answers, suggestions, and even help for those who get stuck.

Aside from reading this book, visiting the community forum is an absolute must. In fact, you should consider visiting the forum any time you have a question or problem with your board. You are most likely going to encounter someone who has been there before, struggling through the same (or very similar) issue, as well as get their (and others') suggestions for how to fix it.

The following lists forums for the more popular MicroPython boards. If you do not see your board here, Google for it next time you are online; then, if you like the forum, bookmark it for faster access:

- *Raspberry Pi Pico*: `www.raspberrypi.com/products/raspberry-pi-pico/`

- *Arduino Nano RP2040*: `https://docs.arduino.cc/tutorials/nano-rp2040-connect/rp2040-01-technical-reference`

- *CircuitPython Forum*: `https://forum.micropython.org/viewtopic.php?f=16&t=2894`

- *General Python Forum (not specific to MicroPython)*: `www.python.org/community/`

Note   I include more tips for interacting with community forums in Chapter 12.

Handle with Care!

You should consider your MicroPython board as a very sensitive device susceptible to electrostatic discharge (ESD). Unless you place your board in a case, you should handle your board carefully, always placing it on a nonconductive surface before powering it on. ESD can be caused by many things (think back to when you were a child with sneakers on carpet). This discharge can harm the board. Always ensure you handle your board so that ESD is controlled and minimized.

You should also never move the board when it is powered on. Why? The MicroPython boards have components soldered on with many pins exposed on both sides. Should any two or more of those pins touch something that conducts electricity, you can risk damaging the board.

Also, always store your board in an ESD safe container – one that is expressly made to store electronics. Your average, everyday, inexpensive plastic box should be avoided. However, if you do not have a container made for electronics, you can use static free bags to place the board in while it is being stored. Many of the boards and components you buy come in such packaging. So, don't throw it away!

You should take care to make sure your body, your workspace, and your project is grounded to avoid electrostatic discharge (ESD). The best way to avoid this is to use a grounding strap that loops around your wrist and attaches to an antistatic mat like these: uline.com/BL_7403/Anti-Static-Table-Mats.

Finally, be extra careful when connecting your USB cable to your board. Most boards come with a micro USB connector, which is prone to breakage (more so than other connectors). In most cases, it is not the cable that breaks but the connector on the board itself. When this happens, it can be very difficult to repair (or may not be repairable). It is also possible that the cable itself will stop working or only work when you hold the cable in place. If this happens, try a new cable and if that fixes the problem, throw the old one away. If it does not fix the problem, it may be the connector on the board. Fortunately, extra care when plugging and unplugging the cable can avoid these issues. For example, always plug the micro USB side first and use the full-size USB end to plug and unplug from your PC. The fewer number of times you use the micro USB connector, the less chance you have of damaging it.

Incorrect Switch Settings

If you work with expansion boards, you may encounter boards with switches that allow you to change power settings. For example, the Grove Shield for Pico from Seeed Studio (www.seeedstudio.com/Grove-Shield-for-Pi-Pico-v1-0-p-4846.html) permits you to choose between 3.3V and 5V for powering the modules connected to the expansion board as shown in Figure 3-4. Be sure to verify the power requirements for any modules used and check the switch to ensure it is in the correct position before powering on your board. Incorrect settings may damage some modules.

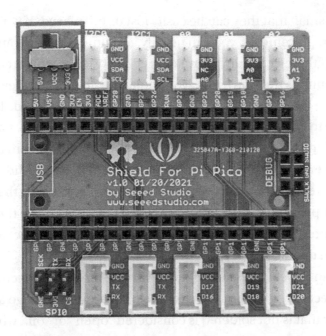

Figure 3-4. Switches on an Expansion Board (Courtesy of seeedstudio.com)

Loose or Missing Jumpers

Another thing that can happen when using a board that has jumpers (small plastic connectors designed to complete a circuit) is the loss of one or more jumpers. Jumpers are used to enable or disable certain features. Figure 3-5 shows an example of what jumpers and their pins look like.

Figure 3-5. Jumpers (Courtesy of sparkfun.com)

Jumpers are so small that they can be easily lost or misplaced. If you lose your jumpers and need replacements, you can usually get some from a computer repair shop in your area. If there aren't any computer repair shops in your area, if you find a PC enthusiast who builds their own PCS, you should be able to get a few jumpers from them. Why? Because those guys normally have a ton of them on hand. The bottom line is you shouldn't have to buy them – someone around you, I am certain, has a few spares.

If one or more jumpers fall off, you can tighten them to make them harder to remove. To tighten the jumpers, use a pair of needle-nose pliers and gently (did I mention gently?) compress the female sockets. There's a bit of a trick to doing that. You can also gently bend the jumper pins slightly out at the top of the pin to make the jumpers fit more snugly. Of course, you can find that computer enthusiast and get a new one if it is still too loose or you damage it.

Jumpers can also appear as small, soldered surface mount connections where the "jumper" connects two or more pads to enable a feature or change a setting. A surface pad jumper that is not soldered is considered "open" or "off," whereas a surface pad jumper with solder connecting two or more pins is considered "closed" or "on." Figure 3-6 shows an example of two soldered jumpers (enlarged for detail). The one on the left is enabled (soldered), and the one on the right is not soldered.

Figure 3-6. *Soldered Jumpers (Courtesy of sparkfun.com)*

Now that we've had a look at some considerations for getting started with MicroPython boards, let's start our tour of the available boards starting with those that have MicroPython loaded and ready to use. Each section includes a brief overview of the board as well as notes on how to get started using the board and where you can buy the board.

MicroPython RP2040 Boards

The first category of boards we will explore are those boards that come with MicroPython installed and use the Raspberry Pi RP2040 chip. These boards are those that you do not need to install any software to use (though you may need to update the firmware periodically or install a driver on your PC). Thus, these boards are the best choices for those new to MicroPython and electronics in general. However, that doesn't mean the boards are not powerful – they are! In fact, the projects in this book are demonstrated using these boards, and you will find they are more than adequate for most small- to medium-sized IoT projects.

The MicroPython-ready boards at the time of this writing are numerous, but we will be using two of the most popular boards: the Raspberry Pi Pico and Arduino Nano RP2040 Connect. Both are good choices, and both use the revolutionary Raspberry Pi RP2040 chip, but as we will see, one is a bit easier to use for MicroPython IoT projects. Let's first explore why this chip (and the Raspberry Pi platform) is important for MicroPython projects.

Origins of the RP2040

The Raspberry Pi foundation (`raspberrypi.org`) has changed the world by providing powerful, low-cost computer boards. The Raspberry Pi is by far the biggest selling and most popular of the many small computer boards available. Perhaps even more important is the Raspberry Pi is designed for education. Educators can use the Raspberry Pi to teach computer science, electronics, hardware automation, and Internet of Things (IoT) projects using Python, Java, or C++ programming languages.

Better still, the ability to run a powerful desktop operating system means you can use a Raspberry Pi just like your laptop or desktop to build your project and connect it to other hardware via the general-purpose input/output (GPIO) pins. With those accolades, it was only a matter of time before the Raspberry Pi foundation extended their global dominance.

The Raspberry Pi Pico (www.raspberrypi.com/products/raspberry-pi-pico/) family of microcontrollers is a departure from the dominance of the Raspberry Pi small computer boards because it isn't another small computer board. So, it doesn't have the ability to run an operating system; there are no video ports, no USB host ports, or even a power connector. Rather, the Raspberry Pi Pico is the first microcontroller to use a small Raspberry Pi–based chip (RP2040).

Tip   Yes, you can program your Raspberry Pi Pico from your Raspberry Pi computer!

Why is this important? It means the Raspberry Pi is one of the newest contenders in the microcontroller field, and, as we will see, the Raspberry Pi foundation has risen to the challenge with a very powerful, very affordable microcontroller that runs MicroPython (Python for microcontrollers), making the Raspberry Pi Pico easy to program and easier to use.

Introducing the RP2040

Let's begin with the name. The name may seem strange at first. Normally, we think the number is some sort of revision or version,[3] but this is not the case for the RP2040. Figure 3-7 depicts the nomenclature of the name. As you can see, it is an encoded phrase to represent four characteristics of the microprocessor. It is likely we will see variants of this microprocessor in the future, and we should expect its name (number) to vary according to this nomenclature.

---

[3] No, this isn't an Edison-like discovery where there were 2039 unsuccessful versions prior to the moment of enlightenment.

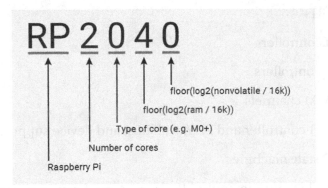

Figure 3-7. RP2040 Nomenclature (Courtesy of raspberrypi.org)

The RP2040 is a single chip combining memory, a dual-core processor, interfaces, and supporting electronics. In many ways, it is a self-contained powerhouse of a microcontroller. The chip is built to deliver high performance with low power consumption. In fact, it can also support extended execution using battery power. And, best of all, it boasts the ability to run MicroPython, making programming very easy, breaking the programming learning curve common to microcontrollers. In other words, you don't have to have a degree in programming or electronics to be able to use it.

The many features of the RP2040 are listed as follows:

- Dual ARM Cortex-M0+ @ 133MHz

- 264kB on-chip SRAM in six independent banks

- Support for up to 16MB of off-chip Flash memory via a dedicated QSPI bus

- DMA controller

- Fully connected AHB crossbar

- Interpolator and integer divider peripherals

- On-chip programmable LDO to generate core voltage

- 2 on-chip PLLs to generate USB and core clocks

- 30 GPIO pins, 4 of which can be used as analog inputs

- Peripherals include

- 2 UARTs

- 2 SPI controllers

- 2 I2C controllers

- 16 PWM channels

- USB 1.1 controller and PHY, with host and device support

- 8 PIO state machines

So, what is all of that mumbo jumbo? For most, these features may not mean a whole lot, but in essence, we're talking about a seriously capable chip. Those features you may be most interested in include the SPI and I2C controllers (2 of each), the 16 pulse wave modulation channels, and the 30 GPIO pins. Suffice it to say, it can handle just about anything you would need for your electronics project. Cool!

Tip   For a complete description of the features of the RP2040, see the datasheet at `https://datasheets.raspberrypi.org/rp2040/rp2040-datasheet.pdf`.

The RP2040 microprocessor can be purchased separately, and there are a growing number of vendors building boards around the RP2040. We will see a few of them in a later section. But first, let's look at the hardware of the Pico in more detail.

Raspberry Pi Pico/Pico W

The Raspberry Pi Pico W, hence Pico (`https://thepihut.com/products/raspberry-pi-pico-w`), is a small, green printed circuit board the size of a stick of gum. Along either long side are the GPIO pins with a micro USB connector on one of the shorter ends. On the other end is a set of debugging pins that you can use for advanced diagnostics. Figure 3-8 shows the Pico from before oriented with the USB port to the right with the WiFi chip (under the large silver cover), and the antenna is located on the left.

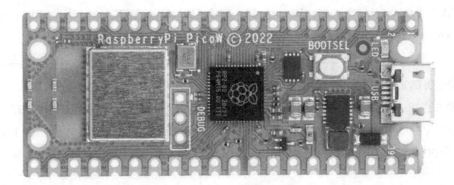

Figure 3-8. *The Raspberry Pi Pico W – Top View (Courtesy of raspberrypi.org)*

Notice the GPIO headers on the top and bottom edges. The three pins on the left are the debugging pins. The only other component on the board we need to know about is the *BOOTSEL* (boot selection) switch located in the upper right of the figure. This switch is used to place the Pico in either boot mode where it runs the MicroPython platform or, if held down while the USB cable is connected to your computer, it will connect as a removable drive, allowing you to load new files or change the base platform files. We will see how to do this later in this section.

Figure 3-9 shows the underside of the Pico (without WiFi). Notice here we see the GPIO pins are labeled, making it easy to locate a specific pin. The places labeled with "TP" are test points that you can use to test voltage should you need to perform any advanced diagnostics of the board. Once again, the pins on the left are for the serial wire debug (SWD) interface. We will not be using that interface in this book, but you can read more about it in Chapter 6 of the Pico datasheet (book): `https://datasheets.raspberrypi.org/pico/getting-started-with-pico.pdf`.

Figure 3-9. *The Raspberry Pi Pico – Bottom View (Courtesy of raspberrypi.org)*

The "W" in the name means this version of the Pico has WiFi, and thus you can connect your Pico to your network and the Internet. Nice.

Tip   The previous version of the Raspberry Pi Pico did not include WiFi but uses the same processor and GPIO (`https://thepihut.com/products/raspberry-pi-pico`). Thus, you can use the older Pico (without WiFi) for many of the introductory projects in this book that do not connect to the Internet.

The heart of the Pico is the large (relative to the board) black chip located in the center of the board on the top side. This is the RP2040 microprocessor, and it provides all of the features that make up the Pico.

Hardware Overview

So, what is the Pico? Simply, the Pico is a printed circuit board built around the RP2040 along with supporting circuitry to create a small microcontroller board about the size of a stick of gum. It breaks out (think wiring) all of the interfaces supported by the RP2040 along with power and ground pins to help round out the GPIO pins.

The Pico is a low-cost board that offers more features than any other board in the price range. In fact, you can find the Pico for as little as $4.00! That's amazing considering what you get. For that price, you will get a Pico without headers attached, and you can buy the headers (male or female pins) cut to length. If you do not know how to solder, you can get the Pico with headers soldered on for a couple of dollars more. Even so, it's still well below what you'd expect to pay for a full-featured microcontroller board.

Let's talk about those header pins for a moment. If you look closely, you will see the pins have what appear to be two rows – one hole closer to the center of the board and another half hole on the edge giving the long edges of the board a serrated look. This design, called castellations, allows you to solder the board in a surface mount configuration or use male header pins for use with a breadboard or female header pins to allow the use of jumper wires to connect components to the Pico. Figure 3-10 shows the header in more detail.

Figure 3-10. *Close-Up of the Pico Header (Courtesy of raspberrypi.org)*

Tip   For a complete guide on how to solder headers onto the Raspberry Pi Pico, visit https://magpi.raspberrypi.org/articles/how-to-solder-gpio-pin-headers-to-raspberry-pi-pico.

Along with the features of the RP2040, the Pico has been designed with the following features:

- RP2040 microcontroller chip designed by Raspberry Pi in the United Kingdom

  - Dual-core ARM Cortex M0+ processor, flexible clock running up to 133MHz

  - 264kB of SRAM and 2MB of onboard Flash memory

- Infineon CYW43439 wireless chip

  - IEEE 802.11n wireless LAN

  - WPA3

- Low-power sleep and dormant modes

- Drag and drop programming using mass storage over USB

- 21x51 1mm thick PCB with 0.1" through-hole pins also with edge castellations

- 40-pin GPIO header

  - Exposes 26 multifunction 3.3V general-purpose I/O (GPIO)

  - 23 GPIO are digital-only and 3 are ADC capable

  - Can be surface mounted as a module

- 3-pin ARM Serial Wire Debug (SWD) port

- Micro USB B port for power and data (and for reprogramming the Flash)

- Can be powered via the micro USB, external supplies, or batteries

- USB 1.1 host and device support

- Real-time clock (RTC)

- Temperature sensor

- Comprehensive SDK, software examples and documentation

Tip   For a complete description of the features of the Pico, see the datasheet at `https://datasheets.raspberrypi.org/pico/pico-datasheet.pdf`.

Getting Started

To connect to your board, use a USB to micro USB cable connecting one end to your Pico and the other end to your PC. If this is a new Pico, the very first time you plug your Pico into your computer, you should see after a few moments a drive mounted named RPI-RP2 (or on Windows, a new drive letter appears in the file explorer tree). When you see your board as a USB drive, it means the board has booted into USB mass storage mode that permits you to copy files and load the firmware.

Loading Firmware

There are two main reasons to load new firmware. First, you may want to reload the firmware if you have used the board for several projects and want to reset it. Second, you may want to load new firmware periodically. This applies to all boards regardless of whether they are MicroPython ready. This is because the version of MicroPython continues to be refined and defects are being repaired.

Thus, to ensure you have the very latest updates, you should update your firmware at least once when you get the board and only when needed later, such as when a new hardware component is added to the library. Loading firmware is easy with the Thonny IDE, but some boards that support MicroPython may require manual loading. Check the vendor website for firmware installation instructions if you cannot use Thonny.

There are several steps involved in loading the MicroPython firmware with Thonny. You must place your board into USB mass media mode first, then use Thonny to download and install the firmware, and finally wait for your board to reboot.

Place Board in USB Mass Media Mode

To place your board in USB mass media mode, you must disconnect the board from your PC, then press and hold the BOOTSEL (boot select) button located near the USB connector on the Pico as shown in Figure 3-11.

Figure 3-11. *Locating the BOOTSEL Button (Pico)*

While holding down the BOOTSEL button, plug your board into your PC with Thonny open. You should hear a tone from your computer (if you have sound enabled) when the USB drive is detected. When you hear the tone, you can release the BOOTSEL button.

Install Firmware in Thonny

In Thonny, click in the lower-right corner and choose *Install MicroPython...* as shown in Figure 3-12.

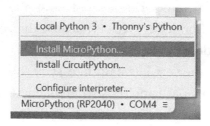

Figure 3-12. *Install MicroPython (Thonny)*

When you click the menu item, you will see the Install or update MicroPython (UF2) dialog as shown in Figure 3-13.

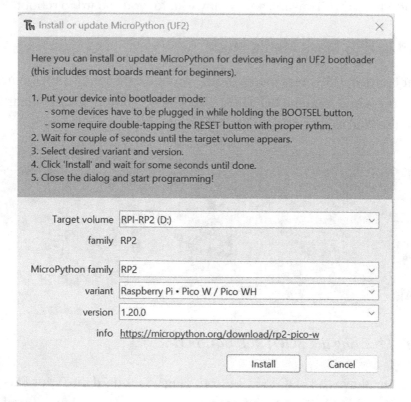

Figure 3-13. *Install or Update MicroPython (UF2) Dialog (Thonny)*

In this dialog, you should see the *Target volume* set to your board (RPI-RP2) as shown. Next, be sure to select RP2 for the *MicroPython family*, then select the correct *variant* (Pico or Pico W). When these selections are correct, click *Install*. The dialog will change to show you the installation progress as shown in Figure 3-14.

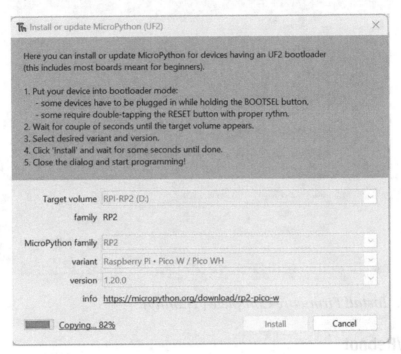

Figure 3-14. *Install Firmware Progress (Thonny)*

When the installation is complete, click the Close button as shown in Figure 3-15.

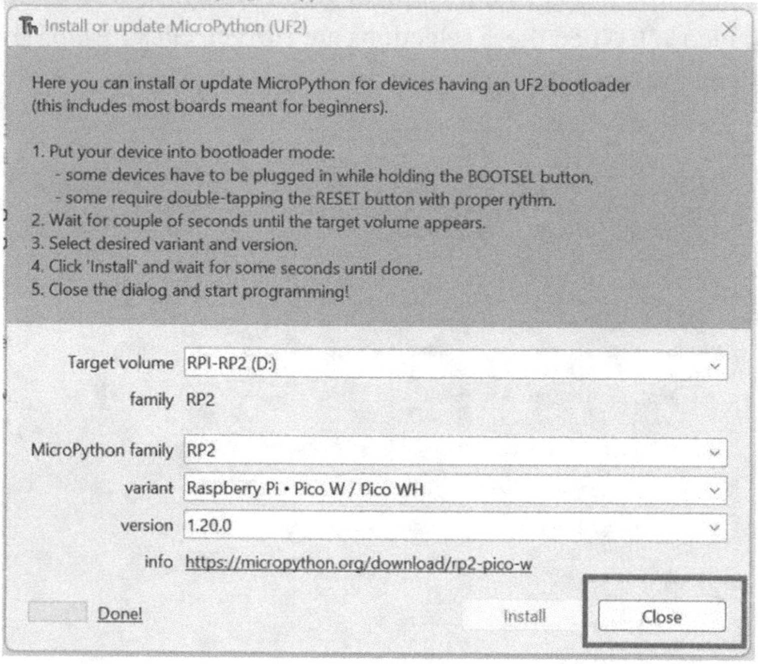

Figure 3-15. *Install Firmware Complete (Thonny)*

Reconnect/Reboot

Once the installation is complete, your board will reboot and Thonny will reconnect. If the board does not connect, click the board in the lower-right corner of Thonny and select your board from the list. If Thonny does not recognize the board, you can disconnect and reconnect your board to your PC. In Thonny, you should then see the board appear and the REPL console connect. You can use the following code to check the firmware version loaded:

```
>>> import os
>>> os.uname()
(sysname='rp2', nodename='rp2', release='1.20.0', version='v1.20.0 on
2023-04-26 (GNU 12.1.0 MinSizeRel)', machine='Raspberry Pi Pico W with
RP2040')
>>>
```

Here, we see the firmware version is 1.20.0, which at the time of this writing was the latest available. It also shows the date the firmware was loaded as well as the name of the firmware file. Finally, we also see the board name.

Your First MicroPython Script

Now that we have our board loaded with the latest firmware, we can try out the board by writing our first script. If you have followed along in the previous chapters and have run the example, you likely have already run some code snippets. This is an example of a complete, simple MicroPython script to print to the REPL console. Yes, this is the essential "Hello, World!" code that everyone who writes code learns as a first step.[4] The code is simply a single line of code as follows:

```
print("Hello, World!")
```

Rather than run this code in the REPL console, we will save it to a file. In Thonny, with your board connected, click the *File ➤ New* menu. You will see a new file as shown in Figure 3-16. Type in the line of code as shown earlier.

---

[4] Some have come to loathe this example, but it does serve a very instructive purpose because it helps confirm your development environment (in this case, Thonny) is set up correctly.

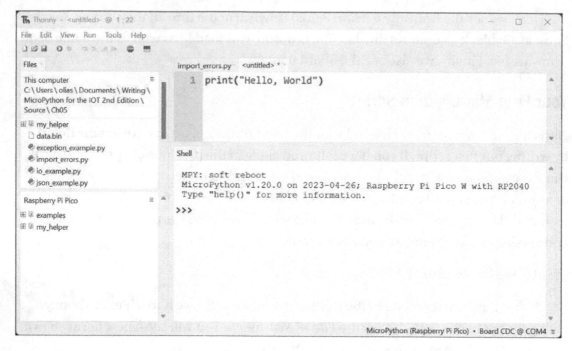

Figure 3-16. *New File (Thonny)*

Next, click the File ➤ Save menu and then select the location to store your program. In this case, choose the Pico as shown in Figure 3-17.

Figure 3-17. *Choose Save Location (Thonny)*

Next, click the Run button as shown in Figure 3-18 and observe the result in the REPL console.

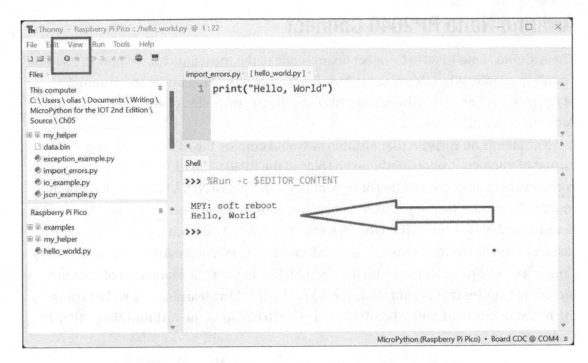

Figure 3-18. *Running the Code (Thonny)*

If you see the output as shown in the image, congratulations! You've written your first MicroPython script (program), saved it to your board, and executed it from your board.

Where to Buy

You can find the Raspberry Pi Pico at any retail or online store that carries the Raspberry Pi line of small computers and accessories. The following are my favorite online vendors to purchase Raspberry Pi boards and components. They are available with or without headers:

- The Pi Hut (https://thepihut.com/collections/pico)

- SparkFun (www.sparkfun.com/categories/395)

- Adafruit (www.adafruit.com/category/437)

Arduino Nano RP2040 Connect

The Arduino Nano RP2040 Connect board is one of the most anticipated new RP2040 boards available. Why? Because the Arduino has been the king under the mountain of microcontrollers. If you have used any other microcontroller, chances are it was an Arduino or Arduino variant.

It comes as no surprise that Arduino.cc would employ the RP2040 in their own format of microcontrollers. Arduino has placed the RP2040 on their Nano format board complete with all of the features of an Arduino Nano plus a NINA WiFi and Bluetooth module. There are so many features that it's no wonder the expectations are high for this board. It is slightly smaller than the Pico with fewer GPIO pins but has the castellated header of the Pico and the same micro USB connector. While the Arduino Nano RP2040 Connect can be programmed with the Arduino IDE in the C-like language of Arduino, including features that permit using the board for machine learning, we will be using the board in this book with MicroPython. Figure 3-19 shows the Arduino Nano RP2040 Connect.

Figure 3-19. *Arduino Nano RP2040 Connect (Courtesy of arduino.cc)*

For a complete description of this board, see `https://store.arduino.cc/nano-rp2040-connect-with-headers`.

Hardware Overview

The Arduino Nano RP2040 Connect is very similar to the Raspberry Pi Pico because it shares the same RP2040 chip. However, there are components and features that differ from the Raspberry Pi Pico. Rather than repeat the same features, the following lists the differences between the boards:

- U-blox Nina W102 WiFi/Bluetooth Module

    - IEEE 802.11b/g/n single-band 2.4GHz WiFi operation

    - Bluetooth 4.2

- 4x 12-bit ADC

- 3x I2C, SDIO, CAN, QSPI

- Memory: AT25SF128A 16MB NOR Flash

- 6-axis sensor (ST LSM6DSOXTR)

    - 3D gyroscope ±2/±4/±8/±16 g full scale

    - 3D accelerometer ±125/±250/±500/±1000/±2000 dps full scale

    - Advanced pedometer, step detector, and step counter

    - Significant motion detection, tilt detection

    - Programmable finite state machine: accelerometer, gyroscope, and external sensors

    - Embedded temperature sensor

- Microphone (ST MP34DT06JTR)

    - 64 dB signal-to-noise ratio

    - Omnidirectional sensitivity

    - –26 dBFS ± 1 dB sensitivity

- RGB LED

    - Connected to U-blox Nina W102 GPIO

- Cryptographic coprocessor with secure hardware-based key storage

    - Microchip ATECC608A Crypto

    - I2C, SWI

    - Hardware support for symmetric algorithms

        - SHA-256 and HMAC Hash including off-chip context save/restore

        - AES-128: Encrypt/decrypt, Galois field multiply for GCM

- Internal high-quality NIST SP 800-90A/B/C Random Number Generator (RNG)

- GPIO

  - 14x digital pins

  - 8x analog pins

Perhaps the most significant difference for those choosing this board over the Pico is the pinout of the GPIO. Figure 3-20 shows the pinout for the Arduino Nano RP2040 Connect.

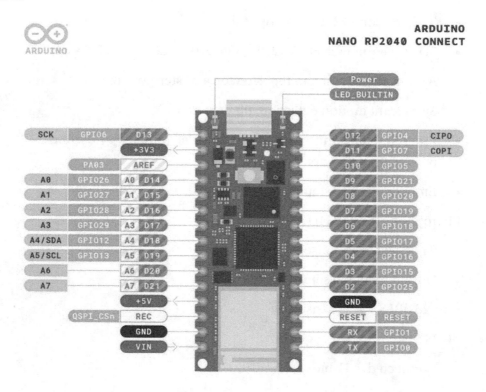

Figure 3-20. *Arduino Nano RP2040 Connect Pinout (Courtesy of arduino.cc)*

Getting Started

You can program the Arduino Nano RP2040 Connect using Thonny once you have installed the MicroPython firmware. New boards do not have the firmware loaded, and thus you will need to install the MicroPython firmware before using it.

Like the Pico, you can place the board into USB mass storage mode that permits you to copy files and load the firmware. However, the process is different than the Pico.

Loading Firmware

To install the firmware on the Arduino Nano RP2040 Connect, you must first download the latest firmware file, put the board into USB mass media mode, and manually copy the file to the board, then reboot the board.

Downloading the Latest Firmware

To download the firmware file written for the Arduino Nano RP2040 Connect (a file with a `.uf2` file extension), navigate to `https://docs.arduino.cc/micropython/`, then scroll down and expand the section for the board as shown in Figure 3-21. Select the latest stable file and download it. For example, we will choose the file named `20230426-v1.20.0.uf2` as shown in the image.

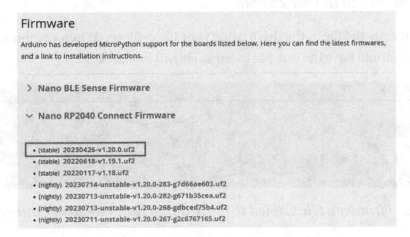

Figure 3-21. *Downloading the Firmware (Arduino Nano RP2040 Connect)*

Place Board in USB Mass Media Mode

To place your board in USB mass media mode, you must first connect the board to your PC, then quickly double-click the BOOTSEL (boot select) button located near the USB connector on the board as shown in Figure 3-22.

Figure 3-22. *Locating the BOOTSEL Button (Arduino Nano RP2040 Connect)*

You should hear a tone on your computer and see the RPI-RP2 drive appear in your file explorer.

Copy the File to the RPI-RP2 Drive

Next, you can copy the file to the drive using your file explorer. When complete, your board (drive) should have the one file listed as shown in Figure 3-23.

Figure 3-23. *Firmware File Copied to the Arduino Nano RP2040 Connect*

Reconnect/Reboot

Once the installation is complete, you can reboot your board by clicking the BOOTSEL button once, and then Thonny will connect. If the board does not connect, click the board in the lower-right corner of Thonny and select your board from the list. If Thonny does not recognize the board, you can disconnect and reconnect your board to your PC. In Thonny, you should then see the board appear and the REPL console connect. You can use the following code to check the firmware version loaded:

```
>>> import os
>>> os.uname()
```

```
(sysname='rp2', nodename='rp2', release='1.20.0', version='v1.20.0 on
2023-04-26 (GNU 12.1.0 MinSizeRel)', machine='Arduino Nano RP2040 Connect
with RP2040')
>>>
```

Here, we see the firmware version is 1.20.0, which at the time of this writing was the latest available. It also shows the date the firmware was loaded as well as the name of the firmware file. Finally, we also see the board name.

Where to Buy

Like the Pico, the Arduino Nano RP2040 is available at any retail or online store that carries the Arduino line of small computers and accessories. The following are my favorite online vendors to purchase Arduino boards and components. They are available with or without headers:

- Arduino Store (`https://store-usa.arduino.cc/collections/boards/products/arduino-nano-rp2040-connect`)

- The Pi Hut (`https://thepihut.com/collections/arduino-store`)

- DigiKey (`www.digikey.com/en/products/detail/arduino/ABX00052/14123941`)

Other RP2040 Boards

There are also a growing number of vendors incorporating the RP2040 chip into their own MicroPython boards. Perhaps the most significant alternative to the Pico and Arduino Nano is the Seeed Studio XIAO[5] RP2040 (`www.seeedstudio.com/XIAO-RP2040-v1-0-p-5026.html`), which offers the power of the RP2040 ecosystem in a compact size. The board itself measures 21 × 17.5mm, which is a fraction of the size of other boards, making it an excellent choice for installations with space limitations, such as wearable devices. Figure 3-24 shows the Seeed Studio XIAO RP2040.

---

[5] Pronounced (roughly) "She-ow" and is the name of a Chinese flute.

Figure 3-24. *Seeed Studio XIAO RP2040 (Courtesy of seeedstudio.com)*

Hardware Overview

The Seeed Studio XIAO RP2040 is tiny and lacks many of the features (components) of the larger boards.[6] The most significant difference is the small number of GPIO pins. The XIAO has the following pins and features. As you can see, it is a viable alternative to the other RP2040 boards. Perhaps the biggest difference is the XIAO uses a USB-C cable rather than a micro USB cable.

- 2 buttons

- 11 digital pins

- 4 analog pins

- 1 I2C interface

- 1 UART port

- 1 SPI port

- 1 SWD Bonding pad interface

- RGB LED

Getting Started

You can program the Seeed Studio XIAO RP2040 using Thonny once you have installed the MicroPython firmware. New boards do not have the firmware loaded, and thus you will need to install the MicroPython firmware before using it.

---

[6] That said, the Raspberry Pi Pico is still a small board. The XIAO is tiny in comparison.

Like the Pico, you can place the board into USB mass storage mode that permits you to copy files and load the firmware. However, the process is different than the Pico.

Loading Firmware

To install the firmware on the Seeed Studio XIAO RP2040, you can follow the same instructions as we used to load the firmware on the Raspberry Pi Pico/Pico W. In fact, Seeed Studio documents the process on their documentation portal (`https://wiki.seeedstudio.com/XIAO-RP2040-with-MicroPython/`).

Where to Buy

You can find RP2040-compatible MicroPython boards on online electronic stores that cater to electronics enthusiasts. The following are my favorite online vendors to purchase MicroPython boards and components:

- The Pi Hut (`https://thepihut.com`)

- SparkFun (`https://sparkfun.com`)

- Mouser (`www.mouser.com`)

- Seeed Studio (`www.seeedstudio.com`)

MicroPython-Compatible Boards

There are many other boards you can use with MicroPython that do not use the RP2040 chip. This section briefly lists some of the more popular alternatives for working with MicroPython. The projects in this book focus on the Raspberry Pi Pico and Arduino Nano RP2040 Connect, but if you have one or more of these alternatives, you may be able to use them in your future MicroPython projects.

BBC micro:bit

The BBC micro:bit board is specially designed to be very easy to use. In fact, it is designed to help instruct children more about hardware and software. In that, the BBC micro:bit is an enormous success. Part of that success is in how easy the board is to use – its form factor measures only approximately 52mm × 42mm with components on both sides.

On one side is an array of programmable LEDs and two buttons. On the other side are the components including the processor, micro USB connector, reset button, and battery connector. The board has its GPIO header arranged along the bottom edge and is also two sided. A set of large-holed pins (called alligator pins) are spaced evenly that allow you to ground, power (3V), and (3) GPIO pins. This makes using the board with an edge connector simple. Figure 3-25 shows the front and back of the original BBC micro:bit board. Newer boards add additional sensors and a radio module for connecting to other boards.

Figure 3-25.   *The BBC micro:bit Board (Front and Back)*

Another reason for the success of this board is the software created to support it.

The developers have created an easy-to-use software for working with the board. Since the board is intended to be used like an Arduino coding in a C-like language, the software available is beyond the scope of this book, but you can read more about it at `http://microbit.org/`. However, we will see shortly a special application that enables us to create, edit, and run MicroPython on the BBC micro:bit. Cool.

Hardware Overview

The original BBC micro:bit does not have networking but does have Bluetooth, which you can use to connect to another device to forward data to the Internet. The newer BBC micro:bit boards add a radio that permits you to communicate with other micro:bit boards. It can be used for IoT projects, but it is not quite as easy as the Pico and may require an intermediate node, such as a PC or small computer like a Raspberry Pi or even an Arduino.

The following lists an overview of some of the hardware features of the BBC micro:bit board. You can also access the onboard USB drive when the board is connected to your PC via a USB cable.

- 32-bit ARM Cortex processor

- 16K RAM

- Compass for detecting orientation

- Temperature sensor

- Speaker (latest boards)

- Microphone and LED (latest boards)

- Red power LED (latest boards)

- Yellow USB LED (latest boards)

- Touch area (latest boards)

- Accelerometer for detecting changes in movement (speed)

- Low-energy Bluetooth (BLE)

- (2) Programmable buttons

- A 5 × 5 array of programmable LEDs

- (3) Alligator digital/analog pins

- (20) GPIO pins on edge connector

- Battery connector

Now that we've had a brief tour of the hardware, let's look at how to use the board with MicroPython.

Getting Started

The BBC micro:bit board is the easiest alternative board to use with MicroPython. This is due to two software applications – an application named *Mu* (https://codewith.mu/en/download) and a command-line tool named uFlash (https://uflash.readthedocs.io/en/latest/). Mu is a full editor that you can use on your PC and, when connected to your BBC micro:bit via a USB cable, can save and execute the scripts. The uFlash tool can be used to manually transfer Python scripts to the board. Both options are available for use on Windows, macOS, and Linux. Figure 3-26 shows an example of using Mu to write a short MicroPython script to print a message. You can still access the board with the REPL console through the Mu application by clicking the REPL button.

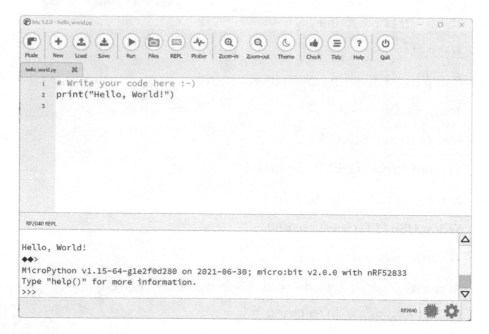

Figure 3-26. *The Mu Editor for MicroPython on the BBC micro:bit*

Unlike the other boards where we must first install the firmware to use MicroPython, the BBC micro:bit can be used to run MicroPython scripts using one of these tools. For example, we can use Mu to write our MicroPython script and then "flash" the BBC micro:bit board with a compiled version of the script (called a hex file). Yes, this means you can write your script, compile it, and flash (load the hex file) directly to the board! We simply write the code in the editor and click Flash to load it on the board. Best of all, the board is programmed to always run the script on each boot. So, that means we can load our own code directly to the board without extra work. Cool.

Tip   You can read the very latest on using MicroPython on the BBC micro:bit at https://microbit-micropython.readthedocs.io/en/latest/.

Where to Buy

You can purchase the BBC micro:bit as well as several accessories from retailers that carry the BBC micro:bit line of components and accessories, including the following:

- Adafruit (`www.adafruit.com/?q=micro%3Abit&`)

- SparkFun (`www.sparkfun.com/categories/284`)

- The Pi Hut (`https://thepihut.com/collections/micro-bit-store`)

- Kitronik (`www.kitronik.co.uk/microbit.html`)

If you plan to use the board for IoT projects or with the projects in this book, I recommend also purchasing an edge connector breakout board such as the one from SparkFun (`www.sparkfun.com/products/13989`).

Circuit Playground Express

The next easiest alternative board to use is the Circuit Playground Express board from Adafruit. In fact, the Circuit Playground Express is a curious alternative board. It's patterned after several other Adafruit wearable boards where the board is designed so that it can be incorporated into clothing. As such, it is circular and about 50mm in diameter.

Around the outside of the board are ten pins with large holes (called alligator pads) that can be used with alligator clips or used to sew with conductive thread. Adafruit also sells alligator to male jumpers that you may find essential to using the board with a breadboard. See the Small Alligator Clip to Male Jumper Wire Bundle at `www.adafruit.com/product/3255`. Another interesting feature is a set of ten RGB NeoPixels, which are bright LEDs that you can change the color through code. The board is also loaded with sensors making a suitable alternative to experiment with IoT projects. Figure 3-27 shows the Circuit Playground Express board.

Figure 3-27. *Circuit Playground Express (Courtesy of adafruit.com)*

Hardware Overview

The following lists an overview of some of the hardware features of the Circuit Playground Express board. You can also access the onboard USB drive when the board is connected to your PC via a USB cable:

- ATSAMD21 ARM Cortex M0 Processor, running at 3.3V and 48MHz.

- 2MB of SPI Flash storage, used primarily with CircuitPython to store code and libraries.

- Micro USB port for programming and debugging. The USB port can act like a serial port, keyboard, mouse, joystick, or MIDI.

- 10 x mini RGB NeoPixels.

- Motion sensor.

- Temperature sensor (thermistor).

- Infrared receiver and transmitter.

- Light sensor (phototransistor). Can also act as a color sensor and pulse sensor.

- Sound sensor (MEMS microphone).

- A mini speaker!

- (2) Pushbuttons.

- (1) Slide switch.

- Infrared receiver and transmitter. Can also act as a proximity sensor.

- (8) Alligator clip-friendly input/output pins.

- I2C, UART, 8 pins that can do analog inputs, multiple PWM output.

- (7) Pads can act as capacitive touch inputs, and the 1 remaining is a true analog output.

- A red "#13" programmable LED.

- Reset button.

The Circuit Playground Express does not have any networking capability. So, you must use an external module to connect to your network. The best option I've found is a Bluetooth module, but other modules like the CC3000 may be alternatives.

The board also does not run MicroPython. Instead, it runs a special version of MicroPython called CircuitPython. CircuitPython is a derivative of MicroPython designed and maintained by Adafruit, built especially for the Circuit Playground Express and a host of other boards. CircuitPython is designed to run on a wide array of boards, including the Circuit Playground Express, Feather, and other popular boards. CircuitPython is currently compatible with MicroPython, but it is being updated regularly.

While CircuitPython is compatible with MicroPython, you may need to use different hardware libraries for some features. There are some differences, and these are documented at `https://github.com/adafruit/circuitpython#differences-from-micropython`. But for our uses, it will work nearly exactly like what we would expect from MicroPython.

Adafruit has an excellent set of tutorials and blogs to help you out. For more information about CircuitPython, see `https://github.com/adafruit/circuitpython` and `https://learn.adafruit.com/search?q=circuitpython&`.

Now that we've had a brief tour of the hardware, let's look at how to use the board with MicroPython.

Getting Started

While the Circuit Playground Express board doesn't have a fancy application like the BBC micro:bit, once you install the correct driver, loading CircuitPython binaries (firmware) on the board is surprisingly easy. In fact, all you need to do is download the current binary and copy it to the board's drive. The steps involved are summarized as follows.

Note   If you use Windows, you may need to download Adafruit's driver at `https://github.com/adafruit/Adafruit_Windows_Drivers/releases/download/1.0.0.0/adafruit_drivers.exe`. Simply download and run the installer. The driver supports many of the Adafruit boards.

When you get the installation options page, you can select which boards you want to support. I recommend selecting all the boards so that you can use any of the Adafruit boards that support CircuitPython. As you will see, there are many such options. Figure 3-28 shows an example of the installation options.

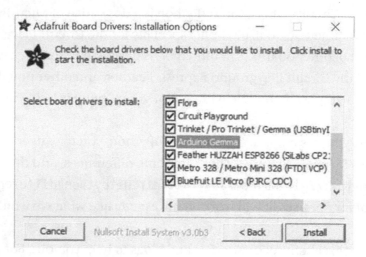

Figure 3-28. *Adafruit Board Drivers – Installation Options*

Next, we need to download the firmware. Adafruit built the firmware in a special format called USB Flashing Format (UF2) at `https://github.com/adafruit/circuitpython/releases` and download the latest version.

Once you download the firmware, you can connect your Circuit Playground Express to your PC, then double-click the reset button (located in the center of the board). When the USB drive mounts (it should be named CIRCUITBOOT), copy the old UF2 file named CURRENT.UF2 to your PC. We will use this as a backup. Next, drag the new UF2 to the CIRCUITPY folder. When the file copy is completed, the board will reboot and run CircuitPython. That's it! You've just loaded CircuitPython! See, that was much easier than any of the other boards, eh?

You should now see the board in Thonny or be able to select the board in Thonny using the button in the lower right of the window. Figure 3-29 shows the REPL console with the Circuit Playground Express connected.

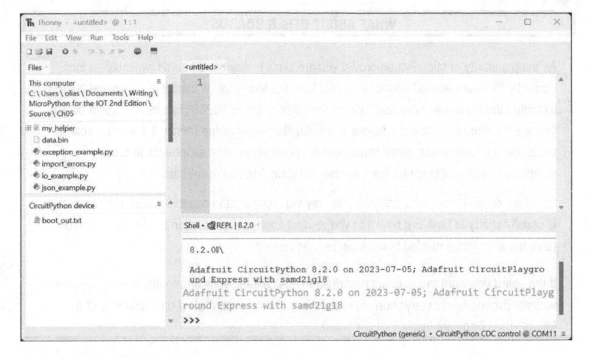

Figure 3-29.   REPL Console on Windows (Circuit Playground Express)

Where to Buy

The Circuit Playground Express board is available from Adafruit and resellers of Adafruit products. You can find the board at www.adafruit.com/product/3333. The cost is approximately $25.

If you decide to try the Circuit Playground Express board, I recommend getting some alligator clips, so you can use the board with a breadboard or connect it to other components. See the Adafruit store for more ideas and accessories for connecting the board to your components.

WHAT ABOUT OTHER BOARDS?

As the popularity of MicroPython grows, you are likely to see more boards available. In fact, currently there are several efforts underway to make MicroPython available on several boards including the Teensy, Arduino, and several variables of the ESP8266 (Espressif) chipset boards. There are some early, limited versions available, like those for the Teensy 3.X version boards, which can be loaded with MicroPython, but the process requires experience in cross-compilation and thus is not for the beginner to tackle (but you're welcome to try!).

However, keep in mind third-party boards may lag somewhat in capability, and documentation is usually spotty at best. But now that you've read about the production boards, you should have the knowledge needed to work with newer boards.

If the board you want to use is not described in this chapter, you can monitor the MicroPython website (`http://micropython.org/download`) for the very latest on availability of a MicroPython firmware install for your board.

Now that we've seen a few of the MicroPython boards that are available, let's dive into the accessories available for you to use to build your projects.

Breakout Boards and Add-Ons

The last bit of hardware we will explore is those boards available for use with the MicroPython board. These can be special, separate modules (called breakout boards) and boards that are specifically designed to be used with a MicroPython board (depending on the board, called shields or skins). The following sections briefly describe some of the breakout boards, shields/skins, and some accessories you may want to consider depending on which board you choose. The list is neither comprehensive nor is it a list of things you must buy. We will see the recommended hardware in each of the example chapters following the discussion on MicroPython.

Breakout Boards

Breakout boards are one of the key elements hobbyists and enthusiasts will use in creating a MicroPython (or any microcontroller-based) IoT solution. This is because breakout boards are small circuit boards that contain all the components needed to support a function such as a sensor, network interface, or even a display. Breakout boards also support one of several communication protocols that require only a few pins to be wired, making them very easy to use. In general, they save the developer a lot of time trying to figure out how to design circuits to support a sensor or chip.

To use breakout boards in our projects, we need only to know which interface to use and how to wire it. Fortunately, most vendors provide a datasheet and other documentation to help you wire your board to it. Even if the vendor only has documentation for an Arduino, it is still helpful to learn how to make the connections. The trick is learning how to write the MicroPython code. We will learn more about the MicroPython libraries and hardware support in Chapters 5 and 6. For now, let's explore some of the breakout boards available. Again, what is shown here is only a very small sample.

In fact, SparkFun has a vast selection of breakout boards. You can find all manner of boards you may find useful. For a full list, see `www.sparkfun.com/categories/20`. Adafruit also has a wide selection of breakout boards. You can see their products at `www.adafruit.com/category/42`. Either vendor has boards that are known to work well and have ample documentation to support them. But, as noted, you may need to adapt them for use with the MicroPython hardware libraries.

The following breakout boards are similar to those we will use in later chapters to read weather data. There are many breakout boards that include sensors for weather data. The most common and easiest to use are those that read temperature, humidity, and barometric pressure. Figure 3-30 shows an example of two such breakout boards: one from Adafruit (`www.adafruit.com/product/992`) and another from SparkFun (`www.sparkfun.com/products/13676`). The Adafruit MPL115A2 reads barometric pressure and temperature, while the SparkFun BME 280 measures barometric pressure, humidity, and temperature. Both use the I2C interface/protocol.

Figure 3-30. *Weather Breakout Boards (Courtesy of adafruit.com and sparkfun.com)*

The next breakout board is often considered a sensor in and of itself because it performs one and only one function, but it is still a breakout board. Many sensors are packaged this way and are often called sensors when they're breakout boards. Fortunately, most people will know what you mean if you use the wrong term. The way you can tell if it is a breakout board is if the board the sensor is mounted on contains other discrete components and a row of header pins.

In this case, the breakout board measures soil moisture and can be handy in creating a plant monitoring solution as we will do in a later chapter. Figure 3-31 shows a soil moisture breakout board from SparkFun (`www.sparkfun.com/products/13322`).

Figure 3-31. *Soil Moisture Sensor (Courtesy of sparkfun.com)*

Notice the unique shape of the board. The two arms or long prongs are part of the sensor apparatus that measures moisture. Notice at the top is a set of pins (no headers installed) that are used to connect to your board. This breakout board does not use a special interface; rather, the sensor produces voltage that you can measure on one of the analog pins on our MicroPython board. In fact, all we need are three wires: 5V, GND, and signal (which connects to an analog pin on our board). Again, we will see how to use this breakout board in a later chapter.

The last breakout board is a special accessory for the BBC micro:bit board. It is an edge connector that you can use to plug in your BBC micro:bit board to a breadboard, making it easier to wire the pins to other components. You can find this breakout board at SparkFun (www.sparkfun.com/products/13989). I highly recommend this or one like it if you choose to use the BBC micro:bit board to run MicroPython.

Figure 3-32 shows the BBC micro:bit Edge Breakout Board from SparkFun.

Figure 3-32. *BBC micro:bit Edge Breakout Board (Courtesy of sparkfun.com)*

Board-Specific Shields/Skins

MicroPython board vendors and indeed vendors of a wide array of microcontroller and similar boards package their components so that they can be used for add-on boards called shields or skins or something similar. For example, the BeagleBone add-on boards are called capes, and the Raspberry Pi add-on boards are called hats. These are boards that have matching headers and are used to plug into (or stack on top of) the main MicroPython board to add functionality. Many shields or skins have pass-through or stacking headers that enable adding more than one shield at a time.

For example, the Arduino and its shield format can be configured with two, three, or more shields added. Similarly, the Arduino Nano RP2040 Connect has several components that can be used with the board, including a nifty Nano Screw Terminal Adapter (https://store-usa.arduino.cc/products/nano-screw-terminal) where the Nano plugs into the shield and each pin has a screw terminal that permits you to make secure connections to your board and thus will help with semipermanent installations. Figure 3-33 shows the Nano Screw Terminal Adapter.

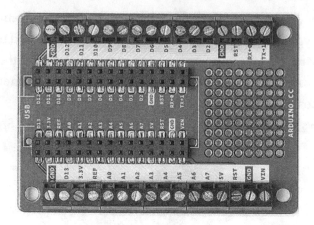

Figure 3-33. *Nano Screw Terminal Adapter (Courtesy of arduino.cc)*

Check with your board vendor to see what board-specific shield/skins are available for your board of choice.

Board-Specific Accessories

The last category of hardware we will discuss is the accessories available for several of the boards discussed in this chapter. Like almost everything in life, we can accessorize our boards to profound (and costly) ends, and, yes, you can reach the nerd-like proportions of the Raspberry Pi or Arduino. In fact, there are several accessories for the Pico and the micro:bit.

That doesn't mean you should rush out and buy them or that they are required for this book; rather, I think you should consider them if you plan to carry on developing with the boards after you complete the examples in this book.

Breadboard for Raspberry Pi Pico/Pico W

The best accessory for the Pico is the Breadboard for Pico available from ThePiHut.com (`https://thepihut.com/products/breadboard-for-pico`). This is a normal, half-sized breadboard that works the same way as any other breadboard but has the pins for the Pico printed on the surface, making this a unique and extremely helpful accessory when building circuits with the Pico. Figure 3-34 shows the Breadboard for Pico with a Pico installed. I highly recommend this board if you plan to use the Pico with the projects in this book.

Figure 3-34. *Breadboard for Pico (Courtesy of thepihut.com)*

BBC micro:bit

The board with the most impressive list of accessories available is the BBC micro:bit. I am sure this is due to its popularity, but it supports our efforts too. You can find kits for building robots, power accessories, cases, and much more!

One of the power options available for the BBC micro:bit that I like is the MI:power board available from Kitronik (`www.kitronik.co.uk/5610-mipower-board-for-the-bbc-microbit.html`). This board is nice because it mounts to your BBC micro:bit board using the large alligator pins (0, 3V, and GND) using only one small 3V coin cell battery for power. It doesn't take up a lot of space when mounted. It includes a switch that allows you to turn the board off and provides a small speaker (hence the connection via the #0 pin), so you can add sound to your project. Figure 3-35 shows the Power Shield from Kitronik.

Figure 3-35. *MI:power Board for the BBC micro:bit*

If you decide to use this battery board, and I highly recommend it over an external battery – especially for the BBC micro:bit – and you decide to use a case, you should know that most cases are not designed to support the MI:power board. However, I did find at least one. As you may surmise, it is made by the same people that made the MI:power!

There are many cases available for the BBC micro:bit with seemingly yet another appearing every day (including those you can print on a 3D printer). However, the one I've found that I like is like others I've used for other boards. It is made from acrylic and uses nylon bolts to join several layers together. It is a clean assembly that allows a clear view of the board, which is nice considering the BBC micro:bit has a lot of LEDs! Figure 3-36 shows the MI:pro case for the BBC micro:bit.

Figure 3-36. *BBC micro:bit MI:pro Case Kit*

Finally, if you are going to be using the BBC micro:bit a lot to run experiments, including those examples in this book as well as the dozens available on the Internet, you should consider the Prototyping System from Kitronik (`www.kitronik.co.uk/5609-prototyping-system-for-the-bbc-microbit.html`). This kit comes with a board that you can mount an included edge connector breakout and breadboard, making the kit a nice and tidy package. Figure 3-37 shows the Prototyping System from Kitronik. This kit is included in the larger Inventor's Kit as described in the following sidebar.

Figure 3-37. *Prototyping System for the BBC micro:bit (Courtesy of kitronik.uk.co)*

Now, let's briefly discuss which board you should buy for use in your MicroPython for the IoT journey.

Which Board Should I Buy?

So, you want to buy a MicroPython board but don't know which to choose. Fortunately, all the boards in this chapter can be an ideal choice. The characteristics that may make some a better fit for some than others include the following:

- *No assembly required*: If you don't know how to solder or don't want to take time to load software, bootstrapping, and firmware, then you should consider a board that is ready to go, such as the Pico or the Arduino Nano. Either can be purchased with headers installed.

- *Connectivity*: If you plan to make your IoT solution public (as opposed to an academic exercise), you should consider boards that have built-in WiFi or similar networking capabilities.

- *Existing hardware*: If you have already invested money and have a platform and devices (add-on boards, breakout boards, etc.), you may want to consider staying with the board. For example, if you have a lot invested in Arduino, you should consider loading MicroPython on an Arduino board. Some Arduino boards are MicroPython compatible. See `https://docs.arduino.cc/learn/programming/arduino-and-python` for a complete list of compatible Arduino boards.

The choice as to which board to buy requires a bit of forethought. Then again, if you're a true enthusiast, you may decide to buy several of these boards, experimenting for yourself as to which fits your project best. Regardless, the boards I feel are best for learning MicroPython for the IoT are the Pico and Nano RP2040. However, the XIAO and micro:bit boards are also great boards to learn MicroPython but require an external module to add networking capabilities.

CONSIDER BUYING A KIT

Many of the boards come packaged with a kit containing an assortment of accessories, including a getting started kit that includes the board and power adapter. Other kits may include breadboards and often sensors or add-on boards. For example, you can purchase several kits for the BBC micro:bit board, including two nice options from SparkFun.

- *BBC micro:bit Go Bundle*: Contains the board and battery pack (`www.sparkfun.com/products/14336`)

- *SparkFun Inventor's Kit for BBC micro:bit*: A version of their wildly popular Inventor's Kit for the BBC micro:bit that includes all the basic electronic components you will need for at least 14 different experiments as well as an easy-to-read instruction booklet (`www.sparkfun.com/products/14300`)

- *micro:climate Kit*: Contains the board, a weather station add-on board, as well as weather sensors (`www.sparkfun.com/products/14217`)

Other vendors may have additional or similar kits for other boards. For example, Kitronik has an excellent Inventor's Kit for the BBC micro:bit (shown as follows – courtesy of kitronik.co.uk) that has many of the parts you will need.

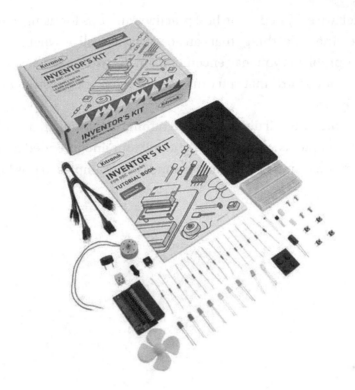

If you are just starting out and don't have any boards or components, a getting started kit may be the most economical option.

Summary

Wow, that was a lot of information. As you can see, there are several MicroPython boards available. Some like the Pico and Nano RP2040 Connect come ready to use and do not require anything more than plugging it in, loading the firmware, and writing your first Python script. Others may require additional work or research to figure out how to use them. However, all the boards presented here are excellent choices for using in the experiments in this book.

In this chapter, we explored some best practices and tips for using your MicroPython board. We covered the usual things that can go wrong as well as where to go to look for solutions to other problems you may encounter. Finally, we looked at several popular add-ons and breakout boards that you can use to develop your project, including those used later in this book.

In the next chapter, we will dive into a programming tutorial on using Python and MicroPython. The chapter is very much a lightning tour and intended to help guide you to the point where you can write (and understand) the examples in this book.

## CHAPTER 4

How to Program in MicroPython

Now that we have a basic understanding of the available MicroPython boards, we can learn more about programming in MicroPython – a very robust and powerful language that you can use to write very powerful applications. Mastering MicroPython is easy, and some may suggest it doesn't require any formal training to use. This is largely true and thus you should be able to write MicroPython scripts with only a little bit of knowledge about the language.

Given that MicroPython is Python, we can learn the basics of the Python language first through examples on our PC. Thus, this chapter presents a crash course on the basics of Python programming, including an explanation about some of the most commonly used language features. As such, this chapter will provide you with the skills you need to understand the Python IoT project examples available on the Internet. The chapter also demonstrates how to program in Python through examples that you can run on your PC or your MicroPython board. So, let's get started!

Note   I use the term Python to describe programming concepts in this chapter that apply to both MicroPython and Python. Concepts unique to MicroPython use the term MicroPython.

Now let's learn some of the basic concepts of Python programming. We will begin with the building blocks of the language, such as variables, modules, and basic statements, then move into the more complex concepts of flow control and data structures. While the material may seem to come at you in a rush, this tutorial on Python covers only the most fundamental knowledge of the language and how to use it on your PC and MicroPython board. It is intended to get you started writing Python IoT applications.

© Charles Bell 2024
C. Bell, *MicroPython for the Internet of Things*, https://doi.org/10.1007/978-1-4842-9861-9_4

If you know the basics of Python programming, feel free to skim through this chapter. However, I recommend working through the example projects at the end of the chapter, especially if you've not written many Python applications.

The following sections present many of the basic features of Python programming that you will need to know to understand the example projects in this book.

Basic Concepts

Python is a high-level, interpreted, object-oriented scripting language. One of the biggest goals of Python is to have a clear, easy-to-understand syntax that reads as close to English as possible. That is, you should be able to read a Python script and understand it even if you haven't learned the language. Python also has less punctuation (special symbols) and fewer syntactical machinations than other languages. The following lists a few of the key features of Python:

- An interpreter processes Python at runtime. No external (separate) compiler is used.

- Python supports object-oriented programming constructs by way of a class.

- Python is a great language for beginner-level programmers and supports the development of a wide range of applications.

- Python is a scripting language but can be used for a wide range of applications.

- Python is very popular and used throughout the world, giving it a huge support base.

- Python has few keywords, simple structure, and a clearly defined syntax. This allows the student to pick up the language quickly.

- Python code is more clearly defined and visible to the eyes.

Python is available for download (`python.org/downloads`) for just about every platform that you may encounter or use – even Windows! Python is a very easy language to learn with very few constructs that are even mildly difficult to learn. Rather than toss out a sample application, let's approach learning the basics of Python in a Python-like way: one step at a time.

Note   If you do not have a MicroPython board and have not installed Python on your PC, you should do so now so that you can run the examples in this chapter.

Code Blocks

The first thing you should learn is that Python does not use a code block demarcated with symbols like other languages. More specifically, code that is local to a construct such as a function or conditional or loop is designated using indentation. Thus, the following lines are indented (by spaces or tabs) so that the starting characters align for the code body of the construct.

Caution   The following shows this concept in action. Python interpreters will complain and could produce strange results if the indentation is not uniform.

```
if (expr1):
    print("inside expr1")
    print("still inside expr1")
else:
    print("inside else")
    print("still inside else")
print("in outer level")
```

Here, we see a conditional or if statement. Notice the function call print() is indented. This signals the interpreter that the lines belong to the construct above it. For example, the two print statements that mention expr1 form the code block for the if condition (and execute when the expression evaluates to true). Similarly, the next two print statements form the code block for the else condition. Finally, the non-indented lines are not part of the conditional and thus are executed after either the if or else depending on the expression evaluation.

As you can see, indentation is a key concept to learn when writing Python. Even though it is very simple, making mistakes in indentation can result in code executing that you did not expect or worse errors from the interpreter.

Note   I use "program" and "application" interchangeably with "script" when discussing Python. While technically Python code saved in a file is a script, we often use it in contexts where "program" or "application" is more appropriate.

There is one special symbol that you will encounter frequently. Notice the use of the colon (:) in the preceding code. This symbol is used to terminate a construct and signals the interpreter that the declaration is complete and the body of the code block follows. We use this for conditionals, loops, classes, and functions.

Comments

One of the most fundamental concepts in any programming language is the ability to annotate your source code with non-executable text that not only allows you to make notes among the lines of code but also forms a way to document your source code.

To add comments to your source code, use the pound sign (#). Place at least one at the start of the line to create a comment for that line, repeating the # symbols for each subsequent line. This creates what is known as a block comment as shown. Notice I used a comment without any text to create whitespace. This helps with readability and is a customary practice for block comments:

```
#
# MicroPython for the IoT Second Edition
#
# Example Python application.
#
# Created by Dr. Charles Bell
#
```

You can also place comments on the same line as the source code. The compiler will ignore anything from the pound sign to the end of the line. For example, the following shows a common style of documenting variables:

```
zip = 35012             # Zip or postal code
address1= "123 Main St."  # Store the street address
```

Arithmetic

You can perform many mathematical operations in Python including the usual primitives, but also logical operations and operations used to compare values. Rather than discuss these in detail, I provide a quick reference in Table 4-1 that shows the operation and example of how to use the operation.

Table 4-1. *Arithmetic, Logical, and Comparison Operators in Python*

Type	Operator	Description	Example
Arithmetic	+	Addition	`int_var + 1`
	-	Subtraction	`int_var - 1`
	*	Multiplication	`int_var * 2`
	/	Division	`int_var / 3`
	%	Modulus	`int_var % 4`
	-	Unary subtraction	`-int_var`
	+	Unary addition	`+int_var`
Logical	&	Bitwise and	`var1 & var2`
	|	Bitwise or	`var1 | var2`
	^	Bitwise exclusive or	`var1 ^ var2`
	~	Bitwise complement	`~var1`
	and	Logical and	`var1 and var2`
	or	Logical or	`var1 or var2`
Comparison	==	Equal	`expr1 == expr2`
	!=	Not equal	`expr1 != expr2`
	<	Less than	`expr1 < expr2`
	>	Greater than	`expr1 > expr2`
	<=	Less than or equal	`expr1 <= expr2`
	>=	Greater than or equal	`expr1 >= expr2`

Bitwise operations produce a result on the values performed on each bit. Logical operators (and, or) produce a value that is either true or false and are often used with expressions or conditions.

Output to Screen

We've already seen a few examples of how to print messages to the screen but without any explanation about the statements shown. While it is unlikely that you would print output from your MicroPython board for projects that you deploy, learning Python is much easier when you can display messages to the screen.

One of the things you may want to print – as we have seen in previous examples – is to communicate what is going on inside your program. This can include simple messages (strings), but can also include the values of variables, expressions, and more.

As we have seen, the built-in print() function is the most common way to display output text contained within single or double quotes. We have also seen some interesting examples using another function named format(). The format() function generates a string for each argument passed. These arguments can be other strings, expressions, variables, etc. The function is used with a special string that contains replacement keys delimited by curly braces { } (called string interpolation[1]). Each replacement key contains either an index (starting at 0) or a named keyword. The special string is called a format string. Let's see a few examples to illustrate the concept. You can run these yourself either on your PC or your MicroPython board. I include the output so you can see what each statement does:

```
>>> a = 42
>>> b = 1.5
>>> c = "seventy"
>>> print("{0} {1} {2} {3}".format(a,b,c,(2+3)))
42 1.5 seventy 5
>>> print("{a_var} {b_var} {c_var} {0}".format((3*3),c_var=c,
b_var=b,a_var=a))
42 1.5 seventy 9
```

---

[1]https://en.wikipedia.org/wiki/String_interpolation

Notice I created three variables (we will talk about variables in the next section), assigning them different values with the equal symbol (=). I then printed a message using a format string with four replacement keys labeled using an index. Notice the output of that print statement. Notice I included an expression at the end to show how the format() function evaluates expressions.

The last line is more interesting. Here, I used three named parameters (a_var, b_var, c_var) and used a special argument option in the format() function where I assign the parameter a value. Notice I listed them in a different order. This is the greatest advantage of using named parameters; they can appear in any order but are placed in the format string in the position indicated.

As you can see, it's just a case of replacing the { } keys with those from the format() function, which converts the arguments to strings. We use this technique anywhere we need a string that contains data gathered from more than one area or type. We can see this in the preceding examples.

Tip   See https://docs.python.org/3/library/string.
html#formatstrings for more information about format strings.

Now let's look at how we can use variables in our programs (scripts).

Tip   Python allows you to terminate a statement with the semicolon (;); however, it is not needed and considered bad form to include it.

Variables

Python is a dynamically typed language, which means the type of the variable (the type of data it can store) is determined by context as it is encountered or used. This contrasts with other languages such as C and C++ where you must declare the type before you use the variable.

Variables in Python are simply named memory locations that you can use to store values during execution. We store values by using the equal sign to assign the value. Python variable names can be anything you want, but there are rules and conventions most Python developers follow. The rules are listed in the Python coding standard.[2]

However, the general, overriding rule requires variable names that are descriptive, have meaning in context, and can be easily read. That is, you should avoid names with random characters, forced abbreviations, acronyms, and similar obscure names. By convention, your variable names should be longer than a single character (with some acceptable exceptions for loop counting variables) and short enough to avoid overly long code lines.

WHAT IS A LONG CODE LINE?

Most will say a code line should not exceed 80 characters, but this hearkens to the darker days of programming when we used punched cards that permitted a maximum of 80 characters per card and later display devices with the same limitation. With modern, widescreen displays, this is not as big a deal, but I still recommend keeping lines short to ensure better readability. No one likes to scroll down (or right) to read!

Thus, there is a lot of flexibility in what you can name your variables. There are additional rules and guidelines in the PEP8 standard, and should you wish to bring your project source code up to date with the standards, you should review the PEP8 naming standards for functions, classes, and more.

See the PEP8 coding guidelines for Python coding at `www.python.org/dev/peps/pep-0008` for a complete list of the rules and standards.

The following shows some examples of simple variables and their dynamically determined types:

```
# floating point number
length = 10.0
# integer
width = 4
# string
```

---

[2]`www.python.org/dev/peps/pep-0008/`

```
box_label = "Tools"
# list
car_makers = ['Ford', 'Chevrolet', 'Dodge']
# tuple
porsche_cars = ('911', 'Cayman', 'Boxster')
# dictionary
address = {"name": "Joe Smith", "Street": "123 Main", "City": "Anytown",
"State": "New Happyville"}
```

So, how did we know the variable width is an integer? Simply because the number 4 is an integer. Likewise, Python will interpret "Tools" as a string. We'll see more about the last three types and other types supported by Python in the next section.

Tip   For more information about naming conventions governed by the Python coding standard (PEP8), see `www.python.org/dev/peps/pep-0008/#naming-conventions`.

Types

As mentioned, Python does not have a formal type specification mechanism like other languages. However, you can still define variables to store anything you want. In fact, Python permits you to create and use variables based on context, and you can use initialization to "set" the data type for the variable. The following shows several examples:

```
# Numbers
float_value = 9.75
integer_value = 5
# Strings
my_string = "He says, he's already got one."
print("Floating number: {0}".format(float_value))
print("Integer number: {0}".format(integer_value))
print(my_string)
```

For situations where you need to convert types or want to be sure values are typed a certain way, there are many functions for converting data. Table 4-2 shows a few of the more commonly used type conversion functions. I discuss some of the data structures in a later section.

Table 4-2. *Type Conversion in Python*

Function	Description
int(x [,base])	Converts x to an integer. Base is optional (e.g., 16 for hex)
long(x [,base])	Converts x to a long integer
float(x)	Converts x to a floating point
str(x)	Converts object x to a string
tuple(t)	Converts t to a tuple
list(l)	Converts l to a list
set(s)	Converts s to a set
dict(d)	Creates a dictionary
chr(x)	Converts an integer to a character
hex(x)	Converts an integer to a hexadecimal string
oct(x)	Converts an integer to an octal string

However, you should use these conversion functions with care to avoid data loss or rounding. For example, converting a float to an integer can result in truncation. Likewise, printing floating-point numbers can result in rounding.

Now let's look at some commonly used data structures including this strange thing called a dictionary.

Basic Data Structures

What you have learned so far about Python is enough to write the most basic programs and indeed more than enough to tackle the example projects later in this chapter. However, when you start needing to operate on data – either from the user or from sensors and similar sources – you will need a way to organize and store data as well as perform operations on the data in memory. The following introduces three data structures in order of complexity: lists, tuples, and dictionary.

Lists

Lists are a way to organize data in Python. It is a free-form way to build a collection. That is, the items (or elements) need not be the same data type. Lists also allow you to do some interesting operations such as adding things at the end, beginning, or at a special index. The following demonstrates how to create a list:

```python
# List
my_list = ["abacab", 575, "rex, the wonder dog", 24, 5, 6]
my_list.append("end")
my_list.insert(0,"begin")
for item in my_list:
  print("{0}".format(item))
```

Here, we see I created the list using square brackets ([ ]). The items in the list definition are separated by commas. Note that you can create an empty list simply by setting a variable equal to [ ]. Since lists, like other data structures, are objects, there are several operations available for lists such as the following:

- append(x): Add x to the end of the list

- extend(l): Add all items to the end of the list

- insert(pos,item): Insert the item at a position pos

- remove(value): Remove the first item that matches (==) the value

- pop([i]): Remove and return the item at position i or end of the list

- index(value): Return the index of the first item that matches

- count(value): Count occurrences of the value

- sort(): Sort the list (ascending)

- reverse(): Reverse sort the list

Lists are like arrays in other languages and very useful for building dynamic collections of data.

Tuples

Tuples, on the other hand, are a more restrictive type of collection. That is, they are built from a specific set of data and do not allow manipulation like a list. In fact, you cannot change the elements in the tuple. Thus, we can use tuples for data that should not change. The following shows an example of a tuple and how to use it:

```
# Tuple
my_tuple = (0,1,2,3,4,5,6,7,8,"nine")
for item in my_tuple:
  print("{0}".format(item))
if 7 in my_tuple:
  print("7 is in the list")
```

Here, we see I created the tuple using parentheses (). The items in the tuple definition are separated by commas. Note that you can create an empty tuple simply by setting a variable equal to (). Since tuples, like other data structures, are objects, there are several operations available such as the following, including operations for sequences such as inclusion, location, etc.:

- x in t: Determine if t contains x
- x not in t: Determine if t does not contain x
- s + t: Concatenate tuples
- s[i]: Get element i
- len(t): Length of t (number of elements)
- min(t): Minimal (smallest value)
- max(t): Maximal (largest value)

If you want even more structure with storing data in memory, you can use a special construct (object) called a dictionary.

Dictionaries

A dictionary is a data structure that allows you to store key-value pairs where the data is assessed via the keys. Dictionaries are a very structured way of working with data and the most logical form we will want to use when collecting complex data. The following shows an example of a dictionary:

```
# Dictionary
my_dictionary = {
    'first_name': "Chuck",
    'last_name': "Bell",
    'age': 36,
    'my_ip': (192,168,1,225),
    42: "What is the meaning of life?",
}
# Access the keys:
print(my_dictionary.keys())
# Access the items (key, value) pairs
print(my_dictionary.items())
# Access the values
print(my_dictionary.values())
# Create a list of dictionaries
my_addresses = [my_dictionary]
```

There is a lot going on here! We see a basic dictionary declaration that uses curly braces to create a dictionary. Inside that, we can create as many key and value pairs as we want separated by commas. Keys are defined using strings (I use single quotes by convention, but double quotes will work) or integers, and values can be any data type we want. For the my_ip attribute, we are also storing a tuple.

Following the dictionary, we see several operations performed on the dictionary from printing the keys, printing all the values, and printing only the values. The following shows the output of executing this code snippet from the Python interpreter:

```
[42, 'first_name', 'last_name', 'age', 'my_ip']
[(42, 'what is the meaning of life?'), ('first_name', 'Chuck'),
('last_name', 'Bell'), ('age', 36), ('my_ip', (192, 168, 1, 225))]
['what is the meaning of life?', 'Chuck', 'Bell', 36, (192, 168, 1, 225)]
```

```
'42': what is the meaning of life?
'first_name': Chuck
'last_name': Bell
'age': 36
'my_ip': (192, 168, 1, 225)
```

As we have seen in this example, there are several operations (functions or methods) available for dictionaries including the following. Together, this list of operations makes dictionaries a very powerful programming tool:

- `len(d)`: Number of items in d

- `d[k]`: Item of d with key k

- `d[k] = x`: Assign key k with value x

- `del d[k]`: Delete item with key k

- `k in d`: Determine if d has an item with key k

- `d.items()`: Return a list (view) of the (key, value) pairs in d

- `d.keys()`: Return a list (view) of the keys in d

- `d.values()`: Return a list (view) of the values in d

Best of all, objects can be placed inside other objects. For example, you can create a list of dictionaries like I did earlier, a dictionary that contains lists and tuples, and any combination you need. Thus, lists, tuples, and dictionaries are a powerful way to manage data for your program.

In the next section, we will learn how we can control the flow of our programs.

Statements

Now that we know more about the basics of Python, we can discover some of the more complex code concepts you will need to complete your project such as conditional statements and loops.

Conditional Statements

We have also seen some simple conditional statements: statements designed to alter the flow of execution depending on the evaluation of one or more expressions. Conditional statements allow us to direct execution of our programs to sections (blocks) of code based on the evaluation of one or more expressions. The conditional statement in Python is the if statement.

We have seen the if statement in action in our example code. Notice in the example, we can have one or more (optional) else phrases that we execute once the expression for the if conditions evaluate to false. We can chain if/else statements to encompass multiple conditions where the code executed depends on the evaluation of several conditions. The following shows the general structure of the if statement, including the abbreviated else if (elif) inner conditions. Notice in the comments how I explain how execution reaches the body of each condition:

```
if (expr1):
    # execute only if expr1 is true
elif ((expr2) or (expr3)):
    # execute only if expr1 is false *and* either expr2 or expr3 is true
else:
    # execute if both sets of if conditions evaluate to false
```

While you can chain the statement as much as you want, use some care here because the more elif sections you have, the harder it will become to understand, maintain, and avoid logic errors in your expressions.

There is another form of conditional statement called a ternary operator. Ternary operators are more commonly known as conditional expressions in Python. These operators evaluate something based on whether a condition is true or not. Conditional expressions are a shorthand notation for an if-then-else construct used (typically) in an assignment statement as shown in the following:

```
variable = value_if_true if condition else value_if_false
```

129

Here, we see if the condition is evaluated to true, the value preceding the `if` is used, but if the condition evaluates to false, the value following the `else` is used. The following shows a short example:

```
>>> numbers = [1,2,3,4]
>>> for n in numbers:
...    x = 'odd' if n % 2 else 'even'
...    print("{0} is {1}.".format(n, x))
...
1 is odd.
2 is even.
3 is odd.
4 is even.
>>>
```

Conditional expressions allow you to quickly test a condition instead of using a multiline conditional statement, which can help make your code a bit easier to read (and shorter).

Loops

Loops are used to control the repetitive execution of a block of code. There are three forms of loops that have slightly different behaviors. All loops use conditional statements to determine whether to repeat execution or not. That is, they repeat as long as the condition is true. I will explain each with an example.

While Loop

The `while` loop has its condition at the "top" or start of the block of code. Thus, while loops only execute the body if and only if the condition evaluates to true on the first pass. The following illustrates the syntax for a `while` loop. This form of loop is best used when you need to execute code only if some expression(s) evaluate to true, for example, iterating through a collection of things whose number of elements is unknown (loop until we run out of things in the collection):

```
while (expression):
    # do something here
```

For Loop

The For loop is sometimes called counting loops because of their unique form. For loops allow you to define a counting variable and a range or list to iterate over. The following illustrates the structure of the for loop. This form of loop is best used for performing an operation in a collection. In this case, Python will automatically place each item in the collection in the variable for each pass of the loop until no more items are available.

```
for variable_name in list:
  # do something here
```

Range or Counting Loop

You can also do range loops or counting loops. These use a special function called range() that takes up to three parameters, range([start], stop[, step]), where start is the starting number (an integer), stop is the last number in the series, and step is the increment. So, you can count by 1, 2, 3, etc., through a range of numbers. The following shows a simple example:

```
for i in range(2,9):
  # do something here
```

There are other uses for range() that you may encounter. See the documentation on this function and other built-in functions at https://docs.python.org/3/library/functions.html for more information.

Python also provides a mechanism for controlling the flow of the loop (e.g., duration or termination) using a few special keywords as follows:

- break: Exit the loop body immediately

- continue: Skip to the next iteration of the loop

- else: Execute code when the loop ends (not executed if the loop was stopped with a break statement)

There are some uses for these keywords, particularly break, but it is not the preferred method of terminating and controlling loops. That is, professionals believe the conditional expression or error handling code should behave well enough to not need these options.

Modularization: Modules, Functions, and Classes

The last groups of topics are the most advanced and include modularization (code organization). As we will see, we can use functions to group code, to eliminate duplication, and to encapsulate functionality into objects.

Including Modules

Python applications can be built from reusable libraries that are provided by the Python environment. They can also be built from custom modules or libraries that you create yourself or download from a third party. These are often distributed as a set of Python code files (e.g., files that have a file extension of .py). When we want to use a library (function, class, etc.) that is included in a module, we use the import keyword and list the name of the module. The following shows some examples:

```
import os
import sys
```

The first two lines demonstrate how to import a base or common module provided by Python. In this case, we are using or importing modules for the os and sys modules (operating system and Python system functions).

Tip   It is customary (but not required) to list your imports in alphabetical order with built-in modules first, then third-party modules listed next, and finally your own modules.

Functions

Python allows you to use modularization in your code. While it supports object-oriented programming by way of classes (a more advanced feature that you are unlikely to encounter for most Python GPIO examples), on a more fundamental level you can break your code into smaller chunks using functions.

Functions use a special keyword construct (rare in Python) to define a function. We simply use def followed by a name for the function and a comma-separated list of parameters in parentheses. The colon is used to terminate the declaration. The following shows an example:

```
def print_dictionary(the_dictionary):
    for key, value in the_dictionary.items():
        print("'{0}': {1}".format(key, value))

# define some data
my_dictionary = {
    'name': "Chuck",
    'age': 44,
}
```

You may be wondering what this strange code does. Notice the loop is assigning two values from the result of the items() function. This is a special function available from the dictionary object.[3] The items() function returns the key-value pairs: hence the names of the variables.

The next line prints out the values. The use of formatting strings where the curly braces define the parameter number starting at zero is common for Python 3 applications.

See https://docs.python.org/3/library/string.html#format-string-syntax for more information about formatting strings.

Notice that the body of the function is indented. All statements indented under this function declaration belong to the function and are executed when the function is called. We can call functions by name providing any parameters as follows. Notice how I referenced the values in the dictionary by using the key names:

```
print_dictionary(my_dictionary)
print(my_dictionary['age'])
print(my_dictionary['name'])
```

---

[3] Yes, dictionaries are objects! So are tuples and lists and many other data structures.

This example together with the preceding code, when executed, generates the following:

```
$ python
Python 3.11.4 (tags/v3.11.4:d2340ef, Jun  7 2023, 05:45:37) [MSC v.1934 64
bit (AMD64)] on win32
Type "help", "copyright", "credits" or "license" for more information.
>>> def print_dictionary(the_dictionary):
...     for key, value in the_dictionary.items():
...         print("'{0}': {1}".format(key, value))
...
>>> # define some data
... my_dictionary = {
...     'name': "Chuck",
...     'age': 41,
... }
>>> print_dictionary(my_dictionary)
'name': Chuck
'age': 41
>>> print(my_dictionary['age'])
41
>>> print(my_dictionary['name'])
Chuck
```

Now let's look at the most complex concept in Python – object-oriented programming.

Classes and Objects

You may have heard that Python is an object-oriented programming language. But what does that mean? Simply, Python is a programming language that provides facilities for describing objects (things) and what you can do with the object (operations). Objects are an advanced form of data abstraction where the data is hidden from the caller and only manipulated by the operations (methods) the object provides.

Like any technology or concept, there come a certain number of terms that you must learn to be able to understand and communicate with others about the technology. The following briefly describes some of the terms you will need to know to learn more about object-oriented programming:

- *Attribute*: A data element in a class.

- *Class*: A code construct used to define an object in the form of attributes (data) and methods (functions) that operate on the data. Methods and attributes in Python can be accessed using dot notation.

- *Class instance variable*: A variable that is used to store an instance of an object. They are used like any other variable and, combined with dot notation, allow us to manipulate objects.

- *Instance*: An executable form of a class created by assigning a class to a variable initializing the code as an object.

- *Inheritance*: The inclusion of attributes and methods from one class in another.

- *Instantiation*: The creation of an instance of a class.

- *Method overloading*: The creation of two or more methods with the same name but with a separate set of parameters. This allows us to create methods that have the same name but may operate differently depending on the parameters passed.

- *Polymorphism*: Inheriting attributes and methods from a base class adding additional methods or overriding (changing) methods.

There are many more OOP terms, but these are the ones you will encounter most often.

The syntax we use in Python is the `class` statement, which you can use to help make your projects modular. By modular, we mean the source code is arranged to make it easier to develop and maintain. Typically, we place classes in separate modules (code files), which helps organize the code better. While it is not required, I recommend using this technique of placing a class in its own source file. This makes modifying the class or fixing problems (bugs) easier.

So, what are Python classes? Let's begin by considering the construct as an organization technique. We can use the class to group data and methods together. The name of the class immediately follows the keyword class followed by a colon. You declare other class methods like any other method except the first argument must be self, which ties the method to the class instance when executed.

I prefer to use terms that have been adopted by language designers or a community of developers. For example, some use "function" but others may use "method." Still others may use subroutine, routine, procedure, etc. It doesn't matter which term you use, but you should strive to use terms consistently. I use the term method when discussing object-oriented examples. That is, a class has methods, not functions. However, you can use the function in place of method, and you'd still be correct (mostly).

Accessing the data is done using one or more methods by using the class (creating an instance) and using dot notation to reference the data member or function. Let's look at an example. Listing 4-1 shows a complete class that describes (models) the most basic characteristics of a vehicle used for transportation. I created a file named vehicle.py to contain this code.

Listing 4-1. Vehicle Class

```
#
# MicroPython for the IoT Second Edition
#
# Class Example: A generic vehicle
#
# Dr. Charles Bell
#
class Vehicle:
    """Base class for defining vehicles"""
    axles = 0
    doors = 0
    occupants = 0
    def __init__(self, num_axles, num_doors):
        self.axles = num_axles
        self.doors = num_doors
```

```
    def get_axles(self):
        return self.axles
    def get_doors(self):
        return self.doors
    def add_occupant(self):
        self.occupants += 1
    def num_occupants(self):
        return self.occupants
```

Notice a couple of things here. First, there is a method with the name __init__().
This is the constructor and is called when the class instance is created. You place all
your initialization code like setting variables in this method. We also have methods for
returning the number of axles, doors, and occupants. We have one method in this class:
to add occupants.

Also, notice we address each of the class attributes (data) using self.<name>. This is
how we can ensure we always access the data that is associated with the instance created
and not a global variable or other local variable.

Let's see how this class can be used to define a family sedan. Listing 4-2 shows the
code that is used in this class. We can place this code in a file named sedan.py.

Listing 4-2. Using the Vehicle Class

```
#
# MicroPython for the IoT Second Edition
#
# Class Example: Using the generic Vehicle class
#
# Dr. Charles Bell
#
from vehicle import Vehicle
sedan = Vehicle(2, 4)
sedan.add_occupant()
sedan.add_occupant()
sedan.add_occupant()
print("The car has {0} occupants.".format(sedan.num_occupants()))
```

Notice the first line imports the Vehicle class from the vehicle module. Notice I capitalized the class name but not the file name. This is a very common naming scheme. Next in the code, we create an instance of the class. Notice I passed in 2, 4 to the class name. This will cause the __init__() method to be called when the class is instantiated. The variable, sedan, becomes the class instance variable (object) that we can manipulate, and I do so by adding three occupants, then printing out the number of occupants using the method in the Vehicle class.

We can run the code on our PC using the following command. As we can see, it tells us there are three occupants in the vehicle when the code is run. Nice.

```
$ python ./sedan.py
The car has 3 occupants.
```

Now, let's see how we can use the vehicle class to demonstrate inheritance. In this case, we will create a new class named PickupTruck that uses the vehicle class but adds specialization to the resulting class. Listing 4-3 shows the new class. I placed this code in a file named pickup_truck.py. As you will see, a pickup truck is a type of vehicle.

Listing 4-3. Pickup Truck Class

```
#
# MicroPython for the IoT Second Edition
#
# Class Example: Inheriting the Vehicle class to form a
# model of a pickup truck with maximum occupants and maximum
# payload.
#
# Dr. Charles Bell
#
from vehicle import Vehicle
class PickupTruck(Vehicle):
    """This is a pickup truck that has:
    axles = 2,
    doors = 2,
    __max occupants = 3
    The maximum payload is set on instantiation.
    """
```

```
    occupants = 0
    payload = 0
    max_payload = 0
    def __init__(self, max_weight):
        super().__init__(2,2)
        self.max_payload = max_weight
        self.__max_occupants = 3
    def add_occupant(self):
        if (self.occupants < self.__max_occupants):
            super().add_occupant()
        else:
            print("Sorry, only 3 occupants are permitted in the truck.")
    def add_payload(self, num_pounds):
        if ((self.payload + num_pounds) < self.max_payload):
            self.payload += num_pounds
        else:
            print("Overloaded!")
    def remove_payload(self, num_pounds):
        if ((self.payload - num_pounds) >= 0):
            self.payload -= num_pounds
        else:
            print("Nothing in the truck.")
    def get_payload(self):
        return self.payload
```

Notice a few things here. First, notice the class statement: `class PickupTruck(Vehicle):`. When we want to inherit from another class, we add parentheses with the name of the base class. This ensures Python will use the base class, allowing the derived class to use all its accessible data and memory. If you want to inherit from more than one class, you can (called multiple inheritance), just list the base (parent) classes with a comma-separated list.

Next, notice the __max_occupants variable. Using two underscores in a class for an attribute or a method makes, through convention, the item private to the class.[4] That is, it should only be accessed from within the class. No caller of the class (via a class variable/ instance) can access the private items nor can any class that is derived from the class. It is always good practice to hide the attributes (data).

You may be wondering what happened to the occupant methods. Why aren't they in the new class? They aren't there because our new class inherited all that behavior from the base class. Not only that, but the code has been modified to limit occupants to exactly three occupants.

I also want to point out the documentation I added to the class. We use documentation strings (strings that use a set of three double quotes before and after) to document the class. You can put documentation here to explain the class and its methods. We'll see a clever use of this a bit later.

Finally, notice the code in the constructor. This demonstrates how to call the base class method, which I do to set the number of axles and doors. We could do the same in other methods if we wanted to call the base class method's version.

Now, let's write some code to use this class. Listing 4-4 shows the code we used to test this class. Here, we create a file named pickup.py that creates an instance of the pickup truck, adds occupants and payload, then prints out the contents of the truck.

Listing 4-4. Using the PickupTruck Class

```
#
# MicroPython for the IoT Second Edition
#
# Class Example: Exercising the PickupTruck class.
#
# Dr. Charles Bell
#
from pickup_truck import PickupTruck
pickup = PickupTruck(500)
pickup.add_occupant()
pickup.add_occupant()
```

---

[4] Technically, it is called name mangling, which simulates making something private, but can still be accessed if you provide the correct number of underscores. See https://en.wikipedia.org/wiki/Name_mangling

```
pickup.add_occupant()
pickup.add_occupant()
pickup.add_payload(100)
pickup.add_payload(300)
print("Number of occupants in truck = {0}.".format(pickup.num_occupants()))
print("Weight in truck = {0}.".format(pickup.get_payload()))
pickup.add_payload(200)
pickup.remove_payload(400)
pickup.remove_payload(10)
```

Notice I add a couple of calls to the add_occupant() method, which the new class inherits and overrides. I also add calls so that we can test the code in the methods that check for excessive occupants and maximum payload capacity. When we run this code, we will see the results as follows:

```
$ python ./pickup.py
Sorry, only 3 occupants are permitted in the truck.
Number of occupants in truck = 3.
Weight in truck = 400.
Overloaded!
Nothing in the truck.
```

Once again, I ran this code on my PC, but I can run all this code on the MicroPython board and will see the same results.

There is one more thing we should learn about classes: built-in attributes. Recall the __init__() method. Python automatically provides several built-in attributes, each starting with __ that you can use to learn more about objects. The following lists a few of the operators available for classes:

- __dict__: Dictionary containing the class namespace

- __doc__: Class documentation string

- __name__: Class name

- __module__: Module name where the class is defined

- __bases__: The base class(es) in order of inheritance

The following shows what each of these attributes returns for the `PickupTruck` class earlier. I added this code to the `pickup.py` file:

```
print("PickupTruck.__doc__:", PickupTruck.__doc__)
print("PickupTruck.__name__:", PickupTruck.__name__)
print("PickupTruck.__module__:", PickupTruck.__module__)
print("PickupTruck.__bases__:", PickupTruck.__bases__)
print("PickupTruck.__dict__:", PickupTruck.__dict__)
When this code is run, we see the following output.
PickupTruck.__doc__: This is a pickup truck that has:
    axles = 2,
    doors = 2,
    max occupants = 3
    The maximum payload is set on instantiation.
PickupTruck.__name__: PickupTruck
PickupTruck.__module__: pickup_truck
PickupTruck.__bases__: (<class 'vehicle.Vehicle'>,)
PickupTruck.__dict__: {'__module__': 'pickup_truck', '__doc__': 'This is a
pickup truck that has:\n    axles = 2,\n    doors = 2,\n    max occupants = 3\n
The maximum payload is set on instantiation.\n    ', 'occupants': 0, 'payload': 0,
'max_payload': 0, '_PickupTruck__max_occupants': 3, '__init__': <function
PickupTruck.__init__ at 0x1018a1488>, 'add_occupant': <function PickupTruck.
add_occupant at 0x1018a17b8>, 'add_payload': <function PickupTruck.add_payload
at 0x1018a1840>, 'remove_payload': <function PickupTruck.remove_payload at
0x1018a18c8>, 'get_payload': <function PickupTruck.get_payload at 0x1018a1950>}
```

You can use the built-in attributes whenever you need more information about a class. Notice the `_PickupTruck__max_occupants` entry in the dictionary. Recall that we made a pseudo-private variable, `__max_occupants`. Here, we see how Python refers to the variable by prepending the class name to the variable. Remember, variables that start with two underscores (not one) indicates it should be considered private to the class and only usable from within the class.

Tip   See `https://docs.python.org/3/tutorial/classes.html` for more information about classes in Python.

Now, let's see a few examples of Python programs that we can use to practice. Like the previous examples, you can write and execute these either on your PC or on your MicroPython board.

Learning Python by Example

The best way to learn how to program in any language is practicing with examples. In this section, I will present several examples that you can use to practice coding in Python. You can use either your MicroPython board or your PC to run these examples. I present the first two examples using my PC via the Python console and the second two using the MicroPython board via the REPL console.

I explain the code in detail for each example and show example output when you execute the code as well as a challenge for you to try a modification or two of each example on your own. I encourage you to implement these examples and figure out the challenge yourself as practice for the projects later in this book.

Example 1: Using Loops

This example demonstrates how to write loops in Python using the for loop. The problem we are trying to solve is converting integers from decimal to binary, hexadecimal, and octal. Often with IoT projects, we need to see values in one or more of these formats, and in some cases, the sensors we use (and the associated documentation) use hexadecimal rather than decimal. Thus, this example can be helpful in the future not only for how to use the for loop but also how to convert integers into different formats.

Write the Code

The example begins with a tuple of integers to convert. Tuples and lists can be iterated through (values read in order) using a for loop. Recall a tuple is read only, so in this case since it is input, it is fine, but in other cases where you may need to change values, you will want to use a list. Recall, the syntactical difference between a tuple and a list is the tuple uses parentheses and a list uses square brackets.

The for loop demonstrated here is called a "for each" loop. Notice I used the syntax "for value in values," which tells Python to iterate over the tuple named values, fetching (storing) each item into the value variable each iteration through the tuple.

Finally, I use the `print()` and `format()` functions to replace two placeholders `{0}` and `{1}`, to print out a different format of the integer using the methods `bin()` for binary, `oct()` for octal, and `hex()` for hexadecimal that do the conversion for us. Listing 4-5 shows examples of converting integers to different forms.

Listing 4-5. Converting Integers

```
#
# MicroPython for the IoT Second Edition
#
# Example: Convert integer to binary, hex, and octal
#
# Dr. Charles Bell
#

# Create a tuple of integer values
values = (12, 450, 1, 89, 2017, 90125)

# Loop through the values and convert each to binary, hex, and octal
for value in values:
    print("{0} in binary is {1}".format(value, bin(value)))
    print("{0} in octal is {1}".format(value, oct(value)))
    print("{0} in hexadecimal is {1}".format(value, hex(value)))
```

Execute the Code

You can save this code in a file named conversions.py on your PC and then open a terminal (console window) and run the code with the command `python ./conversions.py` (or `python3` if you have multiple versions of Python installed). Listing 4-6 shows the output.

Listing 4-6. Conversions Example Output

```
$ python3 ./conversions.py
12 in binary is 0b1100
12 in octal is 0o14
12 in hexadecimal is 0xc
```

```
450 in binary is 0b111000010
450 in octal is 0o702
450 in hexadecimal is 0x1c2
1 in binary is 0b1
1 in octal is 0o1
1 in hexadecimal is 0x1
89 in binary is 0b1011001
89 in octal is 0o131
89 in hexadecimal is 0x59
2017 in binary is 0b11111100001
2017 in octal is 0o3741
2017 in hexadecimal is 0x7e1
90125 in binary is 0b10110000000001101
90125 in octal is 0o260015
90125 in hexadecimal is 0x1600d
```

Notice all the values in the tuple were converted.

Your Challenge

To make this example better, instead of using a static tuple to contain hard-coded integers, rewrite the example to read the integer from arguments on the command line along with the format. For example, the code would be executed like the following:

```
$ python ./conversions.py 123 hex
123 in hexadecimal is 0x7b
```

To read arguments from the command line, use the argument parser, argparse (https://docs.python.org/3/howto/argparse.html). If you want to read the integer from the command line, you can use the argparse module to add an argument by name as follows:

```
import argparse
# Setup the argument parser
parser = argparse.ArgumentParser()
# We need two arguments: integer, and conversion
parser.add_argument("original_val")
```

```
parser.add_argument("conversion")
# Get the arguments
args = parser.parse_args()
```

When you use the argument parser (`argparse`) module, the values of the arguments are all strings, so you will need to convert the value to an integer before you use the `bin()`, `hex()`, or `oct()` method.

You will also need to determine which conversion is requested. I suggest using only hex, bin, and oct for the conversion and use a set of conditions to check the conversion requested. Something like the following would work:

```
if args.conversion == 'bin':
    # do conversion to binary
elif args.conversion == 'oct':
    # do conversion to octal
elif args.conversion == 'hex':
    # do conversion to hexadecimal
else:
    print("Sorry, I don't understand, {0}.".format(args.conversion))
```

Notice the last `else` communicates that the argument was not recognized. This helps to manage user error.

There is one more thing about the argument parser you should know. You can pass in a help string when adding arguments. The argument parser also gets you the help argument (-h) for free. Observe the following. Notice I added a couple of strings using the help= parameter:

```
# We need two arguments: integer, and conversion
parser.add_argument("original_val", help="Value to convert.")
parser.add_argument("conversion", help="Conversion options:
hex, bin, or oct.")
```

Now when we complete the code and run it with the -h option, we get the following output. Cool, eh?

```
$ python ./conversions.py -h
usage: conversions.py [-h] original_val conversion
positional arguments:
  original_val  Value to convert.
  conversion    Conversion options: hex, bin, or oct.
optional arguments:
  -h, --help    show this help message  and exit
```

Example 2: Using Complex Data and Files

This example demonstrates how to work with the JavaScript Object Notation[5] (JSON) in Python. In short, JSON is a markup language used to exchange data. Not only is it human readable, but it can also be used directly in your applications to store and retrieve data to and from other applications, servers, and even MySQL. In fact, JSON looks familiar to programmers because it resembles other markup schemes. JSON is also very simple in that it supports only two types of structures: (1) a collection containing (name, value) pairs and (2) an ordered list (or array). Of course, you can also mix and match the structures in an object. When we create a JSON object, we call it a JSON document.

The problem we are trying to solve is writing and reading data to/from files. In this case, we will use a special JSON encoder and decoder module named json that allows us to easily convert data in files (or other streams) to and from JSON. As you will see, accessing JSON data is easy by simply using the key (sometimes called fields) names to access the data. Thus, this example can be helpful in the future not only for how to use read and write files but also how to work with JSON documents.

Write the Code

This example stores and retrieves data in files. The data is basic information about pets, including their name, age, breed, and type. The type is used to determine broad categories like fish, dog, or cat.

---

[5]www.json.org/

We begin by importing the JSON module (named json), which is built into the MicroPython platform. Next, we prepare some initial data by building JSON documents and storing them in a Python list. We use the json.loads() method to pass in a JSON formatted string. The result is a JSON document that we can add to our list. The examples use a very simple form of JSON documents – a collection of (name, value) pairs. The following shows an example of one of the JSON formatted strings used:

```
{"name":"Violet", "age": 11, "breed":"dachshund", "type":"dog"}
```

Notice we enclose the string inside curly braces and use a series of key names, a colon, and a value separated by commas. If this looks familiar, it's because it is the same format as a Python dictionary. This demonstrates my comment that JSON syntax looks familiar to programmers.

The JSON method, json.loads(), takes the JSON formatted string, then parses the string checking for validity and returns a JSON document. We then store that document in a variable and add it to the list as follows:

```
parsed_json = json.loads('{"name":"Violet", "age": 11, "breed":"dachshund",
"type":"dog"}')
pets.append(parsed_json)
```

Once the data is added to the list, we then write the data to a file named my_data. json. To work with files, we first open the file with the open() function, which takes a file name (including a path if you want to put the file in a directory) and an access mode. We use "r" for read and "w" for write. You can also use "a" for append if you want to open a file and add to the end. Note that the "w" access will overwrite the file when you write to it. If the open() function succeeds, you get a file object that permits you to call additional functions to read or write data. The open() will fail if the file is not present (and you have requested read access) or you do not have permissions to write to the file.

In case you're curious, Table 4-3 shows the complete list of modes available for the open() function.

Table 4-3. *Python File Access Modes*

Mode	Description
r	Opens a file for reading only. The file pointer is placed at the beginning of the file. This is the default mode
rb	Opens a file for reading only in binary format. The file pointer is placed at the beginning of the file. This is the default mode
r+	Opens a file for both reading and writing. The file pointer is placed at the beginning of the file
rb+	Opens a file for both reading and writing in binary format. The file pointer is placed at the beginning of the file
w	Opens a file for writing only. Overwrites the file if the file exists. If the file does not exist, it creates a new file for writing
wb	Opens a file for writing only in binary format. Overwrites the file if the file exists. If the file does not exist, it creates a new file for writing
w+	Opens a file for both writing and reading. Overwrites the existing file if the file exists. If the file does not exist, it creates a new file for reading and writing
wb+	Opens a file for both writing and reading in binary format. Overwrites the existing file if the file exists. If the file does not exist, it creates a new file for reading and writing
a	Opens a file for appending. The file pointer is at the end of the file if the file exists. That is, the file is in the append mode. If the file does not exist, it creates a new file for writing
ab	Opens a file for appending in binary format. The file pointer is at the end of the file if the file exists. That is, the file is in the append mode. If the file does not exist, it creates a new file for writing
a+	Opens a file for both appending and reading. The file pointer is at the end of the file if the file exists. The file opens in the append mode. If the file does not exist, it creates a new file for reading and writing
ab+	Opens a file for both appending and reading in binary format. The file pointer is at the end of the file if the file exists. The file opens in the append mode. If the file does not exist, it creates a new file for reading and writing

Once the file is open, we can write the JSON documents to the file by iterating over the list. Iteration means to start at the first element and access the elements in the list one at a time in order (the order they appear in the list). Recall, iteration in Python is very easy. We simply say "for each item in the list" with the for loop as follows:

```
for pet in pets:
  // do something with the pet data
```

To write the JSON document to the file, we use the json.dumps() method, which will produce a JSON formatted string, writing that to the file using the file variable and the write() method. Thus, we now see how to build JSON documents from strings and then decode (dump) them to a string.

Once we've written data to the file, we then close the file with the close() function, then reopen it and read data from the file. In this case, we use another special implementation of the for loop. We use the file variable to read all of the lines in the file with the readlines() method, then iterate over them with the following code:

```
json_file = open("my_data.json", "r")
for pet in json_file.readlines():
  // do something with the pet string
```

We use the json.loads() method again to read the JSON formatted string as read from the file to convert it to a JSON document, which we add to another list. We then close the file. Now the data has been read back into our program and we can use it. Finally, we iterate over the new list and print out data from the JSON documents using the key names to retrieve the data we want. Listing 4-7 shows the completed code for this example.

Listing 4-7. Writing and Reading JSON Objects to/from Files

```
#
# MicroPython for the IoT Second Edition
#
# Example: Storing and retrieving JSON objects in files
#
# Dr. Charles Bell
#
import json
```

```python
# Prepare a list of JSON documents for pets by converting JSON to a
dictionary
pets = []
parsed_json = json.loads('{"name":"Violet", "age": 11,
                         "breed":"dachshund", "type":"dog"}')
pets.append(parsed_json)
parsed_json = json.loads('{"name": "JonJon", "age": 20,
                         "breed":"poodle", "type":"dog"}')
pets.append(parsed_json)
parsed_json = json.loads('{"name": "Mister", "age": 9,
                         "breed":"siberian khatru", "type":"cat"}')
pets.append(parsed_json)
parsed_json = json.loads('{"name": "Spot", "age": 12,
                         "breed":"koi", "type":"fish"}')
pets.append(parsed_json)
parsed_json = json.loads('{"name": "Charlie", "age": 11,
                         "breed":"dachshund", "type":"dog"}')
pets.append(parsed_json) # Now, write these entries to a file.
                         # Note: overwrites the file
json_file = open("my_data.json", "w")
for pet in pets:
    json_file.write(json.dumps(pet))
    json_file.write("\n")
json_file.close()
# Now, let's read the JSON documents then print the name and
# age for all of the dogs in the list
my_pets = []
json_file = open("my_data.json", "r")
for pet in json_file.readlines():
    parsed_json = json.loads(pet)
    my_pets.append(parsed_json)
json_file.close()
print("Name, Age")
for pet in my_pets:
    if pet['type'] == 'dog':
        print("{0}, {1}".format(pet['name'], pet['age']))
```

Notice the loop for writing data. We added a second `write()` method passing in a strange string (it is actually an escaped character). The \n is a distinctive character called the newline character. This forces the JSON formatted strings to be on separate lines in the file and helps with readability.

Tip   To learn more about working with files in Python, see the documentation at `https://docs.python.org/3/tutorial/inputoutput.html#reading-and-writing-files`.

So, what does the file look like? The following is a dump of the file using the more utility, which shows the contents of the file. Notice the file contains the JSON formatted strings just like we had in our code:

```
$ more my_data.json
{"age": 11, "breed": "dachshund", "type": "dog", "name": "Violet"}
{"age": 20, "breed": "poodle", "type": "dog", "name": "JonJon"}
{"age": 9, "breed": "siberian khatru", "type": "cat", "name": "Mister"}
{"age": 12, "breed": "koi", "type": "fish", "name": "Spot"}
{"age": 11, "breed": "dachshund", "type": "dog", "name": "Charlie"}
```

Now, let's see what happens when we run this script.

Execute the Code

You can save this code in a file named `rw_json.py` on your PC, then open a terminal (console window) and run the code with the command `python ./rw_json.py` (or `python3` if you have multiple versions of Python installed). The following shows the output:

```
$ python ./rw_json.py
Name, Age
Violet, 11
JonJon, 20
Charlie, 11
```

While the output may not be very impressive, by completing the example, you've learned a great deal about working with files and structured data using JSON documents.

Your Challenge

To make this example more of a challenge, you could modify it to include more information about your pets. I suggest you start with a plain text file and type in the JSON formatted strings for your pets. To increase the complexity, try adding information that is pertinent to the type of pet. For example, you could add some keys for one or more pets, other keys for other pets, and so on. Doing so will show one of the powers of JSON documents; collections of JSON documents do not have to have the same format.

Once you have this file, modify the code to read from the file and print out all the information for each pet by printing the key name and value. Hint: You will need to use special code to print out the key name and the value called "pretty printing." For example, the following code will print out the JSON document in an easily readable format. Notice we use the sort_keys option to print the keys (fields), and we can control the number of spaces to indent:

```
for pet in my_pets:
    print(json.dumps(pet, sort_keys=True, indent=4))
```

When run, the output will look like the following:

```
{
    "age": 11,
    "breed": "dachshund",
    "name": "Violet",
    "type": "dog"
}
{
    "age": 20,
    "breed": "poodle",
    "name": "JonJon",
    "type": "dog"
}
```

153

Example 3: Using Functions

This example demonstrates how to create and use functions. Recall functions are used to help make our code more modular. Functions can also be a key tool in avoiding duplication of code. That is, we can reuse portions of code repeatedly by placing them in a function. Functions are also used to help isolate code for special operations such as mathematical formulae.

The problem we're exploring in this example is how to create functions to perform calculations. We will also explore a common computer science technique called recursion[6] where a function calls itself repeatedly. I will also show you the same function implemented in an iterative manner (typically using a loop). While some would advise avoiding recursion, recursive functions are a bit shorter to write but can be more difficult to debug if something goes wrong. The best advice I can offer is that almost every recursive function can be written as iterative functions, and novice programmers should stick to iterative solutions until they gain confidence using functions.

Write the Code

This example is designed to calculate a Fibonacci series.[7] A Fibonacci series is calculated as the sum of the two preceding values in the series. The series begins with 1 followed by 1 (nothing plus 1), then $1 + 1 = 2$, and so on. For this example, we will ask the user for an integer, then calculate the number of values in the Fibonacci series. If the input is 5, the series is 1, 1, 2, 3, 5.

We will create two functions: one to calculate the Fibonacci series using code that iteratively calculates the series and one to calculate the nth Fibonacci number using a recursive function. Let's look at the iterative function first.

To define a function, we use the syntax `def func_name(<parameters>):` where we supply a function name and a list of zero or more parameters followed by a colon. These parameters are then usable inside the function. We pass in data to the function using the parameters. The following shows the iterative version of the Fibonacci series code. We name this function `fibonacci_iterative`:

```
def fibonacci_iterative(count):
    i = 1
```

---

[6] https://en.wikipedia.org/wiki/Recursion_(computer_science)
[7] https://en.wikipedia.org/wiki/Fibonacci_number

```
    if count == 0:
        fib = []
    elif count == 1:
        fib = [1]
    elif count == 2:
        fib = [1,1]
    elif count > 2:
        fib = [1,1]
        while i < (count - 1):
            fib.append(fib[i] + fib[i-1])
            i += 1
    return fib
```

This code simply calculates the first N values in the series and returns them in a list. The parameter count is the number of values in the series. The function begins by checking to see if the trivial values are requested: 0, 1, or 2 whose values are known. If the count value is greater than 2, we begin with the known series [1, 1], then use a loop to calculate the next value by adding the two previous values together. Take a moment to notice how I use the list index to get the two previous values in the list (i and i-1). We will use this function and the list returned directly in our code to find a specific value in the series and print it.

Now let's look at the recursive version of the function. The following shows the code. We name this function `fibonacci_recursive`:

```
def fibonacci_recursive(number):
    if number == 0:
        return 0
    elif number == 1:
        return 1
    else:
        # Call our self counting down.
value = fibonacci_recursive(number-1) + fibonacci_recursive(number-2)
        return value
```

In this case, we don't return the entire series; rather, we return the specific value in the series – the nth value. Like the iterative example, we do the same thing regarding the trivial values returning the number requested. Otherwise, we call the same function again for each number. It may take some time to get your mind around how this works, but it does calculate the nth value.

Now, you may be wondering where you place functions in the code. We need to place them at the top of the code. Python will parse the functions and continue to execute statements following the definitions. Thus, we place our "main" code after our functions.

The main code for this example begins with requesting the nth value for the Fibonacci series and then uses the recursive function first to calculate the value. We then ask the user if they want to see the entire series, and if so, we use the iterative version of the function to get the list and print it out. We print out the nth value and give the option again to see the entire series to show that the result is the same using both functions. Listing 4-8 shows the completed code for the example. We will name this code fibonacci.py.

Listing 4-8. Calculating Fibonacci Series

```
#
# MicroPython for the IoT Second Edition
#
# Example: Fibonacci series using recursion
#
# Calculate the Fibonacci series based on user input
#
# Dr. Charles Bell
#
# Create a function to calculate Fibonacci series (iterative)
# Returns a list.
def fibonacci_iterative(count):
    i = 1
    if count == 0:
        fib = []
    elif count == 1:
        fib = [1]
```

```
    elif count == 2:
        fib = [1,1]
    elif count > 2:
        fib = [1,1]
        while i < (count - 1):
            fib.append(fib[i] + fib[i-1])
            i += 1
    return fib
# Create a function to calculate the nth Fibonacci number (recursive)
# Returns an integer.
def fibonacci_recursive(number):
    if number == 0:
        return 0
    elif number == 1:
        return 1
    else:
        # Call our self counting down.
        value = fibonacci_recursive(number-1) + fibonacci_
recursive(number-2)
        return value
# Main code
print("Welcome to my Fibonacci calculator!")
index = int(input("Please enter the number of integers in the series: "))
# Recursive example
print("We calculate the value using a recursive algoritm.")
nth_fibonacci = fibonacci_recursive(index)
print("The {0}{1} fibonacci number is {2}."
    "".format(index, "th" if index > 1 else "st", nth_fibonacci))
see_series = str(input("Do you want to see all of the values in the
series? "))
if see_series in ["Y","y"]:
    series = []
    for i in range(1,index+1):
        series.append(fibonacci_recursive(i))
    print("Series: {0}: ".format(series))
```

```
# Iterative example
print("We calculate the value using an iterative algoritm.")
series = fibonacci_iterative(index)
print("The {0}{1} fibonacci number is {2}."
      "".format(index, "th" if index > 1 else "st", series[index-1]))
see_series = str(input("Do you want to see all of the values in the
series? "))
if see_series in ["Y","y"]:
    print("Series: {0}: ".format(series))
print("bye!")
```

Take a few moments to read the code. While the problem being solved is a bit simpler than the previous example, there is a lot more code to read. When you're ready, connect your MicroPython board and create the file. You create the file on your PC for this example and name it fibonacci.py. We'll copy it to our MicroPython board in the next section.

Tip   For more information about defining functions, see the documentation at https://docs.python.org/3/tutorial/controlflow.html#defining-functions.

Now, let's see what happens when we run this script. Recall, we will be running this code on our MicroPython board, so if you're following along, be sure to set up your board and connect it to your PC.

Execute the Code

Recall from Chapter 3, when we want to move code to our MicroPython board, we need to create the file and then copy it to the MicroPython board and then execute it. We can use Thonny to create a new file for the Fibonacci module. If you want to follow along, first connect your MicroPython board to your PC, then open Thonny and click the *File* ➤ *New* menu. You should see a new file as shown in Figure 4-1.

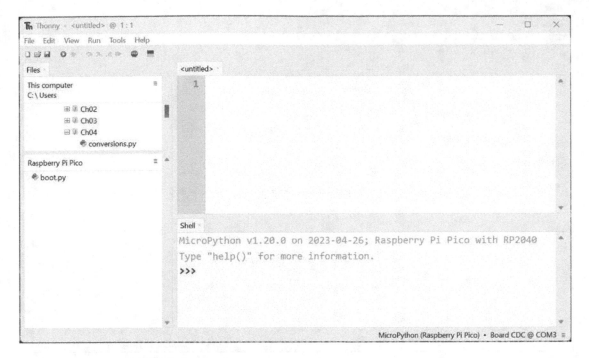

Figure 4-1. *New File (Thonny)*

Next, you can save the file as `fibonocci.py` using the *File* ➤ *Save* menu, then specify you want to save it to your MicroPython Board. You can also save the file to your PC (Thonny will ask you where to save the file). If you are following along, type in the code and then save the file on your MicroPython board. You should see the file appear in the board file menu as shown in Figure 4-2.

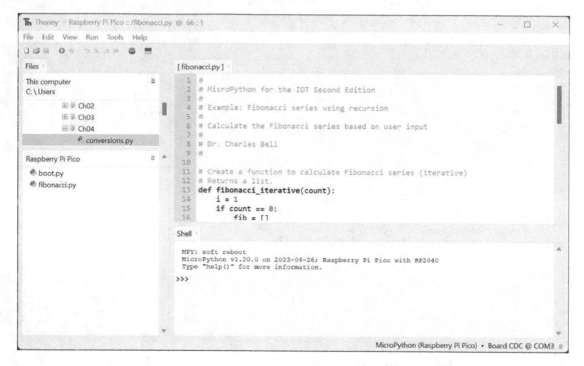

Figure 4-2. *Fibonacci File Saved on MicroPython Board (Thonny)*

Next, we will demonstrate how to use the module using the REPL console located at the bottom of Thonny. You should see the welcome message from MicroPython, followed by the REPL prompt (>>>). From the REPL prompt, issue the following code statement:

```
import fibonacci
```

This code imports the fibonacci.py file we just copied, and when it does, it executes the code. So, it's like we ran it on our PC from the Python console. Go ahead and test the program by requesting the twelfth value in the Fibonacci series. You should see the output shown in Figure 4-3.

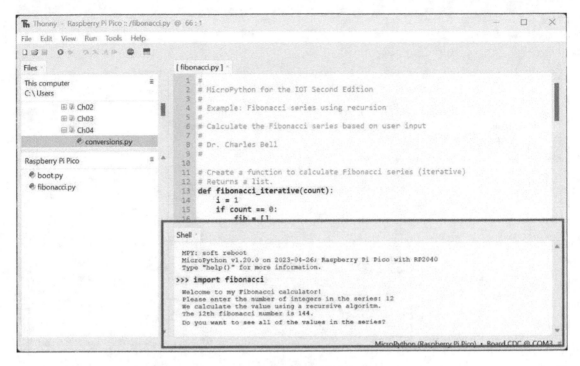

Figure 4-3. *Output of Fibonacci Example (Thonny)*

If you want to see the series, reply Y to the prompt and the code will print the series. Notice also that we see the code has exercised both versions of the function we wrote: iterative and recursive. Finally, we see that the values or output of both functions is the same data. Figure 4-4 shows an example of the output you will see.

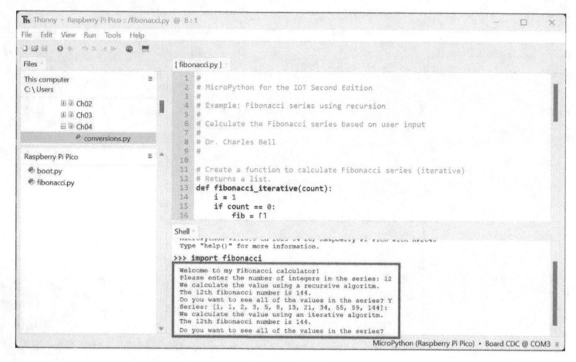

Figure 4-4. *Output with Series (Thonny)*

Note   If you do not yet have a MicroPython board, you can run the code from your PC with the command `python ./fibonacci.py`.

If you run the code again, just press *CTRL+C* to stop the code and *CTRL+D* to do a soft reset, then issue the import statement again. This will rerun the entire code. Or, if you want to run one of the functions, you can call it again by importing it using the following code. The following is how this would look when executed on the MicroPython board:

```
>>> from fibonacci import fibonacci_iterative
>>> fibonacci_iterative(6)
[1, 1, 2, 3, 5, 8]
>>> from fibonacci import fibonacci_recursive
>>> fibonacci_recursive(7)
13
```

Once imported this way, you can run the functions again. Go ahead and try them with different values to show how they behave. Recall, the functions were implemented differently – the iterative version returns the list, and the recursive version returns only the last or nth value.

Your Challenge

To make this example a bit more useful, modify the code to search a Fibonacci series for a specific integer. Ask the user to provide an integer, then determine if the value is a valid Fibonacci value. For example, if the user enters 144, the code should tell the user that the value is valid and is the twelfth value in the series. While this challenge will require you to rewrite most of the code for the "main" functionality, you must figure out how to use the functions in a new way.

Example 4: Using Classes

This example ramps up the complexity considerably by introducing an object-oriented programming concept: classes. Recall from earlier that classes are another way to modularize our code. Classes are used to model data and behavior on that data. Further, classes are typically placed in their own code module (file) that further modularizes the code. If you need to modify a class, you may need only change the code in the class module.

The problem we're exploring in this example is how to develop solutions using classes and code modules. We will be creating two files: one for the class and another for the main code.

Write the Code

This example is designed to convert Roman numerals to integers. That is, we will enter a value like VIII, which is eight, and expect to see the integer 8. To make things more interesting, we will also take the integer we derive and convert it back to Roman numerals.[8] Roman numerals are formed as a string using the characters I for 1, V for 5, X for 10, L for 50, C for 100, D for 500, and M for 1000. Combinations of other numbers

---

[8] https://en.wikipedia.org/wiki/Roman_numerals

are done by adding the character numerical value together (e.g., 3 = III) or a single, lower character before another character to indicate the representative minus that character (e.g., 4 = IV). The following shows some examples of how this works:

```
3 = III
15 = XV
12 = XII
24 = XXIV
96 = LXLVI
107 = CVII
```

This may sound like a lot of extra work, but consider this: if we can convert from one format to another, we should be able to convert back without errors. More specifically, we can use the code for one conversion to validate the other. If we get a different value when converting it back, we know we have a problem that needs to be fixed.

To solve the problem, we will place the code for converting Roman numerals into a separate file (code module) and build a class called `Roman_Numerals` to contain the methods. In this case, the data is a mapping of integers to Roman numerals. However, Python does not "remember" the order in which you define the entries; we must use a subclass of dictionary to preserve the order. The reason we need to preserve the order is that we will use the keys and their values in mathematical calculations. If the entries are not in order, the math will be imprecise, and the conversion will generate incorrect values. We can use the `OrderedDict` subclass to preserve the order of the entries. Notice we simply use the `OrderedDict` as a class and pass in the original dictionary items. Note the location of the parentheses and the use of the `import` statement to use the `OrderedDict` class:

```
from collections import OrderedDict

# Private dictionary of roman numerals
__roman_dict = OrderedDict({
    'I': 1,
    'IV': 4,
    'V': 5,
    'IX': 9,
    'X': 10,
    'XL': 40,
```

```
    'L': 50,
    'XC': 90,
    'C': 100,
    'CD': 400,
    'D': 500,
    'CM': 900,
    'M': 1000,
})
```

Notice the two underscores before the name of the dictionary. This is a special notation that marks the dictionary as a private variable in the class. This is a Python aspect for information hiding, which is a recommended technique to use when designing objects; always strive to hide data that is used inside the class.

Notice also that instead of using the basic characters and their values, I used several other values too. I did this to help make the conversion easier (and cheat a bit). In this case, I added the entries that represent the previous single numeral conversions such as 4 (IV), 9 (IX), etc. This makes the conversion a bit easier (and more accurate).

We will also add two methods: convert_to_int(), which takes a Roman numeral string and converts it to an integer, and convert_to_roman(), which takes an integer and converts it to a Roman numeral. Rather than explain every line of code in the methods, I leave it to you to read the code to see how it works.

Simply, the convert to integer method takes each character and gets its value from the dictionary summing the values. There is a trick there that requires special handling for the lower value characters appearing before higher values (e.g., IX). The convert to Roman method is a bit easier since we simply divide the value by the highest value in the dictionary until we reach zero. Listing 4-9 shows the code for the class module, which is saved in a file named roman_numerals.py.

Listing 4-9. Roman Numeral Class

```
#
# MicroPython for the IoT Second Edition
#
# Example: Roman numerals class
#
# Convert integers to roman numerals
# Convert roman numerals to integers
```

```python
#
# Dr. Charles Bell
#
from collections import OrderedDict

class Roman_Numerals:

    # Private dictionary of roman numerals
    __roman_dict = OrderedDict({
        'I': 1,
        'IV': 4,
        'V': 5,
        'IX': 9,
        'X': 10,
        'XL': 40,
        'L': 50,
        'XC': 90,
        'C': 100,
        'CD': 400,
        'D': 500,
        'CM': 900,
        'M': 1000,
    })

    def convert_to_int(self, roman_num):
        value = 0
        for i in range(len(roman_num)):
            if i > 0 and self.__roman_dict[roman_num[i]] > \
                self.__roman_dict[roman_num[i - 1]]:
                value += self.__roman_dict[roman_num[i]] - 2 * \
                    self.__roman_dict[roman_num[i - 1]]
            else:
                value += self.__roman_dict[roman_num[i]]
        return value
```

```python
def convert_to_roman(self, int_value):
    # First, get the values of all of entries in the dictionary
    roman_values = list(self.__roman_dict.values())
    roman_keys = list(self.__roman_dict.keys())
    # Prepare the string
    roman_str = ""
    remainder = int_value
    # Loop through the values in reverse
    for i in range(len(roman_values)-1, -1, -1):
        count = int(remainder / roman_values[i])
        if count > 0:
            for j in range(0,count):
                roman_str += roman_keys[i]
            remainder -= count * roman_values[i]
    return roman_str
```

If you're following along with the chapter, go ahead and create a file on your PC for this code and name it roman_numerals.py. We'll copy it to our MicroPython board in the next section.

Now let's look at the main code. For this, we simply need to import the new class from the code module as follows. This is a slightly different form of the import directive. In this case, we're telling Python to include the roman_numerals class from the file named Roman_Numerals:

```python
from roman_numerals import Roman_Numerals
```

Note   If the code module were in a subfolder, say roman, we would have written the import statement as from roman import Roman_Numerals where we list the folders using dot notation instead of slashes.

The rest of the code is straightforward. We first ask the user for a valid Roman numeral string, then convert it to an integer and use that value to convert back to Roman numerals, printing the result. So, you see having the class in a separate module has simplified our code, making it shorter and easier to maintain. Listing 4-10 shows the complete main code saved in a file named simply roman.py.

Listing 4-10. Converting Roman Numerals

```
#
# MicroPython for the IoT Second Edition
#
# Example: Convert roman numerals using a class
#
# Convert integers to roman numerals
# Convert roman numerals to integers
#
# Dr. Charles Bell
#
from roman_numerals import Roman_Numerals
roman_str = input("Enter a valid roman numeral: ")
roman_num = Roman_Numerals()
# Convert to roman numerals
value = roman_num.convert_to_int(roman_str)
print("Convert to integer:       {0} = {1}".format(roman_str, value))
# Convert to integer
new_str = roman_num.convert_to_roman(value)
print("Convert to Roman Numerals: {0} = {1}".format(value, new_str))
print("bye!")
```

If you're following along with the chapter, go ahead and create a file on your PC for this code and name it roman.py. We'll copy it to our MicroPython board in the next section.

Now, let's see what happens when we run this script. Recall, we will be running this code on our MicroPython board, so if you're following along, be sure to set up your board and connect it to your PC.

Execute the Code

To execute this example, we want to run the code from our MicroPython board. Use Thonny to copy the files you created on your PC to your MicroPython board. Recall, we use the file explorer in Thonny to navigate to the files on our PC, then right-click each file and choose *Upload to* / as shown in Figure 4-5.

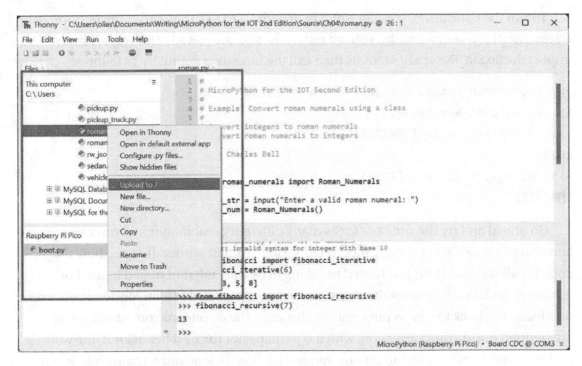

Figure 4-5. *Copying Files to Your MicroPython Board (Thonny)*

Be sure to copy both the `roman.py` and `roman_numerals.py` to your MicroPython board.

Next, use the REPL console in Thonny to run the code. From the REPL prompt, issue the following code statement:

```
>>> import roman
```

This code imports the `roman.py` file we just copied, and when it does, it executes the code, which if you recall will call the code in the roman_numerals.py code module. Once again, issuing the import is like how we ran it on our PC from the Python console.

Once you issue the import statement, the code will be executed. Go ahead and try it out. Start with the value 60, which is LX in Roman numerals:

```
>>> import roman
Enter a valid roman numeral: LX
Convert to integer:        LX = 60
Convert to Roman Numerals: 60 = LVV
bye!
```

To run the code again, you can soft reboot with *CTRL+D*, then rerun the import statement. If this seems clunky, you are right, it is, and there is a better way – simply import the Roman_Numerals module, then call the functions manually as follows:

```
>>> from roman_numerals import Roman_Numerals
>>> rn = Roman_Numerals()
>>> rn.convert_to_int("MMXXIII")
2023
>>> rn.convert_to_roman(2023)
'MMXXIII'
```

Go ahead and try the code out for as many different combinations as you can construct. You can also try using incorrectly formed roman numerals to see how the code handles them. Hint: It will need tweaking to be fully tolerant of bad input. For example, the following shows the use of an incorrectly formed roman numeral converted to integer and back to roman numerals. In this case, the erroneous roman numerals are omitted during the conversion, which is perhaps not the best behavior if one were building a tolerant system, but for our purposes, it is sufficient and remains consistent during the conversion:

```
>>> rn.convert_to_int("MIMVXIII")
2007
>>> rn.convert_to_roman(2007)
'MMVII'
```

Your Challenge

There isn't much to add for this example to improve it other than perhaps some user friendliness (nicer to use). If you want to improve the code or the class itself, I suggest adding a new method named validate() used to validate a Roman numeral string. This method can take a string and determine if it contains a valid series of characters. Hint: To start, check the string has only the characters in the dictionary.

However, you can use this template to build other classes for converting formats. For example, as an exercise, you could create a new class to convert integers to hexadecimal or even octal. Yes, there are functions that will do this for us, but it can be enlightening and satisfying to build it yourself. Go ahead, give it a go – create a new class to convert integers to other formats. I would suggest doing a hexadecimal to integer function first, and when that is working correctly, create the reciprocal to convert integers to hexadecimal.

A more advanced challenge would be to rewrite the class to accept a string in the constructor (when the class variable is created) and use that string to do the conversions instead of passing the string or integer using the convert_to* methods. For example, the class could have a constructor and private member as follows:

```
__roman_str = ""
...
def __init__(self, name):
        self.name = name
```

When you create the instance, you will need to pass the string, or else you will get an error that a required parameter is missing:

```
roman_str = input("Enter a valid roman numeral: ")
roman_num = Roman_Numerals(roman_str)
```

For More Information

Should you require more in-depth knowledge of Python, there are several excellent books on the topic. I list a few of my favorites as follows. A great resource is the documentation on the Python site: python.org/doc/.

- *Pro Python 3, 3rd Edition* (Apress, 2019), J. Burton Browning, Marty Alchin

- *Learning Python, 5th Edition* (O'Reilly Media, 2013), Mark Lutz

- *Automate the Boring Stuff with Python: Practical Programming for Total Beginners, 2nd Edition* (No Starch Press, 2019), Al Sweigart

Summary

Wow! That was a wild ride, wasn't it? I hope that this short crash course in Python has explained enough about the sample programs shown so far that you now know how they work. This crash course also forms the basis for understanding the other Python examples in this book.

If you are learning how to work with IoT projects and don't know how to program with Python, learning Python can be fun given its easy-to-understand syntax. While there are many examples on the Internet you can use, very few are documented in such a way as to provide enough information for someone new to Python to understand or much less get started and deploy the sample! But at least the code is easy to read.

This chapter has provided a crash course in Python that covers the basics of the things you will encounter when examining most of the smaller example projects. We discovered the basic syntax and constructs of a Python application, including a walk-through of building a real Python application that blinks an LED. Through that example, we learned how to work with headless applications, including how to manage a startup background application.

In the next chapter, we'll dive deeper into MicroPython programming. We will see more about the special libraries available for use in your IoT projects written for running on MicroPython boards.

CHAPTER 5

MicroPython Libraries

Now that we have a good grasp on how to write our code in Python and MicroPython, it is time to look at the supporting libraries that make up the firmware. As you will see, the libraries available in MicroPython mirror those in Python. In fact, the libraries in the firmware (sometimes called the application programming interface or API or firmware API) comprise a great deal of the same libraries in Python.

There are some notable exceptions for standard libraries where there is an equivalent library in MicroPython, but it has been renamed to distinguish it from the Python library. In this case, the library has either been reduced in scope by removing the less frequently used features or modified in some ways to fit the MicroPython platform – all to save space (memory).

There are also libraries that are specific to MicroPython and the hardware that provides functionality that may or may not be in some general Python releases. These libraries are designed to make working with the microcontroller and hardware easier.

Thus, there are three types of libraries in the firmware: those that are standard and mostly the same as those in Python, those that are specific to MicroPython, and those that are specific to the hardware. There is another type of library sometimes called user-supplied or simply custom libraries. These are libraries (APIs) we create ourselves that we can deploy to our board and thereby make functionality available to all our projects. We will see an overview of all types of libraries in this chapter.

Note The word module, or code module, is sometimes used to refer to a library; however, a module is commonly a single code file, while a library may consist of many code files. Thus, it is OK to interchange the names if the library is a single file (code module). Another word sometimes used for library is package, which implies multiple files. You may encounter that term too.

© Charles Bell 2024
C. Bell, *MicroPython for the Internet of Things*, https://doi.org/10.1007/978-1-4842-9861-9_5

Rather than simply paraphrase or copy the existing documentation,[1] we will see overviews of the libraries in the form of quick reference tables you can use to become familiar with what is available. Simply knowing what is available can often speed up development and make your programs stronger by not having to reinvent something or spend lots of time trying to find a library that you may (or may not) need. However, there are several libraries that are crucial to learning how to develop MicroPython IoT projects. We will discover those in more detail with code snippets to help you learn them. So, while this chapter is intended to teach you about the more common libraries, it is also a reference guide to a deeper understanding of the MicroPython firmware with links to the official documentation.

Let's begin with a look at those libraries in MicroPython that are "standard" Python libraries.

Built-In and Standard Libraries

As you know, MicroPython is built on Python. Much work was done to trim things down so that most Python libraries can fit on a chip. The resulting MicroPython firmware is considerably smaller than Python on your PC but in no way crippled. That is, MicroPython is Python, and as such MicroPython has many of the same libraries as Python.

Some may call these libraries "built-in," but it is more correct to name them "standard" libraries since these libraries are the same as those in Python. More specifically, they have the same classes with the same functions as those in Python. So, you can write a script on your PC and execute it there and then execute the same script unaltered on your MicroPython board. Nice! As you can surmise, this helps greatly when developing a complex project.

Recall we saw this technique demonstrated in the last chapter. There we saw it is possible to develop part of your script – those parts using standard libraries – and debug them on your PC. That is, once you have them working correctly, you can move on to the next part that requires MicroPython libraries or the hardware libraries. This is because developing on our PC is so much easier. We don't need to power the board on, connect it to our WiFi, etc., to get it to work. Plus, the PC is a lot faster. It's just easier all around. By exercising this practice, we can potentially save ourselves some frustration by ensuring the "standard" parts of our project are working correctly.

---

[1] An altogether deplorable practice.

In this section, we will explore the standard Python libraries beginning with a short overview of what is available, followed by details on how to use some of the more common libraries.

Tip   For more details about the standard MicroPython libraries, see `http://docs.micropython.org/en/latest/library/index.html#python-standard-libraries-and-micro-libraries`.

Overview

The standard libraries in MicroPython contain objects that you can use to perform mathematical functions, operate on programming structures, work with transportable documents (a document store) through JSON, interact with the operating system and other system functions, and even perform calculations on time. Table 5-1 contains a list of the current standard MicroPython libraries. The first column is the name we use in our `import` statement, the second is a short description, and the third contains a link to the online documentation. As you will see, the Python and micro-libraries have a lot to offer.

Table 5-1. *Standard Python Libraries in MicroPython*

Name	Description	Documentation
array	Working with arrays	http://docs.micropython.org/en/latest/library/array.html
asyncio	Asynchronous I/O scheduler	http://docs.micropython.org/en/latest/library/asyncio.html
binascii	Binary/ASCII conversions	http://docs.micropython.org/en/latest/library/binascii.html
builtins	Built-in functions and exceptions	http://docs.micropython.org/en/latest/library/builtins.html
cmath	Complex mathematics	http://docs.micropython.org/en/latest/library/cmath.html

(continued)

Table 5-1. (*continued*)

Name	Description	Documentation
collections	Working with containers	http://docs.micropython.org/en/latest/library/collections.html
errno	Common system errors	http://docs.micropython.org/en/latest/library/errno.html
gc	Working with the garbage collector	http://docs.micropython.org/en/latest/library/gc.html
hashlib	Hashing library	http://docs.micropython.org/en/latest/library/hashlib.html
heapq	Heap queue library	http://docs.micropython.org/en/latest/library/heapq.html
io	Working with I/O streams	http://docs.micropython.org/en/latest/library/io.html
json	JSON encoding and decoding	http://docs.micropython.org/en/latest/library/json.html
math	Math functions	http://docs.micropython.org/en/latest/library/math.html
os	Operating system services	http://docs.micropython.org/en/latest/library/os.html
random	Random number generator	http://docs.micropython.org/en/latest/library/random.html
re	Working with regular expressions	http://docs.micropython.org/en/latest/library/re.html
select	Working with I/O stream events	http://docs.micropython.org/en/latest/library/select.html
socket	Socket library	http://docs.micropython.org/en/latest/library/socket.html
ssl	SSL/TLS library	http://docs.micropython.org/en/latest/library/ssl.html

(*continued*)

Table 5-1. (*continued*)

Name	Description	Documentation
struct	Working with data types	http://docs.micropython.org/en/latest/library/struct.html
sys	System functions	http://docs.micropython.org/en/latest/library/sys.html
time	Time and date functions	http://docs.micropython.org/en/latest/library/time.html
zlib	zlib decompression	http://docs.micropython.org/en/latest/library/zlib.html
_thread	Multithreading support	http://docs.micropython.org/en/latest/library/_thread.html

Most of the libraries presented here are common to most MicroPython boards, but there may be hardware-specific libraries available from the board vendor that permit the use of special hardware features such as onboard sensors. If in doubt, always visit the MicroPython documentation for your board.

Tip   The format of the import statement allows us to specify directories. So, if we use import mylibs.io, MicroPython will attempt to find the library (code module) named io.py in the mylibs folder. This can affect how one uses modules without the u prefix. If we used import io and io.py is not a code module, it will use io as the name of a folder and, if it exists, look for modules in that folder. Thus, you can get yourself in trouble if you use folder names that are the same as the Python library names. Don't do that.

Next, we will look at some of the more commonly used standard libraries and see some code examples for each. But first, there are two categories of standard functions we should discuss.

INTERACTIVE HELP FOR LIBRARIES

A little-known function named `help()` can be, well, very helpful when learning about the libraries in MicroPython. You can use this function in a REPL session to get information about a library, but first be sure to import the library. The following shows an excerpt of the output for the os library:

```
>>> import os
>>> help(os)
object <module 'uos'> is of type module
  __name__ -- uos
  uname -- <function>
  urandom -- <function>
  chdir -- <function>
  getcwd -- <function>
  listdir -- <function>
  mkdir -- <function>
  remove -- <function>
  rename -- <function>
  rmdir -- <function>
  stat -- <function>
  statvfs -- <function>
  unlink -- <function>
  dupterm -- <function>
  ilistdir -- <function>
  mount -- <function>
  umount -- <function>
  VfsFat -- <class 'VfsFat'>
  VfsLfs2 -- <class 'VfsLfs2'>
```

Notice we see the names of all the functions and, if present, constants. This can be a real help when learning the libraries and what they contain. Try it!

Common Standard Libraries

Now let's look at examples of some of the more commonly used standard libraries. What follows is just a sampling of what you can do with each of the libraries. See the online documentation for a full description of all the capabilities. Like most MicroPython libraries, the common standard libraries may be subsets of the full Python3 (CPython) implementation.

Note Some MicroPython implementations name libraries that exist in Python by prepending a u to the name. For example, `uio` is the MicroPython port of the Python `io` library. Most ported libraries are the same as their Python counterpart, and thus you do not need to prepend the u to the name. However, you may encounter situations where you may need to use the MicroPython library by name (by specifying the u prefix).

---

sys

The `sys` (or `usys`) library provides access to the execution system such as constants, variables, command-line options, streams (stdout, stdin, stderr), and more. Most of the features of the library are constants or lists. The streams can be accessed directly, but typically we use the `print()` function, which sends data to the stdout stream by default. The most commonly used functions in this library include the following. Listing 5-1 demonstrates these variables and the `exit()` function.

- `sys.argv`: List of arguments passed to the script from the command line

- `sys.exit(r)`: Exit the program returning the value r to the caller

- `sys.modules`: List of modules loaded (imported)

- `sys.path`: List of paths to search for modules – can be modified

- `sys.implementation`: List of vendor information for MicroPython version

- `sys.platform`: Display platform information such as Linux, MicroPython, etc.

- `sys.byteorder`: The order of the bytes (little vs. big endian)[2]

- `sys.maxsize`: Maximum size (value) stored in integer

- `sys.stderr`: Standard error stream

- `sys.stdin`: Standard input stream

- `sys.stdout`: Standard output stream

- `sys.version`: The version of Python currently executing

- `sys.version_info`: The version number of Python in a tuple

- `sys.exit`: Function for terminating execution

Listing 5-1. Demonstration of the sys Library Features

```
# MicroPython for the IoT Second Edition - Chapter 5
# Example use of the sys library
import sys
print("Modules loaded: " , sys.modules)
sys.path.append("/sd")
print("Path: ", sys.path)
sys.stdout.write("Platform: ")
sys.stdout.write(sys.platform)
sys.stdout.write("\n")
sys.stdout.write("Version: ")
sys.stdout.write(sys.version)
sys.stdout.write("\n")
sys.exit(1)
```

Notice we start with the `import` statement, and after that, we can print the constants and variables in the sys library using the `print()` function. We also see how to append a path to our search path with the `sys.path.append()` function. This is very helpful if we create our own directories to place our code. Without this addition, the `import` statement will fail unless the code module is in the `lib` directory.

---

[2]www.baeldung.com/cs/big-endian-vs-little-endian

At the end of the example, we see how to use the `stdout` stream to write things to the screen. Note that you must provide the carriage return (newline) command to advance the output to a new line (\n). The `print()` function takes care of that for us. The following shows the output of running this script on a MicroPython board:

```
Modules loaded: {'rp2': <module 'rp2' from 'rp2.py'>}
Path: ['', '.frozen', '/lib', '/sd']
Platform: rp2
Version: 3.4.0; MicroPython v1.20.0 on 2023-04-26
```

Notice we see the data as we expect and that this example is running on a Raspberry Pi Pico (rp2) module. Also, notice that there are no command-line arguments. This is because we used an `import` statement. However, if we were to run the code on our PC providing command-line arguments, we would see them. The following shows the output of running this script on a PC:

```
$ python ./sys_example.py
Modules loaded: {'sys': <module 'sys' (built-in)>, 'builtins': <module
'builtins' (built-in)>, '_frozen_importlib': <module '_frozen_importlib'
(frozen)>, '_imp': <module '_imp' (built-in)>, '_thread': <module '_thread'
(built-in)>, '_warnings': <module '_warnings' (built-in)>, '_weakref':
<module '_weakref' (built-in)>, 'winreg': <module 'winreg' (built-in)>,
'_io': <module '_io' (built-in)>, 'marshal': <module 'marshal' (built-in)>,
..., '/sd']
Platform: win32
Version: 3.11.4 (tags/v3.11.4:d2340ef, Jun  7 2023, 05:45:37) [MSC v.1934
64 bit (AMD64)]
```

io

The `io` (or `uio`) library contains additional functions to work with streams and stream-like objects. There is a single function named `io.open()` that you can use to open files (but most people use the built-in function named `open()`) as well as classes for byte and string streams. In fact, the classes have similar file functions, such as `read()`, `write()`, `seek()`, `flush()`, `close()`, as well as a `getvalue()` function, which returns the contents of the stream buffer that contains the data. Let's look at an example.

In this example, we first open a new file for writing and write an array of bytes to the file. The technique used is passing the hex values for each byte to the write() function. When you read data from sensors, they are typically in binary form (a byte or string of bytes). You signify a byte with the escape \x as shown.

After writing the data to the file, we then read the file one byte at a time by passing 1 to the read() function. We then print the values read in their raw form (the value returned from the read(1) call), decimal value, and hex value. Listing 5-2 shows how to read a file in binary mode. The bytes written contain a secret word (one obscured by using hex values) – can you see it?

Listing 5-2. Demonstration of the uio Library Features

```
# MicroPython for the IoT - Chapter 5
# Example use of the io library
import io
# Create the binary file
fio_out = io.open('data.bin', 'wb')
fio_out.write("\x5F\x9E\xAE\x09\x3E\x96\x68\x65\x6C\x6C\x6F")
fio_out.write("\x00")
fio_out.close()
# Read the binary file and print out the results in hex and char.
fio_in = io.open('data.bin', 'rb')
print("Raw,Dec,Hex from file:")
byte_val = fio_in.read(1)  # read a byte
while byte_val:
    print(byte_val, ",", ord(byte_val), hex(ord(byte_val)))
    byte_val = fio_in.read(1)  # read a byte
fio_in.close()
```

Listing 5-3 shows the output when run on a MicroPython board, but you can also run the code on your PC with the same output.

Listing 5-3. Demonstration of the io Library Features

```
Raw,Dec,Hex from file:
b'_' , 95 0x5f
b'\xc2' , 194 0xc2
b'\x9e' , 158 0x9e
```

```
b'\xc2' , 194 0xc2
b'\xae' , 174 0xae
b'\t' , 9 0x9
b'>' , 62 0x3e
b'\xc2' , 194 0xc2
b'\x96' , 150 0x96
b'h' , 104 0x68
b'e' , 101 0x65
b'l' , 108 0x6c
b'l' , 108 0x6c
b'o' , 111 0x6f
b'\x00' , 0 0x0
```

If you're curious what the file looks like, you can use a utility like hexdump to print the contents as follows. Can you see the hidden message?

```
$ hexdump -C data.bin
00000000  5f 9e ae 09 3e 96 68 65  6c 6c 6f 00              |_...>.hello.|
0000000c
```

json

The json (or ujson) library is one of those libraries you are likely to use frequently when working with data in an IoT project. It provides encoding and decoding of JavaScript Object Notation (JSON) documents. This is because many of the IoT services available either require or can process JSON documents. Thus, you should consider getting into the habit of formatting your data in JSON to make it easier to integrate with other systems. The library implements the following functions that you can use to work with JSON documents:

- json.dump(obj, stream): Returns a string decoded from a JSON object to a stream

- json.dumps(obj): Returns a string decoded from a JSON object

- json.loads(stream): Parses the JSON string and returns a JSON object. Will raise an error if not formatted correctly

- json.load(str): Parses the contents of a JSON document. Will raise an error if not formatted correctly

Recall we saw a brief example of JSON documents in the last chapter. That example was written exclusively for the PC, but a small change makes it possible to run it on a MicroPython board. Let's look at a similar example. Listing 5-4 shows an example of using the ujson library.

Listing 5-4. Demonstration of the json Library Features

```
# MicroPython for the IoT Second Edition - Chapter 5
# Example use of the json library
import json

# Prepare a list of JSON documents for pets by converting JSON to a
dictionary
vehicles = []
vehicles.append(json.loads('{"make":"Chevrolet", "year":2015,
"model":"Silverado", "color":"Pull me over red", "type":"pickup"}'))
vehicles.append(json.loads('{"make":"Yamaha", "year":2009, "model":"R1",
"color":"Blue/Silver", "type":"motorcycle"}'))
vehicles.append(json.loads('{"make":"SeaDoo", "year":1997,
"model":"Speedster", "color":"White", "type":"boat"}'))
vehicles.append(json.loads('{"make":"TaoJen", "year":2013,
"model":"Sicily", "color":"Black", "type":"Scooter"}'))

# Now, write these entries to a file. Note: overwrites the file
json_file = open("my_vehicles.json", "w")
for vehicle in vehicles:
    json_file.write(json.dumps(vehicle))
    json_file.write("\n")
json_file.close()

# Now, let's read the list of vehicles and print out their data
my_vehicles = []
json_file = open("my_vehicles.json", "r")
for vehicle in json_file.readlines():
    parsed_json = json.loads(vehicle)
    my_vehicles.append(parsed_json)
json_file.close()
```

```
# Finally, print a summary of the vehicles
print("Year Make Model Color")
for vehicle in my_vehicles:
    print(vehicle['year'],vehicle['make'],vehicle['model'],vehicle['color'])
```

The following shows the output of the script running on MicroPython:

```
Year Make Model Color
2015 Chevrolet Silverado Pull me over red
2009 Yamaha R1 Blue/Silver
1997 SeaDoo Speedster White
2013 TaoJen Sicily Black
```

OS

The os (or uos) library implements a set of functions for working with the base operating system. Some of the functions may be familiar if you have written programs for your PC. Most functions allow you to work with file and directory operations. The following lists several of the more commonly used functions:

- os.chdir(path): Change the current directory

- os.getcwd(): Return the current working directory

- os.listdir([dir]): List the current directory if dir is missing or directory specified

- os.mkdir(path): Create a new directory

- os.remove(path): Delete a file

- os.rmdir(path): Delete a directory

- os.rename(old_path, new_path): Rename a file

- os.stat(path): Get status of a file or directory

In this example, we see how to change the working directory so that we can simplify our import statements. The code for this example requires the json_example.py file we saw earlier placed in a folder on the MicroPython board named examples. Thus, you must create the directory examples on your MicroPython board, then download the json_example.py file into that folder. See Chapter 2 for how to work with files and your MicroPython board.

Tip   For best results, copy all of the source code files for this chapter into the examples folder on your MicroPython board.

We also see how to create a new directory, rename it, create a file in the new directory, list the directory, and finally clean up (delete) the changes. Listing 5-5 shows an example for working with the os library functions.

Listing 5-5. Demonstration of the os Library Features

```
# MicroPython for the IoT Second Edition - Chapter 5
# Example use of the os library
# Note: change os to os to run it on your PC!
import sys
import os

# Create a method to display files in directory
def show_files():
    files = os.listdir()
    sys.stdout.write("\nShow Files Output:\n")
    sys.stdout.write("\tname\tsize\n")
    for file in files:
        stats = os.stat(file)
        # Print a directory with a "d" prefix and the size
        is_dir = True
        if stats[0] > 16384:
            is_dir = False
        if is_dir:
            sys.stdout.write("d\t")
        else:
            sys.stdout.write("\t")
        sys.stdout.write(file)
        if not is_dir:
            sys.stdout.write("\t")
            sys.stdout.write(str(stats[6]))
        sys.stdout.write("\n")
```

```
# List the current directory
show_files()
# Change to the examples directory
os.chdir('examples')
show_files()

# Show how you can now use the import statement with the current dir
print("\nRun the ujson_example with import ujson_example after chdir()")
import json_example

# Create a directory
os.mkdir("test")
show_files()

# Remove the directory
os.rmdir('test')
show_files()
```

While this example is a little long, it shows some interesting tricks. Notice we created a function to print out the directory list rather than printing out the list of files returned. We also checked the status of the file to determine if the file was a directory or not, and if it was, we printed a d to signal the name refers to a directory. We also used the stdout stream to control formatting with tabs (\t) and newline (\n) characters.

You will also see how to use the change directory to improve how we use the import statement. Since we changed the directory to examples, the import json_example will attempt to find that module (library) in the current directory first. This is a nice trick you can use in your own projects to deploy your code to your board in a separate directory, which means you can use this to deploy multiple projects to your board, placing each in its own directory.

Now let's see the output. Listing 5-6 shows the output when run on MicroPython. Take a few moments and look through the output to see how the functions worked. Also, note the output from the JSON example is shown since we imported that code in the middle of the script. Nice.

Listing 5-6. Demonstration of the os Library Features (Output)

```
Show Files Output:
      name        size
      boot.py       17
      data.bin      15
d        examples
      my_vehicles.json      377
      roman.py              612
      roman_numerals.py    1607

Show Files Output:
      name                  size
      exception_example.py   520
      import_errors.py       272
      io_example.py          567
      json_example.py       1326
      my_vehicles.json       377
      os_example.py         1169
      sys_example.py         366
      time_example.py       1420

Run the ujson_example with import ujson_example after chdir()
Year Make Model Color
2015 Chevrolet Silverado Pull me over red
2009 Yamaha R1 Blue/Silver
1997 SeaDoo Speedster White
2013 TaoJen Sicily Black

Show Files Output:
      name                  size
      exception_example.py   520
      import_errors.py       272
      io_example.py          567
      json_example.py       1326
      my_vehicles.json       377
      os_example.py         1169
```

```
        sys_example.py          366
d       test
        time_example.py         1420
Show Files Output:
        name                    size
        exception_example.py    520
        import_errors.py        272
        io_example.py           567
        json_example.py         1326
        my_vehicles.json        377
        os_example.py           1169
        sys_example.py          366
        time_example.py         1420
```

time

The time (or utime) library is another popular library used in many projects. The library is used to get the current time and date, such as calculating time differentials. Note that some of the functions only work with a real-time clock (RTC) installed either as a hardware extension or through a network time server. See Chapter 6 for more details. The following lists several of the more commonly used functions related to inserting delays in our scripts. Delays are helpful when we need to pause processing to allow a sensor to read or to wait for data from/to other sources. Another common use of this library is recording the date and time of an event or sensor data read:

- time.sleep(seconds): Put the board in a sleep mode for the number of seconds specified

- time.sleep_ms(ms): Put the board in a sleep mode for the number of milliseconds specified

- time.sleep_us(us): Put the board in a sleep mode for the number of microseconds specified

Let's see a short example of how to use time delays. Here, we use a random function to sleep for a random period and to provide random values. Don't worry about the time functions. Listing 5-7 shows the code for the time library. We will see more about time and real-time clocks in Chapter 6.

Listing 5-7. Demonstration of the time Library Sleep Features

```python
# MicroPython for the IoT Second Edition - Chapter 5
# Example use of the time library
# Note: This example only works on MicroPython and will not run on your PC.
import machine
import sys
import time
from random import randint

# Init with default time and date
synchTime = time.mktime((2023, 7, 16, 15, 18, 11, 6, 190))
delta = synchTime - int(time.time())

def now():
    return time.localtime(time.time() + delta)

# Format the time (epoch) for a better view
def format_time(tm_data):
    # Use a special shortcut to unpack tuple: *tm_data
    return "{0}-{1:0>2}-{2:0>2} {3:0>2}:{4:0>2}:{5:0>2}".format(*tm_data)

# Generate a random number of rows from 0-25
num_rows = randint(0,25)

# Print a row using random seconds, milleseconds, or microseconds
# to simulate time.
print("Datetime            Value")
print("------------------- --------")
for i in range(0,num_rows):
    # Generate random value for our sensor
    value = randint(0,9999999) / 10000
    # Wait a random number of seconds for time
    time.sleep(randint(1,15))  # sleep up to 10 seconds
    print("{0}  {1:0>{width}.4f}".format(format_time(now()), value,
    width=8))
```

Notice there is a lot going on in this example than simply waiting a random number of seconds. This example shows you how to do that but also how to work with time data and formatting data. You typically must do this when logging data. Let's walk through this a bit.

We create two functions: one to generate the current date and time and another to format the datetime in a user-friendly format.

The `format_time()` function returns a string representing the datetime. Here, we see some advanced formatting options to format the date with the correct digits per part – specifically, four digits for year and two for month, day, hour, minute, and second. The `:0>2` option tells the `format()` function to space the value over two positions (digits) with leading zeros. Cool, eh? Notice the last `print()` statement. Notice we use another trick to pass the width with a named parameter (`width`).

Finally, we get to the example code where we generate a random number of lines from 0 to 25, then loop for those iterations generating a random value (0–999.9999), and then wait (sleep) for a random number of seconds (1–10), then print the new datetime and the value. This simulates a typical loop we would use to read data from sensors. As most sensors need time to read the value, the sleep function allows us to wait for that period.[3]

Now that we know more about what this code is doing, let's see an example of how it works. The following shows the output from running this code on MicroPython:

```
Datetime              Value
-------------------   --------
2023-07-16 15:18:12   003.5471
2023-07-16 15:18:19   429.3827
2023-07-16 15:18:22   987.4546
2023-07-16 15:18:23   113.1418
2023-07-16 15:18:37   239.6263
2023-07-16 15:18:42   338.2216
2023-07-16 15:18:54   315.0221
2023-07-16 15:19:02   086.1253
2023-07-16 15:19:04   533.3747
```

---

[3] Also, keep in mind this interval – called a sampling rate – must also make sense for the project. Sampling the ambient temperature in a controlled climate 30 times a second may generate a considerable amount of data that is useless because it rarely changes.

```
2023-07-16 15:19:12  602.3252
2023-07-16 15:19:22  394.2683
2023-07-16 15:19:26  632.7906
2023-07-16 15:19:41  094.1397
2023-07-16 15:19:42  149.6111
2023-07-16 15:19:54  281.4139
2023-07-16 15:19:59  136.0484
2023-07-16 15:20:08  697.6131
2023-07-16 15:20:18  164.4964
2023-07-16 15:20:23  818.4449
2023-07-16 15:20:35  439.5562
2023-07-16 15:20:41  060.8383
```

There are also built-in functions that are not part of any specific library, and there are exceptions that allow us to capture error conditions. Let's look at those before we dive into some of the more commonly used standard libraries.

Built-In Functions and Classes

Python comes with many built-in functions: functions you can call directly from your script without importing them. There are many classes that you can use to define variables, work with data, and more. They're objects so you can use them to contain data and perform operations (functions) on the data. We've seen a few of these in the examples so far.

Let us see some of the major built-in functions and classes. Table 5-2 includes a short description of each. You can find more information about each at `https://docs.python.org/3/library/functions.html`. While this is Python documentation, it applies to MicroPython too. Classes are designated with "class"; the remainder are functions.

Table 5-2. *MicroPython Built-In Functions and Classes*

Name	Description
abs(x)	Return the absolute value of a number
all(iterable)	Return True if all elements of the iterable are true (or if the iterable is empty)
any(iterable)	Return True if any element of the iterable is true
bin(x)	Convert an integer number to a binary string
class bool([x])	Return a Boolean value, that is, one of True or False
class bytearray([source[, encoding[, errors]]])	Return a new array of bytes
class bytes([source[, encoding[, errors]]])	Return a new "bytes" object, which is an immutable sequence of integers in the range 0 <= x < 256
callable(object)	Return True if the object argument appears callable, False if not
chr(i)	Return the string representing a character whose Unicode code point is the integer i
classmethod(function)	Return a class method for a function
class complex([real[, imag]])	Return a complex number with the value real + imag*1j or convert a string or number to a complex number
delattr(obj, name)	This is a relative of setattr(). The arguments are an object and a string. The string must be the name of one of the object's attributes
class dict()	Create a new dictionary
dir([object])	Without arguments, return the list of names in the current local scope. With an argument, attempt to return a list of valid attributes for that object
divmod(a,b)	Take two (noncomplex) numbers as arguments and return a pair of numbers consisting of their quotient and remainder when using integer division

(continued)

Table 5-2. (*continued*)

Name	Description
enumerate(iterable, start=0)	Return an enumerate object. Iterable must be a sequence, an iterator, or some other object that supports iteration
eval(expression, globals=None, locals=None)	Evaluate an expression using globals and locals as dictionaries in a local namespace
exec(object[, globals[, locals]])	Execute a set of Python statements or object using globals and locals as dictionaries in a local namespace
filter(function, iterable)	Construct an iterator from those elements of iterable for which function returns true
class float([x])	Return a floating-point number constructed from a number or string
class frozenset([iterable])	Return a new frozenset object, optionally with elements taken from iterable
getattr(object, name[, default])	Return the value of the named attribute of the object. Name must be a string
globals()	Return a dictionary representing the current global symbol table
hasattr(object, name)	The arguments are an object and a string. The result is True if the string is the name of one of the object's attributes, False if not
hash(object)	Return the hash value of the object (if it has one). Hash values are integers
hex(x)	Convert an integer number to a lowercase hexadecimal string prefixed with "0x"
id(object)	Return the "identity" of an object
input([prompt])	If the prompt argument is present, it is written to standard output without a trailing newline. The function then reads a line from input, converts it to a string (stripping a trailing newline), and returns that

(*continued*)

Table 5-2. (*continued*)

Name	Description
class int(x)	Return an integer object constructed from a number or string x, or return 0 if no arguments are given
isinstance(object, classinfo)	Return true if the object argument is an instance of the classinfo argument or of a (direct, indirect, or virtual) subclass thereof
issubclass(class, classinfo)	Return true if class is a subclass (direct, indirect, or virtual) of classinfo
iter(object[, sentinel])	Return an iterator object
len(s)	Return the length (the number of items) of an object
class list([iterable])	List sequence
locals()	Update and return a dictionary representing the current local symbol table
map(function, iterable, …)	Return an iterator that applies a function to every item of iterable, yielding the results
max([iterable|arg*])	Return the largest item in an iterable or the largest of two or more arguments
class memoryview(obj)	Return a "memory view" object created from the given argument
min([iterable|arg*])	Return the smallest item in an iterable or the smallest of two or more arguments
next(iterator[, default])	Retrieve the next item from the iterator by calling its __next__() method
class object0	Return a new featureless object. Object is a base for all classes
oct(x)	Convert an integer number to an octal string

(*continued*)

Table 5-2. (*continued*)

Name	Description
`open(file, mode='r', buffering=-1, encoding=None, errors=None, newline=None, closefd=True, opener=None)`	Open a file and return a corresponding file object. Use `close()` to close the file
`ord(c)`	Given a string representing one Unicode character, return an integer representing the Unicode code point of that character
`pow(x, y[, z])`	Return x to the power y; if z is present, return x to the power y, modulo z (computed more efficiently than `pow(x, y) % z`)
`print(*objects, sep=' ', end='\n', file=sys.stdout, flush=False)`	Print objects to the text stream file, separated by `sep` and followed by end. `sep`, end, file, and flush; if present, must be given as keyword arguments
`class property(fget=None, fset=None, fdel=None, doc=None)`	Return a property attribute
`range([stop|[start, stop[, step]]])`	Range sequence
`repr(object)`	Return a string containing a printable representation of an object
`reversed(seq)`	Return a reverse iterator
`round(number[, ndigits])`	Return a number rounded to `ndigits` precision after the decimal point
`class set([iterable])`	Return a new set object, optionally with elements taken from iterable
`setattr(object, name, value)`	This is the counterpart of getattr(). The arguments are an object, a string, and an arbitrary value
`class slice(start, stop[, step])`	Return a slice object representing the set of indices specified by `range(start, stop, step)`

(*continued*)

Table 5-2. (*continued*)

Name	Description
`sorted(iterable[, key][, reverse])`	Return a new sorted list from the items in iterable
`staticmethod(function)`	Return a static method for a function
`class str(object)`	Return a str version of an object
`sum(terable[, start])`	Sums start and the items of an iterable from left to right and returns the total
`super([type[, object-or-type]])`	Return a proxy object that delegates function calls to a parent or sibling class of type
`class tuple([iterable])`	Tuple sequence
`type(object)`	Return the type of an object
`zip(*iterables)`	Make an iterator that aggregates elements from each of the iterables

You should look through this list and explore the links for those you find interesting and refer to the list when developing your projects so that you can use the most appropriate function or class. You may be surprised how much is "built in." However, once again, always check the documentation for your chosen MicroPython board for the latest functions and classes available in your firmware.

Tip See `https://docs.python.org/3/library/functions.html` for more information about the built-in functions and classes. See `http://docs.micropython.org/en/latest/library/builtins.html` for the latest list of built-in functions and classes in MicroPython.

Let's see an example of using one of the classes – the dictionary. The following shows how we can use the built-in class to create a variable of type `dict()` and later use it. Since the class is part of the built-in functionality, it will work on both Python and MicroPython.

```
>>> my_addr = dict()
>>> print(my_addr)
```

```
{}
>>> my_addr['street'] = '123 Main St'
>>> my_addr['city'] = 'Anywhere'
>>> my_addr['zip'] = 90125
>>> print(my_addr)
{'city': 'Anywhere', 'street': '123 Main St', 'zip': 90125}
>>> my_addr = {'street':'201 Cherry Tree Road', 'city':'Gobye',
'zip':12345}
>>> print(my_addr)
{'city': 'Gobye', 'street': '201 Cherry Tree Road', 'zip': 12345}
```

Here, we see we can use the dictionary class to create a variable of that type. We can see this in the first print() call. Recall that the syntax for defining a dictionary is a set of curly braces. Next, we add values to the dictionary using the special syntax for accessing elements. Finally, we reassign the variable a new set of data using the more familiar dictionary syntax.

Now let's talk about a topic we haven't talked a lot about – exceptions. Exceptions are part of the built-in module for Python and can be a very important programming technique you will want to use. Perhaps not right away, but eventually you will appreciate the power and convenience of using exceptions in your code.

Exceptions

There is also a powerful mechanism we can use in Python (and MicroPython) to help manage or capture events when errors occur and execute code for a specific error. This construct is called exceptions, and the exceptions (errors) we can capture are called exception classes. It uses a special syntax called the try statement (also called a clause since it requires at least one other clause to form a valid statement) to help us capture errors as they are generated. Exceptions can be generated anywhere in code with the raise() function. That is, if something goes wrong, a programmer can "raise" a specific, named exception, and the try statement can be used to capture it via an except clause. Table 5-3 shows the list of exception classes available in MicroPython along with a short description of when (how) the exception could be raised.

Table 5-3. *MicroPython Exception Classes*

Exception Class	Description of Use
AssertionError	An assert() statement fails
AttributeError	An attribute reference fails
Exception	Base exception class
ImportError	One or more modules failed to import
IndexError	Subscript is out of range
KeyboardInterrupt	Keyboard CTRL+C was issued or simulated
KeyError	Key mapping in the dictionary is not present in the list of keys
MemoryError	Out of memory condition
NameError	A local or global name (variable, function, etc.) is not found
NotImplementedError	An abstract function has been encountered (it is incomplete)
OSError	Any system-related error from the operating system
RuntimeError	Possibly fatal error encountered on execution
StopIteration	An iterator's next function signaled no more values in iterable object
SyntaxError	Code syntax error encountered

The syntax for the try statement is shown as follows. Each part of the construct is called a clause.

```
try_stmt   ::=  try1_stmt | try2_stmt
try1_stmt ::=  "try" ":" code block
               ("except" [expression ["as" identifier]] ":" code block)+
               ["else" ":" code block]
               ["finally" ":" code block]
try2_stmt ::=  "try" ":" code block
               "finally" ":" code block
```

Notice there are four clauses: try, except, else, and finally. The try clause is where we put our code (code block) – one or more lines of code that will be included in the exception capture. There can be only one try, else, and finally, but you can have any number of except clauses naming an exception class. In fact, the except and else go together such that if an exception is detected running any of the lines of code in the try clause, it will search the except clauses, and if and only if no except clause is met, it will execute the else clause. The finally clause is used to execute after all exceptions are processed and executed. Notice also that there are two versions of the statement: one that contains one or more except and optionally an else and finally and another that has only the try and finally clauses.

Let's look at one of the ways we can use the statement to capture errors in our code. Suppose you are reading data from a batch of sensors and the libraries (modules) for those sensors raise ValueError if the value read is out of range or invalid. It may also be the case that you don't want the data from any other sensors if one or more fail. So, we can use code like the following to "try" to read each of the sensors, and if there is a ValueError, issue a warning and keep going, or if some other error is encountered, flag it as an error during the read. Note that typically we would not stop the program at that point; rather, we would normally log it and keep going. Study the following until you're convinced exceptions are cool:

```
values = []
print("Start sensor read.")
try:
    values.append(read_sensor(pin11))
    values.append(read_sensor(pin12))
    values.append(read_sensor(pin13))
    values.append(read_sensor(pin17))
    values.append(read_sensor(pin18))
except ValueError as err:
    print("WARNING: One or more sensors valued to read a correct
value.", err)
except:
    print("ERROR: fatal error reading sensors.")
finally:
    print("Sensor read complete.")
```

Another way we can use exceptions is when we want to import a module (library), but we're not sure if it is present. For example, suppose there was a module named piano.py that has a function named keys() that you want to import, but the module may or may not be on the system. In this case, we may have other code we can use instead creating our own version of keys(). To test if the module can be imported, we can place our import inside a try block as follows. We can then detect if the import fails and take appropriate steps.

```
# Try to import the keys() function from piano. If not present,
# use a simulated version of the keys() function.
try:
    from piano import keys
except ImportError as err:
    print("WARNING:", err)
    def keys():
        return(['A','B','C','D','E','F','G'])
print("Keys:", keys())
```

If we added code like this and the module were not present, not only can we respond with a warning message, but we can also define our own function to use if the module isn't present.

Finally, you can raise any exception you want including creating your own exceptions. Creating custom exceptions is an advanced topic, but let's see how we can raise exceptions since we may want to do that if we write our own custom libraries. Suppose you have a block of code that is reading values, but it is possible that a value may be out of range. That is, too large for an integer, too small for the valid range of values expected, etc. You can simply raise the ValueError passing in your custom error message as follows with the raise statement and a valid exception class declaration:

```
raise ValueError("ERROR: the value read from the sensor ({0}) is not in
range.".format(val_read))
```

You can then use the try statement to capture this condition since you know it is possible and work your code around it. For example, if you were reading data, you could elect to skip the read and move on – continue the loop. However, if this exception was to be encountered when running your code and there were no try statements, you could get an error like the following, which, even though fatal, is still informative:

```
Traceback (most recent call last):
  File "<stdin>", line 1, in <module>
ValueError: ERROR: the value read from the sensor (-12) is not in range.
```

You can use similar techniques as shown here to make your MicroPython code more robust and tolerant of errors. Better still, you can write your code to anticipate errors and react to them in a graceful, controlled manner.

Tip   For a more in-depth look at Python exceptions, see `https://docs.python.org/3/tutorial/errors.html`.

MicroPython Libraries

There are also libraries that are built expressly for the MicroPython system. These are libraries designed to help facilitate using MicroPython on the hardware. Like the built-in libraries, there are some MicroPython libraries that apply to one board or another and those that differ from one board to another. That is, there are subtle differences in the libraries that prevent them from working on more than one board. Always consult the documentation for the firmware for your board for a complete list of the MicroPython libraries available.

Overview

The MicroPython libraries provide functionality that is specific to the MicroPython implementation of Python. There are libraries with functions for working with the hardware directly, the MicroPython system, and networking. We will see examples of some of the features of each of these libraries in the following sections. Table 5-4 contains a list of the current MicroPython libraries that are common to most boards. The first column is the name we use in our `import` statement, the second is a short description, and the third contains a link to the online documentation.

Table 5-4. *MicroPython-Specific Libraries*

Name	Description	Documentation
bluetooth	Bluetooth library	http://docs.micropython.org/en/latest/library/bluetooth.html
btree	BTree library	http://docs.micropython.org/en/latest/library/btree.html
cryptolib	Cryptographic library	http://docs.micropython.org/en/latest/library/cryptolib.html
framebuf	Frame buffer	http://docs.micropython.org/en/latest/library/framebuf.html
machine	Hardware-related functions	http://docs.micropython.org/en/latest/library/machine.html
micropython	MicroPython internals	http://docs.micropython.org/en/latest/library/micropython.html
neopixel	NeoPixel LED library (WS2812)	http://docs.micropython.org/en/latest/library/neopixel.html
network	Networking	http://docs.micropython.org/en/latest/library/network.html
uctypes	Structured binary data	http://docs.micropython.org/en/latest/library/uctypes.html

Tip For more details about any of the MicroPython libraries, see http://docs.micropython.org/en/latest/library/index.html#micropython-specific-libraries.

Next, we will look at a few of the more common MicroPython libraries and see some code examples for each.

Common MicroPython Libraries

Now let's look at examples of some of the more commonly used MicroPython libraries. What follows is just a sampling of what you can do with each of the libraries. See the online documentation for a full description of all the capabilities.

machine

The machine library contains functions related to the hardware, providing an abstraction layer that you can write code to interact with the hardware. Thus, this library is the main library you will use to access features like timers, communication protocols, CPU, and more. Since this functionality is communicating directly with the hardware, you should take care when experimenting to avoid changing or even potentially damaging the performance or configuration of your board. For example, using the library incorrectly could lead to lockups, reboots, or crashes.

Caution   Take care when working with the low-level machine library to avoid changing or even potentially damaging the performance or configuration of your board.

Since the machine library is a low-level hardware abstraction, we will not cover it in depth in this chapter. Rather, we will see more of the hardware features in the next chapter. In the meantime, let's explore another interesting gem of MicroPython knowledge by showing you how to discover what a library contains through the help function. For example, Listing 5-8 shows an excerpt of what is reported through the REPL console when we issue the statement help(machine). The help() function will display all the functions and constants that are available for use in the library. While it doesn't replace a detailed explanation or even a complete example, it can be useful when encountering a library for the first time.

Listing 5-8. The machine Library Help

```
>>> import machine
>>> help(machine)
object <module 'umachine'> is of type module
  __name__ -- umachine
```

```
unique_id -- <function>
soft_reset -- <function>
reset -- <function>
reset_cause -- <function>
bootloader -- <function>
freq -- <function>
idle -- <function>
lightsleep -- <function>
deepsleep -- <function>
disable_irq -- <function>
enable_irq -- <function>
bitstream -- <function>
time_pulse_us -- <function>
dht_readinto -- <function>
mem8 -- <8-bit memory>
mem16 -- <16-bit memory>
mem32 -- <32-bit memory>
ADC -- <class 'ADC'>
I2C -- <class 'I2C'>
SoftI2C -- <class 'SoftI2C'>
I2S -- <class 'I2S'>
Pin -- <class 'Pin'>
PWM -- <class 'PWM'>
RTC -- <class 'RTC'>
Signal -- <class 'Signal'>
SPI -- <class 'SPI'>
SoftSPI -- <class 'SoftSPI'>
Timer -- <class 'Timer'>
UART -- <class 'UART'>
WDT -- <class 'WDT'>
PWRON_RESET -- 1
WDT_RESET -- 3
```

Notice there is a lot of information there! What this gives us most is the list of classes we can use to interact with the hardware. Here, we see there are classes for UART, SPI, I2C, PWM, and more. Since MicroPython boards from different vendors can contain different hardware, it is always a good idea to check the output of help(machine) on a board you're using for the first time. It may save you a lot of headaches trying to find support for hardware that doesn't exist!

network

The network library is used to install network drivers (classes for interacting with the networking abstraction) and configure the settings. However, it is important to note that only those boards with networking capabilities will have this library. For example, the Raspberry Pi Pico (the original without WiFi) generates an error when attempting to import the library as follows:

```
>>> import network
Traceback (most recent call last):
  File "<stdin>", line 1, in <module>
ImportError: no module named 'network'
```

However, the Raspberry Pi Pico W does support the library as follows:

```
>>> import network
>>> help(network)
object <module 'network'> is of type module
  __name__ -- network
  country -- <function>
  hostname -- <function>
  route -- <function>
  WLAN -- <class 'CYW43'>
  STAT_IDLE -- 0
  STAT_CONNECTING -- 1
  STAT_WRONG_PASSWORD -- -3
  STAT_NO_AP_FOUND -- -2
  STAT_CONNECT_FAIL -- -1
  STAT_GOT_IP -- 3
  STA_IF -- 0
  AP_IF -- 1
```

While other libraries differ from one board to another, this library is one that is quite different among the various MicroPython boards. We will see more about the networking classes and the intriguing Bluetooth class in the next chapter.

Custom Libraries

Building your own custom libraries may seem like a daunting task, but it isn't. What is possibly a bit of a challenge is figuring out what you want the library to do and making the library abstract (enough) to be used by any script. The rules and best practices for programming come into play here, such as data abstraction, API immutability, etc.

We discussed creating our own modules in the last chapter. In this section, we will look at how to organize our code modules into a library (package) that we can deploy (copy) to our MicroPython board and use in all our programs. This example, though trivial, is a complete example that you can use as a template should you decide to make your own custom libraries.

For this example, we will create a library with two modules: one that contains code to perform value conversions for a sensor and another that contains helper functions for our projects – general functions that we want to reuse. We will name the library my_helper. It will contain two code modules: sensor_convert.py and helper_functions.py. Recall we will also need an __init__.py file to help MicroPython import the functions correctly, but we will get back to that in a moment. Let's look at the first code module.

We will place the files in a directory named my_helper (same as the library name). This is a typical convention, and you can put whatever name you want, but you must remember it since we will use that name when importing the library into our code. Figure 5-1 shows an example layout of the files.

Figure 5-1. *Directory/File Layout for the my_helper Sample Library on Raspberry Pi Pico W*

Now let's look at the code. The first module is named helper_functions.py and contains one of the helper functions from a previous example. Since these are generic, we placed them in this code module. However, we want to use this code on all our boards. Listing 5-9 shows the complete code for the module.

Listing 5-9.   The helper_functions.py Module

```python
# MicroPython for the IoT Second Edition - Chapter 5
# Example module for the my_helper library
# This module contains helper functions for general use.

import machine


# Format the time (epoch) for a better view
def format_time(tm_data):
    # Use a special shortcut to unpack tuple: *tm_data
    return "{0}-{1:0>2}-{2:0>2} {3:0>2}:{4:0>2}:{5:0>2}".format(*tm_data)
```

The second code module is named sensor_convert.py and contains functions that are helpful in converting sensor raw values into a string for qualitative comparisons. For example, the function get_moisture_level() returns a string based on the threshold of the raw value. The datasheet for the sensor will define such values, and you should use those in your code until and unless you can calibrate the sensor. In this case, if the value is less than the lower bound, the soil is dry; if greater than the upper bound, the soil is wet. Listing 5-10 shows the complete code for the module.

Listing 5-10. The sensor_convert.py Module

```
# MicroPython for the IoT Second Edition - Chapter 5
# Example module for the my_helper library

# This function converts values read from the sensor to a
# string for use in qualifying the moisture level read.

# Constants - adjust to "tune" your sensor

_UPPER_BOUND = 400
_LOWER_BOUND = 250

def get_moisture_level(raw_value):
    if raw_value <= _LOWER_BOUND:
        return("dry")
    elif raw_value >= _UPPER_BOUND:
        return("wet")
    return("ok")
```

Now let's go over the __init__.py file. This is a very mysterious file that developers often get very confused about. If you do not include one in your library directory, you should import what you want to use manually, that is, with something like import. my_helper.helper_functions. But with the file, you can do your imports at one time, allowing a simple import my_helper statement, which will import all the files. Let's look at the __init__.py file. Listing 5-11 shows the contents of the file.

Listing 5-11. The __init__.py File

```
# MicroPython for the IoT Second Edition - Chapter 5
# Metadata
__name__ = "Chuck's Python Helper Library"
__all__ = ['format_time', 'get_rand', 'get_moisture_level']
# Library-level imports
from my_helper.helper_functions import format_time
from my_helper.sensor_convert import get_moisture_level
```

Notice on the first line we use a special constant to set the name of the library. The next constant limits what will be imported by the * (all) option for the import statement. Since it lists all the methods, it's just an exercise but a good habit to use especially if your library and modules contain many internal functions that you do not want to make usable to others. The last two lines show the import statements used to import the functions from the modules, making them available to anyone who imports the library. The following shows a short example of how to do that along with how to use an alias. Here, we use myh as the alias for my_helper:

```
>>> import my_helper as myh
>>> import time
>>> myh.format_time(time.localtime())
'2023-07-16 16:08:26'
```

We can now access (use) all functions by that alias as follows:

```
>>> import my_helper as myh
>>> import time
>>> myh.format_time(time.localtime())
'2023-07-16 16:12:27'
>>> print(myh.get_moisture_level(750))
wet
```

In case you're wondering, the help function works on this custom library too!

```
>>> import my_helper as myh
>>> help(myh)
object <module 'Chuck's Python Helper Library' from 'my_helper/__init__.
py'> is of type module
```

```
__path__ -- my_helper
get_moisture_level -- <function get_moisture_level at 0x20012f70>
__name__ -- Chuck's Python Helper Library
__file__ -- my_helper/__init__.py
format_time -- <function format_time at 0x20012b00>
helper_functions -- <module 'my_helper.helper_functions' from 'my_helper/
helper_functions.py'>
__all__ -- ['format_time', 'get_rand', 'get_moisture_level']
sensor_convert -- <module 'my_helper.sensor_convert' from 'my_helper/
sensor_convert.py'>
```

Once you have started experimenting with MicroPython and have completed several projects, you may start to build up a set of functions that you reuse from time to time. These are perfect candidates to place into a library. It is perfectly fine if the functions are not part of a larger class or object. So long as you organize them into modules of like functionality, you may not need to worry about making them classes. On the other hand, if data is involved or the set of functions works on a set of data, you should consider making that set of functions a class for easier use and better quality code.

WAIT, WHAT ABOUT CIRCUITPYTHON?

Recall from Chapter 3 we discussed CircuitPython when we looked at the Circuit Playground board from Adafruit. This chapter does not cover CircuitPython in more detail because it is a port of MicroPython, and thus what we learn about MicroPython libraries applies. What is different is some of the board-specific libraries and functions, and CircuitPython has some advanced libraries specific to the Adafruit boards. For more information about CircuitPython, see https://circuitpython.readthedocs.io/en/stable/.

Summary

The MicroPython firmware has a lot of capability for IoT projects. Indeed, there are a lot of different classes we can use to write robust and complex MicroPython programs from built-in functions that give the language a breadth of capability to working with data, performing calculations, and even working with time values to interfacing directly with the hardware.

Working with the hardware is one area that differs the most about MicroPython from one board to another. This is because the boards are quite different. Some have networking, some do not. Some have more onboard features than others, and some have less memory and even fewer GPIO pins. It is no surprise then that the firmware differs from one board to the next when it comes to the hardware abstraction layers.

In this chapter, we explored some of the more commonly used built-in and MicroPython libraries that generally apply to all boards. In the next chapter, we will dive a bit deeper into the lower-level libraries and hardware support in MicroPython.

CHAPTER 6

Low-Level Hardware Support

The MicroPython firmware, at the most basic of functionality, is the same from board to board for all the general Python language supported and many of the built-in functions. However, some of the libraries in the MicroPython firmware have a few minor differences from one board to another. In some cases, there are more libraries or classes available than others, or perhaps the classes are organized differently, but most implement the same core libraries in one form or another. The same cannot be said to be true at the lower-level hardware abstraction layers. This is simply because one board vendor may implement different hardware than others. In some cases, the board has features that are not present on other boards.

In this chapter, we will look at several examples of the low-level hardware support in MicroPython. We will learn about the board-specific libraries as well as some of the lower-level specialized libraries such as those for Bluetooth, SPI, I2C, and more. We will also see short code examples to illustrate the capabilities of the board-specific libraries. Some of these will be short snippets of code rather than actual projects you can implement yourself.

However, there are a few that are complete projects, which you may want to explore, but most are explained without a lot of depth and are intended to be examples rather than detailed walk-throughs. Also, keep in mind they will likely require a specific breakout board and MicroPython board as well as other accessories to implement. Again, these are for demonstration purposes. We will see more complete, step-by-step examples in later chapters, including how to assemble the hardware.

To keep things brief, we will explore the RP2040-specific libraries and some of the features that differ on the Pico and Arduino boards. Other boards may be different further still, but you will need to check the vendor documentation to know how they

213

© Charles Bell 2024
C. Bell, *MicroPython for the Internet of Things*, https://doi.org/10.1007/978-1-4842-9861-9_6

differ. This chapter should provide you with the insight to find those differences. We will also revisit working with breakout boards to demonstrate some of the libraries and hardware protocols and techniques discussed in previous chapters.

Perhaps the one thing you should remember when working with a new MicroPython board for the first time is the firmware at the hardware level is very likely to be different from the last MicroPython board you used. This is especially true when you look at the firmware ports for boards like the BBC micro:bit, Circuit Playground, ESP8266, etc.

Tip   You can see the differences in the low-level library support for other boards at `https://docs.micropython.org/en/latest/library/index.html`. By clicking the links for the other boards listed such as the Pyboard and ESP8266.

Let's begin with a look at the RP2040-specific libraries for the Pico and Arduino RP2040-based boards.

RP2040-Specific Libraries

The RP2040-specific libraries for MicroPython are contained in a module named `rp2`. This library is included with your MicroPython installation for any board that uses the RP2040 chipset. Thus, you do not need to download any additional code to use the library.

There are three classes available in the `rp2` module including the following:

- `Flash`: Built-in flash storage operations

- `StateMachine`: A base class for working with programmable input/output

- `PIO`: Advanced programmable input/output operations

The most interesting class for those new to MicroPython is the Flash class. The other two classes are useful for creating advanced code solutions that take advantage of the RP2040's programmable input/output (PIO) functionality. We briefly discuss each of these features in the following sections.

The Flash Class

The `Flash` class provides the ability to work directly with the flash file system. This may be handy if you want to do some low-level data storage, but in general you are encouraged to use the existing higher-level MicroPython libraries for reading and writing files.

PIO Classes

The `PIO` and `StateMachine` classes provide the ability to add additional interfaces or protocols such as additional serial communication support. This is not likely something most Pico projects will require, but it is there should you find you need one more interface than what is provided by the Pico hardware.

With these classes, you can create your own custom low-level hardware access mechanisms. For example, if you have a sensor that needs a specific timing to read data faster than the existing hardware and software library support or a device requires a specific sequence of commands or responses, you can use these classes to essentially use software to form the hardware interface. These special code segments are loaded and run in a special processing core, allowing up to eight processes to run. You can find a complete guide to using PIO in Chapter 3 of the RP2040 datasheet book (`https://datasheets.raspberrypi.org/rp2040/rp2040-datasheet.pdf`).

Should you wish to explore these classes in greater detail, or you want to learn more about PIO support, you can find example code at `https://github.com/raspberrypi/pico-micropython-examples/tree/master/pio`.

Next, let's look at the board-specific libraries for our featured MicroPython boards.

Board-Specific Libraries

Each MicroPython board may have one or more features (components) that are not included in the base MicroPython libraries. For example, if your board has WiFi or additional sensors, the base MicroPython libraries may contain support for working with those features. Fortunately, most vendors supply additional libraries you can use, hence the name board-specific libraries.

These libraries may be included in a special board-specific MicroPython image or may be available for download and installation. Since our featured boards (Raspberry Pi Pico and Arduino Nano RP2040 Connect) both use the RP2040 chipset, the basic libraries have everything we need. However, the Arduino Nano RP2040 Connect has additional features that require additional libraries.

Tip   If you are using a different MicroPython board, see the vendor's website for additional information concerning the board-specific libraries or images you may need to download and install.

Raspberry Pi Pico–Specific Libraries

The Raspberry Pi Pico has one board-specific feature, the WiFi module, which differs slightly from the Arduino Nano RP2040 Connect. To use WiFi on the Pico, we import the network module and then use the WLAN class and call the connect() method passing in our WiFi name (SSID) and password. We can then loop waiting for a connection by calling the isconnected() and status() methods as shown in Listing 6-1. It shows how easy it is to connect to WiFi on the Pico. We will see more details on working with WiFi in later examples.

Listing 6-1. Connecting to WiFi (Pico)

```
#
# MicroPython for the IoT Second Edition - Chapter 6
#
# Example use of the network library
# WiFi for Raspberry Pi Pico
#
# Dr. Charles Bell
#
import network, time

wlan = network.WLAN(network.STA_IF)
wlan.active(True)
wlan.connect('SSID', 'password')
```

```
while not wlan.isconnected() and wlan.status() >= 0:
    print("Waiting to connect to WiFi:")
    time.sleep(1)

print("Success!\nMy IP address is: {0}".format(wlan.ifconfig()[0]))
```

Arduino Nano RP2040 Connect–Specific Libraries

While the GPIO pinout for the Arduino Nano RP2040 Connect varies from the Raspberry Pi Pico, much of the functionality is the same since they both use the RP2040 Connect. For this reason, the example projects in this book shall provide wiring schematics for both boards with notations for any board-specific code.

However, the Arduino Nano RP2040 Connect provides additional features that are encapsulated in a special application programming interface (API) that is bundled with the latest image for the board. Thus, like the Pico, you do not have to install any special libraries to use the board-specific features.

The Arduino Nano RP2040 provides two sensors, a different WiFi module, and low-energy Bluetooth (BLE). Table 6-1 lists the features that are specific to the board along with sample code on how to use the board in your code. We will see how to use some of these features throughout the examples.

Table 6-1. *Arduino Nano RP2040 Connect–Specific Features and Libraries*

Category	Device	Description	Sample Code
Sensor	IMU (LSM6DSOX)	Accelerometer and gyroscope	`from lsm6dsox import LSM6DSOX`
Sensor	Microphone (MP34DT06JTR)	Audio microphone	`import audio`
Interface	I2C	Communicate over I2C bus	`from machine import Pin, I2C`
Wireless	WiFi	Wireless connectivity	`import network`
Wireless	Bluetooth Low Energy	Communicate over BLE connections	`import bluetooth`

The Arduino Nano RP2040 Connect can also be programmed using an advanced machine vision integrated development environment (IDE) named OpenMV. This IDE provides an alternative (called a fork) of MicroPython that includes visualization features. If you want to learn more about OpenMV or you want to explore any of these features on your own, the Arduino website contains example code for using each of these features.

See `https://docs.arduino.cc/tutorials/nano-rp2040-connect/rp2040-python-api` for the latest documentation for the Arduino Nano RP2040 Connect libraries.

Now that we have had a brief introduction to the RP2040-specific and board-specific libraries, let's discuss how low-level libraries work and why we need them.

Working with Low-Level Hardware

Working with the low-level hardware (some would just say "hardware" or "device") is where all the action and indeed the focus (and relative difficulty) of using MicroPython take place. MicroPython and the breakout board vendors have done an excellent job of making things easier for us, but there is room for improvement in the explanations.

That is, the documentation online is a bit terse when it comes to offering examples of using the low-level hardware. Part of this is because the examples often require additional, specific hardware and software. For example, to work with the I2C interface, you will need an I2C-capable breakout board as well as a software library (or drive) to "talk" to the board. Thus, the online examples provide only the most basic of examples and explanations.

Except for the onboard sensors, most low-level communication will be through I2C, one-wire, analog, or digital pins, or even SPI interfaces. The I2C and SPI interfaces are those where you will likely encounter the most difficulty working with hardware. This is because each device (breakout board) you use will require a very specific protocol. That is, the device may require a special sequence to trigger the sensor or features of the device that differs from other breakout boards. Thus, working with I2C or SPI (and some other) type devices can be a challenge to figure out exactly how to "talk" to them.

Drivers and Libraries to the Rescue!

Fortunately, there are a small but growing number of people making classes and sets of functions to help us work with those devices. These are called libraries or more commonly drivers and come in the form of one or more code modules that you can download, copy to your board, and import the functionality into your program. The developers of the drivers have done all the heavy lifting for you, making it very easy to use the device.

Thus, for most just starting out with MicroPython wanting to work with certain sensors, devices, breakout boards, etc., you should limit what you plan to use to those that you can find a driver that works with it. So, how do you find a driver for your device? There are several places to look.

First and foremost, you should look at the forums and documentation on MicroPython. In this case, don't limit yourself to only those forums that cater to your board of choice. Rather, look at all of them! Chances are, you can find a library that you can adapt with only minor modifications. Most of them can be used with very little or even no effort beyond downloading it and copying it to the board. The following lists the top set of forums and documentation you should frequent when looking for drivers:

- *MicroPython Forums*: https://forum.micropython.org/
- *MicroPython Documentation*: https://docs.micropython.org/en/latest/
- *Adafruit Learning*: https://learn.adafruit.com/
- *Pico Documentation*: www.raspberrypi.org/documentation/rp2040/getting-started/

There are also a number of documents you can download and read offline. The following are some of the more important Pico documents:

- *Pico Datasheet*: https://datasheets.raspberrypi.org/pico/pico-datasheet.pdf
- *RP2040 Datasheet*: https://datasheets.raspberrypi.org/rp2040/rp2040-datasheet.pdf

- *Hardware Design Guide*: https://datasheets.raspberrypi.org/
  rp2040/hardware-design-with-rp2040.pdf

- *Pico MicroPython Manual*: https://datasheets.raspberrypi.org/
  pico/raspberry-pi-pico-python-sdk.pdf

Second, use your favorite Internet search engine and search for examples of the hardware. Use the name of the hardware device and "MicroPython" in your search. If the device is new, you may not find any hits on the search terms. Be sure to explore other search terms too.

Once you find a driver, the fun begins! You should download the driver and copy it to your board for testing. Be sure to follow the example that comes with the driver to avoid using the driver in an unexpected way.

This calls to mind one important thing you should consider when deciding if you want to use the driver. If the driver is well documented and has examples – especially if the example is written for the Pico – you should feel safe using it. However, if the driver isn't documented at all or there is no or little sample code or it is written for a specific board, you may not want to use it. There is a good chance it is half-baked, old, a work in progress, or just poorly coded. Not all those that share can share and communicate well.

We will see several examples of libraries as we work through the example projects in this book. As you will see, not all are as simple as downloading and using.

Let's look at two low-level examples: working with setting the time from the Internet using the network time protocol (NTP) and callbacks through interrupts. We will begin with the NTP example. These are only a small sample of what is available and represents the most common things you will need to work with for this book and most small IoT projects.

Network Time Protocol (NTP)

Some MicroPython boards and several breakout boards have a real-time clock (RTC). The RTC is a special circuit (sometimes an integrated circuit or chip) that keeps time. This is because most processors (microcontroller, microprocessor, etc.) operate in synchronization with a crystal or clock chip that keeps the processor running at a certain speed (e.g., Mhz). Sadly, this is often not divisible easily into a time variable (value). The RTC is used to keep time so that we can use the time to record events.

To use an RTC, we first initialize the starting value with the current date and time (like setting a new desktop clock), and we can read the current date and time whenever we want. However, an RTC without a battery backup will lose its values when the board is powered off. Thus, we must set it every time we start the board. Fortunately, there is a time service on the Internet that we can use to get the current date and time. It's called the network time protocol (NTP).

Note   This example is for demonstration purposes of using the built-in libraries like the `rtc` library. We will examine the code in more detail in a later example project. However, it should be noted that breakout boards with RTC modules may require their own, vendor-provided library that replaces the use of the `rtc` library.

Let's see an example of how to use this service. We will create a program on the Pico that connects the board to our local WiFi, which is connected to the Internet. Once connected, we will use the NTP to set the current time and then perform a test to see what the current date and time are. We should see the exact date and time when we run the code! Listing 6-2 shows the completed example.

Note   The Raspberry Pi Pico has no battery backup, and while you can set the date and time, the values will be lost on reboot.

Listing 6-2. Using an NTP Time Server to set the RTC (Pico)

```
#
# MicroPython for the IoT Second Edition - Chapter 6
#
# Example use of the ntptime library and connecting to an NTP service
#
# Dr. Charles Bell
#
import network, ntptime, time, socket, struct
from machine import RTC
```

```python
NTP_HOST = "us.pool.ntp.org"
TZ_DELTA = 4 * 3600 # num_hours * num_mins_in_hour
NUM_RETRIES = 3 # number of retries for ntp server call

# Return time now adjusted for timezone
def now():
    return time.localtime(time.time() - TZ_DELTA)

# Connect to WiFi
def connect_wifi():
    print("Connecting to WiFi... ", end="")
    wlan = network.WLAN(network.STA_IF)
    wlan.active(True)
    wlan.connect('SSID', 'password')

    while not wlan.isconnected() and wlan.status() >= 0:
        print("retrying... ", end="")
        time.sleep(1)
    print("done.")
    print("Network values: {0}".format(wlan.ifconfig()))

# Connect to NTP server and set localtime
def set_ntp_time():
    print("Contacting NTP Server... ", end=(""))
    for i in range(0, NUM_RETRIES):
        try:
            ntptime.settime()
        except:
            print("retrying... ", end=(""))
            time.sleep(3)
        print("done.")
        break

connect_wifi()
# Begin NPT synchronization
print("Time Before NPT: {0}".format(time.localtime()))
set_ntp_time()
print("Time after NPT : {0}".format(now()))
```

Most of this code should be familiar since we've seen WiFi connect in a previous section. In this example, we place the code in a method to make it a bit easier to use. However, the use of the `ntptime` class is new. Notice all we need to do, once the network connection is made, is to call the `ntp_settime()`. Yes, it's built into the library! Cool. After that, we need only adjust for local timezone, and we're good to go. See the `now()` method for how we do that.

Also, notice the code has been written using methods for each of the major steps (`connect_wifi()`, `set_ntp_time()`, and `now()`). Notice that the `set_ntp_time()` was written using a loop that will help with connection timeouts. If your network is slow, you may need to increase the number of retries.

When you run this on your Pico, you will see output like the following. Notice we print the value of the local time tuple before the NTP call, then print the local time again once the local time has synched with the NTP:

```
Connecting to WiFi... retrying... done.
Network values: ('192.168.1.205', '255.255.255.0', '192.168.1.1',
'192.168.1.1')
Time Before NPT: (2023, 8, 26, 21, 19, 5, 5, 238)
Contacting NTP Server... retrying... done.
Time after NPT : (2023, 8, 26, 17, 19, 15, 5, 238)
```

This example can be very helpful and in some cases a must when reading data for later analysis. It is often crucial to know when the data was saved or sensor was read. You may want to earmark this code for later use in your IoT projects.

Note   We can use a dedicated RTC module that has an onboard clock that keeps the clock synchronized when operating offline or during periods when the board is powered off. We will see how to do this in Chapter 8.

Now, let's look at callbacks, which are programming mechanisms you can use to work with hardware interrupts and timers.

Callbacks

What do you do if you want to have some bit of code executed in reaction to a sensor or user input? Using what we've learned thus far, we could write our program with a loop to poll the sensor or user actionable device (such as a button) and, when triggered, execute the code. This polling technique will work, but there is a better construct called callbacks.

Callbacks are functions we define and associate with the firmware to execute when a certain event occurs. If a hardware abstraction permits the use of a callback, we can use that. Fortunately, the Timer class has such a mechanism. We could also use hardware interrupts in much the same way. However, hardware interrupts are an advanced topic. Let's work with the Timer class to keep things easier.

The use of callbacks allows us to continue executing code to do work such as reading sensors, displaying data, etc., and when the event (interrupt) occurs, MicroPython will execute the callback function and then return to executing our code. This works by tying the callback function to interrupts. The Timer class has an interrupt defined for calling code to do work in a variety of ways. We will be using the periodic option that will call out callback and specified intervals – perfect for blinking LEDs, checking sensors, etc.

There are some caveats to using the Timer callback. First, the callback function cannot take parameters, so you cannot define a callback function and pass it any data. In fact, callback functions are not permitted to create data. For example, you cannot create a dictionary, tuple, etc., inside the function. While callback functions can access global variables, they may throw an exception if you use state variables. Finally, you can turn off (disconnect) the callback. For example, you can disconnect the callback with timer. deinit().

Now, let's see an example. In this example, we want to create a callback to toggle the LED on the board. Setting up the callback is easy. We just specify the callback function for the timer and pass in the name of the function. Let's see the code and you'll see how this works. Listing 6-3 shows the completed code for the callback example for the Pico.

Listing 6-3. Callback Example (Pico)

```
#
# MicroPython for the IoT Second Edition - Chapter 6
#
# Example use of callbacks with the Timer class to blink an LED
#
```

```
# Dr. Charles Bell
#
from machine import Pin, Timer

led = Pin("LED", Pin.OUT)  # Get the onboard LED as output
led.off()                  # Make sure it's off first

# Callback for toggling the LED on/off
def toggle_led(timer):
    global led  # fetch the global led variable
    led.toggle()

# Get instance of Timer class
timer = Timer()
# Initialize the timer to periodically call the callback method
# once every second
timer.init(freq=1, mode=Timer.PERIODIC, callback=toggle_led)
```

Now, let's look at how to communicate with breakout boards using the I2C and SPI protocols.

Using Breakout Boards

Breakout boards are one of the key elements hobbyists and enthusiasts will use in creating a MicroPython (or any microcontroller based) IoT solution. This is because breakout boards are small circuit boards that contain all the components needed to support a function such as a sensor, network interface, or even a display. Breakout boards also support one of several communication protocols that require only a few pins to be wired, making them very easy to use. In general, they save the developer a lot of time trying to figure out how to design circuits to support a sensor or chip.

There are two methods for working with breakout boards: finding a driver you can use or building your own driver. Building your own driver is not recommended for those new to MicroPython and I2C or SPI. It is much easier to take the time to search for a driver that you can use (or adapt) than to try to write one yourself. This is because you must be able to obtain, read, and understand how the breakout board communicates (understand its protocol). Each board will communicate differently based on the sensor or devices supported. That is, a driver for a BMP180 sensor will not look or necessarily work the same as one for a BME280 sensor. You must be very specific when locating and using a driver.

Searching for a driver can be a tedious endeavor, which requires some patience and perhaps several searches on the forums using different search terms such as "micropython BME280". Once you find a driver, you can tell quickly whether it is a viable option by looking at the example included. As mentioned before, if there is no example or the example doesn't resemble anything you've seen in this book or in the online documentation, don't use it.

Let's look at two examples of breakout boards: one that uses the I2C protocol and another that uses the SPI protocol. We will follow a pattern of explaining the examples that is used throughout the book to introduce the project, present the required components, show you how to set up the hardware (connect everything together), write the code, and finally execute it.

THE VALUE OF ONLINE EXAMPLES

If you want to use a breakout board in your IoT project, be sure to spend some time not only in the forums but also looking at various blogs and tutorials such as those on hackaday.com, learn.sparkfun.com, or learn.adafruit.com. The best blogs and tutorials are those that explain not only how to write the code but also what the breakout board does and how to use it. These online references are few, but the ones from these three sites are among the very best. Also, look at some of the videos on the topic too. Some of those are worth the time to watch – especially if they're from the nice folks at Adafruit or SparkFun.

Inter-integrated Circuit (I2C)

The I2C protocol is perhaps the most common protocol that you will find on breakout boards. We've encountered this term a few times in previous chapters, and thus we only know it is a communication protocol. So, what is it?

What Is I2C?

I2C is a fast-digital protocol using two wires (plus power and ground) to read data from circuits (or devices). The protocol is designed to allow the use of multiple devices (slaves) with a single master (the MicroPython board). Thus, each I2C breakout board will have its own address or identity that you will use in the driver to connect to and communicate with the device.

Tip   See `https://learn.sparkfun.com/tutorials/i2c` for an in-depth discussion of I2C.

Overview

Let's look at an example of how to use an I2C breakout board. In this example, we want to use an RGB sensor from Adafruit (`www.adafruit.com/product/1334`) to read the color of objects. Yes, you can make your Pico see in color!

What the code will present is four values read from the sensor. We will see the values for the red, green, and blue spectrum as well as the clear light value. The combination of the red, green, and blue values defines the color. You can use a color picker control from one of several websites like `www.rapidtables.com/web/color/RGB_Color.html` to show you the color. This RGB sensor isn't going to give you a 100% color match, but you may be surprised how well it can distinguish colors. Let's get started.

Required Components

Don't worry if you do not have or do not want to purchase the Adafruit RGB Sensor breakout board (although it is not expensive). This example is provided as a tutorial for working with I2C breakout boards. We will use another I2C breakout board in one of the example projects later in the book. Figure 6-1 shows the Adafruit RGB Sensor. Note that this sensor comes without the header soldered, so you will need to solder a header on the breakout board before you can use it with your Pico.

Figure 6-1. *Adafruit RGB Sensor (Courtesy of adafruit.com)*

Set Up the Hardware

Wiring the breakout board is also very easy since we need only power, ground, Serial clock (SCL), and Serial data (SDA) connections. SCL is the clock signal, and SDA is the data signal. These pins are labeled on your Pico (or in the documentation) as well as the breakout board. When you connect your breakout board, make sure the power requirements match. That is, some breakout boards can take 5V, but many are limited to 3 or 3.3V. Check the vendor's website if you have any doubts.

We need only to connect the 3V, ground, SDA, SCL, and LED pins. The LED pin is used to turn on the bright LED on the breakout board to signal it is ready to read. We will leave it on for ten seconds so that there is time to read the color value and then display it. We will then wait another five seconds to take the next reading.

But to get this to work, we will need to connect the breakout board to the Pico. If you ordered a Pico with headers or you soldered your own headers to the Pico, we can use what is called a breadboard to host the Pico and use wires called jumper wires to connect the Pico GPIO pins to the pins on the breakout board.

Note   We will discuss breadboards and their use in more detail in the next chapter.

Once you place your Pico on a breadboard, you can use (5) male-to-female jumper wires to connect to the breakout board. Figure 6-2 shows the connections you need to make.

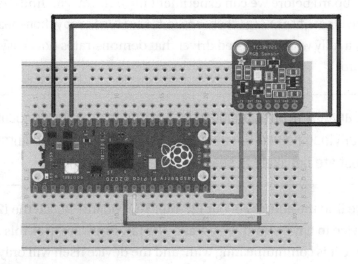

Figure 6-2. *Wiring the RGB Sensor*

The connections we will use are shown in Table 6-2, which shows the pin for the Pico in the first three columns depicting the description, physical pin, and GPIO number with the pin on the breakout board in the last column. Recall, physical pins are numbered 1–20 on the left of the USB connector starting at the top and 21–40 on the right starting from the bottom.

Table 6-2. *Connections for the RGB Sensor*

Pico			RGB Sensor
Function	**Physical Pin**	**GPIO Number**	**Pin Label**
OUT	20	GP15	LED
I2C SDA	11	GP8	SDA
I2C SDC	12	GP9	SCL
3V3	37	N/A	3V3
GND	38	N/A	GND

Write the Code

Once you have the hardware connected, set it aside. We need to download the driver and copy it to the board before we can experiment further. You can find the driver for download on GitHub at https://github.com/adafruit/micropython-adafruit-tcs34725. This is a fully working, tested driver that demonstrates how easy it is to use an I2C breakout board.

Note   This library has been abandoned by Adafruit in an effort to focus on their version of MicroPython named CircuitPython. But don't worry. The library still works very well. We just are not likely to see any updates to the code.

So, how do we find the address of our I2C breakout board? Recall the I2C bus requires each device to have a unique address. The I2C firmware uses this address to know which device it is communicating with, and the device itself will only recognize messages for that specific address.

We check the documentation, or we can check the code for the library. If you open the library you downloaded, you can read through it and look in the initialization code (or constructor) to see what address the library is using. In this case, we find the address in the library is 0x29 as follows, but since address is a parameter, you can override it if you have another breakout board for the same RGB sensor that is at a different address. This means you can use more than one RGB sensor with the same driver!

```
class TCS34725:
    def __init__(self, i2c, address=0x29):
```

To download the driver, you first navigate to https://github.com/adafruit/micropython-adafruit-tcs34725, then click the *Download* button and then the *Download Zip* button. Once the file has been downloaded, unzip it. In the resulting folder, you should find the file named tcs34725.py. This is the driver code module. When ready, copy the module to your Pico and place it in the root folder (same folder as the example code).

Now that the driver has been copied onto our board, we can write the code. In this example, we will set up the I2C connection to the breakout board and run a loop to read values from the sensor. Sounds simple, but there is a bit of a trick to it. We will forego a lengthy discussion of the code and instead offer some key aspects, allowing you to read the code yourself to see how it works.

230

The key components are setting up the I2C, sensor, a pin for controlling the LED, and reading from the sensor. The LED on the board can be turned on and off by setting a pin high (on) or low (off). First, the I2C code is as follows. Here, we initiate an object, then call the init() function, setting the bus to master mode. The scan() function returns a list of addresses found on the bus. We can then print out the device addresses. Notice we define the pins for the SDA and SCL I2C operations too.

Tip If you see an empty set displayed, your I2C wiring is not correct. Check it and try the code again.

```
# Setup the I2C - easy, yes?
sda = Pin(8)
scl = Pin(9)
i2c = SoftI2C(sda=sda,scl=scl,freq=400000)
print("I2C Devices found:", end="")
for addr in i2c.scan():
    print("{0} ".format(hex(addr)))
print("")
```

Notice here we are using something named SoftI2C. This is a special version of the I2C library that supports a different way of communicating with a breakout board. As it turns out, not all I2C devices will work correctly with the firmware implementation of I2C on the Pico. To use the firmware I2C, use the I2C library from the machine module as follows. The only difference besides the name is the first parameter, which tells the I2C we want a master connection.

```
#i2c = I2C(0,sda=sda,scl=scl,freq=400000)
```

It is recommended to try the I2C library first, and if that doesn't work, try the SoftI2C library. This is because the I2C firmware is much faster than the software implementation. We will see specific examples that use I2C and SoftI2C in later chapters.

The next part is the sensor itself. The driver makes this easy. All we need to do is pass in the I2C constructor function as shown:

```
# Setup the sensor
sensor = tcs34725.TCS34725(i2c)
```

Setting up the LED pin is also easy. All we need to do is call the `Pin()` class constructor passing in the pin name (P15) and setting it for output mode as follows:

```
# Setup the LED pin
led_pin = Pin(15, Pin.OUT)
led_pin.value(0)
```

Finally, we read from the sensor with the `sensor.read()` function passing in True, which tells the driver to return the RGBC values. We will then print these out in order.

If you are following along with the sample code downloaded from the Apress book site, the name of the file is `adafruit_rgb_sensor.py`. If you want to create the file yourself, you can use that name and save it to your Pico.

Listing 6-4 shows the completed code. Take a few moments to read through it so that you understand how it works.

Listing 6-4. Using the Adafruit RGB Sensor

```
#
# MicroPython for the IoT Second Edition - Chapter 6
#
# Example of using the I2C interface via a driver
# for the Adafruit RGB Sensor tcs34725
#
# Requires library:
# https://github.com/adafruit/micropython-adafruit-tcs34725
#
from machine import I2C, SoftI2C, Pin
import sys
import tcs34725
import utime

# Method to read sensor and display results
def read_sensor(rgb_sense, led):
    sys.stdout.write("Place object in front of sensor now...")
    led.value(1)                   # Turn on the LED
    utime.sleep(5)                 # Wait 5 seconds
    sys.stdout.write("reading.\n")
    data = rgb_sense.read(True)  # Get the RGBC values
```

```
        print("Color Detected: {")
        print("    Red: {0:03}".format(data[0]))
        print("  Green: {0:03}".format(data[1]))
        print("   Blue: {0:03}".format(data[2]))
        print("  Clear: {0:03}".format(data[3]))
        print("}\n")
        led.value(0)

# Setup the I2C - easy, yes?
sda = Pin(8)
scl = Pin(9)
i2c = SoftI2C(sda=sda,scl=scl,freq=400000)
print("I2C Devices found:", end="")
for addr in i2c.scan():
    print("{0} ".format(hex(addr)))
print("")

# Setup the sensor
sensor = tcs34725.TCS34725(i2c)

# Setup the LED pin
led_pin = Pin(15, Pin.OUT)
led_pin.value(0)
print("Reading object color every 10 seconds.")
print("When LED is on, place object in front of sensor.")
print("Press CTRL-C to quit.")
while True:
    utime.sleep(10)             # Sleep for 10 seconds
    read_sensor(sensor, led_pin)  # Read sensor and display values
```

Once you have the code, you can copy it to your board in the similar manner we did for the driver. All that is left is running the example and testing it.

Execute

After copying the code to the Pico, go ahead and run it from Thonny. Listing 6-5 shows an example of the code running. Note that you will get differing results for each object you test in a mixture of the RGB values as shown.

Listing 6-5. Output from Using the Adafruit RGB Sensor

```
I2C Devices found:0x29
Reading Colors every 10 seconds.
When LED is on, place object in front of sensor.
Press CTRL-C to quit.
Place object in front of sensor now...reading.
Color Detected: {
    Red: 057
  Green: 034
   Blue: 032
  Clear: 123
}
Place object in front of sensor now...reading.
Color Detected: {
    Red: 054
  Green: 069
   Blue: 064
  Clear: 195
}
Place object in front of sensor now...reading.
Color Detected: {
    Red: 012
  Green: 013
   Blue: 011
  Clear: 036
}
...
```

If you wanted another exercise, you could take these values from the sensor and map them to an RGB LED. Yes, you can do that! Go ahead, try it. See the example GitHub project at `https://github.com/JanBednarik/micropython-ws2812` for inspiration. Tackle it after you've read the next section on SPI.

Serial Peripheral Interface (SPI)

The Serial Peripheral Interface (SPI) is designed to allow sending and receiving data between two devices using a dedicated line for each direction. That is, it uses two data lines along with a clock and a slave select pin. Thus, it requires six connections for bidirectional communication or only five for reading or writing only. Some SPI devices may require a seventh pin called a reset line.

Tip   See `https://learn.sparkfun.com/tutorials/serial-peripheral-interface-spi` for an in-depth discussion of SPI.

Overview

Let's look at an example of how to use an SPI breakout board. In this example, we want to use the Adafruit Thermocouple Amplifier MAX31855 breakout board (`www.adafruit.com/product/269`) and a Thermocouple Type-K sensor (`www.adafruit.com/product/270`) to read high temperatures. It can also read low or room temperature, so don't worry. You won't need to put this in a heater or oven to use it!

In fact, we're going to use this example to show how easy it is to read one of the most common measurements (samples) taken – temperature. Once the code is running, you can simply touch the thermocouple and watch the values respond (change) as it heats up and again when you let go. A touchable project, cool!

Required Components

Don't worry if you do not have or do not want to purchase the Adafruit Thermocouple Amplifier MAX31855 breakout board (although it is not expensive). This example is provided as a tutorial for working with SPI breakout boards. We will use another I2C breakout board in one of the example projects later in the book. Figure 6-3 shows the Adafruit Thermocouple Amplifier and Type-K sensor from Adafruit.

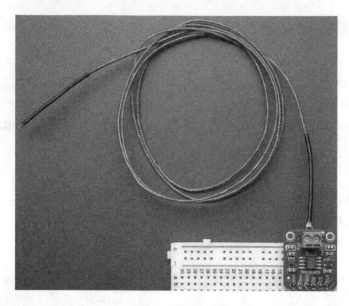

Figure 6-3. *Adafruit Thermocouple Breakout Board and Type-K Sensor (Courtesy of adafruit.com)*

The sensor can be used to measure high temperatures either through proximity or touch. The sensor can read temperature in the range –200°C to +1350°C output in 0.25 degree increments. One possible use of this sensor is to read the temperature of nozzles on 3D printers or any similar high heat output. It should be noted that the breakout board comes unassembled, so you will need to solder the header and terminal posts.

Set Up the Hardware

Now, let's see how to wire the breakout board to our Pico. We will use only five wires since we are only reading data from the sensor on the breakout board. This requires a connection to power, ground (GND), the master input (MOSI), clock (CLK), and chip select (CS). We only receive information from the sensor, so the MISO (transmit) pin isn't needed. Figure 6-4 shows the connections.

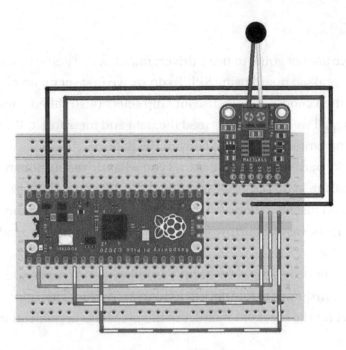

Figure 6-4. *Wiring the Adafruit Thermocouple Module*

The connections we will use are shown in Table 6-3, which shows the pin for the Pico in the first three columns depicting the description, physical pin, and GPIO number with the pin on the breakout board in the last column. Recall, physical pins are numbered 1–20 on the left of the USB connector starting at the top and 21–40 on the right starting from the bottom.

Table 6-3. *Connections for the MAX31855*

Pico			RGB Sensor
Function	**Physical Pin**	**GPIO Number**	**Pin Label**
GND	38	N/A	GND
3V3	37	N/A	3V3
SPI RX/MOSI	6	GP4	SDO
SPI CS	2	GP1	CS
SPI CLK	9	GP6	CLK

Now, let's look at the code!

Write the Code

In this example, we are not going to use a driver; rather, we're going to see how to read directly from the breakout board using SPI. To do so, we first set up an object instance of the SPI interface, then choose a pin to use for chip select (also called code or even slave select). From there, all we need to do is read the data and interpret it. We will read the sensor in a loop and write a function to convert the data.

This is the tricky part. This example shows you what driver authors must do to make using the device easier. In this case, we must read the data from the breakout board and interpret it. We could just read the raw data, but that would not make any sense since it is in binary form. Thus, we can borrow some code from Adafruit that reads the raw data and makes sense of it.

The function is named normalize_data() as follows, and it does some bit shifting and arithmetic to transform the raw data to a value in Celsius. This information comes from the datasheet for the breakout board, but the nice folks at Adafruit made it easy for us.

```python
# Create a method to normalize the data into degrees Celsius
def normalize_data(data):
    temp = data[0] << 8 | data[1]
    if temp & 0x0001:
        return float('NaN')
    temp >>= 2
    if temp & 0x2000:
        temp -= 16384
    return (temp * 0.25)
```

Setting up the SPI class is easy. We initiate an SPI object using the class constructor passing in the SPI option. We will use zero for the first SPI implementation. The other parameters tell the SPI class to set up the SCK, MISO, and MOSI pins (even though we are not using the MOSI pin) and set the baudrate, polarity, and phase (which can be found on the datasheet). We also set the CS pin and turn it on (set to high) after initializing the SPI library. The following shows the code we need to activate the SPI interface:

```
...
spi_cs = Pin(1)
spi = SPI(0, baudrate=1000000, sck=Pin(6), miso=Pin(4), mosi=Pin(3))
spi_cs.high()
...
```

Now, let's look at the completed code. If you are following along with the sample code downloaded from the Apress book site, the name of the file is adafruit_thermocouple.py. If you want to create the file yourself, you can use that name and save it to your Pico.

Listing 6-6 shows the complete code to use the Thermocouple Amplifier breakout board from Adafruit.

Listing 6-6. The Adafruit Thermocouple Module Example

```
#
# MicroPython for the IoT Second Edition - Chapter 6
#
# Example of using the SPI interface via direct access
# for the Adafruit Thermocouple Module MAX31855
#
from machine import Pin, SPI
import utime

# Create a method to normalize the data into degrees Celsius
def normalize_data(data):
    temp = data[0] << 8 | data[1]
    if temp & 0x0001:
        return float('NaN')
    temp >>= 2
    if temp & 0x2000:
        temp -= 16384
    return (temp * 0.25)

spi_cs = Pin(1)
spi = SPI(0, baudrate=1000000, sck=Pin(6), miso=Pin(4), mosi=Pin(3))
spi_cs.high()
```

```
# read from the chip
print("Reading temperature every second.")
print("Press CTRL-C to stop.")
while True:
    spi_cs.low()
    utime.sleep(1)
    print("Temperature is {:05.2F} C".format(normalize_data(spi.read(4))))
    spi_cs.high()
```

Execute

At this point, you can make the hardware connections and plug in your Pico. Then, you can copy the file to your Pico and run it. Let it run for a few readings, then try to gently grasp the silver portion (the far end) of the thermocouple with two fingers. Be sure not to turn the Pico or the breakout board. You should see a change in temperature. You can let go and also see the temperature return to near room temperature.

```
Reading temperature every second.
Press CTRL-C to stop.
Temperature is 24.50 C
Temperature is 24.50 C
Temperature is 24.25 C
Temperature is 24.25 C
Temperature is 25.75 C
Temperature is 25.50 C
Temperature is 25.75 C
Temperature is 26.25 C
Temperature is 26.00 C
Temperature is 26.50 C
Temperature is 26.50 C
Temperature is 27.00 C
Temperature is 27.25 C
Temperature is 27.00 C
Temperature is 27.50 C
Temperature is 27.50 C
Temperature is 27.00 C
...
```

Once you run the example, you should see it produce values in degrees Celsius. If you see 00.00, or NaN, you likely do not have the SPI interface connected properly. Check your wiring against the figure above. If you see values but they go down when you expose the thermocouple tip to heat, you need to reverse the wires. Be sure to power off the board first to avoid damaging the sensor, breakout board, or your Pico!

Summary

Accessing the low-level hardware through the firmware is where the true elegance and in some cases complexity of using MicroPython begin. Given that the available boards differ, it should be no surprise that the low-level support in the firmware also differs. Thus, when planning MicroPython IoT projects, we must consider what we want to do and whether our board (and firmware) supports it. We also need to know what breakout boards and devices we want to connect to and if there are drivers or other libraries we can use to access them. In this case, most breakout boards with I2C or SPI interfaces will require some form of driver.

In this chapter, we explored some of the low-level support in the firmware and specialized support for the RP2040 chipset and the unique features of the Raspberry Pi Pico and Arduino Nano RP2040 Connect. As we discovered, this is where the code becomes very specialized. As we saw, it sometimes is a matter of choosing a different library to import, but sometimes the classes, functions, and even how to use the functions differ from one board to another.

We also saw a few code examples and snippets that are meant to be examples for you to see how things are done rather than projects to implement on your own (although you're welcome and encouraged to do so). We will see more hands-on projects with a greater level of detail in later chapters.

In the next chapter, we take a short detour in the form of a short tutorial on electronics. If you've never worked with electronics before, the next chapter will give you the information you need to complete the projects in this book and prepare you for an exciting new hobby – building MicroPython IoT projects!

CHAPTER 7

Electronics for Beginners

If you are new to working with hardware and have little or no experience with electronics, you may be curious as to how you can complete the projects in this book. Fortunately, the projects in this book show you how to connect the various electronic parts together with your MicroPython board. That is, you can complete the projects without additional skill or experience.

However, if you want to know what the components do, you will need a bit more information than "plug this end in here." This is especially so if something goes wrong. Furthermore, if you want to create projects on your own, you need to know enough about how the components work to successfully complete your project – whether that is completing the examples in this book or examples found elsewhere on the Internet.

Fortunately, you don't need formal training or even a college degree in theory to learn how to work with electronics. You can learn quite a lot about working with electronics at the hobbyist level without devoting months or years of research.[1] To ensure success even at a basic level, you will need to know more than simply how to plug the components together.

Rather than attempt to present a comprehensive tutorial on electronics, which would take several volumes, this chapter presents an overview of electronics for those who want to work with the types of electronic components commonly found in IoT projects. I include an overview of some of the basics, descriptions of common components, and a look at sensors. If you are new to electronics, this chapter will give you the extra boost you need to understand the components used in the projects in this book.

If you have experience with electronics either at the hobbyist or enthusiast level or have experience or formal training in electronics, you may want to skim this chapter or read the sections with topics on which you may want a refresher.

---

[1] However, there is no substitute for formal training! If you want to explore electronics beyond the tutorial in this chapter, you may want to consider formal training or even a self-paced course as described in the sidebar, "I Want to Learn More!"

© Charles Bell 2024
C. Bell, *MicroPython for the Internet of Things*, https://doi.org/10.1007/978-1-4842-9861-9_7

Let's begin with a look at the basics of electronics. Once again, this is in no way a tutorial that covers all there is to know, but it will get you to the point where the projects make sense in how they connect and use components.

The Basics

This section presents a short overview of some of the most common tools and techniques you will need to use when working with electronics. As you will see, you only need the most basic of tools, and the skills or techniques are not difficult to learn. However, before we get into those, let's look at some of the tools you will need to work on your IoT projects.

Tools

The clear majority of tools you will need to construct your IoT projects are common hand tools (screwdrivers, small wrenches, pliers, etc.). For larger projects or for creating enclosures, you may need additional tools such as power tools, but I will concentrate only on those tools for building the projects. The following is a list of tools I recommend to get you started:

- Breadboard

- Breadboard wires (also called jumpers)

- Electrostatic discharge (ESD) safe tweezers

- Helping hands or printed circuit board (PCB) holder

- Multimeter

- Needle-nose pliers

- Screwdrivers – assorted sizes (micro, small)

- Solder

- Soldering iron

- Solder remover (solder sucker)

- Tool case, roll, or box for storage

- Wire strippers

However, you cannot go wrong if you prefer to buy a complete electronics toolset such as those from SparkFun (sparkfun.com/categories/47) or Adafruit (adafruit.com/categories/83). You can often find electronics kits at major brand electronics stores and home improvement centers. If you are fortunate enough to live near a store that carries electronic components and kits, you can find just about any electronics tool made. Most electronics kits will have all the hand tools you will need. Some even come with a multimeter, but more often you must buy them separately.

Most of the tools in the list do not need any explanation except to say you should purchase the best tools that your budget permits. The following paragraphs describe some of the tools that are used for special tasks, such as stripping wires, soldering, and measuring voltage and current.

Multimeter

A multimeter is one of those tools that you will need when building IoT solutions. You will also need it to do almost any electrical repair on your circuits. There are many different multimeters available with prices ranging from inexpensive, basic units to complex, feature-rich, incredibly expensive units. For most IoT projects, including most IoT kits, a basic unit is all you will need. However, if you plan to build more than one IoT solution or want to assemble your own electronics, you may want to invest a bit more in a more sophisticated multimeter. Figure 7-1 shows a basic digital multimeter (costing about $10) on the left and a professional multimeter from BK Precision on the right.

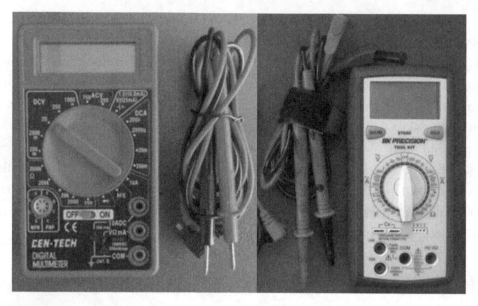

Figure 7-1. *Digital Multimeters*

Notice the better meter has more granular settings and more features. Again, you probably won't need more than the basic unit. You will need to measure voltage, current, and resistance at a minimum. Whichever meter you buy, make sure it has modes for measuring AC and DC voltage, continuity testing (with an audible alert), and checking resistance. I will explain how to use a multimeter in a later section.

Tip   Most multimeters including the inexpensive ones come with a small instruction booklet that shows you how to measure voltage, resistance, and other functions of the unit.

Soldering Iron

A soldering iron is not required for any of the projects in this book because we will use a breadboard to lay out and connect the components. However, if you plan to build a simple IoT solution where you will need to solder wires together, or maybe a few connectors, a basic soldering iron from an electronics store such as RadioShack is all you will need. On the other hand, if you plan to assemble your own electronics, you may want to consider getting a good, professional soldering iron such as a Hakko.

The professional models include features that allow you to set the temperature of the wand, have a wider array of tips available, and tend to last a lot longer. Figure 7-2 shows a well-used entry-level one from RadioShack.

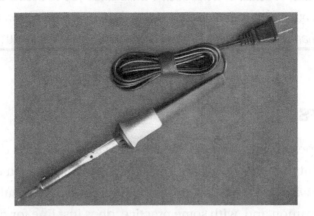

Figure 7-2. *Entry-Level Soldering Iron*

Figure 7-3 shows a professional model Hakko soldering iron.

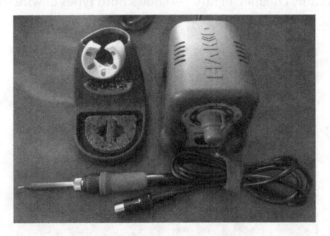

Figure 7-3. *Professional Soldering Iron*

Tip   For best results, choose a solder with a low lead content in the 37%–40% range. If you use a professional soldering iron, adjust the temperature to match the melting point of the solder (listed on the label).

DO I NEED TO LEARN TO SOLDER?

If you do not know how to solder or it has been a while since you've used a soldering iron, you may want to check out the book *Getting Started with Soldering: A Hands-On Guide to Making Electrical and Mechanical Connections* by Marc de Vinck (O'Reilly Media, 2017).

Wire Strippers

There are several types of wire strippers. In fact, there are probably a dozen or more designs out there. But there are two kinds: ones that only grip and cut the insulation as you pull it off the wire and those that grip, cut, and remove the insulation. The first type is more common and, with some practice, does just fine for most small jobs (like repairing a broken wire), but the second type makes a larger job – such as wiring electronics from bare wire (no prefab connectors) – much faster. As you can imagine, the first type is considerably cheaper. Figure 7-4 shows both types of wire strippers. Either is a good choice.

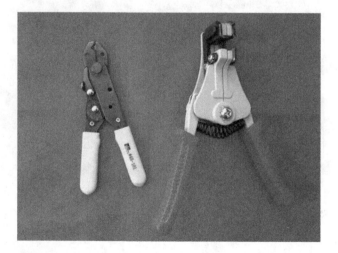

Figure 7-4. *Wire Strippers*

Helping Hands

There is one other tool that you may want to get, especially if you need to do any soldering: it's called the helping hand or third hand tool. Most have a pair of alligator clips to hold wires, printed circuit boards, or components while you solder. Figure 7-5 shows an example of a simple helping hand tool.

Figure 7-5. *Helping Hand Tool*

Now let's look at some of the skills you are likely to need when working with advanced IoT projects.

ESD IS THE ENEMY

You should take care to make sure your body, your workspace, and your project are grounded to avoid electrostatic discharge (ESD). ESD can damage your electronics – permanently. The best way to avoid this is to use a grounding strap that loops around your wrist and attaches to an antistatic mat like these at uline.com/BL_7403/Anti-Static-Table-Mats.

Let's look at how to use the one tool you will likely use more than any other when learning electronics – the multimeter.

Using a Multimeter

The electrical skills needed for IoT projects can vary from plugging in wires on a breadboard – as we saw with the projects so far – to needing to solder components together or to printed circuit boards (PCBs). Regardless of whether you need to solder the electronics, you will need to be able to use a basic multimeter to measure resistance and check voltage and current.

A multimeter is a very useful and essential tool for any electronics hobbyist and downright required for any enthusiast of worth. A typical multimeter has a digital display[2] (typically an LCD or similar numeric display), a dial, and two or more posts or ports for plugging in test leads with probe ends. Most multimeters have ports for lower current (that you will use most) and ports for larger current. Test leads use red for positive and black for negative (ground). The ground port is where you plug in the black test lead and is often marked with a dash or COM for common. Which of the other ports you use will depend on what you are testing.

One thing to note on the dial is that there are many settings (with some values repeated) or those that look similar. For example, you will see a set of values (sometimes called a scale) for ohms, one or two sets of values for amperage, and one or two sets of values for volts. The set of values for voltages that has a V with a solid and a dashed line is for DC, whereas the range that has a V with a wavy line is for AC. Amperage ranges are marked in the same manner. Figure 7-6 shows a close-up of a multimeter dial labeled with the sets of values I've mentioned.

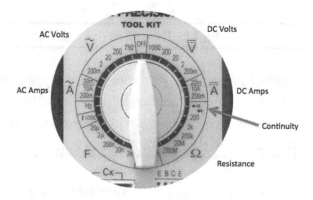

Figure 7-6. *Multimeter Dial (Typical)*

---

[2] Older multimeters have an analog gauge. You can still find them if you want a bit of old school feel.

Tip   When not in use, be sure to turn your multimeter dial to off or one of the voltage ranges if it has a separate off button.

There is a lot you can do with a multimeter. You can check voltage, measure resistance, and even check continuity. Most basic multimeters will do these functions. However, some multimeters have a great many more features such as testing capacitors and the ability to test AC as well as DC.

Let's see how we can use a multimeter to perform the most common tasks we will need for IoT projects: testing continuity, measuring voltage in a DC circuit, measuring resistance, and measuring current.

Testing Continuity

We test for continuity to determine if there is a path for the charged particles to flow: that is, our wires and components are connected properly. For example, you may want to check to ensure a wire has been spliced correctly.

To test for continuity, turn your multimeter dial to the position marked with an audible symbol, bell, or triangle with an arrow through it. Plug the black test lead into the COM port and the red test lead in the port marked with Hz VÙ or similar. Now you can touch the probe end of the test leads together to hear an audible tone or beep. Some multimeters don't have an audible tone but instead may display "1" or the like to indicate continuity. Check your manual for how your multimeter indicates continuity. Figure 7-7 shows how to set a multimeter to check for continuity including which ports to plug in the test leads.

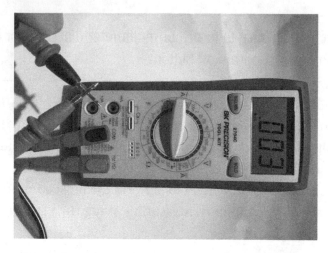

Figure 7-7. *Settings for Checking Continuity*

Notice in the photo I simply touched the probes together to demonstrate how to check for continuity. I like to do this just to ensure my multimeter is turned on and on the correct setting.[3]

Another excellent use for the continuity test is when diagnosing or discovering how cables are wired. For example, you can use the continuity test to discover which connector is connected on each end of the cable (sometimes called wire sorting or ringing out from the old telephone days).

Measuring Voltage

Our IoT projects use DC. To measure voltage in the circuit, we will use the DC range on the multimeter. Notice the DC range has several stops. This is a scale selection. Choose the scale that closely matches the voltage range you want to test. For example, for our IoT projects we will often measure 3.3–12V, so we choose 20 on the dial. Next, plug the black test lead into the COM port and the red test lead into the port labeled Hz VÙ.

Now we need something to measure! Take any battery you have in the house and touch the black probe to the negative side and the red probe to the positive side. You should see a value appear on the display that is close to the range for the battery. For example, if we used a 1.5V battery, we should see close to 1.5V. It may not be exactly 1.5–1.6V if the battery is depleted. So now you know how to test batteries for freshness! Figure 7-8 shows how to measure voltage of a battery.

---

[3] Yes, a bit of OCD there. Check, double-check, check again.

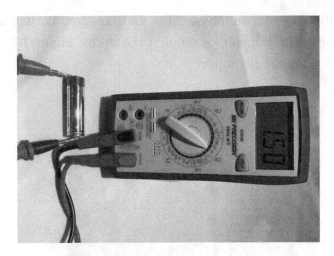

Figure 7-8. *Measuring Voltage of a Battery*

Notice the readout displays 1.50, which is the correct voltage for this AA battery. If I had reversed the probes – the red one on negative and the black on positive – the display would have read –1.50. This is OK because it shows the current is flowing in the opposite direction of how the probes are oriented.

Note   If you use the wrong probe when measuring voltage in a DC circuit, most multimeters will display the voltage as a negative number. Try that with your battery. It won't hurt the multimeter (or the battery)!

We can use this technique to measure voltage in our projects. Just be careful to place the probes in the appropriate positions and try not to cross or short by touching more than one component at a time with a single probe tip.

Measuring Current

Current is measured as amperage (milliamps – mA). Thus, we will use the range marked with an A with a straight and dashed line (not the wavy one – that's AC). We measure current in series. That is, we must place the multimeter in the circuit. This can be a little tricky because we must interrupt the flow of current and put the meter inline.

If you are familiar with how to use a breadboard, you can follow along with this experiment. However, if you haven't used a breadboard, you may want to read this experiment, then return to it once you finish reading this chapter. For this experiment, we will use a breadboard power supply, an LED, and a resistor. We will wire the circuit such that we will use the multimeter to complete the circuit. Figure 7-9 shows how to set up the circuit with the multimeter inline.

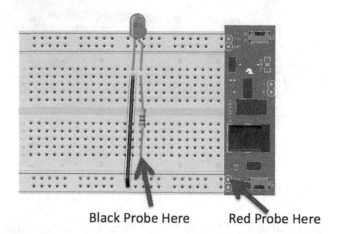

Black Probe Here   Red Probe Here

Figure 7-9. *Measuring Current*

Before powering on your breadboard power supply, plug the black test lead into the COM port and the other test leads into the port labeled mA. Some multimeters use the same port for measuring voltage as well as current. Turn the dial on the multimeter to the 200mA setting. Then power on the breadboard power supply and touch the leads to the places indicated. Be careful to touch only the VCC pin on the breadboard power supply. Once the circuit is powered on, you should see a value on the multimeter. Figure 7-10 shows how to use a multimeter to measure current in a circuit.

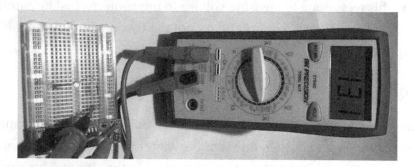

Figure 7-10. *Measuring Current*

There is one other tricky thing about measuring current. If you attempt to measure current that is greater than the maximum for the port, you may damage your meter (e.g., the meter in the photo has a maximum of 20mA on the one port). If I exceeded that by, say, 5A, I would likely blow a fuse in the multimeter. This is not desirable, but at least there is a fuse that we can replace should we make a mistake and choose the wrong port.

Measuring Resistance

Resistance is measured in ohms (Ù). The most common component we will use to introduce resistance in a circuit is a resistor. We can test the resistance of the charge through the resistor with our multimeter. To test resistance, choose the ohm scale that is closest to the rating of the resistor. For example, I am going to test a resistor that I believe is about 200 ohms, but since I am not sure, I will choose the 2k setting.

Next, plug the black test lead into the COM port and the red test lead into the port labeled HzVÙ. Now, touch one probe to one side of a resistor and the other probe to the other side. It doesn't matter which side you choose – a resistor works in both directions. Notice the readout. The meter will read one of three things: 0.00, 1, or the actual resistor value.

In this case, the meter reads 0.219, meaning this resistor has a value of 220Ù. Recall, I used the 2k scale, which means a resistor of 1k would read 1.0. Since the value is a decimal, I can move the decimal point to the left to get a whole number.

If the multimeter displays another value such as 0 or 1, it indicates the scale is wrong and you should try a higher scale. This isn't a problem. It just means you need to choose a larger scale. On the other hand, if the display shows 0 or a small number, you need to choose a lower scale. I like to go one tick of the knob either way when I am testing resistance in an unknown circuit.

Figure 7-11 shows an example of measuring resistance for a resistor. Notice the display reads 219. I am testing a resistor rated at 220 ohms. The reason it is 219 instead of 220 is because the resistor I am using is rated at 220 +/- 5%. Thus, the acceptable range for this resistor is 209–231 ohms.

Figure 7-11. *Measuring Resistance of a Resistor*

Now we know how to test a resistor to discover its rating. As we will see, those rings around the body of the resistor are the primary way we know its rating, but we can always test it if we're unsure, someone has painted over it (hey, it happens), or we're too lazy to look it up.

Now, let's discuss the most fundamental concept you must understand when working with electronics – powering your project!

Powering Your Electronics

Electricity[4] is briefly defined as the flow of electric charge and when used provides power for our electronics – from a common light bulb or ceiling fan to our high-definition television or our new tablet. Whether you are powering your electronics with batteries or a power supply, you are initiating a circuit where electrons flow in specific patterns. There are two forms (or kinds) of power you will be using. Your home is powered by alternating current, and your electronics are powered by direct current.

The term alternating current (AC) is used to describe the flow of charged particles that changes direction periodically at a specific rate (or cycle) reversing the voltage along with the current. Thus, AC systems are designed to work with a specific range of cycles as well as voltage. Typically, AC systems use higher voltages than direct current systems.

---

[4]https://learn.sparkfun.com/tutorials/what-is-electricity

The term direct current (DC) is used to describe the flow of charged particles that do not change direction and thus always flow in a specific "direction." Most electronics systems are powered with DC voltages and are typically at lower voltages than AC systems. For example, IoT projects typically run on lower direct current (DC) voltages in the range 3.3–24V.

Tip   For more information about AC and DC current and the differences, see https://learn.sparkfun.com/tutorials/alternating-current-ac-vs-direct-current-dc.

Since DC flows in a single direction, components that operate on DC have a positive and a negative "side" where current flows from positive to negative. The orientation of these sides – one to positive and one to negative – is called polarity. Some components such as resistors can operate in "direction," but you should always be sure to connect your components per its polarity. Most components are clearly marked, but those that are not have a well-known arrangement. For example, the positive pole (side) of an LED is the longer of the two legs called anode, whereas the negative or shorter leg is called the cathode.

Despite the lower voltages, we mustn't think that they are completely harmless or safe. Incorrectly wiring electronics (reversing polarity) or shorting (connecting positive and negative together) can damage your electronics and in some cases cause overheating, which, in extreme cases, causes electronics to catch fire.

Caution   Don't be tempted to think working with 3.3 or 5.5 volts is "safe." Even a small amount of voltage improperly connected can lead to potentially devastating results. Don't assume low DC voltage is harmless.

I had a lesson in just how real this scenario can be a couple of years ago. I was changing the batteries in our smoke detectors. I took the old batteries out and placed them in my pocket. I had forgotten I had a small penknife in the same pocket. One of the batteries shorted on the knife, and within about ten minutes, the battery heated to an alarming temperature. It wasn't enough to burn, but had I left something like that unattended, it could have been bad.

That's a scary thought, isn't it? Consider it an admonishment as well as a warning; we should never relax our safe handling practices even for lower voltage projects.

Finally, DC components are often rated for a specific voltage range. Recall from our discussion on the various low-cost computing boards and GPIO headers, some boards operate at 5V, whereas others operate at 3.3V (or less). Fortunately, there are several ways we can adapt components that work at different voltages – by using other components!

Note   I have deliberately kept the discussion on power simple. There is far more to electrical current – even DC – than what I've described here. Once you understand these basics, you'll be able to work with the projects in this book.

Electronic Components

Aside from learning how to use a multimeter and possibly learning to solder, you also need to know something about the electronic components available to build your projects. In this section, I provide a short list and description of some of the common components in alphabetical order by name that you will encounter when building IoT solutions. I also cover breakout boards and logic circuits, which are small circuits built with a set of components that provide a feature or solve a problem. For example, you can get breakout boards for USB host connections, Ethernet modules, logic shifters, real-time clocks, and more.

Button

A button (sometimes called a momentary button) is a mechanism that makes a connection when pressed. More specifically, a button connects two or more poles together while it is pressed. A common (and perhaps overused) example of a button is a home doorbell. When pressed, it completes a circuit that triggers a chime, bell, tone, or music to play. Some older doorbells continue to sound while the button is pressed.

In IoT projects, we will use buttons to trigger events, start and stop actions, and similar operations. A button is a simple form of a switch, but unlike a switch, you must continue to press the button to make the electrical connections. Most buttons have at least two legs (or pins) that are connected when the button is pressed. Some have more than two legs connected in pairs, and some of those can permit multiple connections. Figure 7-12 shows several buttons.

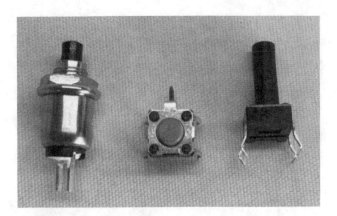

Figure 7-12. *Momentary Buttons*

There is a special variant of a momentary button called a latching momentary button. This version uses a notch or detent to keep the poles connected until it is pushed again. If you've seen a button on a stereo or in your car that remains depressed until pressed again, it is likely a latching momentary button.

There are all kinds of buttons from those that can be used with breadboards (the spacing of the pins allow it to be plugged into a breadboard), can be mounted to a panel, or those made for soldering to printed circuit boards.

Capacitor

A capacitor is designed to store charges. As current flows through the capacitor, it accumulates charge and can discharge after the current is disconnected. In this way, it is like a battery, but unlike a battery, a capacitor charges and discharges very fast. We use capacitors for all manner of current storage from blocking current, reducing noise in power supplies, in audio circuits, and more. Figure 7-13 shows several capacitors.

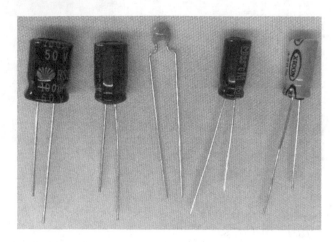

Figure 7-13. *Capacitors*

There are several types of capacitors, but we will most often encounter capacitors when building power supplies for IoT projects. Most capacitors have two legs (pins) that are polarized. That is, one is positive and the other negative. Be sure to connect the capacitor with the correct polarity in your circuit.

Diode

A diode is designed to allow current to flow in only one direction. Most are marked with an arrow pointing to a line, which indicates the direction of flow. A diode is often used as rectifiers in AC-to-DC converters (devices that convert AC to DC voltage), used in conjunction with other components to suppress voltage spikes or protect components from reversed voltage. They are often used to protect against current flowing into a device.

Most diodes are shaped like a small cylinder, and they are usually black with silver writing and have two legs. They look a little like resistors. We use a special variant called a Zener diode in power supplies to help regulate voltages. Figure 7-14 shows several diodes.

Figure 7-14. *Diodes*

Fuse

A fuse is designed to protect a device (the entire circuit) from current greater than what the components can safely operate. Fuses are placed inline on the positive pole. When too much current flows through the fuse, the internal parts trigger a break in the flow of current.

Some fuses use a special wire inside that melts or breaks (thereby rendering it useless but protecting your equipment), while other fuses use a mechanism that operates like a switch (many of these are resettable). When this happens, we say the fuse has "blown" or "tripped." Fuses are rated at a certain current in amperage indicating the maximum amps that the fuse will permit to flow without tripping.

Fuses come in many shapes and varieties and can work with AC or DC voltage. Those we will use are of the disposable variety. Figure 7-15 shows an example of two fuses: an automotive-style blade fuse on the left and a glass cartridge fuse on the right.

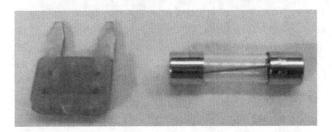

Figure 7-15. *Fuses*

If you are familiar with the electrical panel in your home that houses the circuit breakers, they are resettable fuses. So, the next time one of them goes "click" and the lights go out, you can say, "Hey, a fuse has tripped!" Better still, now you know why – you have exceeded the maximum rating of the circuit breaker.

This is probably fine in situations where you accidentally left that infrared heater on when you dropped the toast and started the microwave (it happens), but if you are tripping breakers frequently without any load, you should call an electrician to have the circuit checked.

Light-Emitting Diode (LED)

As we learned in Chapter 3, an LED has two legs where the longer leg is positive and the shorter negative. LEDs also have a flat edge that indicates the negative leg. They come in a variety of sizes ranging from as small as 3mm to 10mm. Figure 7-16 shows an example of some smaller LEDs.

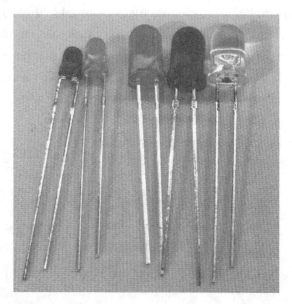

Figure 7-16. *Light-Emitting Diodes*

Recall we also needed to use a resistor with an LED. We need this to help reduce the flow of the circuit to lower the current flowing through the LED. LEDs can be used with lower current (they will burn a bit dimmer than normal) but should not be used with a higher current.

To determine what size resistor we need, we need to know several things about the LED. This data is available from the manufacturer who provides the data in the form of a datasheet or, in the case of commercially packaged products, lists the data on the package. The data we need includes the maximum voltage, the supply voltage (how many volts are coming to the LED), and the current rating of the LED.

For example, if I have an LED like the one we used in the last chapter, in this case a 5mm red LED, we find on Adafruit's website (sparkfun.com/products/12062) that the

LED operates at 1.8–2.2V and 20mA of current. Let's say we want to use this with a 5V supply voltage. We can then take these values and plug them into this formula:[5]

```
R = (Vcc-Vf)/I
```

Using more descriptive names for the variable, we get the following:

```
Resistor = (Volts_supply - Volts_forward) / Desired_current
```

Plugging our data in, we get this result. Note that we have mA so we must use the correct decimal value (divide by 1000). In this case, it is 0.020 and we will pick a voltage in the middle.

```
Resistor = (5 - 2.0) / 0.020
         = 3.0 / 0.020
         = 150
```

Thus, we need a resistor of 150 ohms. Cool. Sometimes, the formula will produce a value that does not match any existing resistors. In that case, choose one closest to the value but a bit larger. Remember, we want to limit and thus err on the side of more restrictive than less restrictive. For example, if you found you need a resistor of 95 ohms, you can use one rated at 100 ohms, which is safer than using one rated at 90 ohms.

Tip   Always err on the side of the more restrictive resistor when the formula produces a value for which there is no resistor available.

Also, if you use LEDs in serial or parallel, the formula is a little different. See https://learn.adafruit.com/all-about-leds for more information about using LEDs in your projects and calculating the size of resistors to use with LEDs.

Relay

A relay is an interesting component that helps us control higher voltages with lower voltage circuits. For example, suppose you wanted to control a device that is powered by 12V from your MicroPython board, which only produces a maximum of 3V. A relay can be used with a 3V circuit to turn on (or relay) power from that higher source.

---

[5] A variant of Ohm's law (https://en.wikipedia.org/wiki/Ohm's_law).

In this example, we would use the MicroPython board output to trigger the relay to switch on the 12V power. Thus, relays are a form of switch. Figure 7-17 shows a typical relay and how the pins are arranged.

Figure 7-17. *Relay*

Relays can take a lot of different forms and typically have slightly different wiring options, such as where the supply voltage is attached and where the trigger voltage attaches as well as whether the initial state is open (no flow) or close (flow) and thus the behavior of how it controls voltage. Some relays come mounted on a PCB with clearly marked terminals for changing its switching feature and where everything plugs in. If you want to use relays in your projects, always check the datasheet to make sure you are wiring it correctly based on its configuration.

You can also use relays to allow your DC circuit to turn AC appliances on and off like those from Adafruit (`www.adafruit.com/product/2935`).

Resistor

A resistor is one of the standard building blocks of electronics. Its job is to impede current and impose a reduction in voltage (which is converted to heat). Its effect, known as resistance, is measured in ohms. A resistor can be used to reduce voltage to other components, limiting frequency response, or protect sensitive components from overvoltage. Figure 7-18 shows several resistors.

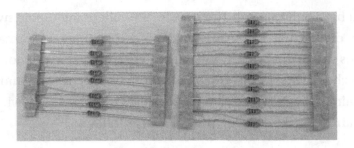

Figure 7-18. *Resistors*

When a resistor is used to pull up voltage (by attaching one end to positive voltage) or pull down voltage (by attaching one end to ground) (resistors are bidirectional), it eliminates the possibility of the voltage floating in an indeterminate state. Thus, a pull-up resistor ensures that the stable state is positive voltage, and a pull-down resistor ensures that the stable state is zero voltage (ground).

Switch

A switch is designed to control the flow of current between two or more pins. Switches come in all manner of shapes, sizes, and packaging. Some are designed as a simple on/off while others can be used to change current from one set of pins to another. Like buttons, switches come in a variety of mounting options from PCB (also called through hole) to panel mount for mounting in enclosures. Figure 7-19 shows a variety of switches.

Figure 7-19. *Various Switches*

Switches that have only one pole (leg or side) are called single-pole switches. Switches that can divert current from one set of poles to another set are called two-pole switches. Switches where there is only one secondary connection per pole are called single-throw switches. Switches that disconnect from one set of poles and connect to another while maintaining a common input are called double-throw switches. These are often combined and form the switch type (or kind) as follows:

- *SPST*: Single pole, single throw

- *DPST*: Double pole, single throw

- *SPDT*: Single pole, double throw

- *DPDT*: Double pole, double throw

- *3PDT*: Three pole, double throw

There may be other variants that you could encounter. I like to keep it straight like this; if I have just an on/off situation, I want a single throw switch. How many poles depends on how many wires or circuits I want to turn on or off at the same time. For double-throw switches, I use these when I have an "A" condition and "B" condition that I want A on when B is off and vice versa. I sometimes use multiple-throw switches when I want an "A," "B," and off situations where I use the center position (throw) as off. You can be very creative with switches!

Transistor

A transistor (a bipolar transistor) is designed to switch current on/off in a cycle or amplify fluctuations in current. Interestingly, transistors used to amplify current replaced vacuum tubes. If you are an audiophile, you likely know a great deal about vacuum tubes. When a resistor operates in switching mode, it behaves like a relay, but its "off" position still allows a small amount of current to flow. Transistors are used in audio equipment, signal processing, and switching power supplies. Figure 7-20 shows two varieties of transistors.

Figure 7-20. *Transistors*

Transistors come in all manner of varieties, packaging, and ratings that make it suitable for one solution or another.

Voltage Regulator

A voltage regulator (linear voltage regulator) is designed to keep the flow of current constant. Voltage regulators often appear in electronics when we need to condition or lower current from a source. For example, we want to supply 5V to a circuit but only have a 9V power supply. Voltage regulators accomplish this (roughly) by taking current in and dissipating the excess current through a heat sink. Thus, voltage regulators have three legs: positive current in, negative, and positive current out. They are typically shaped like those shown in Figure 7-21, but other varieties exist.

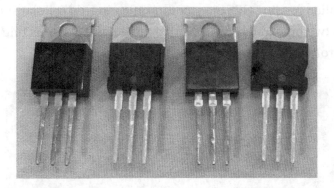

Figure 7-21. *Voltage Regulators*

The small hole in the plate that extends out of the voltage regulator is where the heat sink is mounted. Voltage regulators are often numbered to match their rating. For example, an LM7805 produces 5V, whereas an LM7833 produces 3.3V.

An example of using a voltage regulator to supply power to a 3.3V circuit on a breadboard is shown in Figure 7-22. This circuit was designed with capacitors to help smooth or condition the power. Notice the capacitors are rated with μF, which means microfarad.

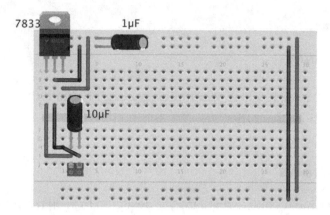

Figure 7-22. *Power Supply Circuit on a Breadboard with Voltage Regulator*

Breakout Boards and Circuits

Breakout boards are our modular building blocks for IoT solutions. They typically combine several components together to form a function such as measuring temperature, enabling reading GPS data, communicating via cellular services, and more. Figure 7-23 shows two breakout boards. Notice the holes for connecting the breakout board to your MicroPython board via a breadboard.

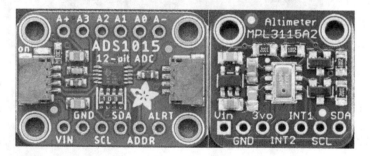

Figure 7-23. *Breakout Boards (Courtesy of adafruit.com)*

On the left is an analog-to-digital converter (www.adafruit.com/product/1083), and on the right is a barometric pressure sensor (www.adafruit.com/product/1893). Both products are available from Adafruit.

Whenever you design a circuit or IoT solution, you should consider using breakout boards as much as possible because they simplify the use of the components. Take the barometric pressure sensor, for example. Adafruit has designed this board so that all we need to do to use it is to attach power and connect it to our IoT device on its I2C bus. An I2C bus is a fast digital protocol that uses two wires (plus power and ground) to read data from circuits (or devices).

Thus, there is no need to worry about how to connect the sensor to other components to use it – just connect it up like any I2C device and start reading data! We will use several breakout boards in the projects later in this book.

Using a Breadboard to Build Circuits

If you have been following along with the projects thus far in the book, you have already encountered a breadboard to make a very simple circuit. Recall from Chapter 3 that a breadboard is a tool we use to plug components into to form circuits. Technically, we're using a solderless breadboard. A solder breadboard has the same layout, except it has only through-hole solder points on a PCB.

WHY ARE THEY CALLED BREADBOARDS?

In the grand old days, microelectronics and discrete components became widely available for experimentation, when we wanted to prototype a circuit, some would use a piece of wood with nails driven into it (sometimes in a grid pattern) where connections were made (called "runs") by wrapping wire around the nails. Some used a breadboard from the kitchen to build their wire wrap prototypes. The name has stuck ever since.

A breadboard allows us to create prototypes for our circuits or simply temporary circuits without having to spend the time (and cost) to make the printed circuit board. Prototyping is the process of experimenting with a circuit by building and testing your ideas. In fact, once we've got our circuit to work correctly, we can use the breadboard layout to help us design a PCB. Figure 7-24 shows several breadboards.

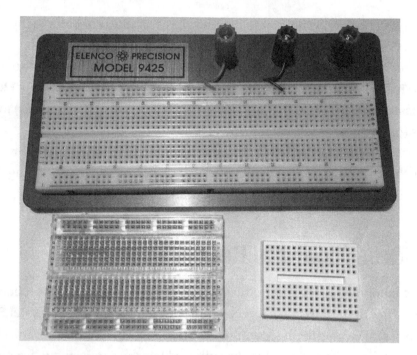

Figure 7-24. *Assorted Breadboards*

Recall that most breadboards (there are several varieties) have a center groove (called a ravine) or a printed line down the center of the board. This signifies the terminal strips that run perpendicular to the channel are not connected. That is, the terminal strip on one side is not connected to the other side. This allows us to plug integrated circuits (IC) or chips that are packaged as two rows of pins. Thus, we can plug the IC into the breadboard with one set of pins on each side of the breadboard. We see this in the following example.

Most breadboards also have one or more sets of power rails that are connected together parallel to the ravine. If there are two sets, the sets are not connected together. The power rails may have a colored reference line, but this is only for reference; you can make either one positive with the other negative. Finally, some breadboards number the terminal strip rows. These are for reference only and have no other meaning. However, they can be handy for making notes in your engineering notebook. Figure 7-25 shows the nomenclature of a breadboard and how the terminal strips and power rails are connected together.

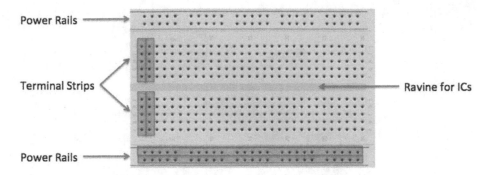

Figure 7-25. *Breadboard Layout*

Note   The sets of power rails are not connected together. If you want to have power on both sides of the breadboard, you must use jumpers to connect them.

FRITZING: A BREADBOARDING SOFTWARE APPLICATION

The drawings of breadboards in this book were made with a program named Fritzing (https://fritzing.org/). This inexpensive application allows you to create a digital representation of a circuit on a breadboard. It is quite handy to use. If you find yourself wanting to design a prototype circuit, using Fritzing can help save you a lot of trial and error. As a bonus, Fritzing allows you to see the same circuit in an electronic schematic or PCB layout view. I recommend downloading and trying this application out.

It is sometimes desirable to test a circuit out separately from code. For example, if we want to make sure all our devices are connected together properly, we can use a breadboard power supply to power the circuit. This way, if something goes horribly wrong, we don't risk damaging our IoT device. Most breadboard power supplies are built on a small PCB with a barrel jack for a wall wart power supply, two sets of pins to plug into the power rails on the breadboard, and an off switch (very handy), and some can generate different voltages. Figure 7-26 shows one of my favorite breadboard power supplies available from SparkFun (www.sparkfun.com/products/13157).

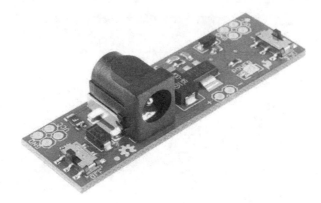

Figure 7-26. *Breadboard Power Supply (Courtesy of sparkfun.com)*

Should our circuits require more room than what is available on a single breadboard, you can use multiple breadboards by simply jumping the power rails and continuing the circuit. To facilitate this, some breadboards can be connected using small nubs and slots on the side. Finally, most breadboards also come with an adhesive backing that you can use to mount on a plate or inside an enclosure or similar workspace. If you decide to use the adhesive backing, be forewarned that they cannot be unstuck easily – they stay put quite nicely.

Now that we know more about how breadboards work, let's discuss the component our IoT solutions will employ to collect data: sensors.

What Are Sensors?

A sensor is a device that measures phenomena of the physical world. These phenomena can be things you see, like light, gases, water vapor, and so on. They can also be things you feel, like temperature, electricity, water, wind, and so on. Humans have senses that act like sensors, allowing us to experience the world around us. However, there are some things your sensors can't see or feel, such as radiation, radio waves, voltage, and amperage. Upon measuring these phenomena, it's the sensor's job to convey a measurement in the form of either a voltage representation or a number.

There are many forms of sensors. They're typically low-cost devices designed for a single purpose and with a limited capability for processing. Most simple sensors are discrete components; even those that have more sophisticated parts can be treated as separate components. Sensors are either analog or digital and are typically designed to measure only one thing. But an increasing number of sensor modules are designed to measure a set of related phenomena, such as the Weather Shield from SparkFun Electronics (www.sparkfun.com/products/10586).

The following sections examine how sensors measure data, how to store that data, and examples of some common sensors.

How Sensors Measure

Sensors are electronic devices that generate a voltage based on the unique properties of their chemical and mechanical construction. One of the common misconceptions some have about sensors is they do not manipulate the phenomena (change the event or data) they're designed to measure. Rather, sensors sample some physical variable and turn it into a proportional electric signal (voltage, current, digital, and so on).

For example, a humidity sensor measures the concentration of water (moisture) in the air. Humidity sensors react to these phenomena and generate a voltage that the microcontroller or similar device can then read. A typical humidity sensor reads data on a scale, such as the low-cost humidity sensor called the DHT-20 (www.adafruit.com/product/5183). Figure 7-27 shows a typical DHT-20 sensor.

Figure 7-27. *DHT-20 Humidity Sensor (Courtesy of adafruit.com)*

The DHT-20 is designed to measure temperature as well as humidity. It generates a digital signal on the output (data pin). Although simple to use, it's a bit slow and should be used to track data at a reasonably slow rate (no more frequently than about once every three or four seconds).

When this sensor generates data, that data is transmitted as a series of high (interpreted as a 1) and low (interpreted as a 0) voltages that the microcontroller can read and use to form a value. In this case, the microcontroller reads a value 40 bits in length (40 pulses of high or low voltage) – that is, 5 bytes – from the sensor and places it in a program variable. The first two bytes are the value for humidity, the second two are for temperature, and the fifth byte is the checksum value to ensure an accurate read. Fortunately, all this challenging work is done for you in the form of a special library designed for the DHT-20 and similar sensors.

The DHT-20 produces a digital value. Not all sensors do this; some generate a voltage range instead. These are called analog sensors. Let's take a moment to understand the differences. This will become essential information as you plan and build your sensor nodes.

Analog Sensors

Analog sensors are devices that generate a voltage range, typically between 0 and 5 volts. An analog-to-digital circuit is needed to convert the voltage to a number. But it isn't that simple (is it ever?). Analog sensors work like resistors and, when connected to GPIO pins, often require another resistor to "pull up" or "pull down" the voltage to avoid spurious changes in voltage known as floating. This is because voltage flowing through resistors is continuous in both time and amplitude.

Thus, even when the sensor isn't generating a value or measurement, there is still a flow of voltage through the sensor that can cause spurious readings. Your projects require a clear distinction between OFF (zero voltage) and ON (positive voltage). Pull-up and pull-down resistors ensure that you have one of these two states. It's the responsibility of the A/D converter to take the voltage read from the sensor and convert it to a value that can be interpreted as data.

When sampled (when a value is read from a sensor), the voltage read must be interpreted as a value in the range specified for the given sensor. Remember that a value of, say, 2 volts from one analog sensor may not mean the same thing as 2 volts from another analog sensor. Each sensor's datasheet shows you how to interpret these values.

As you can see, working with analog sensors is a lot more complicated than using the DHT-20 digital sensor. With a little practice, you will find that most analog sensors aren't difficult to use once you understand how to attach them to a microcontroller and how to interpret their voltage on the scale in which the sensor is calibrated to work.

Digital Sensors

Digital sensors like the DHT-20 are designed to produce a string of bits using serial transmission (one bit at a time). However, some digital sensors produce data via parallel transmission (one or more bytes[6] at a time). As described previously, the bits are represented as voltage, where high voltage (say, 5 volts) or ON is 1 and low voltage (0 or even –5 volts) or OFF is 0. These sequences of ON and OFF values are called discrete values because the sensor is producing one or the other in pulses – it's either ON or OFF.

Digital sensors can be sampled more frequently than analog signals because they generate the data more quickly and because no additional circuitry is needed to read the values (such as A/D converters and logic or software to convert the values to a scale). Thus, digital sensors are generally more accurate and dependable than analog sensors. But the accuracy of a digital sensor is directly proportional to the number of bits it uses for sampling data.

The most generic form of digital sensor is the pushbutton or switch. What, a button is a sensor? Why, yes, it's a sensor. Consider for a moment the sensor attached to a window in a home security system. It's a simple switch that is closed when the window is closed and open when the window is open. When the switch is wired into a circuit, the flow of current is constant and unbroken (measuring positive volts using a pull-up resistor) when the window is closed and the switch is closed, but the current is broken (measuring zero volts) when the window and switch are open. This is the most basic of ON and OFF sensors.

Most digital sensors are small circuits of several components designed to generate digital data. Unlike analog sensors, reading their data is easy because the values can be used directly without conversion (except to other scales or units of measure). Some may suggest this is more difficult than using analog sensors, but that depends on your point of view. An electronics enthusiast would see working with analog sensors as easier, whereas a programmer would think digital sensors are simpler to use.

Now let's look at some of the sensors available and the types of phenomena they measure.

Examples of Sensors

An IoT solution that observes something may use at least one sensor and a means to read and interpret the data. You may be thinking of all manner of useful things you can measure in your home or office or even in your yard or surroundings. You may want to measure the temperature changes in your new sunroom, detect when the mail carrier

---

[6] This depends on the width of the parallel buffer. An 8-bit buffer can communicate 1 byte at a time, a 16-bit buffer can communicate 2 bytes at a time, and so on.

has tossed the latest circular in your mailbox, or perhaps keep a log of how many times your dog uses his doggy door. I hope that by now you can see these are just the tip of the iceberg when it comes to imagining what you can measure.

What types of sensors are available? The following sections describe some of the more popular sensors and what they measure. I also provide a few hints on how you might want to use the sensor in an IoT project. However, this is just a sampling of the growing array of sensors available. Perusing the catalogs of online electronics vendors like Mouser Electronics (`www.mouser.com`), SparkFun Electronics (`www.sparkfun.com`), and Adafruit Industries (`www.adafruit.com`) will reveal many more examples.

I also include photos of popular examples for some of the sensor types.

Accelerometers

These sensors measure motion or movement of the sensor or whatever it's attached to. They're designed to sense motion (velocity, inclination, vibration, and so on) on several axes. Some include gyroscopic features. Most are digital sensors. A Wii Nunchuck (or WiiChuck) contains a sophisticated accelerometer for tracking movement. Aha, now you know the secret of those funny little thingamabobs that came with your Wii! You may want to add accelerometers if your IoT project involves something in motion and the observation of that motion provides useful information.

Audio Sensors

Perhaps this is obvious, but microphones are used to measure sound. Most are analog, but some of the better security and surveillance sensors have digital variants for higher compression of transmitted data. IoT projects such as home security, child monitoring, ghost hunting, or auditory health can all benefit from integrating audio sensors.

Barcode Readers

These sensors are designed to read barcodes. Most often, barcode readers generate digital data representing the numeric equivalent of a barcode. Such sensors are often used in inventory-tracking systems to track equipment through a plant or during transport. They're plentiful, and many are economically priced, enabling you to incorporate them into your own projects. If your IoT project requires capturing data from an object, you may want to consider barcodes.

For example, if you want to sense when parking lot subscribers enter or exit an unattended parking lot, you could position a barcode reader at the gates that read barcodes that you design and distribute to your subscribers. When the car pulls up to the gate, the barcode reader can read the barcode, log the entry, and raise the gate. If you've ever lived in a large city, worked in a controlled office complex, or were a commuter student, you may have encountered parking solutions like this.

Biometric Sensors

A sensor that reads fingerprints, irises, or palm prints contains a special sensor designed to recognize patterns. Given the uniqueness inherent in patterns such as fingerprints and palm prints, they make excellent components for a secure access system. Most biometric sensors produce a block of digital data that represents the fingerprint or palm print. IoT projects that require a greater level of security may want to include a biometric sensor to help identify the user of the system.

Capacitive Sensors

A special application of capacitive sensors, pulse sensors are designed to measure your pulse rate and typically use a fingertip for the sensing site. Special devices known as pulse oximeters (called pulse-ox by some medical professionals) measure pulse rate with a capacitive sensor and determine the oxygen content of blood with a light sensor.

If you own modern electronic devices, you may have encountered touch-sensitive buttons that use special capacitive sensors to detect touch and pressure. If your IoT project needs to measure any sort of movement, or respond to touch, capacitive sensors can help provide a futuristic non-tactile interface. The Touch Bar on the latest MacBook Pro is an example of such a solution.

Figure 7-28 shows two examples of touch-sensitive modules that you can buy from Adafruit: a momentary switch (`www.adafruit.com/product/1374`) and a toggle switch (`www.adafruit.com/product/1375`).

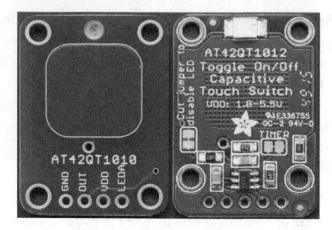

Figure 7-28. *Touch Capacitive Sensor Breakout Boards (Courtesy of adafruit.com)*

Coin Sensors

This is one of the most unusual types of sensors. These devices[7] are like the coin slots on a typical vending machine. Like their commercial equivalent, they can be calibrated to sense when a certain size of coin is inserted. Although not as sophisticated as commercial units that can distinguish fake coins from real ones, coin sensors can be used to add a new dimension to your projects. A great, practical IoT project for parents would be a coin-operated WiFi station where the children have to buy their own Internet time. Not only will this keep them from using the Internet too much, it may also help teach them how to budget their allowance. Now, that should keep the kids from spending too much time on the Internet!

Current Sensors

These are designed to measure voltage and amperage. Some are designed to measure change, whereas others measure load. IoT projects that integrate circuits or need to monitor the flow of electricity will need a current sensor. These may be some of the more esoteric projects, but you can use these sensors to monitor the behavior of existing solutions without modifying them.

---

[7]www.sparkfun.com/products/11719

For example, if you wanted to adapt sensors to observe a manufacturing machine, you could add sensors that monitor the current to the various components. That is, you may be able to record when voltage is applied to motors, actuators, or even warning lights to determine when (or how much) the devices are activated. However, as a hobbyist, you are more likely interested in building your own multimeter or similar tool.

Flex/Force Sensors

Resistance sensors measure flexes in a piece of material or the force or impact of pressure on the sensor. Flex sensors may be useful for measuring torsional effects or to measure finger movements (like in a Nintendo Power Glove). Flex-sensor resistance increases when the sensor is flexed. For example, if you want to create an IoT solution that reports your fishing experience in real time, you might want to use a flex sensor on your fishing rod to report every time you cast or got a hit on your lure.

Gas Sensors

There are a great many types of gas sensors. Some measure potentially harmful gases such as LPG and methane and other gases such as hydrogen, oxygen, and so on. Other gas sensors are combined with light sensors to sense smoke or pollutants in the air. The next time you hear that telltale and often annoying low-battery warning beep[8] from your smoke detector, think about what that device contains. Why, it's a sensor node! If your IoT project needs to observe or detect any form of gas, especially if it involves reacting to certain gases or levels thereof, you will need to use the appropriate gas sensors.

Light Sensors

Sensors that measure the intensity or lack of light are special types of resistors: light-dependent resistors (LDRs), sometimes called photo resistors or photocells. Thus, they're analog by nature.

---

[8] I subscribe to the more is better theory and have many detectors in our home, which is great, but when the batteries run down, I can never tell which detector is beeping! This becomes maddeningly frustrating when they beep only once or twice, then go silent. Fortunately, I've replaced nearly all of them with the newest ten-year battery variants. No more wild beep goose chases!

If you own a Mac laptop, chances are you've seen a photo resistor in action when your illuminated keyboard turns itself on in low light. Special forms of light sensors can detect other light spectrums such as infrared (as in older TV remotes). For example, if you want your IoT project to automatically adjust the brightness of its display, a light sensor is the component you need.

The following figures show two examples of light sensors. Figure 7-29 shows a typical mini photocell (`www.sparkfun.com/products/9088`).

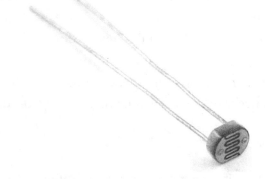

Figure 7-29. *Mini Photocell (Courtesy of sparkfun.com)*

Figure 7-30 shows a breakout board that combines proximity, light, and RGB (color) sensors onto a single, small board (`www.adafruit.com/product/3595`).

Figure 7-30. *Proximity, Light, and RGB Sensor Breakout Board (Courtesy of adafruit.com)*

Liquid-Flow Sensors

These sensors resemble valves and are placed inline in plumbing systems. They measure the flow of liquid as it passes through. Basic flow sensors use a spinning wheel and a magnet to generate a Hall effect (rapid ON/OFF sequences whose frequency equates to how much water has passed). If your IoT project involves any form of liquid, such as a garden pond or irrigation system, knowing the flow of the water may be helpful in learning or observing something.

Liquid-Level Sensors

A special resistive solid-state device can be used to measure the relative height of a body of water. One example generates low resistance when the water level is high and higher resistance when the level is low. Like liquid-flow sensors, liquid-level sensors are typically used in the same solution. Figure 7-31 shows a typical liquid-level sensor that operates as a switch where the float closes the switch when the water level rises.

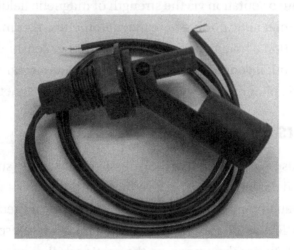

Figure 7-31. *Water-Level Sensor*

Location Sensors

Modern smartphones have GPS sensors for sensing location, and of course GPS devices use the GPS technology to help you navigate. Fortunately, GPS sensors are available in low-cost forms, enabling you to add location sensing to your project. GPS sensors generate digital data in the form of longitude and latitude, and most can also sense altitude. If your IoT project needs to report its location, a GPS sensor can give you very accurate readings. However, like most sensors, GPS sensors can have a degree of inaccuracy. Depending on how close you need to locate something, you may need to spend a bit more on a more accurate GPS sensor.

Magnetic-Stripe Readers

These sensors read data from magnetic stripes (like that on a credit card) and return the digital form of the alphanumeric data (the actual strings). IoT projects that include a security component may want to use a magnetic-stripe reader to help identify a user. When combined with a password and a biometric sensor, security can be increased considerably. That is, someone would have to know something (a password or pin), possess something (security card with a magnetic stripe encoded with a key phrase, number, user ID, etc.), and be validated as someone (fingerprint) before gaining access.

Magnetometers

These sensors measure orientation via the strength of magnetic fields. A compass is a sensor for finding magnetic north. Some magnetometers offer multiple axes to allow even finer detection of magnetic fields. This is another sensor that you may not encounter very often, but if your IoT project needs to measure magnetic fields from motors or atmospheric phenomena, you may want to look at magnetometers.

Moisture Sensors

Moisture sensors measure the amount of moisture in a substance (such as soil) or in the air. They typically send data in the form of a voltage reading where low values indicate less moisture. You often find moisture sensors in atmospheric projects or even plant monitoring solutions. Figure 7-32 shows a typical soil moisture sensor (`www.sparkfun.com/products/17731`). Notice the prongs are the portion of the sensor inserted into the soil.

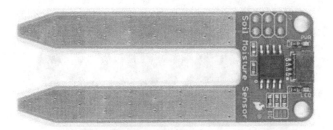

Figure 7-32. *Soil Moisture Sensor (Courtesy of sparkfun.com)*

Proximity Sensors

Often thought of as distance sensors, proximity sensors use infrared or sound waves to detect distance, movement, or the range to/from an object. Made popular by low-cost robotics kits, the Parallax Ultrasonic Sensor uses sound waves to measure distance by sensing the amount of time between pulse sent and pulse received (the echo). For approximate distance measuring,[9] it's a simple math problem to convert the time to distance. If you're building an IoT project that detects movement or proximity, such as a motion-sensing camera, you may want to use proximity sensors.

The following figures show two types of proximity sensors. Figure 7-33 shows a popular passive infrared sensor (PIR) motion sensor (`www.sparkfun.com/products/13285`).

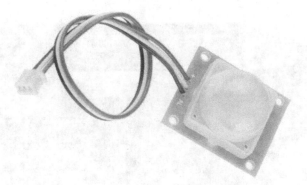

Figure 7-33. *PIR Motion Sensor (Courtesy of sparkfun.com)*

Figure 7-34 shows an ultrasonic sensor (`www.sparkfun.com/products/15569`) used in many projects from robots to drones.

---

[9]Accuracy may depend on environmental variables such as elevation, temperature, and so on.

Figure 7-34. *Ultrasonic Proximity Sensor (Courtesy of sparkfun.com)*

Radiation Sensors

Among the more serious sensors are those that detect radiation. This can also be electromagnetic radiation (there are sensors for that too), but a Geiger counter uses radiation sensors to detect harmful ionizing. In fact, it's possible to build your very own Geiger counter using a sensor and an Arduino (and a few electronic components). This is one sensor that you may not encounter as a hobbyist. However, there are several kits for building your own Geiger counter such as those from Adafruit (`www.adafruit.com/product/483`). Figure 7-35 shows the kit fully assembled.

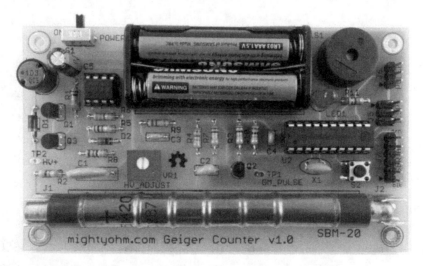

Figure 7-35. *Geiger Counter Kit – Radiation Sensor (Courtesy of adafruit.com)*

RFID Sensors

Radio frequency identification uses a passive device (sometimes called an RFID tag) to communicate data using radio frequencies through electromagnetic induction. For example, an RFID tag can be a credit card–sized plastic card, a label, or something similar that contains a special antenna, typically in the form of a coil, thin wire, or foil layer that is tuned to a specific frequency.

When the tag is placed near the reader, the reader emits a radio signal; the tag can use the electromagnet energy to transmit a nonvolatile message embedded in the antenna, in the form of radio signals, which is then converted to an alphanumeric string.[10] RFID sensors are another excellent choice for security systems. If you have pets, you may want to visit your veterinarian to inquire about RFID sensors that act as hidden owner identification tags. If you know the frequency, you can even use it to help detect when your pet goes through a pet door.

Figure 7-36 shows an RFID reader (sensor) that you can use to read RFID tags via USB (www.sparkfun.com/products/9963).

Figure 7-36. *USB RFID Reader*

Speed Sensors

Like flow sensors, simple speed sensors like those found on many bicycles use a magnet and a reed switch to generate a Hall effect. The frequency combined with the circumference of the wheel can be used to calculate speed and, over time, distance traveled. If your IoT solution needs to read movement, you can use a magnetic switch

---

[10] http://en.wikipedia.org/wiki/Radio-frequency_identification

and a magnet to detect rotation. For example, bicycle speedometers often use a magnet and magnetic switch to detect the number of rotations, circumference of the wheel, and frequency of the actions to calculate speed.

Switches and Pushbuttons

These are the most basic of digital sensors used to detect if something is set (ON) or reset (OFF). Even so, you can use switches and buttons to build a user interface, for controlling other devices, or even turning the thing on!

Tilt Switches

These sensors can detect when a device is tilted one way or another. Although very simple, they can be useful for low-cost motion detection sensors. They are digital and are essentially switches. If your IoT solution needs to detect when the device is leaning, you can use tilt sensors to trigger at a certain lean angle. For example, some modern motorcycles use tilt sensors to turn on cornering lights – headlamps angled to improve vision around a turn at night.

Touch Sensors

The touch-sensitive membranes formed into keypads, keyboards, pointing devices, and the like are an interesting form of sensor. You can use touch-sensitive devices like these for collecting data from humans. Touch sensors can help you build a user interface for your IoT project that can be presented in a low-profile form or to save space in a console, project box, etc.

Video Sensors

As mentioned previously, it's possible to obtain very small video sensors that use cameras and circuitry to capture images and transmit them as digital data. If you want to incorporate a video element to your IoT project such as a security solution, you can add a camera or video sensor to capture a visual component that can help provide information beyond the incident measurements. That is, you can review a photo and learn more than simply something moved or approached the device. For example, you can build an IoT project that detects movement and takes a photo if something gets close enough or, perhaps, moves faster than a certain threshold.[11]

Weather Sensors

Sensors for temperature, barometric pressure, rainfall, humidity, wind speed, and so on are all classified as weather sensors. Most generate digital data and can be combined to create comprehensive environmental solutions. Figure 7-37 shows a common breakout board for the BMP280 pressure and temperature sensor (`www.adafruit.com/product/2651`).

Figure 7-37. *BMP280 Pressure and Temperature Sensor (Courtesy of adafruit.com)*

With this and other easy-to-use sensors, it's possible to build your own weather station from about a dozen inexpensive sensors, your MicroPython board, and a bit of programming to interpret and combine the data. In fact, we'll do that in Chapter 10!

Tip   If you want to see more sensors, you can purchase any number of sensors from Adafruit (`www.adafruit.com/category/35`) or SparkFun (`www.sparkfun.com/categories/23`).

---

[11] Have you ever thought it would be great if you could catch a photo of whatever critter is eating your garden? Build your own critter camera with a proximity sensor and an infrared camera!

I WANT TO LEARN MORE!

If you find you need or want to learn more about electronics than what I've presented in this chapter or you want to learn more about the electronics you will need for a more advanced IoT project, you may want to consider taking a course at a community college or try a self-paced course on electronics.

One of the best self-paced courses I've found include the set of electronics books by Charles Platt. I've found these books to be very well written, opening the door for many to learn electronics without having to spend years learning the tedious (but no less important) theory and mathematics of electronics. Best of all, they are not written in the dreary textbook fact-fact-fact-question pace. They are written by a world-renown expert with a gift of presenting the material in an easy-to-read and comprehend style. I recommend the following books for anyone wanting to learn more about electronics:

- *Make: Electronics, Third Edition* (O'Reilly, 2021), Charles Platt

- *Make: More Electronics* (O'Reilly, 2014), Charles Platt

- *Encyclopedia of Electronic Components Volume 1* (O'Reilly, 2012), Charles Platt

- *Encyclopedia of Electronic Components Volume 2* (O'Reilly, 2014), Charles Platt

- *Encyclopedia of Electronic Components Volume 3* (O'Reilly, 2016), Charles Platt

The third volume in his encyclopedia series includes an in-depth study of sensors: necessary for advanced IoT projects.

Maker Shed (www.makershed.com/collections/electronics) sells companion kits that contain all the parts you need to complete the experiments in the *Make: Electronics* and *Make: More Electronics* books. The books together with the kits make for an excellent self-paced learning experience.

Summary

Learning how to work with electronics as a hobby or to create an IoT solution does not require a lifetime of study or a change of vocation. Indeed, learning how to work with electronics is all part of the fun of experimenting with the IoT! I have met many people who have learned electronics on their own, and while most will admit formal study is essential for mastering the topic, you can learn quite a lot on your own – enough to become proficient working with the basic electronic components typically found in IoT projects.

This chapter presented the basics of electronic components, including the use of breadboards, common components, and example circuits. This and a bit of key knowledge of how to use a multimeter will get you a long way toward becoming proficient with electronics. We also learned about one of the key components of an IoT solution – sensors. We discovered two ways they communicate (digital and analog) and a bit of what types of sensors are available.

In the next chapter, we will dive into our first electronics project – the equivalent of a "hello, world!" project for hardware. We'll see how to connect our MicroPython board to a few components and write a Python program to control them. Cool!

Project: Hello, World! MicroPython Style

Here, we are at the most fun part of this book – working on MicroPython projects! It is at this point that we have learned how to write in MicroPython and now know a lot more about the hardware and even how to use discrete electronics and breakout boards.

This chapter represents an introduction to building MicroPython projects. As such, there are a few more things we need to learn, including techniques and procedures for installing and running our projects on our MicroPython boards. This chapter will introduce those things you need to make your MicroPython projects successful. Thus, the chapter is a bit longer and should be considered required reading even if you do not plan to implement the project.

As you will see, the format for all the project chapters is the same; an overview of the project is presented, followed by a list of the required components and how to assemble the hardware. Once we have a grasp of how to connect the hardware, we then see how to connect everything and begin writing the code. Each chapter will close with how to execute the project along with a sample of it running and suggestions for embellishing the project.

Before we jump into our first electronics project for the Pico, let's discuss a few best practices and other practical advice for developing projects. These apply to all projects in this chapter and likely any future project you may have in mind.

Getting Started with MicroPython Projects

If you have never worked with microcontrollers before, you have no knowledge of building electronics projects, or you are not familiar with the hardware on the Pico, you may be wondering how to get started building such projects.

© Charles Bell 2024
C. Bell, *MicroPython for the Internet of Things*, https://doi.org/10.1007/978-1-4842-9861-9_8

In this section, we will see some helpful tips and best practices for how to get started working with the Pico hardware. Most of this advice applies to any electronics or microcontroller project. They are included here for the beginner and those that need a refresher.

One Step at a Time!

Another very common mistake beginners make is sitting down and wiring all of their electronics together, then writing all their code in one pass without testing anything ahead of time. This creates a situation where if something doesn't work, a host of problems can mask it.

For example, if there is some logic error or data produced is incorrect, it may cause other parts of the project to fail or produce incorrect results. This is made worse when the project doesn't work at all – there are too many parts to try and diagnose what went wrong. This often places beginners in a desperate situation of confusion and frustrations. You students out there know exactly what I am talking about.

This can be avoided easily by building your project one step at a time. That is, build your project one aspect at a time. For example, if you're working with LEDs to signal something, get that part working first. Similarly, if you're reading data from a sensor, ensure you can do that correctly in isolation before wiring it all together and hoping it all works. Even the very experienced can make this mistake, but they are more equipped to fix it if something goes wrong (and they know better, but it's a do as I say not as I do situation). We will build the examples in this book one step at a time. Some are small enough that there may be only one step, but the practice is one you should heed for any project you undertake.

Some Assembly Required

Some vendors offer Pico and breakout boards with and without headers soldered. Not soldering the headers saves on production and in some cases shipping costs and makes the boards a bit cheaper. If you know how to solder (or know someone who does), you may be able to save a little going with the boards without headers.

Another reason you may want a board without headers is if you want to install your board in a project enclosure or some other form of embedded installation. In this case, having the headers soldered may take up more space than you have or make the completed project a bit bulkier.

You may also encounter some add-on boards, breakout boards, or other discrete components that are not soldered with headers (or connectors). If you want to use these, you may have to solder the header or connector yourself. For example, most of the breakout boards from Adafruit (`adafruit.com`) and SparkFun (`sparkfun.com`) do not come with the headers soldered.

Handle with Care!

You should consider your Pico as a very sensitive device susceptible to electrostatic discharge (ESD). Unless you place your board in a case or on a nonmetal surface, you should handle your board carefully, always placing it on a nonconductive surface before powering it on. ESD can be caused by many things (think back to when you were a child with sneakers on carpet). This discharge can harm the board. Always ensure you handle your board so that ESD is controlled and minimized.

You should also never move the board when it is powered on. Why? The board has components soldered on with many pins exposed on both sides. Should any two or more of those pins touch something that conducts electricity, you can risk damaging the board.

Also, always store your board in an ESD-safe container – one that is expressly made to store electronics. Your average, everyday inexpensive plastic box should be avoided (many generate static electricity when handled). However, if you do not have a container made for electronics, you can use static free bags to place the board in while it is being stored. Many of the boards and components you buy come in such packaging. So, don't throw it away!

You should take care to make sure your body, your workspace, and your project is grounded to avoid electrostatic discharge (ESD). ESD can damage your electronics – permanently. The best way to avoid this is to use a grounding strap that loops around your wrist and attaches to an antistatic mat like these: `uline.com/BL_7403/Anti-Static-Table-Mats`.

Finally, be extra careful when connecting your USB cable to your board. The micro USB connector is prone to breakage (more so than other connectors). In most cases, it is not the cable that breaks but the connector on the board itself. When this happens, it can be very difficult to repair (or may not be repairable). It is also possible that the cable itself will stop working or only work when you hold the cable in place. If this happens, try a new cable, and if that fixes the problem, throw the old one away. If it does not fix the problem, it may be the connector on the board. Fortunately, extra care when plugging and unplugging the cable can avoid these issues. For example, always plug the micro USB side first and use the full-sized USB end to plug and unplug from your PC. The fewer times you use the micro USB connector, the less chance you have of damaging it.

Now, let's get started on our very first MicroPython project!

Overview

In this chapter, we will design and build a MicroPython clock. We will use both an SPI and I2C breakout board. We will use a small organic light-emitting diode (OLED) display that uses an SPI interface and a hardware-based real-time clock (RTC) that uses the DS1307 chip and a battery for keeping time while the project is turned off. Rather than simply connecting to a network time protocol (NTP) server on the Internet, we will use the hardware-based RTC and display the current date and time on the small OLED display. This not only keeps the project a bit smaller but also demonstrates how to use an RTC for projects that may not be connected to the Internet.

While the Pico has a hardware RTC, it must be initialized each time you connect the board to your PC (via Thonny or rshell), making it less than ideal for a project that you power on periodically. To make it possible for the Pico to know what time it is even after being powered off and on again without connecting to your PC, we will use an external RTC.

As you will see, there is a fair amount of wiring needed, and an understanding of the hardware capabilities is imperative to write the code, which is why we spent time in previous chapters talking about the firmware and various low-level hardware control. You will need those skills and knowledge to complete this project.

While a clock may sound rather simple, this project will walk you through all the steps needed to assemble the hardware and write the code. Further, the project is small and simplistic, so we can focus on the process, which we can then apply to more advanced projects. In fact, we will see that even a relatively simple project can have an unexpected level of difficulty. But don't worry, as this chapter documents all the things you need to do to complete the project.

The sources for this project are many. The following links include background data used for this project, including documentation and links to the MicroPython library (also called a driver) we will need to download for this project:

- *OLED display information*: `https://learn.adafruit.com/monochrome-oled-breakouts/wiring-128x32-spi-oled-display`

- *OLED display library*: https://github.com/adafruit/micropython-adafruit-ssd1306

- *RTC breakout board documentation*: https://learn.adafruit.com/ds1307-real-time-clock-breakout-board-kit

- *RTC library*: https://github.com/adafruit/Adafruit-uRTC

Note   The Adafruit MicroPython libraries are marked as deprecated, which only means no one is actively maintaining them; however, they will work with your Pico board without modification.

Notice the sites used. A good practice is to start with the Adafruit and MicroPython learning, blobs, and forums. Then check out the libraries. That is, do the research first and find all the references you can. If you find nice tutorials like those from Adafruit or SparkFun, you may want to download them to your PC or tablet or print them out for later reading. More importantly, take the time to read the references so that you understand as much as you can before you start working with the hardware or writing your code. You can save yourself a lot of time by understanding simple things like how to wire your board to the device and how the library is expected to be used.

WHICH LIBRARY DO I USE?

You may encounter a situation where you find more than one library for the hardware you want to use. In fact, I found several libraries for the OLED display. The differences among them are subtle, and it appears at least one does not support text, another is written for a specific platform, and another is written in C++ for the Pico.

The one listed earlier is the best one to use. Even so, it needs some minor changes for use. I will show you those changes, and, as you will see, they are not too difficult to spot and fix (e.g., when MicroPython throws exceptions, it will show you the source of the issue).

If you encounter a comparable situation – having more than one library to choose from – you may want to try each until you find one that works best for your hardware and project. Sometimes, and in this case it is true, one library may not be viable, or another may be lacking features you need. The trick is to find the library that works best with the least amount of modification.

Now let's see what components are needed for this project, then we will see how to wire everything together.

Required Components

Table 8-1 lists the components you will need in addition to your Pico board. You can purchase the components separately from Adafruit (`adafruit.com`), SparkFun (`sparkfun.com`), or any electronics store that carries electronic components. Links to vendors are provided should you want to purchase the components. When listing multiple rows of the same object, you can choose one or the other – you do not need both. Also, you may find other vendors that sell the components. You should shop around to find the best deal. Costs shown are estimates and do not include any shipping costs.

Table 8-1. *Required Components*

Component	Qty	Description	Cost	Links
OLED display	1	ssd1306-based SPI display	$17.5	www.adafruit.com/product/661
RTC breakout board	1	RTC module with battery backup	$15.95	www.sparkfun.com/products/12708
			$7.50	www.adafruit.com/product/3296
Breadboard	1	Prototyping board, full-sized	$5.95	www.sparkfun.com/products/12615
			$5.95	www.adafruit.com/product/239
Jumper wires	11	M/M jumper wires, 7" (set of 30)	$2.25	www.sparkfun.com/products/9838
		M/M jumper wires, 6" (set of 20)	$1.95	www.adafruit.com/product/1950
Coin cell battery	1	CR1225 (SparkFun RTC)	$1.95	www.sparkfun.com/products/337
		CR1220 (Adafruit RTC)	$0.95	www.adafruit.com/product/380

The OLED breakout board used in this project is a small module from Adafruit. It has a tiny but bright display that you can mount on the breadboard. The resolution is 128 pixels wide by 32 pixels high. The OLED breakout board comes without headers installed, but they are easy to add if you know how to solder (now might be a fun time to practice), or you can get a friend to help you. Figure 8-1 shows the Adafruit OLED SPI breakout board.

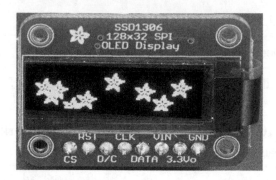

Figure 8-1. *Monochrome 128x32 SPI OLED Graphic Display (Courtesy of adafruit.com)*

There are several OLED breakout boards available, and so long as they have the SPI interface and use the ssd1306 controller chip (the description will tell you this), you can use an alternate OLED display. The reason we need to use one with that controller chip is because the library is written for that controller. Other controller chips will require a different library.

The RTC breakout board used in this project is a DS1307 breakout board from Adafruit. The board also comes without headers installed (but includes them), nor does it come with a battery, so you must purchase a CR1220 coin cell battery. Adafruit has those as well if you want to save yourself a trip to the store. Figure 8-2 shows the RTC breakout board.

Figure 8-2. *DS1307 Real-Time Clock Assembled Breakout Board (Courtesy of adafruit.com)*

There are several DS1307 RTC clocks available. In fact, SparkFun has one or you can build your own! See the sidebar, "Building Your Own RTC Module," for more details. Fortunately, the library we will use supports breakout boards with DS1307, DS3231, or PCF8523 RTC chips.

Tip   Small, discrete components like LEDs, resistors, etc., and even jumper wires and breadboards can be found in the kits mentioned in Chapter 2 – the Adafruit Parts Pal (www.adafruit.com/product/2975) or the SparkFun Beginner Parts Kit (www.sparkfun.com/products/13973). I recommend one of these kits.

Now, let's see how to wire the components together.

Set Up the Hardware

This project has a lot of connections. There are seven needed for the OLED and four needed for the RTC. To help keep things easier, we will plan for how things should connect. We will use a full-sized breadboard to mount the breakout boards, making the connections easier. We will use male/male jumper wires to make these connections via a breadboard.

We will see how to make the connections for both the Raspberry Pi Pico and the Arduino Nano RP2040 Connect. As you will see, the connections are similar in that you will wire the breakout boards with the same connections and number of wires, but where those wires connect to the board differs. Let's begin with the Pico.

Connections for the Raspberry Pi Pico

But first, we will learn what connections are needed for each component and where they need to be connected to our board, writing them down to keep things straight. Doing this small amount of homework will save you time later (and a small bit frustration).

As you will see, mapping out the connections like this makes it easy to check the connections. This table along with a wiring drawing is the tool you will see in this book and other example projects on the Internet or elsewhere. Thus, learning how to read maps and wiring drawings is a skill you should have to make your project successful.

Table 8-2 shows the connections needed for this project. Traditionally, we use black for ground (negative), red for power (positive) at a minimum, but you can use whatever color wires you want. We will start with physical pin 40 and work our way down to the lowest number pin used. As you will see in the drawing, this is working clockwise.

Table 8-2. *Connections for the MicroPython Clock (Pico)*

Physical Pin	GPIO Num/Function	Breakout Board	Pin Label
40	VBUS	RTC	VCC
37	GND	RTC	GND
37	GND	OLED	GND
26	GP20	OLED	RST
25	GP19	OLED	DATA
24	GP18	OLED	CLK
22	GP17	OLED	D/C
21	GP16	OLED	CS
10	GP9	RTC	SCL
9	GP8	RTC	SDA

Wow, that's a lot of connections! As we saw in Chapter 5, a breadboard allows us to plug our components in and use jumper wires to make the connections. This simplifies wiring the project and allows you to move things around if you need to make more room.

When plugging in components, always make sure the pins are mounted parallel to the center channel. Recall breadboards have the pins wired together in rows perpendicular to the center channel. This allows you to make more than one connection to the component (or pin on the board).

Caution   Never plug or unplug jumper wires when the project is powered on.

Finally, always make sure you wire your project carefully, double-checking all the connections – especially power, ground, and any pins used for signaling (will be set to "high" or "on"), such as those pins used for SPI interfaces. Most importantly, never plug or unplug jumper wires when the project (or your board) is powered on. This will very likely damage your board or components.

For this project, I mounted the Pico on the left side of the breadboard with the OLED in the center above the center channel and the RTC module on the right below the channel. Notice the RTC board uses a different power connection. The OLED board uses 3.3V and the RTC board 5V. Always check the power requirements of your components before powering on the project. Double-check and triple-check your connections.

If you chose a different RTC board than the one shown in the drawing, be sure to adjust the connections as needed. For example, the SparkFun DS1307 breakout board has the pins in a different order, so don't go by this drawing alone – especially if you use alternative components!

Figure 8-3 shows the wiring drawing for the MicroPython clock project. Notice that the image shows the Raspberry Pi Pico, but you can substitute the Raspberry Pi Pico W without any changes.

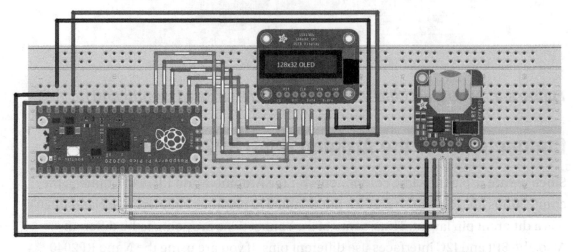

Figure 8-3. *Wiring the Clock Project (Pico on a Full-Sized Breadboard)*

If you do not have a full-sized breadboard, you can use two of the more popular half-sized breadboards and clip them together. If you look closely, you will see nubs on two sides and corresponding notches on the other.

Note   While you can use a half-sized breadboard for most of the projects in this book, a full-sized breadboard is a bit easier to use.

If you'd rather use a single half-sized breadboard, you can, but the wiring will get a bit complex as shown in Figure 8-4.

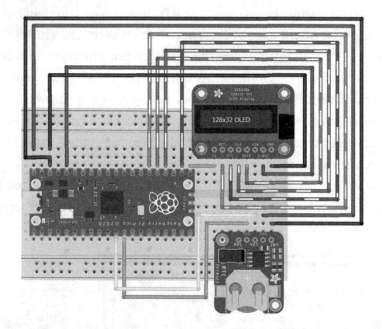

Figure 8-4.   *Wiring the Clock Project (Pico on a Half-Sized Breadboard)*

Connections for the Arduino Nano RP2040 Connect

Since we are using the same components for the Arduino Nano RP2040 Connect, the connections are going to be similar, but as noted in previous chapters, the Nano RP2040 has a different pin layout. Thus, some of the connections are going to be different. Also, the SPI and I2C interfaces use different pins. If you are using the Nano RP2040 for this project, double-check the connections as shown in Table 8-3 to ensure you are connecting everything correctly.

Table 8-3. *Connections for the MicroPython Clock (Nano RP2040)*

Physical Pin	GPIO Num/Function	Breakout Board	Pin Label
12	5V	RTC	5V
14	GND	RTC	GND
19	GND	OLED	GND
26	GP20	OLED	RST
29	MOSI/COPI	OLED	DATA
1	SCK	OLED	CLK
23	GP17	OLED	D/C
22	GP16	OLED	CS
9	SCL	RTC	SCL
8	SDA	RTC	SDA

Caution   Always double- and triple-check your connections, especially all power and ground connections. Be sure to examine the power connections to ensure the correct power (3V or 5V) is being connected to the components correctly. Connecting the wrong voltage can damage the component.

Figure 8-5 shows the wiring diagram for this project using the Arduino Nano RP2040 Connect instead of the Raspberry Pi Pico. Since the Nano RP2040 is a bit shorter than the Pico, there is a bit more room to work on the half-sized breadboard.

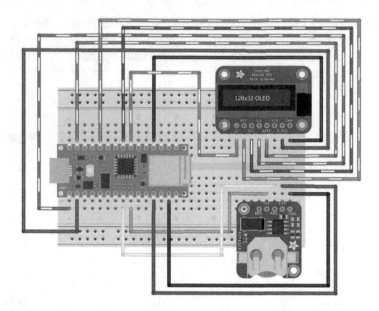

Figure 8-5. *Wiring the Clock Project (Nano RP2040 on a Half-Sized Breadboard)*

Enabling the 5V Pin on the Arduino Nano RP2040 Connect

The Arduino Nano RP2040 Connect comes with the 5V pin disabled. This is a cautionary measure since fewer breakout boards and components use 5V (most are 3.3V). Since this project and many others in this book use 5V, we need to enable the pin. Fortunately, we can do so with a jumper located on the bottom of the board as shown in Figure 8-6.

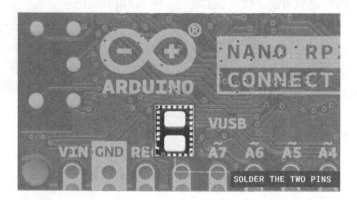

Figure 8-6. *5V Pin Enable Jumper on the Bottom of Nano RP2040 (Courtesy of arduino.cc)*

Unfortunately, the jumper is comprised of two surface mount solder pads. You will need to solder each pad, then bridge the pads with solder. If you do not know how to solder, this is a wonderful time to learn!

Once again, always make sure to double-check your connections before powering the board on. Now, let's talk about the code we need to write. Don't power on your board just yet – there is a fair amount of discussion needed before we're ready to test the project.

Write the Code

Now it's time to write the code for our project. While there are some minor differences that will be noted between the GPIO pins used for the Pico vs. the Nano RP2040, the code is the same for both boards. The code differences are isolated into a few lines that will be identified as we proceed.

Note   Unless otherwise stated or identified, the code presented works on both the Pico and Nano RP2040.

Since we are working with several new components, I will introduce the code for each in turn. The code isn't overly complicated but may not be as clear as some of the code from previous projects. Let's begin with a look at the design of the project.

Design

Once you have the hardware sorted out and how to connect the components to your board, it is time to start designing the code. Fortunately, this project is small enough to make the design simple. In short, we want to display the time on our OLED once every second. Thus, the "work" of the code is to read the date and time from the RTC and then display it on the OLED. The following lists the steps that summarize how to design and implement the code for this project or any project for that matter:

- *Libraries*: We will need to select and import libraries for the RTC and OLED.

- *Setup*: We will need to set up the interfaces for I2C and SPI.

- *Initialize*: We will need to initialize object instances for the classes in the libraries.

- *New functions*: We will write some helper functions to better organize the code.

- *Core code*: We will write the core code for the project.

- *Test the breakout boards*: We will take an extra step to test each breakout board separately before trying to execute the entire code.

- *Copy to the board*: Name the file `main.py` (or whatever you'd like) and copy the file to the board.

These elements are what we will use for most of the projects in this book, and, indeed, it is a good pattern to follow for all your MicroPython projects. The new function step allows us to wrap the operational portion of the code in a separate function to make it easy to call from the main function. We'll see more about this later when we execute and test the project.

Now that we know how the project code will be implemented, let's review the libraries needed.

Libraries Needed

Recalling from earlier, we need two libraries: one for the OLED display and another for the RTC. The library for the OLED display is found at `https://github.com/adafruit/micropython-adafruit-ssd1306`, and the library for the RTC can be found at `https://github.com/peter-l5/DS1307/tree/main`.

Go ahead and download both libraries now. You should be able to go to the sites and click the *Clone* or *Download* link and then the *Download Zip* button to download the files to your PC. Then, open the location of the downloaded files and unzip them. You should find the following files:

- `ssd1306.py`: The OLED display library

- `ds1307.py`: The RTC library

Ordinarily, we would create a new folder for each project we want to place on our board, but since we will be making this project run on the board when it is booted (powered on), the main code file will have to be named `main.py` and placed in the root folder. However, you can name the file whatever you'd like.

However, we will be creating a new folder to place the library files (drivers) for the breakout boards. Once you have your Pico connected, create a new folder named `project1` in the root folder by right-clicking the Pico in Thonny and select `New directory`.... Then, double-click the `project1` folder on the Pico and upload the library files to that folder. You should see a folder structure and file list similar to Figure 8-7.

Figure 8-7. *New Project Folder and Files (Thonny)*

Now that we have the libraries copied, let's look at the code we will need to write.

Planning the Code

Now that we have our design and have downloaded and modified the libraries, we can begin writing the code. Rather than show you a long listing and say, "comprehend or perish," let's walk through all the parts of the code first so that we understand each part. As we walk through the code, feel free to test the parts yourself, but if you prefer to wait until the end to test the code, you can. Some of this will be familiar and perhaps rudimentary to those who've worked with the examples so far in this book, but a little refresher never hurts. Let's begin with a look at the imports section.

Imports

The imports section for the project comes before all other statements but after the comment block at the top of the file. You should also include some level of documentation at the top of the file to explain what the code does. You don't have to write a lengthy tutorial – just a short statement or so that describes the program, including your name and other information. This is important if you want to share your code with others and if you ever go back to the code later to reuse it.

If you want to type in the code as we go along, you can open a new file named main. py on your PC with Thonny or your favorite code (or text) editor. We will copy the file to the Pico in a later step.

The following shows the imports for this project:

```
# Import libraries
from project1.ds1307 import DS1307
from project1.ssd1306 import SSD1306_SPI
from utime import sleep
from machine import SPI, Pin, SoftI2C
```

Notice we specified project1 in the first two imports because we placed these libraries (drivers) in the project1 folder. The main.py file will be copied to the root of the Pico file system. Also, we use the SoftI2C library instead of I2C because the ds1307 library doesn't work well with the I2C library.

Setup

Next, we need to set up the interfaces for I2C and SPI for use in the ds1307 and ssd1306 libraries. That is, the classes in those libraries need object instances of the interfaces passed to the constructor. The code we will use is like the code we saw in previous examples. The following shows the interface setup code:

```
#
# I2C for the RTC
# Arduino Nano RP2040 Connect uses sda=12, scl=13
#sda = Pin(12)
#scl = Pin(13)
#
```

```
# Raspberry Pi Pico uses sda=8, scl=9
sda = Pin(8)
scl = Pin(9)
#
# Software I2C (bit-banging) for the RTC
i2c = SoftI2C(sda=sda, scl=scl, freq=100000)
#
# SPI for the OLED
#
# Arduino Nano RP2040 Connect uses mosi=7, sck=6
#spi = SPI(0, 100000, mosi=Pin(7), sck=Pin(6))
#
# Raspberry Pi Pico uses mosi=18, sck=18
spi = SPI(0, 100000, mosi=Pin(19), sck=Pin(18))
#
```

Notice we use different parameters for the SPI, and we specify pins for the I2C. You can use other pins if you'd like, but just remember to use the correct pins when you wire the components together.

Notice also that we have comments that designate differences between the Pico and Nano RP2040. To use the correct code, simply comment out (place a # on the line to the left of the code) what you do not need. For the Pico, I2C uses pins 8 and 9 for SDA and SCL, and for SPI, the Pico uses 19 and 18 for MOSI and SCK. Conversely, the Nano RP2040 uses pins 12 and 13 for I2C and 7 and 6 for SPI. Those are the only changes needed for this project to run on either board.

Initialize

Next, we initialize object instances for the classes in the libraries. This is the point where you need to read the documentation for each library to understand what is needed to initialize the objects. For the ssd1306 library, the class constructor requires the number pixels (resolution is number of pixels in rows, columns) for the display, the interface instance (SPI from the last section), and the pins we will use for the D/C, RST, and CS pins. For the RTC library, we need only pass in interface instance (SoftI2C from the last section). The following shows how to do both steps:

```
# Initialize class instance variables for RTC, OLED
rtc = DS1307(i2c)
# (year, month, day, hours, minutes, seconds, weekday: integer: 0-6 )
# rtc.datetime = (2023,09,11,16,15,30,2)
oled = SSD1306_SPI(128, 32, spi, dc=Pin(17), res=Pin(20), cs=Pin(16))
```

Note   This code is not in error. We will be using the same pins for DC, RES, and CS for both the Pico and Nano RP2040.

Notice there are some commented out lines in there. When we first use the RTC or when we replace the battery, we must initialize the date and time. We can use the library features to do this. In this case, we simply call the datetime function, which is written to accept a tuple (instead of calling the function using parameters) for the RTC instance assigning a tuple containing the new start date and time – the order of the tuple elements are shown as follows. Once set, we do not need to run it again. In fact, running it again will reset the RTC, and we don't need to do that. Thus, we leave this code commented out for normal operation and uncomment it when we need to reset the RTC. When you run your project for the first time, uncomment this code supplying the correct current date and time, but later comment it out.

New Helper Functions

Now that all the setup and initialization code have been figured out, we can create a few helper functions to allow us to organize the code.

Recall we want the project to read the date and time from the RTC and display it on the OLED once every second. Thus, we expect to see some sort of loop that performs these two steps. However, we must again refer to the library documentation where we find that the RTC returns data as a tuple (year, month, day, weekday, hour, minute, second, millisecond). This means we must format the date and time to make it easier for humans to read and to fit on the small OLED screen. This is a perfect candidate for a helper function.

Let's create a function named `write_time()` that takes an instance of the OLED display and the RTC, then read the date and time with the `datetime()` function (with no parameters) and print it to the OLED screen using the `text()` function, which takes a starting column (called the X position in the documentation) and row (Y position) for the location on the screen to print the message when the `show()` function is called. This is the essence of the project. Placing it in a separate function allows you to isolate the behavior and make it easier to maintain or modify the code – because the "core" is in one place.

```
# Display the date and time
def write_time(oled, rtc):
    # Get datetime
    dt = rtc.datetime
    # Print the date
    oled.text("Date: {0:02}/{1:02}/{2:04}".format(dt[1], dt[2], dt[0]),
              0, 0)
    # Print the time
    oled.text("Time: {0:02}:{1:02}:{2:02}".format(dt[3], dt[4], dt[5]),
              0, 10)
    # Print the day of the week
    oled.text("Day:  {0}".format(get_weekday(dt[6])), 0, 20)
    # Update the OLED
    oled.show()
```

Notice we use the `text()` function and the `format()` function to take the data from the RTC and format it in an expected format that most clocks use: `HH:MM::SS` and `MM/DD/YYYY`. Notice there is an additional function here named `get_weekday()`. This function takes the number of the day of the week as returned from the RTC and returns a string for the name of the day. The following shows the code for this function:

```
# Return a string to print the day of the week
def get_weekday(day):
    if day == 1: return "Sunday"
    elif day == 2: return "Monday"
    elif day == 3: return "Tuesday"
    elif day == 4: return "Wednesday"
```

```
    elif day == 5: return "Thursday"
    elif day == 6: return "Friday"
    else: return "Saturday"
```

There is one more function added – a function to clear the screen. This function simply blanks the screen to allow us to overwrite the screen with new data. Normally, this is not needed, but it is a good practice to clear the screen in case the library doesn't do it for you. In this case, it does now. This function is named `clear_screen()` and is shown as follows. It simply uses the `fill()` and `show()` functions from the ssd1306 library. Passing in 0 for the `fill()` function tells the library to fill the screen with no data (blank or off).

```
# Clear the screen
def clear_screen(oled):
    oled.fill(0)
    oled.show()
```

Core Code

Now we are ready to code the new `main()` function for the project. We have our helper functions developed, so we need only call them and wait for a second on each pass. We will use a `main()` function so that when the script is executed (the name check will fail if the code is imported from another script), the `main()` function is called. We do this with the following code:

```
if __name__ == '__main__':
    try:
        main()
    except (KeyboardInterrupt, SystemExit) as err:
        print("\nbye!")
        sys.exit(0)
```

We use a `try...except` block so that we can capture the keyboard interrupt (*CTRL+C*) so that we can stop it. This construct is typical of how we would write scripts that are intended to be executed.

Recall, when a Python script is loaded (read), each line of code is executed. If we place all of our code in functions (or a class), we need some way to start execution in a controlled manner. The preceding code accomplishes this task, and we will use it in all of our projects. It does not matter what you call the function for the core code, but main is a common practice.

Next, we can create the main() function. The following shows the function with the setup and initialization code discussed earlier:

```python
def main():
    #
    # I2C for the RTC
    # Arduino Nano RP2040 Connect uses sda=12, scl=13
    sda = Pin(12)
    scl = Pin(13)
    #
    # Raspberry Pi Pico uses sda=8, scl=9
    #sda = Pin(8)
    #scl = Pin(9)
    #
    # Software I2C (bit-banging) for the RTC
    i2c = SoftI2C(sda=sda, scl=scl, freq=100000)
    #
    # SPI for the OLED
    #
    # Arduino Nano RP2040 Connect uses mosi=7, sck=6
    spi = SPI(0, 100000, mosi=Pin(7), sck=Pin(6))
    #
    # Raspberry Pi Pico uses mosi=18, sck=18
    #spi = SPI(0, 100000, mosi=Pin(19), sck=Pin(18))
    #
    # Initialize class instance variables for RTC, OLED
    rtc = DS1307(i2c)
    # (year, month, day, hours, minutes, seconds, weekday: integer: 0-6 )
    # rtc.datetime = (2023,09,11,16,15,30,2)
    oled = SSD1306_SPI(128, 32, spi, dc=Pin(17), res=Pin(20), cs=Pin(16))
```

```
for i in range(10):
    clear_screen(oled)
    write_time(oled, rtc)
    sleep(1)
```

Notice how "clean" this function is – we can see only three statements: clear the screen, show the time, and wait for one second.

Let's put this code together with the imports section and the helper functions. Listing 8-1 shows the complete code for the main.py file.

Listing 8-1. Completed Code for the MicroPython Clock (main.py)

```
#
# MicroPython for the IoT Second Edition - Chapter 8
#
# Chapter 08 - Digital Timepiece
#
# This example uses an I2C real time clock (RTC) to store the current
# date and time. It displays the time, date, and day of the week on
# an SPI OLED.
#
# Dr. Charles Bell
#
# Import libraries
from project1.ds1307 import DS1307
from project1.ssd1306 import SSD1306_SPI
from utime import sleep
from machine import SPI, Pin, SoftI2C

# Return a string to print the day of the week
def get_weekday(day):
    if day == 1: return "Sunday"
    elif day == 2: return "Monday"
    elif day == 3: return "Tuesday"
    elif day == 4: return "Wednesday"
    elif day == 5: return "Thursday"
    elif day == 6: return "Friday"
    else: return "Saturday"
```

```python
# Display the date and time
def write_time(oled, rtc):
    # Get datetime
    dt = rtc.datetime
    # Print the date
    oled.text("Date: {0:02}/{1:02}/{2:04}".format(dt[1], dt[2],
    dt[0]), 0, 0)
    # Print the time
    oled.text("Time: {0:02}:{1:02}:{2:02}".format(dt[3], dt[4],
    dt[5]), 0, 10)
    # Print the day of the week
    oled.text("Day:  {0}".format(get_weekday(dt[6])), 0, 20)
    # Update the OLED
    oled.show()

# Clear the screen
def clear_screen(oled):
    oled.fill(0)
    oled.show()

def main():
    #
    # I2C for the RTC
    # Arduino Nano RP2040 Connect uses sda=12, scl=13
    sda = Pin(12)
    scl = Pin(13)
    #
    # Raspberry Pi Pico uses sda=8, scl=9
    #sda = Pin(8)
    #scl = Pin(9)
    #
    # Software I2C (bit-banging) for the RTC
    i2c = SoftI2C(sda=sda, scl=scl, freq=100000)
    #
    # SPI for the OLED
    #
```

```python
    # Arduino Nano RP2040 Connect uses mosi=7, sck=6
    spi = SPI(0, 100000, mosi=Pin(7), sck=Pin(6))
    #
    # Raspberry Pi Pico uses mosi=18, sck=18
    #spi = SPI(0, 100000, mosi=Pin(19), sck=Pin(18))
    #
    # Initialize class instance variables for RTC, OLED
    rtc = DS1307(i2c)
    # (year, month, day, hours, minutes, seconds, weekday: integer: 0-6 )
    # rtc.datetime = (2023,09,11,16,15,30,2)
    oled = SSD1306_SPI(128, 32, spi, dc=Pin(17), res=Pin(20), cs=Pin(16))
    for i in range(10):
        clear_screen(oled)
        write_time(oled, rtc)
        sleep(1)

if __name__ == '__main__':
    try:
        main()
    except (KeyboardInterrupt, SystemExit) as err:
        print("\nbye!")
        sys.exit(0)
```

Take some time to read the code so you can see how it is organized. We will use this as a template in future projects. You can save it to your PC, but don't execute it on the Pico yet because we need to test the code for the breakout boards.

Test the Breakout Boards

Now that we have planned the code and know how to code each of the parts, we have one more thing to do – test the breakout boards separately. We do this by wiring one breakout board and testing it, then powering off and unwiring that breakout board, and then wiring the other breakout board and testing it.

This is a good practice to get into the habit of doing for one primary reason. You will save yourself a lot of grief by testing the individual parts of the project – especially the hardware – one at a time. This not only makes it easier to narrow down any issues, but it also ensures you can identify the source of the problem. That is, if you plugged all the hardware in and wired everything and wrote the code, deployed it, then powered it on, and nothing works, how do you know which part is to blame? This is one of my mantras: build and test one piece at a time.

Tip   Testing code one part at a time is a familiar pattern to me, and it is highly recommended you adopt the process yourself. That is, coding a part of the project at a time and testing each individually.

For this project, there are two parts – the RTC and the OLED. Let's see how to test them individually. The code presented is intended to be run via a REPL console via Thonny.

Test the RTC Breakout Board

To test the RTC, use the following code. Listing 8-2 is a condensed form of the code we saw in Listing 8-1 with only the bare minimum code added. You can name this file test_ rtc.py if you'd like to save it, but we will execute the code via the REPL console. You will also notice we included the code for both boards, so be sure to comment out and uncomment out the ones you need for whichever board you are using.

Listing 8-2. Test Code for the RTC Breakout Board (test_rtc.py)

```
#
# MicroPython for the IoT Second Edition - Chapter 8
#
# Chapter 08 - Digital Timepiece
#
from project1.ds1307 import DS1307
from utime import sleep
from machine import Pin, SoftI2C

#
# I2C for the RTC
# Arduino Nano RP2040 Connect uses sda=12, scl=13
#sda = Pin(12)
#scl = Pin(13)
```

```
#
# Raspberry Pi Pico uses sda=8, scl=9
sda = Pin(8)
scl = Pin(9)
#
# Software I2C (bit-banging) for the RTC
i2c = SoftI2C(sda=sda, scl=scl, freq=100000)
rtc = DS1307(i2c)
# (year, month, day, hours. minutes, seconds, weekday: integer: 0-6 )
rtc.datetime = (2023,09,11,16,15,30,2)
for i in range(0,10):
    # Get datetime
    dt = rtc.datetime
    print("\nTest:", i+1)
    # Print the date
    print("Date: {0:02}/{1:02}/{2:04}".format(dt[1], dt[2], dt[0]))
    # Print the time
    print("Time: {0:02}:{1:02}:{2:02}".format(dt[3], dt[4], dt[5]))
    sleep(3)
```

Notice we set the date and time for this test. When you run this for yourself, you should change the date and time tuple to include the current date and time when you run the test. What you should see in the REPL console is a tuple representing the date and time. It should be the same as what you set since the code will execute much less than a second from the time you set it to the time you query the RTC. Go ahead and reenter that last statement several times to ensure the time changes as you'd expect. That is, wait a few seconds and try it again – several seconds should have elapsed. Listing 8-3 shows what the output should look like for a successful test.

Listing 8-3. Test RTC Output

```
Test: 1
Date: 09/11/2023
Time: 16:15:30

Test: 2
Date: 09/11/2023
Time: 16:15:30
```

Test: 3
Date: 09/11/2023
Time: 16:15:30

Test: 4
Date: 09/11/2023
Time: 16:15:30

Test: 5
Date: 09/11/2023
Time: 16:15:30

Test: 6
Date: 09/11/2023
Time: 16:15:30

Test: 7
Date: 09/11/2023
Time: 16:15:30

Test: 8
Date: 09/11/2023
Time: 16:15:30

Test: 9
Date: 09/11/2023
Time: 16:15:30

Test: 10
Date: 09/11/2023
Time: 16:15:30

If any of the statements fail, be sure to check your wiring and look for any typos. Also, ensure you are using the correct, modified version of the libraries (and that you have copied them to the board).

Test the OLED Breakout Board

To test the OLED, use the following code. Listing 8-4 is a condensed form of the code we saw in Listing 8-1 with only the bare minimum code added. You can name this file test_oled.py if you'd like to save it, but we will execute the code via the REPL console. You will also notice we included the code for both boards, so be sure to comment out and uncomment out the ones you need for whichever board you are using.

Listing 8-4. Test Code for the OLED Breakout Board (test_oled.py)

```
#
# MicroPython for the IoT Second Edition - Chapter 8
#
# Chapter 08 - Digital Timepiece
#
from project1.ssd1306 import SSD1306_SPI
from machine import Pin, SPI
from utime import sleep_ms

#
# SPI for the OLED
#
# Arduino Nano RP2040 Connect uses mosi=7, sck=6
#spi = SPI(0, 100000, mosi=Pin(7), sck=Pin(6))
#
# Raspberry Pi Pico uses mosi=18, sck=18
spi = SPI(0, 100000, mosi=Pin(19), sck=Pin(18))
#
oled = SSD1306_SPI(128, 32, spi, dc=Pin(17), res=Pin(20), cs=Pin(16))
for i in range(40):
    for j in range(32):
        oled.fill(0)
        oled.show()
        oled.text("HELLO WORLD",i,j)
        oled.show()
        sleep_ms(100)
```

When you run this code, you should see the screen blank (it should be blank from the start), then display the hello message in various places in the range of the OLED screen, and may "scroll" off the screen (can you spot why?).

If you do not see any output, power off your board and check all the connections, verifying the correct pins are used, and that you have the correct modified version of the library copied to your board.

Tip   The OLED breakout boards from Adafruit (and presumably others) come with a protective cover over the lens. You can and should leave that in place to ensure the lens does not get damaged. Plus, the OLED is bright enough to see through the protective cover.

OK, now we're ready to execute and test the completed project.

Execute

We are finally at the point where we can copy all the files to our board and execute the project code. There are several recommended steps in this process as shown in the following. You should follow this process each time you want to deploy and test a project:

1. Double-check all hardware connections (wiring).

2. Connect your Pico to your PC.

3. Copy the libraries and code file to the board.

4. Test the code, fix any issues found, and recopy the file(s) if needed.

5. Disconnect and reconnect the board.

The first step cannot be overstated. Always check your wiring connections every time before you power on the board. This is in case curious hands have wandered by and "examined" your project or you've moved it, or some other event has occurred to unplug wires. It never hurts to be extra careful.

Next, we connect the board to our PC to power on the board and check for any issues. Yes, this is the smoke test! Simply make sure all LEDs that are supposed to illuminate do (like those on the board) and that things that should not be on are off.

For example, if you see a solid bar on the OLED when you power it on, that's not a good sign. If ever in doubt, disconnect the Pico and check your connections. If things still aren't right, disconnect everything and test your board. Sometimes, a damaged component can cause strange behavior.

Next, we copy all the libraries and code we want to use to the board. Recall, we copy the libraries for the RTC and OLED to a folder on the board named `project1` and copy the `main.py` file to the root folder on the board.

Caution   Be sure to uncomment out the lines to initialize the RTC on your first execution. You can comment them out immediately after your test!

At this point, the code isn't running, but we can execute it via Thonny. Simply click the Run button and watch your code run! If everything is connected correctly, and the code is correct, you will see the date and time appear on the OLED. You should see something like Figure 8-8, which shows the project running in all its glory.

Figure 8-8. *A MicroPython Clock!*

Notice in the figure I am using two half-sized breadboards connected together, which is the same size as a full-sized breadboard. Notice all of the wiring. If we used a single half-sized breadboard, the wiring would be a snaggle that could obscure the OLED. Ever the neat freak, I've zip tied the wiring so that it is out of the way.

If something doesn't work, go back, and check your code. If you left the two lines of code to initialize the RTC uncommented, you may see the same date and time appear each time you run the code. Be sure to comment those out on subsequent executions. Or, if you forgot to uncomment out those lines, you may see some strange date and time values.

It is at this point that you should bask in the wonder of your first successful MicroPython hardware project. Take some time to bask in your delight of a job well done.

However, we're not done. There's one more step. Disconnect your Pico and exit Thonny, then reconnect it to your PC to power it on again. If the date and time show up after a few seconds, you've done it! You have successfully created a project where you can package and run anywhere you want, and, so long as the coin cell battery has a charge, it won't lose time.

Taking It Further

This project has a lot of potential for embellishment. If you liked the project, you should consider taking time to explore some embellishments. Here are a few you may want to consider. Some are easy and some may be a challenge:

- Use a different RTC.

- Calculate AM/PM and display it.

- Use a larger display and display the Julian date.

- Use a light sensor to turn off the dim display in direct sunlight.

- Add a speaker and implement an alarm feature (hint: some RTCs have this feature).

- Format the date and time using different world standards such as YYYY/MM/DD.

Of course, if you want to press on to the next project, you're welcome to do so, but take some time to explore these potential embellishments – it will be good practice.

If you're thinking this project is rudimentary now that we have solved the problems with the libraries, consider this: most sensor-based projects and indeed most projects that generate data that must be associated with a date and time when the events are sampled. Thus, using an RTC to read the date and time will be a consideration for many IoT projects.

BUILDING YOUR OWN RTC MODULE

If you're like me and like to tinker, you can build your own RTC module using an RTC DS1307 chip, two resistors, a crystal, and a coin cell battery breakout board. You can find these components at most online electronics stores such as Adafruit (www.adafruit.com), SparkFun (www.sparkfun.com), and Mouser (www.mouser.com). The component list is as follows:

- DS1307 chip

- Coin cell battery breakout board

- 3V coin cell battery

- 32.768kHz crystal

- (2) 1K resistor

That's it! The following shows how to connect the components on a breadboard.

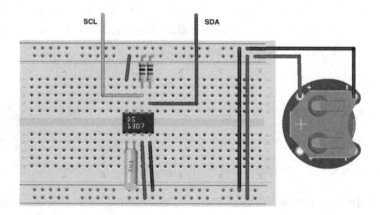

See www.learningaboutelectronics.com/Articles/DS1307-real-time-clock-RTC-circuit.php for an example walk-through for assembling this side project.

If you plan to build a lot of projects that use an RTC, buying these components in bulk and wiring up your own RTC 1307 module may be more cost effective. Plus, it ups the cool factor of your kit.

Summary

Working with hardware such as breakout boards and the libraries we need to talk to them over specialized interfaces such as I2C and SPI can be a challenge. Sometimes, like we saw in this chapter, you need the Soft version of the SPI or I2C libraries. The reason for this is the growing array of boards that vendors are creating specialized versions of the MicroPython firmware that may not work 100% with the Pico and Nano RP2040.

The trick then is understanding why the changes are necessary and taking the time to make the changes yourself. It is so easy to just give up when something doesn't work – don't do that! Take your time and understand the problem, then solve it systematically.

In this chapter, we saw a detailed walk-through of a MicroPython clock. We used an OLED display to display time we read from an RTC. Along the way, we learned how to plan our projects, make hardware connections, and write code for use in deploying on our Pico.

In the next chapter, we will explore a project that uses more low-level hardware in the form of discrete components, such as LEDs, resistors, and buttons. These are the building blocks you will need to form more complex solutions.

Project: Pedestrian Crossing

Now that we've had a tutorial of how to design, wire, and implement a MicroPython project, let's now look at a more advanced project. In this case, we will use some very basic components to learn further how to work with hardware. The hardware of choice for this project will be LEDs, resistors, and a button. A button is the most basic of sensors. That is, when the button is pressed, we can make our MicroPython code respond to that action.

Working with LEDs is perhaps more of a "Hello, World!" style project for hardware because turning LEDs on and off is easy, and except for figuring out what size of current limiting resistor is needed, wiring LEDs is also easy.

However, to make it more interesting and a bit of a challenge, we will be implementing a simulation. More specifically, we will implement a traffic light and a pedestrian walk button. The walk button is a button pedestrians can use to trigger the traffic signal to change and stop traffic, so they can cross the street.

Simulation projects can be a lot of fun because we already have an idea of how it should work and by simulating something we have encountered. For example, unless you've lived in a very rural area, you most likely have encountered a traffic signal at an intersection that included walk/don't walk signs with a button. If you live in the city, you will have encountered these in various configurations. When a pedestrian (or bicyclist) presses the walk button, the traffic lights all cycle to red, and the walk sign is illuminated. After some time (30 seconds or so), the walk sign flashes, and then about 15 seconds later, the walk signal cycles to don't walk, and the traffic signals resume their normal cycle.

Note The word "cycle" refers to a set of states that are linear in action. Thus, cycle refers to the changing of one state to another.

© Charles Bell 2024
C. Bell, *MicroPython for the Internet of Things*, https://doi.org/10.1007/978-1-4842-9861-9_9

Overview

In this chapter, we will implement a traffic signal with a pedestrian walk button. This project works with LEDs, which allows us to see the state of our code as it executes. For the traffic light (also called a stoplight), we will use red, yellow, and green LEDs to match the same colored lights on the traffic light. We will also use red and yellow LEDs to correspond to the don't walk (red) and walk (yellow) lights.

We will use a pushbutton (also called a momentary button) because it triggers (is on) only when pushed. When released, it is no longer triggered (is off). Trigger is the word used to describe the state of the button where triggered means the connections from one side of the button to another are connected (on). A button that remains triggered (latched) is called a latching button, which typically must be pressed again to turn off.

We will simulate the traffic light and walk signal by first turning on only the green traffic light LED and the red walk LED signal. This is the normal state we will use. When the button is pressed, the traffic light will cycle to yellow for a few seconds, then cycle to red. After a few seconds, the walk signal will cycle to yellow and after a few seconds will begin flashing. After a few more seconds, the walk signal will cycle back to red and the traffic light to green.

Now let's see what components are needed for this project, then we will see how to wire everything together.

Required Components

Table 9-1 lists the components you will need in addition to your MicroPython board and USB cable. Links to vendors are provided should you want to purchase the components. I include both value packages as well as single unit prices where available.

Table 9-1. *Required Components*

Component	Qty	Description	Cost	Links
Red LED	2	Pack of 25	$4.00	www.adafruit.com/product/299
		Single	$0.35	www.sparkfun.com/products/9590
Yellow LED	2	Pack of 25	$4.95	www.adafruit.com/product/2700
		Single	$0.35	www.sparkfun.com/products/9594
Green LED	1	Pack of 25	$4.00	www.adafruit.com/product/298
		Single	$0.35	www.sparkfun.com/products/9592
220 or 330 ohm resistors	5	Variety kit	$7.95	www.sparkfun.com/products/10969
		Pack of 25	$0.75	www.adafruit.com/product/2780
Button	1	Momentary button, breadboard friendly (pack)	$2.50	www.adafruit.com/product/1119
		Single	$0.50	www.sparkfun.com/products/9190
Breadboard	1	Prototyping board, full-sized	$5.95	www.sparkfun.com/products/12615
			$5.95	www.adafruit.com/product/239
Jumper wires	11	M/M jumper wires, 7" (set of 30)	$2.25	www.sparkfun.com/products/9838
		M/M jumper wires, 6" (set of 20)	$1.95	www.adafruit.com/product/1950

You can purchase the components separately from Adafruit (adafruit.com), SparkFun (sparkfun.com), or any electronics store that carries electronic components. Costs shown are estimates and do not include any shipping costs.

Some components such as the LEDs and button can be found in a beginning electronics kit like those from the Parts Pal kit from Adafruit that we saw in Chapter 2. Other vendors may have similar kits. Buying basic components like LEDs, buttons, and resistors is much cheaper when bought in a kit.

Similarly, you can pick up a set of resistors of various sizes much cheaper than if you bought a few at a time. In fact, you most likely will find buying a small set of five or ten of each size resistor you will eventually need will be far more expensive than if you purchased a set. The set from SparkFun will provide you all the resistors you need for most projects.

Recall from Chapter 7 that LEDs require a current limiting resistor that reduces the current to safe levels for the LED. To determine what size resistor we need, we need to know several things about the LED. This data is available from the manufacturer who provides the data in the form of a datasheet or, in the case of commercially packaged products, lists the data on the package. The data we need includes the maximum voltage, the supply voltage (how many volts are coming to the LED), and the current rating of the LED.

For example, if I have an LED like the ones in the Adafruit Parts Pal, in this case a 5mm red LED, we find on Adafruit's website (adafruit.com/products/297) that the LED operates at 1.8–2.2V and 20mA of current. Let's say we want to use this with a 5V supply voltage. We can then take these values and plug them into this formula:

```
R = (Vcc-Vf)/I
```

Using more descriptive names for the variable, we get the following:

```
Resistor = (Volts_supply - Volts_forward) / Desired_current
```

Plugging our data in, we get this result. Note that we have mA, so we must use the correct decimal value (divide by 1000). In this case, it is 0.020, and we will pick a voltage in the middle.

```
Resistor = (5 - 1.8) / 0.020
         = 3.2 / 0.020
         = 160
```

Thus, we need a resistor of 160 ohms. However, there is no resistor with that rating. When this happens, we use the next size up. For example, if you have only 220 or even 330 ohm resistors, you can use those. The result will be the LEDs will not be as bright, but having a higher resistor is much safer than using one that is too small. Too much current and an LED will burn out.

Now, let's see how to wire the components together.

Set Up the Hardware

Before we look at the wiring, let's review some tips for wiring components. The best way to wire components to your board is to use a breadboard. As we saw in Chapter 2, a breadboard allows us to plug our components in and use jumper wires to make the connections. In this project, we will use one jumper wire for ground from the Pico board to the breadboard power and ground rails (those that run along the top and bottom marked with a red line for power and blue or black for ground) and then jumpers on the breadboard to connect to the button. In fact, we will use the ground rail on one side of the breadboard to plug in one side of the LEDs.

The button works in either position so long as the pins are oriented with two legs on each side of the center trough. If you orient the button with the legs that can reach either side of the trough, it will be oriented correctly. If you get it off by 90 degrees, the button either will not work or will always be triggered. If you have any doubts, use a multimeter to test the continuity of the button connections. You should find the connections open when not pressed and closed when pressed.

The only component that is polarized is the LED (it has a positive and negative leg). When you look at the LED, you will see one leg (pin) of the LED is longer than the other. This longer side is the positive side. We will plug the LEDs in so that the negative leg is plugged into the ground rail and the positive side is plugged into the main area of the breadboard. We then plug the resistor in to jump over the center trough connecting the resistor to the GPIO pin on the board. It doesn't matter which direction you plug the resistor in – they will work both directions.

We will see how to make the connections for both the Raspberry Pi Pico and the Arduino Nano RP2040 Connect. As you will see, the connections are similar in that you will wire the breakout boards with the same connections and number of wires, but where those wires connect to the board differs. Let's begin with the Pico.

Connections for the Raspberry Pi Pico

Table 9-2 shows the connections needed for this project. Traditionally, we use black for ground (negative) and red for power (positive) at a minimum, but you can use whatever color wires you want. We will start with physical pin 40 and work our way down to the lowest number pin used. As you will see in the drawing, this is working clockwise.

Table 9-2. *Connections for the Pedestrian Crossing Simulation (Pico)*

Physical Pin	GPIO Num/Function	Connection
40	VBUS	Breadboard power (top)
37	GND	Breadboard ground (bottom)
17	GP13	Resistor for red LED (stoplight)
16	GP12	Resistor for yellow LED (stoplight)
15	GP11	Resistor for green LED (stoplight)
12	GP9	Button side B (bottom)
11	GP8	Resistor for red LED (walk light)
10	GP7	Resistor for green LED (walk light)
N/A	Breadboard power (top)	Button side A (bottom)
N/A	Breadboard ground	All LED negative side
N/A	Resistor	All LED positive side

Wow, that's a lot of connections! As we saw in Chapter 2, a breadboard allows us to plug our components in and use jumper wires to make the connections. This simplifies wiring the project and allows you to move things around if you need to make more room.

Figure 9-1 shows the wiring drawing for the project on the Pico.

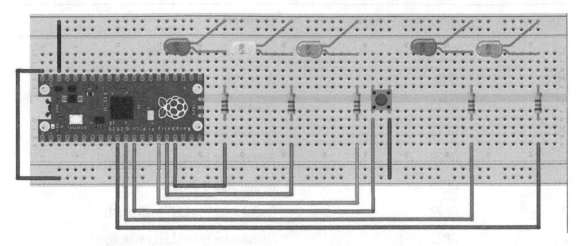

Figure 9-1. *Wiring the Pedestrian Crossing Project (Pico)*

Connections for the Arduino Nano RP2040 Connect

Since we are using the same components for the Arduino Nano RP2040 Connect, the connections are going to be similar, but as noted in previous chapters, the Nano RP2040 has a different pin layout. Thus, some of the connections are going to be different.

Table 9-3 shows the connections needed for this project. Traditionally, we use black for ground (negative) and red for power (positive) at a minimum, but you can use whatever color wires you want. We will start with physical pin 40 and work our way down to the lowest number pin used. As you will see in the drawing, this is working clockwise.

Table 9-3. *Connections for the Pedestrian Crossing Simulation (Nano RP2040)*

Physical Pin	GPIO Num/Function	Connection
12	5V	Breadboard power (top)
19	GND	Breadboard ground (bottom)
11	GP13	Resistor for red LED (stoplight)
10	GP12	Resistor for yellow LED (stoplight)
9	GP29	Resistor for green LED (stoplight)
20	GP25	Button side B (bottom)
7	GP27	Resistor for red LED (walk light)
6	GP27	Resistor for green LED (walk light)
N/A	Breadboard power (top)	Button side A (bottom)
N/A	Breadboard ground	All LED negative side
N/A	Resistor	All LED positive side

Notice most of the connections are the same. What differs is where the jumper wires connect to the board.

Figure 9-2 shows the wiring drawing for the project on the Nano RP2040.

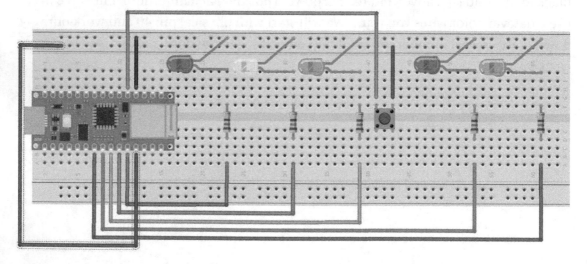

Figure 9-2. *Wiring the Pedestrian Crossing Project (Nano RP2040)*

Caution   Never plug or unplug jumper wires when the project is powered on. You risk damaging your board or the components.

Once again, always make sure to double-check your connections before powering the board on. Now, let's talk about the code we need to write. Don't power on your board just yet – there is a fair amount of discussion needed before we're ready to test the project.

Write the Code

Now it's time to write the code for our project. The code isn't overly complicated, but it is a bit longer than the examples thus far. We will see how to write code to simulate the pedestrian crosswalk button and traffic light. We will need to monitor the button and, when pressed, cycle the lights as described earlier. We also need code to initialize the LEDs, setting them to off initially. We can write functions for monitoring the button and cycling the LEDs. We will use an interrupt to tie the function for the button to the hardware so that we can avoid using a polling loop.

Imports

The imports for the project will require the `Pin` class from the machine library and the time library. The following shows the imports for the project:

```
from machine import Pin
import time
```

Setup

The setup code for this project will need to initialize the button and LED instances, then turn off all the LEDs (as a precaution), and turn on the green stoplight LED and the red walk signal LED. Listing 9-1 shows the code for setup and initialization. Notice we have two sets of pin setup: one for the Raspberry Pi Pico and another for the Arduino Nano RP2040 Connect. Be sure to uncomment the one that matches your board.

Listing 9-1. Setup and Initialization of the Button and LEDs

```
# Pins for the Arduino Nano RP2040 Connect
#stoplight_red = Pin(13, Pin.OUT)
#stoplight_yellow = Pin(12, Pin.OUT)
#stoplight_green = Pin(29, Pin.OUT)
#button = Pin(25, Pin.IN, Pin.PULL_DOWN)
#pedestrian_red = Pin(27, Pin.OUT)
#pedestrian_green = Pin(26, Pin.OUT)

# Pins for the Pico
stoplight_red = Pin(13, Pin.OUT)
stoplight_yellow = Pin(12, Pin.OUT)
stoplight_green = Pin(11, Pin.OUT)
button = Pin(9, Pin.IN, Pin.PULL_DOWN)
pedestrian_red = Pin(8, Pin.OUT)
pedestrian_green = Pin(7, Pin.OUT)

# Setup lists for the LEDs
stoplight = [stoplight_red, stoplight_yellow, stoplight_green]
pedestrian_signal = [pedestrian_red, pedestrian_green]

# Turn off the LEDs
for led in stoplight:
    led.off()
for led in pedestrian_signal:
    led.off()

# Start with green stoplight and red pedestrian_signal
stoplight[2].on()
pedestrian_signal[0].on()
```

One thing to notice is how the button is initialized. This is a Pin object instance that is set up as an input (read), and the pull-up resistors are turned on. This allows the board to detect when the button is pressed because the value of the pin will be a positive value when the connection is made (the button is pressed).

Notice also in the Arduino Nano RP2040 Connect section we use GPIO25. This is because we need a digital pin, and the pins on the same side as the LED connections are all analog pins.

Notice also I create a list that contains the LEDs for the stoplight and walk signal (named pedestrian_signal in the code). This is mostly for demonstration, so you can see how to manage lists of class objects. As you can see, it makes it easier to call the same function for all the objects in the list using a loop. Take note of this technique as you will need it from time to time in other projects.

Functions

There are two functions needed for this part of the project. First, we need a function to cycle through the lights. Second, we need a function to monitor the button press. Let's look at the cycle light function.

We will name the cycle light function cycle_lights(). Recall we need to control how the lights change state. We do this with a specific cycle as described earlier. To recap, we call this function when we want to simulate changing the stoplight when the walk request button is pressed. Thus, this function will be called from the code for the button. Listing 9-2 shows the code for the cycle_lights() button. As you will see, the code is rather straightforward. The only tricky part may be the loop used to flash the yellow walk LED. Be sure to read through it so that you understand how it works.

Listing 9-2. The cycle_lights() Function

```
# We need a method to cycle the stoplight and pedestrian_signal
#
# We toggle from green to yellow for 2 seconds
# then red for 20 seconds.
def cycle_lights():
    # Go yellow.
    stoplight[2].off()
    stoplight[1].on()
    # Wait 2 seconds
    utime.sleep(2)
    # Go red and turn on walk light
    stoplight[1].off()
```

```
stoplight[0].on()
utime.sleep_ms(500)  # Give the pedestrian a chance to see it
pedestrian_signal[0].off()
pedestrian_signal[1].on()
# After 10 seconds, start blinking the walk light
utime.sleep(1)
for i in range(0,10):
    pedestrian_signal[1].off()
    utime.sleep_ms(500)
    pedestrian_signal[1].on()
    utime.sleep_ms(500)

# Stop=green, walk=red
pedestrian_signal[1].off()
pedestrian_signal[0].on()
utime.sleep_ms(500)  # Give the pedestrian a chance to see it
stoplight[0].off()
stoplight[2].on()
```

We will name the button function button_pressed(). This function is used as a callback for the button press interrupt. Technically, we tell MicroPython to associate this method with the pin interrupt, but we will see that in a moment. However, there is another element to this function that requires explanation.

When we use a component like a button and the user (you) presses the button, the contacts in the button do not go from an off state to an on state instantaneously. There is a very small period where the value read is erratic. Thus, we cannot simply say "when the pin goes high" because the value read on the pin may "bounce" from low to high (or high to low) rapidly. This is called bouncing. We can overcome this artificially with code (as well as other techniques) – called debouncing.

In this case, we can check the value of the pin (button) over time and only "trigger" the button press if and only if the value remains stable during that time. The code for debouncing the pin is shown in Listing 9-3. Notice in the loop we wait for a value of 50. This is 50 milliseconds. If the trigger is long enough, we call the cycle_lights() function.

Listing 9-3. The button_pressed() Function

```
# Create callback for the button
def button_pressed(line):
    cur_value = button.value()
    active = 0
    while (active < 50):
        if button.value() != cur_value:
            active += 1
        else:
            active = 0
        utime.sleep_ms(1)
        print("")
    if active:
        cycle_lights()
    else:
        print("False press")
```

Tip   For more information about debouncing and the techniques available to avoid
it, see www.eng.utah.edu/~cs5780/debouncing.pdf.

Finally, we need to set up the button to call the button_pressed() function when the
board detects the interrupt. The following sets the callback function using the interrupt
setting for the button pin:

```
# Create an interrupt for the button
button.irq(trigger=Pin.IRQ_RISING, handler=button_pressed)
```

Now we're all set to test the code. Go ahead and open a new file named pedestrian_
crossing.py and enter the preceding code. Listing 9-4 shows the complete code for the
project.

Listing 9-4. Pedestrian Crossing Simulation Code

```
#
# MicroPython for the IoT Second Edition - Chapter 09
#
# Chapter 09 - Pedestrian Crosswalk
#
# This example implements a Pedestrian Crosswalk Simulator
# controlling LEDs and button as input
#
# Dr. Charles Bell
#
# Import libraries
from machine import Pin
import time

# Setup the button and LEDs

# Pins for the Arduino Nano RP2040 Connect
#stoplight_red = Pin(13, Pin.OUT)
#stoplight_yellow = Pin(12, Pin.OUT)
#stoplight_green = Pin(29, Pin.OUT)
#button = Pin(25, Pin.IN, Pin.PULL_DOWN)
#pedestrian_red = Pin(27, Pin.OUT)
#pedestrian_green = Pin(26, Pin.OUT)

# Pins for the Pico
stoplight_red = Pin(13, Pin.OUT)
stoplight_yellow = Pin(12, Pin.OUT)
stoplight_green = Pin(11, Pin.OUT)
button = Pin(9, Pin.IN, Pin.PULL_DOWN)
pedestrian_red = Pin(8, Pin.OUT)
pedestrian_green = Pin(7, Pin.OUT)

# Setup lists for the LEDs
stoplight = [stoplight_red, stoplight_yellow, stoplight_green]
pedestrian_signal = [pedestrian_red, pedestrian_green]
```

```
# Turn off the LEDs
for led in stoplight:
    led.off()
for led in pedestrian_signal:
    led.off()

# Start with green stoplight and red pedestrian_signal
stoplight[2].on()
pedestrian_signal[0].on()

# We need a method to cycle the stoplight and pedestrian_signal
#
# We toggle from green to yellow for 2 seconds
# then red for 20 seconds.
def cycle_lights():
    print("HERE")    # Go yellow.
    stoplight[2].off()
    stoplight[1].on()
    # Wait 2 seconds
    time.sleep(2)
    # Go red and turn on walk light
    stoplight[1].off()
    stoplight[0].on()
    time.sleep_ms(500)  # Give the pedestrian a chance to see it
    pedestrian_signal[0].off()
    pedestrian_signal[1].on()
    # After 10 seconds, start blinking the walk light
    time.sleep(1)
    for i in range(0,10):
        pedestrian_signal[1].off()
        time.sleep_ms(500)
        pedestrian_signal[1].on()
        time.sleep_ms(500)

    # Stop=green, walk=red
    pedestrian_signal[1].off()
    pedestrian_signal[0].on()
```

```
    time.sleep_ms(500)  # Give the pedestrian a chance to see it
    stoplight[0].off()
    stoplight[2].on()

# Create callback for the button
def button_pressed(line):
    cur_value = button.value()
    active = 0
    while (active < 50):
        if button.value() != cur_value:
            active += 1
        else:
            active = 0
        time.sleep_ms(1)
        print("")
    if active:
        cycle_lights()
    else:
        print("False press")

# Create an interrupt for the button
button.irq(trigger=Pin.IRQ_RISING, handler=button_pressed)
```

OK, now we're ready to execute the project.

Execute

We are finally at the point where we can copy all the files to our board and execute the project code. Once again, be sure to check all hardware connections before connecting the Pico to your PC. Then, copy the code files to your Pico and execute the script. You can create a directory on your Pico to place the code if you'd like to keep things tidy as shown in Figure 9-3.

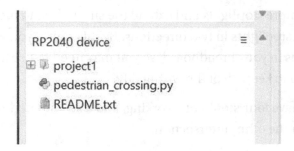

Figure 9-3. *Pedestrian Crossing Files on the MicroPython Board*

Once you've downloaded the file (`pedestrian_crossing.py`) to your Pico, simply click the *Run* button and watch your code run! If everything is connected correctly, and the code is correct, you will see the green LED for the stoplight illuminated and the red LED for the pedestrian crosswalk illuminated.

You can then press the button and watch the stoplight change from green to yellow and then red. The crosswalk will then change from red to green and start flashing. When the timer expires, the crosswalk will change from green to red and the stoplight from red to green. If something doesn't work, go back, and check your code.

Taking It Further

This project shows excellent prospects for reusing the techniques in other projects. This is especially true since we have now learned how to use analog devices (LEDs). You should now consider taking time to explore some embellishments. Here are a few you may want to consider. Some are easy and some may be a challenge or require more research and more complex coding:

- Use NeoPixels (`www.adafruit.com/category/168`) instead of LEDs. These are RGB LEDs, so you need only two – one for the stoplight and one for the walk light. See `https://github.com/JanBednarik/micropython-ws2812` for more information and examples.

- Use OLED from the last project in place of the LEDs for the walk sign to show "WALK" or "DON'T WALK."

- Add another stoplight to complete the simulation for a pedestrian crossing.

- Add three more stoplights and extend the simulation to include controlling stoplights in two directions. By this point, you will have a lot of wires in your breadboard, so you may need to use a second breadboard to keep all of the wiring tidy.

- Once you have four stoplights working, add a second pedestrian crossing for the other intersection.

Of course, if you want to press on to the next project, you're welcome to do so, but take some time to explore these potential embellishments – it will be good practice.

Summary

Working with discrete electronic components can be a lot of fun. Just making the circuit work is a real thrill when you're just starting out with electronics. Now that we know a lot more about controlling our Pico and hardware connected to the GPIO, we can see how powerful having an easy-to-program language like MicroPython at our disposal to make things easy.

In this chapter, we implemented a simulation of a pedestrian crossing button and stoplight. We used a series of LEDs to represent the stoplight and walk signal. We also added a hardware button to simulate pressing the real walk. If you liked this project, you would enjoy the next two projects even more.

In the next chapter, we will explore a project that helps you around the house to keep your plants well watered. We will also see how to view the data from the sensors on a web page.

Project: Plant Monitoring

One of the most common forms of electronics projects is those that monitor events using sensors providing the data either to another machine, cloud service, or local server (like a web server). One way to do that is to wire your MicroPython board up to a set of sensors and then log the data. You can find several examples of general data loggers on the Internet, but few combine the logging of data with a visualization component. Indeed, making sense of the data is the key to making a successful project.

In this chapter, we won't jump directly into making our project run on the Internet. Rather, we will start with the basics and explore combining data logging with data visualization using a web server that we will run on our MicroPython board. How cool is that?

We will also see how to use an analog sensor that produces analog data that we will then have to interpret. In fact, we will rely on the analog-to-digital conversion (ADC) capabilities of our Pico to change the voltage read to a value we can use. Finally, we will be reusing the RTC module from Chapter 8.

As you will see, the code used in this chapter is more modular and uses more functions than previous projects, but not much more than the previous examples. As you will see, the code isn't difficult to learn and uses concepts we have seen in previous chapters. It is the web server and analog hardware that are the most challenging.

Overview

In this chapter, we will implement a plant soil moisture monitoring solution (plant monitor for brevity). This will involve using one or more soil moisture sensors connected to our MicroPython board. We will set up a timer alarm (an interrupt) to run periodically to read the data from the sensors and store it in a comma-separated value (CSV) file.

© Charles Bell 2024
C. Bell, *MicroPython for the Internet of Things*, https://doi.org/10.1007/978-1-4842-9861-9_10

Figure 10-1 depicts a conceptual drawing of the project. The MicroPython board will read the data from the soil moisture sensors and then display it via an HTML web page upon request.

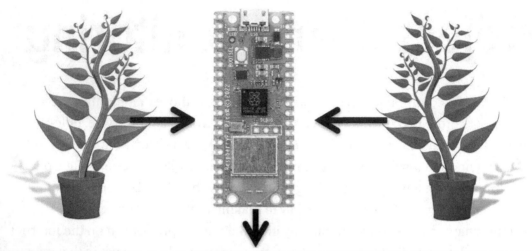

Datetime	Name	Raw Value	Moisture	Location
9/23/2023 16:20	Ivy	585	ok	Green ceramic pot on top shelf
9/23/2023 16:20	Fern	800	wet	Fern on bottom shelf
9/23/2023 17:05	Ivy	500	ok	Green ceramic pot on top shelf
9/23/2023 17:06	Fern	825	wet	Fern on bottom shelf

Figure 10-1. *Plant Monitoring Project Concept*

The user interface for this project is a web page that consists of a table that includes all the data read from the log file. This is how we can overcome potential issues of running the HTML server in a loop. That is, we do not have to interrupt the loop to read the sensors – that's done via the read timer.

By separating the sensor reading from the display, we can reuse or modify either without confusing ourselves as we dig into the code. For example, so long as the visualization component reads the sensor data from the file, it doesn't matter to the sensor reading code how it is used. The only interface or connection between these two parts is the format of the file, and since we're using a CSV file, it is very easy to read and use in our code.

To make things more interesting and to make it easier to code, we will place all the sensor code in a separate code module. Recall, this is a technique used to help reduce the amount of code in any one module, thereby making it easier to write and maintain.

Now let's see what components are needed for this project, and then we will see how to wire everything together.

Required Components

Table 10-1 lists the components you will need in addition to your MicroPython board and USB cable. Links to vendors are provided should you want to purchase the components. When listing multiple rows of the same object, you can choose one or the other – you do not need both. Also, you may find other vendors that sell the components. You should shop around to find the best deal. Costs shown are estimates and do not include any shipping costs.

Table 10-1. *Required Components*

Component	Qty	Description	Cost	Links
Soil moisture sensor	1+	Soil moisture sensor	$6	www.sparkfun.com/products/13637
Real-time clock	1	RTC	$10+	www.sparkfun.com/products/12708
			$7.50	www.adafruit.com/product/3296
Jumper wires	3*	M/M jumper wires, 6"	$4	www.sparkfun.com/products/8431

Soil moisture sensors come in a variety of formats, but most have two prongs that are inserted into the soil and, using a small electrical charge, measure the resistance between the prongs. The higher the value read, the more moisture is in the soil. However, there is a bit of configuration needed to obtain dependable or realistic thresholds. While the manufacturer will have threshold recommendations, some experimentation may be needed to find the right values.

These sensors can also be affected by environmental factors including the type of pot the plant is in, the soil composition, and other factors. Thus, experimenting with a known overwatered soil, dry soil, and properly tended soil will help you narrow down the thresholds for your environment.

Figure 10-2 shows a soil moisture sensor from SparkFun that has a terminal mount instead of pins. You can find several varieties of these sensors. Just pick the one you want to use, keeping in mind you may need different jumpers to connect it to your board.

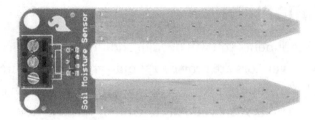

Figure 10-2. *Soil Moisture Sensor (Courtesy of sparkfun.com)*

Of special note is how these soil moisture sensors work. If you were to leave the sensors powered on, they can degrade over time. The metal on the prongs can become degraded due to electrolysis, thereby dramatically reducing its lifespan. You can use the technique of a GPIO pin to power the sensor by turning the pin on when you want to read a value. Keep in mind there will be a small delay while the sensor settles, but we can use a simple delay to wait and then read the value and turn the sensor off. In this way, we can extend the life of the sensor greatly.

Fortunately, the wiring for this project is less complex than the last two projects. Now, let's see how to wire the components together.

Set Up the Hardware

The hardware setup for this project will show only two sensors, but you can add several more if you'd like. However, it is recommended you start with one sensor until you get the project working and then add additional sensors. If it is easier, you can use a breadboard to connect the sensors to the MicroPython board, but depending on where you plan to place the board, you may not need it. It is your choice.

Of course, you must insert the soil moisture sensors into the soil of your plants. If your plants are located further away from your power source, you may need to use longer wires to connect the sensors. You should start with a single, small plant and one sensor (or for testing, two sensors in one plant) that you can place close to your PC (or power source).

We will see how to make the connections for both the Raspberry Pi Pico and the Arduino Nano RP2040 Connect. As you will see, the connections are similar in that you will wire the breakout boards with the same connections and number of wires, but where those wires connect to the board differs. Let's begin with the Pico.

Connections for the Raspberry Pi Pico

Table 10-2 shows the connections needed for this project for the Raspberry Pi Pico. If you purchased the soil moisture sensors from SparkFun, they use screw terminals rather than female headers. These will work, but you will need a small screwdriver to attach the male jumpers to the screw terminals.

Table 10-2. *Connections for the Plant Monitoring Project (Pico)*

Physical Pin	GPIO Num/Function	Connection
27	GP20	Sensor 1 – SIG
32	GP27	Sensor 1 – VCC
N/A	Breadboard GND	Sensor 1 – GND
29	GP21	Sensor 2 – SIG
34	GP28	Sensor 2 – VCC
N/A	Breadboard GND	Sensor 2 – GND
28	GND	Breadboard Ground (top)
40	5V	RTC – VCC
N/A	Breadboard GND	RTC – GND
11	GP8	RTC – SDA
12	GP9	RTC – SCL

Figure 10-3 shows the wiring drawing for the project on the Pico.

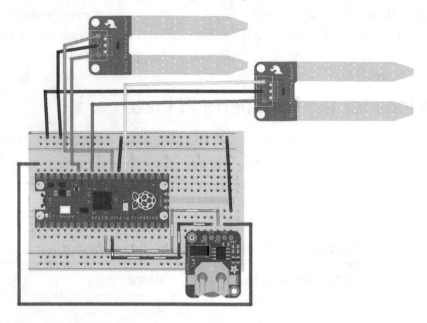

Figure 10-3. *Wiring the Plant Monitoring Project (Pico)*

Caution   You will need soil moisture sensors that can operate at 3.3–5V. Some MicroPython boards may limit output on the pins to 3.3V. The sensors from SparkFun are compatible.

Connections for the Arduino Nano RP2040 Connect

Since we are using the same components for the Arduino Nano RP2040 Connect, the connections are going to be similar, but as noted in previous chapters, the Nano RP2040 has a different pin layout. Thus, some of the connections are going to be different. Table 10-3 shows the connections needed for the Nano RP2040.

Table 10-3. *Connections for the Plant Monitoring Project (Nano RP2040)*

Physical Pin	GPIO Num/Function	Connection
5	GP20	Sensor 1 – SIG
27	GP27	Sensor 1 – VCC
N/A	Breadboard GND	Sensor 1 – GND
6	GP21	Sensor 2 – SIG
26	GP28	Sensor 2 – VCC
N/A	Breadboard GND	Sensor 2 – GND
28	GND	Breadboard Ground (top)
12	5V	RTC – VCC
14	GND	RTC – GND
8	SDA	RTC – SDA
9	SCL	RTC – SCL

Notice most of the connections are the same. What differs is where the jumper wires connect to the board.

Figure 10-4 shows the wiring drawing for the project on the Nano RP2040.

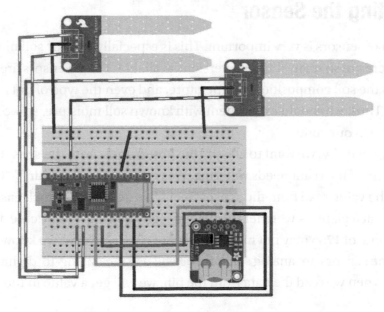

Figure 10-4. *Wiring the Plant Monitoring Project (Nano RP2040)*

Once again, always make sure to double-check your connections before powering the board on. Now, let's talk about the code we need to write. Don't power on your board just yet – there is a fair amount of discussion needed before we're ready to test the project.

Write the Code

Now it's time to write the code for our project. Fortunately, the code can run on both the Pico and Nano RP2040 Connect with only a minor change, which will be identified as we discuss the main portion of the code.

The code is longer than what we've seen thus far, and due to all the bits and bobs we're working with, it is best to divide the project into parts. So, we are going to write the code in two stages. We won't have a working project until the end, so most of the discussion will be about the individual parts. We will put it all together before testing the project.

Recall from the overview, we will have two major components: the main code and a code module that encapsulates the soil sensors. We will place the HTML server code and supporting functions in the main code module. However, before we embark on the code for the project, we should calibrate our sensors. Let's do that now.

Calibrating the Sensor

Calibration of sensors is very important. This is especially true for soil moisture sensors because there are so many different versions available. These sensors are also very sensitive to the soil composition, temperature, and even the type of pot in which the plant lives. Thus, we should experiment with known soil moisture, so we know what ranges to use in our code.

More specifically, we want to classify the observation from the sensor so that we can determine if the plant needs watering. We will use the values "dry," "Ok," and "wet" to classify the value read from the sensor. Seeing these labels is much easier for us to determine – at a glance – whether the plant needs watering. In this case, the raw data such as a value of 1756 may not mean much, but if we see "dry," we know it needs water.

Since the sensors are analog sensors, we will use the analog-to-digital conversion on the board. When we read the data from the pin, we will get a value in the range of 0–4096.

This value is related to the resistance the sensor reads in the soil. Low values indicate dry soil, and high values indicate wet soil.

However, the sensors from different vendors can vary widely in the values read. For example, sensors from SparkFun tend to read values in the range 0–1024, but sensors from other vendors can read as high as 4096. Fortunately, they all seem to be consistent in that the lower the value, the drier the soil.

So, we must determine thresholds for the three classifications. Again, there are several factors that can influence the values read from the sensor. Thus, you should select several pots of soil including one that you feel is dry, another that is correctly watered, and a third that is overwatered. The best thing to do is select one that is dry, take measurements, then water it until the soil moisture is correct, measure that, then water it again until there is too much water.[1]

To determine the threshold, we must first write a short bit of code to set up our board for reading values from the sensor. This includes choosing a GPIO pin that supports ADC. Check the reference drawing for your board to be certain which GPIO pins are included.

We also need to choose a pin to use to power the board. This is also an analog output pin. Finally, we will write a loop to read several values every five seconds and then average them. Five seconds is an arbitrary value, and it was derived from reading the datasheet for the sensor. Check your sensors to see how much time is needed for the read to settle (maybe under the heading of frequency of reads). Listing 10-1 shows the code needed to set up the analog-to-digital channel, a pin to use for powering the sensor, and a loop for reading ten values and averaging them.

Listing 10-1. Calibrating the Soil Moisture Threshold

```
#
# MicroPython for the IoT Second Edition - Chapter 10
#
# Chapter 10 - Plant Monitoring
#
# This file contains code to capture the range of values
# for a soil moisture sensor.
#
```

---

[1] Be sure to choose a plant hearty enough to withstand overwatering.

```
# Dr. Charles Bell
#
# Import libraries
from machine import ADC, Pin
import time

print("MicroPython for the IoT - Soil Moisture threshold test.")
# Setup the GPIO pin for powering the sensor.
power = Pin(21, Pin.OUT)
# Setup the ADC for the signal pin
adc = ADC(Pin(27))
# Turn sensor off
power.low()

# Loop 10 times and average the values read
print("Reading 10 values.")
total = 0
for i in range (0,10):
    # Turn power on
    power.high()
    # Wait for sensor to power on and settle
    time.sleep(5)
    # Read the value
    value = adc.read_u16()
    print("Value read ({0:02}): {1}".format(i+1, value))
    total += value
    # Turn sensor off
    power.low()

# Now average the values
print("The average value read is: {0}".format(total/10))
```

If you enter this code in a file named threshold.py, you can copy it to your
MicroPython board and execute it. Listing 10-2 shows the output of running this
calibration code in a plant that is correctly watered.

Listing 10-2. Running the Calibration Code

```
>>> import threshold
Reading 10 values.
Value read: 1724
Value read: 1983
Value read: 1587
Value read: 1702
Value read: 1634.
Value read: 1525
Value read: 1874
Value read: 1707
Value read: 1793
Value read: 1745
The average value read is: 1727.4
>>>
```

Here, we see an average value of 1727 (always round the number – you need integers). Further tests running the code on dry soil resulted in a value of 425 and for a wet plant, 3100. Thus, the thresholds for this example are 500 for dry and 2500 for wet. However, your results may vary greatly, so make sure to run this code with your sensors, board, and plant of choice.

Tip   To make things easier for calibrating the thresholds, use sensors from the same vendor. Otherwise, you may have to use a separate set of thresholds for each sensor supported.

Notice the values read. As you can see, the values can vary from one moment to another. This is normal for these sensors. They are known for producing some jumpy values. Thus, you should consider sampling the sensor more than once to get an average over a brief period rather than a single value. Even taking an average can be skewed slightly if one or more of the samples are off by a large margin. However, sampling even ten values and averaging will help reduce the possibility of getting an anomalous reading. We will do this in our project code.

Now that we have our threshold values for our sensors, we can begin with the code module for the sensors.

Part 1: Sensor Code Module

The first part of the project will be to create a code module to contain a new class named SoilMoisture that contains all the functionality to read data from the sensors and save the data to a file. In this section, we will see how to write the code for the module. Open a new file and name it soil_moisture.py. Let's start by looking at the high-level design.

High-Level Design

As we learned earlier, it is a clever idea to create a design for each code module (class) we want to use. We will use the code module from the main code. Thus, we need functions to tell the class to read the sensors and a way to get the file name the class uses for the data.

Typically, one would design a code module to completely hide a file and all operations on it, but in this case, the class is only concerned with reading the sensors and writing the data. We will use a timer interrupt to read the sensors. This allows us to set up a function to be called periodically without the need to monitor or poll the time and call the function directly.

We provide a clear log function as a convenience. Thus, we will only need two public functions: one to clear the log and another to fetch the file name. Aside from initializing the class, we only need to get the file name when we want to refresh the data (send it to the client). Table 10-4 shows the functions for the Soil Moisture class.

Table 10-4. *High-Level Design (Functions) Soil Moisture Class*

Function	Parameters	Description
__init__()	rtc, csv_filename, sensor_list	Initialization for the class (the constructor)
clear_log()		Clear the log
_format_time()		Format the time for display and save to the log
_get_value()	adc, power	Read the sensor ten times and average the values read
read_sensors()		Read the values and save them to the log
_convert_value()	value	Convert the raw sensor value to an enumeration

Notice the first function named __init__(). This is the constructor for the class and will be called when the class is instantiated from our main code. Notice also the private methods are named with a single underscore.

The following sections explain the initialization code and the functions needed. We will see the complete code in a later section.

Setup and Initialization

In this section, we discuss the code we need to set up and initialize the code module. First, there are a few imports we need, including those for the analog-to-digital converter, pin, and the operating system libraries.

We will also need some constants defined for the class. Recall we want to classify the soil moisture read with an enumeration. To do so, we will need to use the thresholds we determined for the classification. We can use constants at the top of the file to make it easier to change them later should we need to adjust the code for use with other sensors or the conditions of our plants change (different pot, soil, environment, etc.). We can use the same philosophy to set the name of the file to contain the data.

We also use a constant to define the frequency for reading the sensors. Since we will use a loop to read the sensor waiting 5 seconds for each read, we will need a minimum of 50–55 seconds to read ten values. Thus, we cannot set the update frequency to anything less than about one minute. The frequency is in seconds. While you may want to set this to a low value for testing, you certainly do not want to check the soil moisture of your plants every minute. How often do you check your plants normally? Once every few days or once a day? Why check it sooner than normal?

SAMPLING FREQUENCY

How often you sample data from a sensor (also called sampling rate) is often overlooked when designing sensor networks. The tendency is to store as many values as you can, thinking more data is better. But that is not applicable in the general case. Consider the plant monitoring project. If you normally check your plants once per day, how can sampling the sensors once every five minutes benefit you? It won't and it only results in excess data!

Sampling rate must be calculated carefully to deliver the data you need to draw conclusions without creating too much data. While more data is always better than too little data, saving data too often at unrealistic frequencies can generate so much data that it could exceed the storage capacity of your device.

You should carefully consider sampling rate when designing projects that sample sensors. Choose a sampling rate that is based on realistic expectations. Generally, if you are sampling data that can change very slowly, the sampling rate should be low. Sampling data that can change more quickly should have a higher (shorter time between samples) sampling rate.

Finally, we need a function that converts a time structure to a string. Recall from an earlier example, we can use a simple format specification. We will use a module-level private function for that feature.

Listing 10-3 shows the code for the setup and initialization section. Place this at the top of the file.

Listing 10-3. Soil Moisture Class Setup and Initialization

```python
import os
import time
from machine import ADC, Pin

# Thresholds for the sensors
LOWER_THRESHOLD = 500
UPPER_THRESHOLD = 2500
UPDATE_FREQ = 120    # seconds

# Format the time (epoch) for a better view
def _format_time(tm_data):
    # Use a special shortcut to unpack tuple: *tm_data
    return "{0}-{1:0>2}-{2:0>2} {3:0>2}:{4:0>2}:{5:0>2}".format(*tm_data)
```

Constructor

The constructor for the class is where all the major work takes place. There are several things we need to do, including the following:

- Initialize all class variables
- Set up the sensors in a dictionary stored in a list

We use a dictionary for each sensor, so we can define the pin for the sensor, pin for powering the sensor, sensor number (an arbitrary identification), and the location of the sensor. We then place the dictionaries in a list to make it easy to read all the sensors at the same time using a loop.

Listing 10-4 shows the code for the class constructor.

Listing 10-4. Soil Moisture Class Constructor

```
# Initialization for the class (the constructor)
def __init__(self, rtc, csv_filename, sensor_list):
    self.rtc = rtc

    # Try to access the file system and make the new path
    self.sensor_file = csv_filename

    # Loop through the sensors specified and setup a new dictionary
    # for each sensor that includes the power and ADC pins defined.
    self.sensors = []
    for sensor in sensor_list:
        # Setup the dictionary for each soil moisture sensor
        soil_moisture = {
            'sensor': ADC(Pin(sensor['pin'])),
            'power': Pin(sensor['power'], Pin.OUT),
            'location': sensor['location'],
            'nick': sensor['nick']
        }
        self.sensors.append(soil_moisture)
    print("Soil moisture sensors are ready...")
```

Public Functions

There are only two public functions. The first, clear_log(), simply opens the file for writing and closes it. This effectively empties the file. The function is provided for convenience. The second function, read_sensors(), reads the sensor(s) and records the data in the log file.

Private Functions

There are three private functions. The _get_value() function is the same code as our threshold calibration code where we sample the sensor ten times and average the value. The _convert_value() function is a helper function to determine the classification of the soil based on the sensor data. This function returns a string or "dry," "Ok," or "wet." The _format_time() function gets the current time and formats the time for writing to the log.

Complete Code

Now that we have seen all the parts of the code module, let's look at the completed code. Listing 10-5 shows the complete code for the Plant Monitor code module. Once again, we can save this file as soil_moisture.py.

Listing 10-5. Soil Moisture Code Module Complete Code

```
#
# MicroPython for the IoT Second Edition - Chapter 10
#
# MicroPython Plant Monitoring
#
# Soil Moisture class
#
import os
import time
from machine import ADC, Pin

# Thresholds for the sensors
LOWER_THRESHOLD = 500
UPPER_THRESHOLD = 2500
UPDATE_FREQ = 120    # seconds

# Format the time (epoch) for a better view
def _format_time(tm_data):
    # Use a special shortcut to unpack tuple: *tm_data
    return "{0}-{1:0>2}-{2:0>2} {3:0>2}:{4:0>2}:{5:0>2}".format(*tm_data)
```

```
class SoilMoisture:
    """

    This class reads soil moisture from one or more sensors and writes the
    data to a comma-separated value (csv) file as specified in the
    constructor.

    It also requires a list (array) or sensor dictionaries in the
    following form.

    sensor = {
      'pin': sensor_pin,
      'power': power_pin,
      'location': location or description
      'nick': nickname for the sensor
    }

    Sensors are numbered in the order they appear in the list.

    Note: Intermediate calls to get_values() will return the last
    value(s) read or None if no sensors have been read.
    """

    # Initialization for the class (the constructor)
    def __init__(self, rtc, csv_filename, sensor_list):
        self.rtc = rtc

        # Try to access the file system and make the new path
        self.sensor_file = csv_filename

        # Loop through the sensors specified and setup a new dictionary
        # for each sensor that includes the power and ADC pins defined.
        self.sensors = []
        for sensor in sensor_list:
            # Setup the dictionary for each soil moisture sensor
            soil_moisture = {
                'sensor': ADC(Pin(sensor['pin'])),
                'power': Pin(sensor['power'], Pin.OUT),
                'location': sensor['location'],
                'nick': sensor['nick']
```

```python
        }
        self.sensors.append(soil_moisture)
    print("Soil moisture sensors are ready...")

# Clear the log
def clear_log(self):
    log_file = open(self.sensor_file, 'w')
    log_file.close()

# Format the time (epoch) for a better view
def _format_time(self):
    # Get datetime
    dt = self.rtc.datetime
    # (year, month, day, hours. minutes, seconds, weekday:
    integer: 0-6 )
    return "{0:02}/{1:02}/{2:04} {3:02}:{4:02}:{5:02}".format(
            dt[1], dt[2], dt[0], dt[3], dt[4], dt[5])
# Read the sensor 10 times and average the values read
def _get_value(self, adc, power):
    total = 0
    # Turn power on
    power.high()
    # Wait for sensor to power on and settle
    time.sleep(5)
    for i in range (0,10):
        time.sleep(1)
        # Read the value
        value = adc.read_u16()
        total += value
    # Turn sensor off
    power.low()
    return int(total/10)

# Monitor the sensors, read the values, and save them
def read_sensors(self):
    log_file = open(self.sensor_file, 'a')
    self.values_read = []
```

```
    for sensor in self.sensors:
        # Read the data from the sensor and convert the value
        value = self._get_value(sensor['sensor'], sensor['power'])
        print("Value read: {0}".format(value))
        # datetime,num,value,enum,location
        message = ("{0},{1},{2},{3},{4}"
                   "".format(self._format_time(), sensor['nick'], value,
                             self._convert_value(value),
                                 sensor['location']))
        log_file.write("{0}\n".format(message))
    log_file.close()

# Convert the raw sensor value to an enumeration
def _convert_value(self, value):
    # If value is less than lower threshold, soil is dry else if it
    # is greater than upper threshold, it is wet, else all is well.
    if (value <= LOWER_THRESHOLD):
        return "dry"
    elif (value >= UPPER_THRESHOLD):
        return "wet"
    return "ok"
```

Wow, that's a lot of code! Take some time to read it until you understand all the parts of the code.

There is one thing missing from this class: the read event to read the sensors. Recall, we do not want the HTML code (web server) to have to read the sensors because it will be designed to wait for connections from clients. Thus, we need a way to periodically read the sensors. Let's look at the read timer code.

Part 2: Read Timer Code

The read timer code consists of a class named ReadTimer. We will use a timer event and callback in this chapter to keep things simpler, but we will see a more advanced technique in the next chapter. The class constructor sets up a Timer instance and uses a method in the class to execute (called a callback) when the Timer event fires. We will use a constant to establish the frequency of the read event (DATA_READ_INTERVAL) in milliseconds. Rather than link this class to the SoilMoisture class, we will provide two public functions: one to see if it is time to read, time_to_read(), and another to reset the timer, reset().

So, how do we use this class? Once instantiated, we can call time_to_read(), which returns true when the timer has fired, and thus we can use it to determine whether we can read the sensors. Savvy readers will note that this method isn't particularly exact and that the read event can occur sometime after the read event fires. However, once again, we will see a better technique in the next chapter.

Listing 10-6 shows the complete code for the ReadTimer class. You can save this file as read_event.py.

Listing 10-6. Read Timer Code Module Complete Code

```
#
# MicroPython for the IoT Second Edition - Chapter 10
#
# Chapter 10 - Plant Monitoring
#
# This file contains a class to display data from one or more soil
# moisture sensors.
#
# Dr. Charles Bell
#
# Import libraries
from machine import Timer

# Constants
DATA_READ_INTERVAL = 30000          # Increase this interval as needed

# Class to control reading data with a timer
class ReadTimer:
    def __init__(self, interval=DATA_READ_INTERVAL):
        # Create and start the timer interrupt to read data
        self.interval = interval
        self.data_read_event = True
        self.read_timer = Timer()
        self.read_timer.init(period=self.interval, mode=Timer.PERIODIC,
```

```
                            callback=self.read_data_event)

    # Callback for reading the data on the interval.
    def read_data_event(self, timer_obj):
        self.data_read_event = True
        self.read_timer.deinit()

    # Check to see if it is time to read
    def time_to_read(self):
        return self.data_read_event

    # Reset the read event boolean (timer doesn't reset)
    def reset(self):
        self.read_timer.init(period=self.interval, mode=Timer.PERIODIC,
                                callback=self.read_data_event)
        self.data_read_event = False
```

Take some time to read the code and ensure you know how it works.

OK, now we're ready to look at the main code.

Part 3: Main Code

The main will use a file to store the HTML code (since it doesn't change) and a single HTML string for populating an HTML table with the data from the file. We will also add code to read the date and time from the RTC.

Instead of using an HTML button, we can format a command manually on the URL. We can use this technique to allow access to commands without using buttons or other user interface features. It also helps to make these commands harder to use to prevent overuse. For example, we can provide a clear log command. We would use a URL like http://192.168.42.140/CLEAR_LOG, which submits a GET request to the HTML server. We can capture that command and clear the log when it is issued.

Caution   If you build commands like this, be sure to use them carefully. That is, setting your URL to http://192.168.42.140/CLEAR_LOG and pressing enter issue the command. Refreshing the page will reissue the command! When you use the command, be sure to clear your URL before refreshing or, better, use it once and close the page/tab.

The following sections explain the initialization code and the functions needed. We will see the complete code in a later section. Let's start with the HTML code.

HTML Code (Files)

We will store the HTML code needed in files to save memory. Recall by reading a row at a time – we do not have to take up space with the strings in our code. As your projects grow in complexity, this could become an issue. Thus, this project demonstrates a way to save some memory.

The HTML for this project creates a web page with a simple table that includes all the data in the file at the time of the request. To make things easier, we will use three files. The first file (named part1.html) will contain the HTML code up to the table rows; the second file (named plant_data.csv) will be populated by the data in csv format; and the third (named part2.html) will contain the remaining HTML code.

The first file, part1.html, is shown in Listing 10-7. This file establishes the table HTML code. It also establishes characteristics for the table including text alignment, border size, and padding – all through cascading style (<style> tag). Don't worry if this looks strange or alien. You can google for W3C standards to see how we use the tag to control the style of the web page.

Listing 10-7. HTML Code (part1.html)

```
<!DOCTYPE html>
<html>
  <head>
    <title>MicroPython for the IoT 2nd Edition - Plant Monitor</title>
    <meta http-equiv="refresh" content="30">
    <style>
      table, th, td {
          border: 1px solid black;
          border-collapse: collapse;
      }
      th, td {
          padding: 5px;
      }
      th {
          text-align: left;
```

```
    }
  </style>
</head>
<center><h2>MicroPython for the IoT 2nd Edition - Plant Monitor</h2></
center><br>
<center>A simple project to demonstrate how to retrieve sensor data over
the Internet.</center>
<center><br><b>Plant Monitoring Data</b><br><br>
  <table style="width:75%">
    <col width="180">
    <col width="120">
    <col width="100">
    <col width="100">
    <tr><th>Datetime</th><th>Name</th><th>Raw Value</th><th>Moisture<//
    th><th>Location</th></tr>
```

Notice the table code. Again, don't worry if this seems strange. It works and it is very basic. Those familiar with HTML may want to embellish and improve the code. The last line establishes the header for the table.

The second file, `plant_data.csv`, contains the data. We will use a constant to populate a properly formatted HTML table row. The following shows an example of what a row of data would look like in the file and how that data is transformed to HTML. We will see the HTML for the table row in the next section.

```
# Raw data
9/23/2023 17:05,Ivy,500,ok,Green ceramic pot on top shelf
# HTML table row
<tr><td>2023-09-23 17:05</td><td>Ivy</td><td>500</td><td>ok</td><td>Green
ceramic pot on top shelf </td></tr>
```

The last file, `part2.html`, contains the closing tags, so it isn't very large. But since we're reading from files, we include this file. The following shows the code in the second file:

```
  </table>
  </center>
</html>
```

So, how do we use these files? When we send a response back to the client (the web page), we read the first file sending one row at a time, then read the data file sending one row at a time, then read the last file sending one row at a time. We will use a helper function to read the data file. Listing 10-8 shows the code used to do this.

Listing 10-8. Reading the HTML and Data File

```
# Read HTML from file and send to client a row at a time.
def send_html_file(filename, client):
    html = open(filename, 'r')
    for row in html:
        client.send(row)
    html.close()

# Send the sensor data to the client.
def send_sensor_data(client, filename):
    send_html_file("project3/part1.html", client)
    log_file = open(filename, 'r')
    for row in log_file:
        cols = row.strip("\n").split(",") # split row by commas
        # build the table string if all parts are there
        if len(cols) >= 5:
            html = HTML_TABLE_ROW.format(cols[0], cols[1], cols[2],
                                         cols[3], cols[4])
            # send the row to the client
            client.send(html)
            time.sleep(0.50)
    log_file.close()
    send_html_file("project3/part2.html", client)
```

Imports

The imports we need for the project include those for the select, sys, socket, Pin, SoftI2C, RTC (DS1307), SoilMoisture, and the ReadEvent class. The complete list of imports is shown as follows. If you want to follow along, open a new file and name it plants.py.

```
import network, select, socket, sys, time
from machine import Pin, SoftI2C
```

```
from project3.ds1307 import DS1307
from project3.soil_moisture import SoilMoisture
from project3.read_timer import ReadEvent
```

We also need two constants. First, we need a string for the log file name, and we need a string we can use to create the rows for the table. The HTML code that occurs before this line is saved in files as described earlier. The following shows the string used. Notice we use replacement syntax so that we can use the `format()` function to fill in the details:

```
# Constants
DATA_FILENAME = 'plant_data.csv'

# HTML web page for the project
HTML_TABLE_ROW = "<tr><td>{0}</td><td>{1}</td><td>{2}</td><td>{3}</
td><td>{4}</td></tr>"
```

The Main() Function

The HTML server portion of the `main()` function is like the last project, but instead of processing form requests, we send the web page back to the client by default. The only command supported is the `CLEAR_LOG` command, which requires specifying it on the URL on the client as described earlier.

Another difference is instead of placing code in the global section of the code file (so that it executes when we import the file in our REPL console or `plants.py` file), we use functions to connect to the network, set up the RTC, and send the HTML code to the client. This is an escalation of complexity that you should start using as general practice. We did not see this in earlier projects so that we could concentrate on getting the code complete. When writing your own projects, be sure to use functions to contain code and call the functions from your other code.

Since this is different from the last project, we will look at the code. Listing 10-9 shows the code for the `main()` function.

Like the previous chapters, we must add special code for the Pico and Nano RP2040. See the comments in the listing for instructions on how to change the `SoftI2C` setup for each board or refer to Chapters 8 and 9 for more details.

Listing 10-9. Plant Monitor main() Function

```python
# Main function
def main():
    # Setup the socket and respond to HTML requests
    # Connect to the network
    if not connect():
        sys.exit(-1)
    #
    # I2C for the RTC
    # Arduino Nano RP2040 Connect uses sda=12, scl=13
    #sda = Pin(12)
    #scl = Pin(13)
    #
    # Raspberry Pi Pico uses sda=8, scl=9
    sda = Pin(8)
    scl = Pin(9)
    #
    # Software I2C (bit-banging) for the RTC
    i2c = SoftI2C(sda=sda, scl=scl, freq=100000)
    #
    # NOTE: We only need to set the datetime once. Uncomment these
    #       lines only on the first run of a new RTC module or
    #       whenever you change the battery.
    rtc = DS1307(i2c)
    # (year, month, day, hours. minutes, seconds, weekday: integer: 0-6 )
    # rtc.datetime = (2023,09,23,16,15,30,2)
    #

    # Setup the sensors
    sensor_list = [
        {
            # Arduino Nano RP2040 Connect and Raspberry Pi Pico
            # use pin=27, power=20
            'pin': 27,
            'power': 20,
```

```
        'location': 'Green ceramic pot on top shelf',
        'nick': 'Ivy',
    },
    {
        # Arduino Nano RP2040 Connect and Raspberry Pi Pico
        # use pin=28, power=21
        'pin': 28,
        'power': 21,
        'location': 'Fern on bottom shelf',
        'nick': 'Fern',
    }
]

# Setup the soil moisture object instance from the SoilMoisture class
plants = SoilMoisture(rtc, DATA_FILENAME, sensor_list)

# Setup the socket and wait for connections
addr = socket.getaddrinfo('0.0.0.0', 80)[0][-1]
sock = socket.socket()
sock.bind(addr)
sock.listen(5)

# Setup read event handler
data_read_event = ReadTimer(120000)
print("Ready for connections...")
while True:
    # Since the socket.accept() method is blocking, the easiest way to
    # make it non-blocking is to use the select module which provides
    # functions to efficiently wait for events on multiple streams.
    # See https://docs.micropython.org/en/latest/library/select.html
    # for more details.
    read_event, write_event, error = select.select((sock,), (), (), 1)
    if read_event:
        for readable in read_event:
            try:
                client, address = sock.accept()
            except OSError as err:
```

```
                    time.sleep(0.50)
                    continue
                print("Got a connection from a client at: %s" % str(address))
                request = client.recv(1024)

                # Allow for clearing of the log but be careful!
                # The auto refresh will resend this command if you do not
                # clear it from your URL line.
                if (request[:14] == b'GET /CLEAR_LOG'):
                    print('Requesting clear log.')
                    plants.clear_log()
                else:
                    send_sensor_data(client, DATA_FILENAME)
                client.close()
        if data_read_event.time_to_read():
            data_read_event.reset()
            print("Reading data...")
            plants.read_sensors()
        time.sleep(1)
    sock.close()
```

Take a moment to read this code. Notice how we implement the function in a more modular way. Not only does placing common code in functions help with how you break a problem down into parts, but it also makes your main code (the main() function) shorter.

Notice also there is the use of the select class. This is a special class that permits us to use the socket class, which is a form of stream class, without blocking (waiting for a client before returning). See https://docs.micropython.org/en/latest/library/select.html for more information about using the select class.

Let's look at the completed code.

Complete Code

Now that we have seen all the parts of the code module, let's look at the completed code. Listing 10-10 shows the complete code for the Plant Monitor code module. Once again, we can save this file as plants.py.

Notice we also have the WiFi code we used in the previous chapters. Be sure to set the SSID and password for your local WiFi setup.

Listing 10-10. Plant Monitor Main Code

```
#
# MicroPython for the IoT Second Edition - Chapter 10
#
# Chapter 10 - Plant Monitoring Web Server
#
# Required Components:
# - (N) Soil moisture sensors (one for each plant)
#
# Imports for the project
import network, select, socket, sys, time
from machine import Pin, SoftI2C
from project3.ds1307 import DS1307
from project3.soil_moisture import SoilMoisture
from project3.read_timer import ReadTimer

# Constants
DATA_FILENAME = 'plant_data.csv'

# HTML web page for the project
HTML_TABLE_ROW = "<tr><td>{0}</td><td>{1}</td><td>{2}</td><td>{3}</
td><td>{4}</td></tr>"

# Setup the board to connect to our network.
def connect():
    wlan = network.WLAN(network.STA_IF)
    wlan.active(True)
    wlan.connect('SSID', 'PASSWORD')
    while not wlan.isconnected() and wlan.status() >= 0:
        print("Waiting to connect...")
        time.sleep(1)
    if not wlan.isconnected():
        print("Cannot find SSID!")
        sys.exit(0)
```

```python
    print("Connected!")
    print("My IP address is: {0}".format(wlan.ifconfig()[0]))
    return True

# Read HTML from file and send to client a row at a time.
def send_html_file(filename, client):
    html = open(filename, 'r')
    for row in html:
        client.send(row)
    html.close()

# Send the sensor data to the client.
def send_sensor_data(client, filename):
    send_html_file("project3/part1.html", client)
    log_file = open(filename, 'r')
    for row in log_file:
        cols = row.strip("\n").split(",") # split row by commas
        # build the table string if all parts are there
        if len(cols) >= 5:
            html = HTML_TABLE_ROW.format(cols[0], cols[1], cols[2],
                                         cols[3], cols[4])
            # send the row to the client
            client.send(html)
            time.sleep(0.50)
    log_file.close()
    send_html_file("project3/part2.html", client)

# Main function
def main():
    # Setup the socket and respond to HTML requests
    # Connect to the network
    if not connect():
        sys.exit(-1)
    #
    # I2C for the RTC
    # Arduino Nano RP2040 Connect uses sda=12, scl=13
    #sda = Pin(12)
```

```
#scl = Pin(13)
#
# Raspberry Pi Pico uses sda=8, scl=9
sda = Pin(8)
scl = Pin(9)
#
# Software I2C (bit-banging) for the RTC
i2c = SoftI2C(sda=sda, scl=scl, freq=100000)
#
# NOTE: We only need to set the datetime once. Uncomment these
#       lines only on the first run of a new RTC module or
#       whenever you change the battery.
rtc = DS1307(i2c)
# (year, month, day, hours. minutes, seconds, weekday: integer: 0-6 )
# rtc.datetime = (2023,09,23,16,15,30,2)
#

# Setup the sensors
sensor_list = [
    {
        # Arduino Nano RP2040 Connect and Raspberry Pi Pico
        # use pin=27, power=20
        'pin': 27,
        'power': 20,
        'location': 'Green ceramic pot on top shelf',
        'nick': 'Ivy',
    },
    {
        # Arduino Nano RP2040 Connect and Raspberry Pi Pico
        # use pin=28, power=21
        'pin': 28,
        'power': 21,
        'location': 'Fern on bottom shelf',
        'nick': 'Fern',
    }
]
```

```python
# Setup the soil moisture object instance from the SoilMoisture class
plants = SoilMoisture(rtc, DATA_FILENAME, sensor_list)

# Setup the socket and wait for connections
addr = socket.getaddrinfo('0.0.0.0', 80)[0][-1]
sock = socket.socket()
sock.bind(addr)
sock.listen(5)

# Setup read event handler
data_read_event = ReadTimer(120000)
print("Ready for connections...")
while True:
    # Since the socket.accept() method is blocking, the easiest way to
    # make it non-blocking is to use the select module which provides
    # functions to efficiently wait for events on multiple streams.
    # See https://docs.micropython.org/en/latest/library/select.html
    # for more details.
    read_event, write_event, error = select.select((sock,), (), (), 1)
    if read_event:
        for readable in read_event:
            try:
                client, address = sock.accept()
            except OSError as err:
                time.sleep(0.50)
                continue
            print("Got a connection from a client at: %s" %
            str(address))
            request = client.recv(1024)

            # Allow for clearing of the log but be careful!
            # The auto refresh will resend this command if you do not
            # clear it from your URL line.
            if (request[:14] == b'GET /CLEAR_LOG'):
                print('Requesting clear log.')
                plants.clear_log()
            else:
```

```
            send_sensor_data(client, DATA_FILENAME)
                client.close()
        if data_read_event.time_to_read():
            data_read_event.reset()
            print("Reading data...")
            plants.read_sensors()
        time.sleep(1)
    sock.close()

if __name__ == '__main__':
    try:
        main()
    except (KeyboardInterrupt, SystemExit) as err:
        print("\nbye!\n")
sys.exit(0)
```

Take some time to read the code to ensure you understand how it works. Aside from building a simple web server, the code isn't as complex as we have seen in previous chapters.

Now, let's run this project!

WAIT, WHAT ABOUT THE DATA FILE?

If you are wondering about the data file, you need not worry. The code is designed to create the file even if it doesn't exist. The following shows a mockup of data you can use in your tests:

```
2023-09-23 15:42:05,1,99,dry,Small fern on bottom shelf on porch

2023-09-23 15:42:10,2,204,dry,Green pot creeper thing on floor in living room

2023-09-23 15:42:22,1,215,dry,Small fern on bottom shelf on porch

2023-09-23 15:43:11,2,89,dry,Green pot creeper thing on floor in living room
```

If you want to start with some sample data, you can do so, but just make sure it is comma separated with no spaces and one line of data per row.

Execute!

Now is the fun part! We've got the code all set up to read soil moisture from our plants and send all the sensor data collected to the client. Recall, we need to copy the code to our board. We will need to copy the files we created to our MicroPython board. Recall from the code walk-through that the code modules we created are referenced from a folder, project3, as follows:

```
from project3.ds1307 import DS1307
from project3.soil_moisture import SoilMoisture
from project3.read_timer import ReadTimer
```

This means we need to create a directory on our MicroPython board named project3 and copy those files there (soil_moisture.py and read_timer.py). Recall that you can do this from Thonny. We also need to copy the two HTML files (part1.html and part2.html) to the folder along with the RTC module (ds1307.py) that we used in Chapter 8. Finally, we can copy the main code (plants.py) into the root folder on the MicroPython board. When all of the files are copied, you should see the file structure similar to what is shown in Figure 10-5.

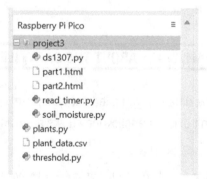

Figure 10-5. *Sample File Layout for the Plant Monitoring Project*

Copy the files as shown, and then you are ready to test the project.

All we need now is the IP address of that board to point our web browser. We can get that from our debug statements by running the code. Listing 10-11 shows the initial run for the project.

Listing 10-11. Running the Plant Monitor

```
Waiting to connect...
Waiting to connect...
Waiting to connect...
Waiting to connect...
Waiting to connect...
Connected!
My IP address is: 10.0.0.14
Soil moisture sensors are ready...
Ready for connections...
Reading data...
Got a connection from a client at: ('10.0.0.13', 51754)
Got a connection from a client at: ('10.0.0.13', 51755)
```

Notice in this case the IP address is 10.0.0.14. All we need to do is put that in our browser as shown in Figure 10-6. Depending on your WiFi setup, you may see an address in the 192.168.X.X network, which is fine provided it matches the same subnet as your PC.

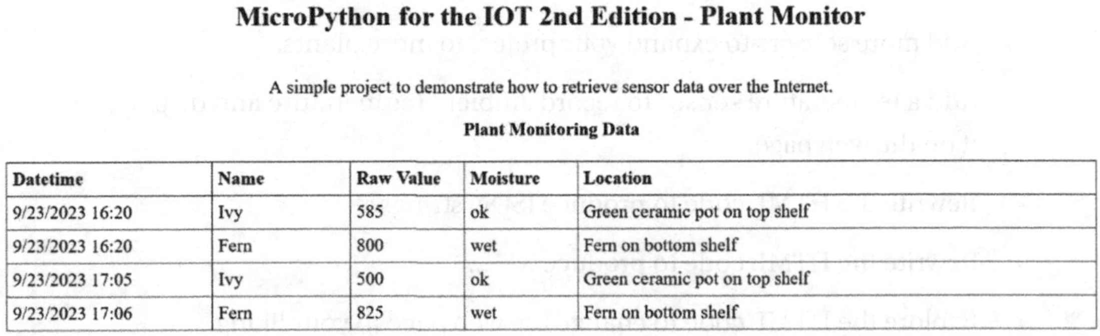

MicroPython for the IOT 2nd Edition - Plant Monitor

A simple project to demonstrate how to retrieve sensor data over the Internet.

Plant Monitoring Data

Datetime	Name	Raw Value	Moisture	Location
9/23/2023 16:20	Ivy	585	ok	Green ceramic pot on top shelf
9/23/2023 16:20	Fern	800	wet	Fern on bottom shelf
9/23/2023 17:05	Ivy	500	ok	Green ceramic pot on top shelf
9/23/2023 17:06	Fern	825	wet	Fern on bottom shelf

Figure 10-6. *Plant Monitoring Project*

Once you enter the URL, you should see a web page like the image shown. If you don't, be sure to check the HTML in your code to ensure it is exactly like what is shown; otherwise, the page may not display properly.

Caution   It is possible you may receive an error code EADDRINUSE, which can occur when running the code multiple times. It means the MicroPython board has found the address is still in use and thus will not initialize. When this happens, you can simply power off (unplug) the board and power it back on (plug it back into your PC USB port).

You should also ensure the network your PC is connected to can reach the network to which your board is connected. If your home office is set up like mine, there may be several WiFi networks you can use. It is best if your board and your PC are on the same network (and same subnet).

At this point, you've completed another real MicroPython IoT project. In this case, we saw an IoT project that collects and displays data. Cool!

Taking It Further

This project, like the last one, shows excellent prospects for reusing the techniques in other projects. This is especially true for the HTML server aspect. If you liked seeing your sensor data over the Internet, you should consider taking time to explore some embellishments. Here are a few you may want to consider. Some are easy and some may be a challenge or require more research:

- Add more sensors to expand your project to more plants.

- Add a temperature sensor to record ambient temperature and display it on the web page.

- Rewrite the HTML code to produce JSON strings.

- Rewrite the HTML code to produce XML.

- Explore the HTML code to change the web page to your liking. Consider using cascading style sheets to change the background of the button when pressed.

- Connect your board to the Internet and call a friend to connect to your board and try it out.

- Add LEDs to your board to illuminate when the plants need watering.

Of course, if you want to press on to the next project, you're welcome to do so, but take some time to explore these potential embellishments – it will be good practice.

Summary

IoT solutions can take many forms. One of the more common forms is those that generate data that we can view over the Internet (sometimes called data collectors). The implementation of data collectors can vary greatly, but they generally store the data in some location and provide a way to view the data. The simplest forms are those that log the data (sometimes called data loggers) locally, on a remote server, in a database, or in a cloud service. The visualization of the data can also vary with the most basic providing the data via a web page.

In this chapter, we saw a MicroPython IoT project that logs data read from a series of soil moisture sensors. We created a plant monitoring solution that saved the data to the MicroPython board. The project also served the data via an HTML server so that we can see the data at any time. This project can be used as a template for a host of data collection projects. You can simply follow the pattern established in this chapter and build your own HTML-based data logger.

In the next chapter, we will see another project that uses a web server. We will build a small project to help track the humidity, barometric pressure, and temperature. Cool!

Project: Using Weather Sensors

Perhaps one of the ubiquitous projects that you will find on the Internet is a simple weather station. A basic weather station is a great project because it shows what is possible for sensing the environment, and it's a project almost anyone can relate to. After all, the weather is often a topic in almost every polite social interaction. If you had your own weather station, particularly one you created yourself, you could contribute a bit more to the conversation!

In this chapter, we will create a basic weather station. It isn't a full weather station because it doesn't include some of the more frequent sensors such as wind speed and rainfall totals (but you could add them). Rather, we're going to start with the basic observations for temperature, humidity, and barometric pressure.

Like the last chapter, we will be implementing this project as a web server to give us more practice on interfacing with sensors, logging data, and displaying results via a web page. Since we covered how to set up the web server code in the last chapter, the code for this project will focus on the changes rather than explain how the web server works. If you have not worked on the project from Chapter 10, you may want to refer to the main code section for details on the web server omitted from this chapter.

As you will see, the code used in this chapter is similar to the code in the last chapter, but with some subtle but significant changes in how we read data from the sensors.

Overview

In this chapter, we will implement a basic weather monitoring solution. This will involve using a weather sensor connected to our MicroPython board. We will use threading to read the data from the sensors and store it in a comma-separated value (CSV) file. Threading allows for faster, more dependable (predictable) reads.

383

© Charles Bell 2024
C. Bell, *MicroPython for the Internet of Things*, https://doi.org/10.1007/978-1-4842-9861-9_11

Now let's see what components are needed for this project, and then we will see how to wire everything together.

Required Components

Table 11-1 lists the components you will need. You can purchase the components separately from Adafruit (`adafruit.com`), SparkFun (`sparkfun.com`), or any electronics store that carries electronic components. Links to vendors are provided should you want to purchase the components. When listing multiple rows of the same object, you can choose one or the other - you do not need both. Also, you may find other vendors that sell the components. You should shop around to find the best deal. Costs shown are estimates and do not include any shipping costs.

Table 11-1. *Required Components*

Component	Qty	Description	Cost	Links
BME280	1	Weather sensor	$20	`www.sparkfun.com/products/13676`
			$15	`www.adafruit.com/product/2652`
Real-time clock	1	RTC	$10+	`www.sparkfun.com/products/12708`
			$7.50	`www.adafruit.com/product/3296`
Jumper wires	8	M/M jumper wires, 6" (cost is for a set of 10 jumper wires)	$4	`www.sparkfun.com/products/8431`

BME280 breakout board atmospheric sensors can support either I2C or SPI interfaces. The BME280 from SparkFun supports both, which makes it ideal for an IoT parts kit. Figure 11-1 shows the BME280 weather sensor from SparkFun. If you have one from another vendor, make sure it supports I2C (or adjust the code in this project and the wiring diagram accordingly). It does not come with headers, so you can add those yourself. Just order a set when you order the sensor and solder them yourself (or get a friend to help you).

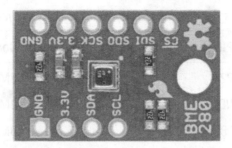

Figure 11-1. *Atmospheric Sensor Breakout (Courtesy of sparkfun.com)*

Fortunately, the wiring for this project is less complex than the last two projects. Now, let's see how to wire the components together.

Set Up the Hardware

The hardware setup for this project is easier than those for the last chapter. We have only the RTC and the BME280 sensor. However, the RTC module uses 5V and the BME280 uses 3.3V, so we will use different power connections.

Caution   Always check and double-check your power connections to ensure the power routed to the device matches its specifications. Powering a 3.3V sensor or breakout board with 5V (or more) may damage the components.

We will see how to make the connections for both the Raspberry Pi Pico and the Arduino Nano RP2040 Connect. As you will see, the connections are similar in that you will wire the breakout boards with the same connections and number of wires, but where those wires connect to the board differs. Let's begin with the Pico.

Connections for the Raspberry Pi Pico

Table 11-2 shows the connections needed for this project for the Raspberry Pi Pico.

Table 11-2. *Connections for the Weather Monitoring Project (Pico)*

Physical Pin	GPIO Num/Function	Connection
29	GP21	BME280 – 3.3V
38	GND	BME280 – GND
11	GP8	BME280 – SDA
12	GP9	BME280 – SCL
40	5V	RTC – VCC
38	GND	RTC – GND
11	GP8	RTC – SDA
12	GP9	RTC – SCL

Notice that we are connecting the RTC and the BME280 on the same pins for SDA and SCL (I2C). This is perfectly fine and will work since each device on the I2C bus must have its own address. Figure 11-2 shows the wiring drawing for the project on the Pico.

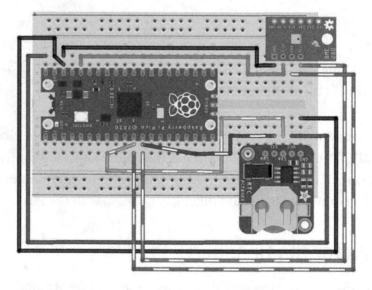

Figure 11-2. *Wiring the Weather Monitoring Project (Pico)*

Connections for the Arduino Nano RP2040 Connect

Since we are using the same components for the Arduino Nano RP2040 Connect, the connections are going to be similar, but as noted in previous chapters, the Nano RP2040 has a different pin layout. Thus, some of the connections are going to be different. Table 11-3 shows the connections needed for the Nano RP2040.

Table 11-3. *Connections for the Weather Monitoring Project (Nano RP2040)*

Physical Pin	GPIO Num/Function	Connection
2	3.3V	BME280 – 3.3V
19	GND	BME280 – GND
8	SDA	BME280 – SDA
9	SCL	BME280 – SCL
12	5V	RTC – VCC
14	GND	RTC – GND
8	SDA	RTC – SDA
9	SCL	RTC – SCL

Notice most of the connections are the same. What differs is where the jumper wires connect to the board. Figure 11-3 shows the wiring drawing for the project on the Nano RP2040.

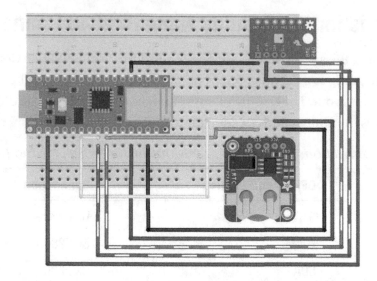

Figure 11-3. *Wiring the Weather Monitoring Project (Nano RP2040)*

Once again, always make sure to double-check your connections before powering the board on. Now, let's talk about the code we need to write. Don't power on your board just yet – there is a fair amount of discussion needed before we're ready to test the project.

Write the Code

Now it's time to write the code for our project. Fortunately, the code can run on both the Pico and Nano RP2040 Connect with only a minor change, which will be identified as we discuss the main portion of the code.

Like the last chapter, the code is a bit long, so we will divide the project into parts. We will put it all together before testing the project. Like the last chapter, we will write a module for the weather sensor. We will place the HTML server code and supporting functions in the main code module.

However, unlike the project in the last chapter, we will use threading to execute two parts of the project simultaneously: the main code and a loop to read the sensor and save the data to the log file. Since these two parts of the project will be accessing the log file where the main code reads and the sensor module writes, we will use a special construct of the threading module called a lock that we can use to place around the read and write functionality to ensure only one thread accesses the critical data (sometimes called a critical section of code) at a time. This concept will become clear as we look into the code.

Before we begin with the code, we should discuss the library (driver) we will need to read data from the BME280 sensor. It is a good practice to write a short test program to test new libraries and sensors. Let's do that first.

Testing the BME280 Module

The library we need to use to read the BME280 data is available from GitHub, and it is a library originally provided by Adafruit, but modified since. You can find and download the library from `https://github.com/gloveboxes/MicroPython-ESP8266-Environmental-Data-Streaming/blob/master/bme280.py`. You should download this to your PC as we will need it to download to our MicroPython board.

We will write a simple endless loop program to read the sensor using the `ReadTimer` class from Chapter 10. A quick look at the documentation for the `bme280.py` library reveals that one can read from the sensor after initializing the I2C connection with the class variables (a property that is actually a function) `sensor.raw_values` for raw values and `sensor.values` for human-readable format values as follows:

```
i2c = SoftI2C(sda=sda, scl=scl, freq=100000)
sensor = BME280(i2c=i2c, address=0x77)
print("Raw Data ->", sensor.raw_values)
print("Human Readable ->", sensor.values)
```

OK, so that's now so bad. Notice the `BME280()` initialization call (the class constructor) and the address parameter. We need to pass this parameter with this value (`0x77`) because the library is set up with a default address of `0x76` as follows. You could simply edit the library and set the constant to `0x77`, but the constructor allows you to pass in the address by value:

```
# BME280 default address.
BME280_I2CADDR = 0x76
```

Unfortunately, that is not the only surprise waiting for us to use this library. We also need to retrieve the raw values from the sensor, but this library does not provide such a function. Thus, we will have to edit the file and add it. Listing 11-1 shows the new function named `raw_values` that we need to add to the library. You can place this function at the end of the `bme280.py` files.

Listing 11-1. New Function: read_value for the BME280 Library

```
@property
def raw_values(self):
    """ human readable values """

    t, p, h = self.read_compensated_data()

    p = p // 256
    pi = p // 100
    pd = p - pi * 100

    hi = h // 1024
    hd = h * 100 // 1024 - hi * 100
    return ("{}".format(t / 100), "{}.{:02d}".format(pi, pd),
            "{}.{:02d}".format(hi, hd))
```

Notice the @property decorator. This permits MicroPython to treat the function as a property like the read_values property. Take a few moments to read the code, so you know how it works. You can compare it to the read_values function above it.

The need to add new functions is typical when looking for a library for your projects. Thus, this is a good example of how to take something that is almost what we need and modify it accordingly. Nice. Now, let's look at the completed test code.

Listing 11-2 shows the code for a test program named test_bme280.py that you can use to test your connections to the BME280 sensor. Notice the code is written for both the Pico and Nano RP2040 (just add/remove comments as discussed in previous chapters).

Listing 11-2. Test Code for BME280

```
#
# MicroPython for the IoT Second Edition - Chapter 11
#
# Chapter 11 - MicroPython Weather Web Server
#
# Test BME280 sensor with required modifications.
#
import network, socket, sys, time
```

```
from machine import Pin, SoftI2C
from project4.bme280 import BME280
from project4.read_timer import ReadTimer

#
# I2C for the RTC
# Arduino Nano RP2040 Connect uses sda=12, scl=13
#sda = Pin(12)
#scl = Pin(13)
#
# Raspberry Pi Pico uses sda=8, scl=9
sda = Pin(8)
scl = Pin(9)
#
# Software I2C (bit-banging) for the RTC
i2c = SoftI2C(sda=sda, scl=scl, freq=100000)
# Now, setup the sensor
print("setting up sensor...")
sensor = BME280(i2c=i2c, address=0x77)
# Setup read event handler
data_read_event = ReadTimer()
while True:
    if data_read_event.time_to_read():
        print("reading...", end="")
        data_read_event.reset()
        print("Raw Data ->", sensor.raw_values)
        print("Human Readable ->", sensor.values)
    time.sleep(1)
```

To run this code, you will need to create a folder on your MicroPython board named project4 and place in it the bme280.py and read_timer.py (from Chapter 10) files. Then, you can download the test_bme280.py code file and run it. When you run the code, you should see output similar to Listing 11-3. If things do not work, go back, and check to make sure you have wired the module correctly. Listing 11-3 shows the output of running this test program.

Listing 11-3. Running the Test BME280 Code

```
setting up sensor...
reading...Raw Data -> ('16.89', '1001.69', '65.00')
Human Readable -> ('16.84C', '1001.73hPa', '65.02%')
reading...Raw Data -> ('16.84', '1001.79', '65.02')
Human Readable -> ('16.83C', '1001.76hPa', '65.02%')
reading...Raw Data -> ('16.84', '1001.82', '65.00')
Human Readable -> ('16.84C', '1001.80hPa', '65.01%')
reading...Raw Data -> ('16.84', '1001.79', '65.03')
Human Readable -> ('16.83C', '1001.76hPa', '65.02%')
reading...Raw Data -> ('16.84', '1001.74', '65.04')
Human Readable -> ('16.83C', '1001.75hPa', '65.03%')
...
```

Now that the BME280 sensor has been tested, we are ready to create the code module to read the sensor.

Part 1: Sensor Code Module

The first part of the project will be to create a code module to contain a new class named WeatherSensor that contains all the functionality to read data from the sensor and save the data to a file. In this section, we will see how to write the code for the module. Open a new file and name it weather_sensor.py. Let's start by looking at the high-level design.

High-Level Design

Like the last chapter, we will create the functions to read data from the sensor and clear the log. However, this code module will be designed to provide a callback function that uses the ReadTimer class (once again, the same file from Chapter 10) to periodically read data from the sensor. Table 11-4 shows the functions for the Weather Sensor class.

Table 11-4. *High-Level Design (Functions) Weather Sensor Class*

Function	Parameters	Description
__init__()	csv_filename, i2c, rtc, rwlock	Initialization for the class (the constructor)
clear_log()		Clear the log
format time()		Format the time for display and saving to the lob
read_ sensor()		Read the values, and save them to the log
run()	value	Run the sensor read in a thread (callback function)

Notice the first function named __init__(). This is the constructor for the class and will be called when the class is instantiated from our main code. Notice also the private methods are named with a single underscore.

The following sections explain the initialization code and the functions needed. We will see the complete code in a later section.

Setup and Initialization

In this section, we discuss the code we need to set up and initialize the code module. First, there are a few imports we need, including those for the threading module, I2C, time, and the operating system libraries. We also need the libraries for the BME280 and Read Timer class. Listing 11-4 shows the code for the setup and initialization section. Place this at the top of the file.

Listing 11-4. Weather Sensor Class Setup and Initialization

```
import _thread, time
from machine import SoftI2C
from project4.bme280 import BME280
from project4.read_timer import ReadTimer
```

Constructor

The constructor for the class is where all the major work takes place. There are several things we need to do including the following:

- Initialize all class variables
- Set up the BME280 sensor
- Initialize the Read Timer

Listing 11-5 shows the code for the class constructor.

Listing 11-5. Weather Sensor Class Constructor

```
# Constructor
def __init__(self, csv_filename, i2c, rtc, rwlock):
    self.csv_filename = csv_filename
    self.i2c = i2c
    self.rtc = rtc
    self.rwlock = rwlock

    # Now, setup the sensor
    self.sensor = BME280(i2c=i2c, address=0x77)
    time.sleep(0.100)

    # Setup read event handler
    self.data_read_event = ReadTimer(60000)
    print("Weather Monitor Client is ready.")
```

Public Functions

There are only two public functions. The first, `clear_log()`, simply opens the file for writing and closes it. This effectively empties the file. The function is provided for convenience. The second function, `read_sensor()`, reads the sensor and records the data in the log file. Finally, we supply a `run()` function for running the code in a thread.

Private Functions

The `_format_time()` function is the same function we used in Chapter 10. Recall, it gets the current time and formats the time for writing to the log.

Complete Code

Now that we have seen all the parts of the code module, let's look at the completed code. Listing 11-6 shows the complete code for the Plant Monitor code module. Once again, we can save this file as weather_sensor.py.

Listing 11-6. Weather Sensor Code Module Complete Code

```
#
# MicroPython for the IoT Second Edition - Chapter 11
#
# Chapter 11 - MicroPython Weather Web Server - BME280 Weather Class
#
# Imports for the project
import _thread, time
from machine import SoftI2C
from project4.bme280 import BME280
from project4.read_timer import ReadTimer

class WeatherSensor:
    """"Sensor node using a BME280 sensor to read temperature, humidity, and
        barometric pressure."""

    # Constructor
    def __init__(self, csv_filename, i2c, rtc, rwlock):
        self.csv_filename = csv_filename
        self.i2c = i2c
        self.rtc = rtc
        self.rwlock = rwlock

        # Now, setup the sensor
        self.sensor = BME280(i2c=i2c, address=0x77)
        time.sleep(0.100)
        # Setup read event handler
        self.data_read_event = ReadTimer(60000)
        print("Weather Monitor Client is ready.")

    # Format the time (epoch) for a better view
```

```python
    def _format_time(self):
        # Get datetime
        dt = self.rtc.datetime
        # (year, month, day, hours. minutes, seconds, weekday: integer: 0-6 )
        return "{0:02}/{1:02}/{2:04} {3:02}:{4:02}:{5:02}".format(
                dt[1], dt[2], dt[0], dt[3], dt[4], dt[5])

    # Clear the log
    def clear_log(self):
        if self.rwlock.acquire():
            print("Lock available for clearing log!")
            return    # skip the read
        log_file = open(self.csv_filename, 'w')
        log_file.close()
        self.rwlock.release()

    # Reads the sensor data
    def read_sensor(self):
        time.sleep_ms(50)
        raw_values = self.sensor.raw_values
        temperature = raw_values[0]
        humidity = raw_values[2]
        pressure = raw_values[1]
        print("Acquiring lock...")
        # Wait for the lock
        while not self.rwlock.acquire():
            print("Waiting on lock for writing...")
            time.sleep(1)
        print("Writing...")
        data_file = open(self.csv_filename, "a")
        message = ("{0},{1},{2},{3}"
                    "".format(self._format_time(), temperature,
                    humidity, pressure))
        data_file.write("{0}\n".format(message))
        data_file.close()
        self.rwlock.release()
```

```
        print("Lock released.")
        print("Data read:", self.sensor.values)
    # Run the sensor read in a thread
    def run(self):
        while True:
            if self.data_read_event.time_to_read():
                self.data_read_event.reset()
                self.read_sensor()
            time.sleep(1)
```

Wow, that's a lot of code! Take some time to read it until you understand all the parts of the code. Don't worry about the run() function and how it is called. We will see how to do that in the main code.

Part 2: Read Timer Code

We will reuse the Read Timer from Chapter 10. You can copy the file directly, but be sure to change the constant for how frequently you want to read the sensor. This is always a critical item to consider, avoiding reading too much data or data that doesn't change too frequently. See the section on the Read Timer code in Chapter 10 for more details.

OK, now we're ready to look at the main code.

Part 3: Main Code

The main will use a file to store the HTML code (since it doesn't change) and a single HTML string for populating an HTML table with the data from the file. We will also add code to read the date and time from the RTC.

Instead of using an HTML button, we can format a command manually on the URL. We can use this technique to allow access to commands without using buttons or other user interface features. It also helps to make these commands harder to use to prevent overuse. For example, we can provide a clear log command. We would use a URL like http://192.168.42.140/CLEAR_LOG, which submits a GET request to the HTML server. We can capture that command and clear the log when it is issued.

Caution   If you build commands like this, be sure to use them carefully. That is, setting your URL to `http://192.168.42.140/CLEAR_LOG` and pressing enter issues the command. Refreshing the page will reissue the command! When you use the command, be sure to clear your URL before refreshing or, better, use it once and close the page/tab.

The following sections explain the initialization code and the functions needed. We will see the complete code in a later section. Let's start with the HTML code.

HTML Code (Files)

The HTML files are similar to the files used in Chapter 10. Recall that the first file (named `part1.html`) will contain the HTML code up to the table rows; the second file (named `weather_data.csv`) will be populated by the `WeatherSensor` class; and the third (named `part2.html`) will contain the remaining HTML code. The only difference between the .html files for this project and Chapter 10 are the title, column names, and the rows for the `part1.html` file as shown in Listing 11-7. The `part2.html` is the same as Chapter 10, and the `weather_data.csv` file is created by the Weather Sensor class.

Listing 11-7. HTML Code (part1.html)

```
<!DOCTYPE html>
<html>
  <head>
    <title>MicroPython for the IoT 2nd Edition - Weather Sensor</title>
    <meta http-equiv="refresh" content="30">
    <style>
      table, th, td {
          border: 1px solid black;
          border-collapse: collapse;
      }
      th, td {
          padding: 5px;
      }
      th {
```

```
            text-align: left;
      }
   </style>
</head>
<center><h2>MicroPython for the IoT 2nd Edition - Weather Sensor</h2>
</center><br>
<center>A simple project to demonstrate how to retrieve sensor data over
the Internet.</center>
<center><br><b>Weather Data</b><br><br>
   <table style="width:75%">
     <col width="180">
     <col width="120">
     <col width="100">
     <col width="100">
     <tr><th>Datetime</th><th>Temperature</th><th>Humidity</th><th>
     Pressure</th></tr>
```

See Chapter 10 for more details about these files and how they are used in the main function.

Imports

The imports we need for the project include those for the select, sys, socket, Pin, SoftI2C, RTC (DS1307), and the WeatherSensor class. The complete list of imports is shown as follows. If you want to follow along, open a new file and name it weather.py.

```
import network, select, socket, sys, time, _thread
from machine import Pin, SoftI2C
from project4.ds1307 import DS1307
from project4.weather_sensor import WeatherSensor
```

We also need two constants. First, we need a string for the log file name, and we need a string we can use to create the rows for the table. The HTML code that occurs before this line is saved in files as described earlier. The following shows the string used. Notice we use replacement syntax so that we can use the format() function to fill in the details.

```
# Constants
DATA_FILENAME = 'weather_data.csv'
```

```
# HTML web page for the project
HTML_TABLE_ROW = "<tr><td>{0}</td><td>{1}</td><td>{2}</td><td>{3}</
td></tr>"
```

The Main() Function

The HTML server portion of the main() function is like the last project, but instead of processing form requests, we send the web page back to the client by default. The only command supported is the CLEAR_LOG command, which requires specifying it on the URL on the client as described earlier. Listing 11-8 shows the code for the main() function.

Like the previous chapters, we must add special code for the Pico and Nano RP2040. See the comments in the listing for instructions on how to change the SoftI2C setup for each board or refer to Chapters 8 and 9 for more details.

Listing 11-8. Plant Monitor main() Function

```
# Main function
def main():
    # Setup the socket and respond to HTML requests
    # Connect to the network
    if not connect():
        sys.exit(-1)
    #
    # I2C for the RTC
    # Arduino Nano RP2040 Connect uses sda=12, scl=13
    #sda = Pin(12)
    #scl = Pin(13)
    #
    # Raspberry Pi Pico uses sda=8, scl=9
    sda = Pin(8)
    scl = Pin(9)
    #
    # Software I2C (bit-banging) for the RTC
    i2c = SoftI2C(sda=sda, scl=scl, freq=100000)
    #
    # NOTE: We only need to set the datetime once. Uncomment these
```

```
#       lines only on the first run of a new RTC module or
#       whenever you change the battery.
rtc = DS1307(i2c)
# (year, month, day, hours. minutes, seconds, weekday: integer: 0-6 )
# rtc.datetime = (2023,09,23,16,15,30,2)
#
# Read/Write lock
rwlock = _thread.allocate_lock()
# Setup the weather sensor
weather = WeatherSensor(DATA_FILENAME, i2c, rtc, rwlock)
# Start the weather sensor in a thread
weather_thread = _thread.start_new_thread(weather.run, ())

# Setup the socket and wait for connections
addr = socket.getaddrinfo('0.0.0.0', 80)[0][-1]
sock = socket.socket()
sock.bind(addr)
sock.listen(5)

print("Ready for connections...")
while True:
    try:
        client, address = sock.accept()
    except OSError as err:
        time.sleep(0.50)
        continue
    print("Got a connection from a client at: %s" % str(address))
    request = client.recv(1024)

    # Allow for clearing of the log but be careful! The auto refresh
    # will resend this command if you do not clear it from your URL
    # line.
    if (request[:14] == b'GET /CLEAR_LOG'):
        print('Requesting clear log.')
        weather.clear_log()
    else:
        if not rwlock.acquire():
```

```
                print("Lock unavailable for reading!")
                continue   # skip the read
            send_sensor_data(client, DATA_FILENAME)
            rwlock.release()
        client.close()
        time.sleep(1)
    sock.close()
    weather_thread.exit()
```

Take a moment to read this code. Notice how we implement the function in a more modular way. Not only does placing common code in functions help with how you break a problem down into parts, but it also makes your main code (the main() function) shorter.

Notice also there is the use of the select class. This is a special class that permits us to use the socket class, which is a form of stream class, without blocking (waiting for a client before returning). See https://docs.micropython.org/en/latest/library/select.html for more information about using the select class.

Threading Code

The threading code is very short. We simply create the lock that we will use to control access to the read and write functions for the log file and start the weather sensor in another thread supplying the run() function as follows. When the code is complete, we also stop the thread.

```
    rwlock = _thread.allocate_lock()
    # Start the weather sensor in a thread
    weather_thread = _thread.start_new_thread(weather.run, ())
...
    weather_thread.exit()
```

That's it! Threading, while it sounds really complicated, isn't provided you are careful with locking and do not need to call into another thread. For more information about threading, see https://docs.micropython.org/en/latest/library/_thread.html.

Let's look at the completed code.

Complete Code

Now that we have seen all the parts of the code module, let's look at the completed code. Listing 11-9 shows the complete code for the Plant Monitor code module. Once again, we can save this file as `weather.py`. Notice we also have the WiFi code we used in the previous chapters. Be sure to set the SSID and password for your local WiFi setup.

Listing 11-9. Weather Monitor Main Code

```
#
# MicroPython for the IoT Second Edition - Chapter 11
#
# Chapter 11 - MicroPython Weather Web Server
#
# Required Components:
# - (1) BME280 Weather Sensor
#
# Imports for the project
import network, select, socket, sys, time, _thread
from machine import Pin, SoftI2C
from project4.ds1307 import DS1307
from project4.weather_sensor import WeatherSensor

# Constants
DATA_FILENAME = 'weather_data.csv'

# HTML web page for the project
HTML_TABLE_ROW = "<tr><td>{0}</td><td>{1}</td><td>{2}</td><td>{3}</
td></tr>"

# Setup the board to connect to our network.
def connect():
    wlan = network.WLAN(network.STA_IF)
    wlan.active(True)
    wlan.connect('SSID', 'PASSWORD')
    while not wlan.isconnected() and wlan.status() >= 0:
        print("Waiting to connect...")
        time.sleep(1)
```

403

```
    if not wlan.isconnected():
        print("Cannot find SSID!")
        sys.exit(0)

    print("Connected!")
    print("My IP address is: {0}".format(wlan.ifconfig()[0]))
    return True

# Read HTML from file and send to client a row at a time.
def send_html_file(filename, client):
    html = open(filename, 'r')
    for row in html:
        client.send(row)
    html.close()

# Send the sensor data to the client.
def send_sensor_data(client, filename):
    send_html_file("project4/part1.html", client)
    try:
        log_file = open(filename, 'r')
    except OSError as e:
        print("Log file not found. Creating new file.")
        log_file = open(filename, 'w')
        log_file.close()
        log_file = open(filename, 'r')
    for row in log_file:
        cols = row.strip("\n").split(",") # split row by commas
        # build the table string if all parts are there
        if len(cols) >= 4:
            html = HTML_TABLE_ROW.format(cols[0], cols[1], cols[2], cols[3])
            # send the row to the client
            client.send(html)
            time.sleep(0.05)
    log_file.close()
    send_html_file("project4/part2.html", client)

# Main function
```

```python
def main():
    # Setup the socket and respond to HTML requests
    # Connect to the network
    if not connect():
        sys.exit(-1)
    #
    # I2C for the RTC
    # Arduino Nano RP2040 Connect uses sda=12, scl=13
    #sda = Pin(12)
    #scl = Pin(13)
    #
    # Raspberry Pi Pico uses sda=8, scl=9
    sda = Pin(8)
    scl = Pin(9)
    #
    # Software I2C (bit-banging) for the RTC
    i2c = SoftI2C(sda=sda, scl=scl, freq=100000)
    #
    # NOTE: We only need to set the datetime once. Uncomment these
    #       lines only on the first run of a new RTC module or
    #       whenever you change the battery.
    rtc = DS1307(i2c)
    # (year, month, day, hours. minutes, seconds, weekday: integer: 0-6 )
    # rtc.datetime = (2023,09,23,16,15,30,2)
    #
    # Read/Write lock
    rwlock = _thread.allocate_lock()
    # Setup the weather sensor
    weather = WeatherSensor(DATA_FILENAME, i2c, rtc, rwlock)
    # Start the weather sensor in a thread
    weather_thread = _thread.start_new_thread(weather.run, ())

    # Setup the socket and wait for connections
    addr = socket.getaddrinfo('0.0.0.0', 80)[0][-1]
    sock = socket.socket()
    sock.bind(addr)
```

405

```python
    sock.listen(5)

    print("Ready for connections...")
    while True:
        try:
            client, address = sock.accept()
        except OSError as err:
            time.sleep(0.50)
            continue
        print("Got a connection from a client at: %s" % str(address))
        request = client.recv(1024)

        # Allow for clearing of the log but be careful! The auto refresh
        # will resend this command if you do not clear it from your URL
        # line.
        if (request[:14] == b'GET /CLEAR_LOG'):
            print('Requesting clear log.')
            weather.clear_log()
        else:
            if not rwlock.acquire():
                print("Lock unavailable for reading!")
                continue    # skip the read
            send_sensor_data(client, DATA_FILENAME)
            rwlock.release()
        client.close()
        time.sleep(1)
    sock.close()
    weather_thread.exit()

if __name__ == '__main__':
    try:
        main()
    except (KeyboardInterrupt, SystemExit) as err:
        print("\nbye!\n")
sys.exit(0)
```

Take some time to read the code to ensure you understand how it works. Aside from building a simple web server, the code isn't as complex as we have seen in previous chapters.

Now, let's run this project!

Execute!

Now is the fun part! We've got the code all set up to read Weather Sensor from our plants and send all the sensor data collected to the client. Recall, we need to copy the code to our board. We will need to copy the files we created to our MicroPython board. Recall from the code walk-through that the code modules we created are referenced from a folder, project4, as follows:

```
from project4.ds1307 import DS1307
from project4.weather_sensor import WeatherSensor
```

Recall we also have these imports in the WeatherSensor class:

```
from project4.bme280 import BME280
from project4.read_timer import ReadTimer
```

This means we need to create a directory on our MicroPython board named project4 and copy those files there (weather_sensor.py and read_timer.py). Recall that you can do this from Thonny. We also need to copy the BME280 library (bme280.py) and the two HTML files (part1.html and part2.html) to the folder along with the RTC module (ds1307.py) that we used in Chapter 8. Finally, we can copy the main code (weather.py) into the root folder on the MicroPython board. When all of the files are copied, you should see the file structure similar to what is shown in Figure 11-4.

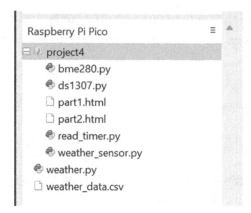

Figure 11-4. *Sample File Layout for the Weather Monitoring Project*

Copy the files as shown and then you are ready to test the project.

All we need now is the IP address of that board to point our web browser. We can get that from our debug statements by running the code. Listing 11-10 shows the initial run for the project.

Listing 11-10. Running the Weather Monitor

```
Waiting to connect...
Waiting to connect...
Waiting to connect...
Waiting to connect...
Waiting to connect...
Waiting to connect...
Connected!
My IP address is: 10.0.0.14
Weather Monitor Client is ready.
Ready for connections...
Acquiring lock...
Writing...
Lock released.
Data read: ('17.26C', '1002.43hPa', '65.83%')
Got a connection from a client at: ('10.0.0.13', 52937)
Got a connection from a client at: ('10.0.0.13', 52935)
Got a connection from a client at: ('10.0.0.13', 52936)
Got a connection from a client at: ('10.0.0.13', 52943)
```

```
Acquiring lock...
Writing...
Lock released.
Data read: ('17.05C', '1002.48hPa', '65.75%')
Got a connection from a client at: ('10.0.0.13', 52950)
Got a connection from a client at: ('10.0.0.13', 52951)
Got a connection from a client at: ('10.0.0.13', 52952)
```

Notice in this case the IP address is 10.0.0.14. All we need to do is put that in our browser as shown in Figure 11-5. Depending on your WiFi setup, you may see an address in the 192.168.X.X network, which is fine provided it matches the same subnet as your PC.

MicroPython for the IOT 2nd Edition - Weather Sensor

A simple project to demonstrate how to retrieve sensor data over the Internet.

Weather Data

Datetime	Temperature	Humidity	Pressure
9/25/2023 22:30	21.94	64.47	1009.31
9/25/2023 22:39	21.93	64.52	1009.32
9/25/2023 22:39	21.8	64.47	1009.38
9/25/2023 22:39	21.79	64.48	1009.36
10/17/2023 18:33:29	17.18	64.46	1002.43

Figure 11-5. *Weather Monitor Project*

Once you enter the URL, you should see a web page like the image shown. If you don't, be sure to check the HTML in your code to ensure it is exactly like what is shown; otherwise, the page may not display properly.

Caution   It is rare, but possible, to corrupt the file storage on your MicroPython board. If you see strange data or files are incomplete or always empty, you may have corrupted your filesystem. To fix this problem, reload a different .uf2 image. For example, try https://github.com/dwelch67/raspberrypi-pico/blob/main/flash_nuke.uf2 and then reinstall the correct image to fully erase your flash.

You should also ensure the network your PC is connected to can reach the network to which your board is connected. If your home office is set up like mine, there may be several WiFi networks you can use. It is best if your board and your PC are on the same network (and same subnet).

At this point, you've completed another real MicroPython IoT project. Cool!

Taking It Further

This project, like the last one, shows excellent prospects for reusing the techniques in other projects. This is especially true for the HTML server aspect. If you liked seeing your sensor data over the Internet, you should consider taking time to explore some embellishments. Here are a few you may want to consider. Some are easy and some may be a challenge or require more research:

- Add more sensors to expand your project to more weather phenomena.

- Rewrite the HTML code to produce JSON strings.

- Rewrite the HTML code to produce XML.

- Explore the HTML code to change the web page to your liking. Consider using cascading style sheets to change the background of the button when pressed.

- Connect your board to the Internet and call a friend to connect to your board and try it out.

Of course, if you want to press on to the next project, you're welcome to do so, but take some time to explore these potential embellishments – it will be good practice.

Summary

In this chapter, we saw another MicroPython IoT project that logs data read from a weather sensor. We created a plant monitoring solution that saved the data to the local MicroPython board. The project also served the data via an HTML server so that we can see the data at any time. This project can be used as a template for a host of data collection projects. You can simply follow the pattern established in this chapter and build your own HTML-based data logger.

In the next chapter, we will revisit the topic of cloud computing and discuss what is available for consumers to use to build IoT projects. We will follow that chapter with tutorials on three of the most popular IoT cloud services, taking three of our previous IoT projects to the next level with cloud services.

CHAPTER 12

Cloud Computing

Thus far in the book, we have learned that the Raspberry Pi Pico and Arduino Nano RP2040 Connect are great small microcontrollers that have a lot of power in such a small package. They are inexpensive and easy to program, and now that we've built a good foundation of experience working with basic electronics, including how to write code to use sensors, respond to inputs (e.g., buttons), and display data as well as how to create a simple web server solution, it's time to take our IoT skills to a new level.

In previous chapters, you've seen a number of projects, ranging from very basic to advanced in difficulty; it is time to discuss how to make your IoT data viewable by others via the cloud. More specifically, you will get a small glimpse at what is possible with the more popular cloud computing services and solutions.

I say a glimpse because it is not possible to cover all viable solutions available in cloud services solutions for IoT in a single chapter. Once again, this is a case learning a little bit about something, and seeing it in practice will help you get started.

In this chapter, we will get an overview of what the cloud is and how it is used for IoT solutions. The chapter also presents a concise overview of the popular cloud systems for IoT.

THE CLOUD: ISN'T THAT JUST MARKETING HYPE?

Don't believe all the hype or sales talk about any product that includes "cloud" in its name. Cloud computing services and resources should be accessible via the Internet from anywhere, available to you via subscription (fee or for free), and permit you to consume or produce and share the data involved. Also, consider the fact that you must have access to the cloud to get your data. Thus, you have no alternative if the service is unreachable (or down).

© Charles Bell 2024
C. Bell, *MicroPython for the Internet of Things*, https://doi.org/10.1007/978-1-4842-9861-9_12

Since the technologies presented are quite unique in implementation (but straightforward in concept), I keep the project hardware and programming to a minimal effort.

Overview

Unless you live in a very isolated location, you have been bombarded with talk about the cloud and IoT. You've seen advertisements in magazines and on television, or read about it in other books, or attended a seminar or conference. Unless you've spent time learning what cloud means, you are wondering what all the fuss is about.

What Is the Cloud?

Simply stated,[1] the cloud is a name tagged to services available via the Internet. These can be servers you can access (running as a virtual machine on a larger server), systems that provide access to a specific software or environment, or resources such as disks or IP addresses that you can attach to other resources. The technologies behind the cloud include grid computing (distributed processing), virtualization, and networking. The correct scientific term is cloud computing. Although a deep dive into cloud computing is beyond the scope of this book, it is enough to understand that you can use cloud computing services to store your sensor data.

What Is Cloud Computing Then?

The term *cloud computing* is sadly overused and has become a marketing term for some. True cloud computing solutions are services that are provided to subscribers (customers) via a combination of virtualization, grid computing (distributed processing and storage), and facilities to support virtualized hardware and software, such as IP addresses that are tied to the subscription rather than a physical device. Thus, you can use and discard resources on the fly to meet your needs.

---

[1] Experienced cloud researchers will tell you there is a lot more to learn about the cloud.

These resources, services, and features are priced by usage patterns (called *subscription plans* or *tiers*), in which you can pay for as little or as much as you need. For example, if you need more processing power, you can move up to a subscription level that offers more CPU cores, more memory, and so forth. Thus, you only pay for what you need, which means that organizations can potentially save a great deal on infrastructure.

A classic example of this benefit is a case where an organization experiences a brief and intense level of work that requires additional resources to keep their products and services viable. Using the cloud, organizations can temporarily increase their infrastructure capability and, once the peak has passed, scale things back to normal. This is a lot better than having to rent or purchase a ton of hardware for that one event.

Sadly, there are some vendors that offer cloud solutions (typically worded as *cloud enabled* or simply *cloud*) that fall far short of being a complete solution. In most cases, they are nothing more than yesterday's Internet-based storage and visualization. Fortunately, Microsoft Azure is authentic: a full cloud computing solution with an impressive array of features to support almost any cloud solution you can dream up.

Tip   If you would like to know more about cloud computing and its many facets, see `https://en.wikipedia.org/wiki/Cloud_computing`.

How Does the Cloud Help IoT?

OK, so now that we know what cloud systems are, how do they help me with my IoT projects? There are a variety of ways, but most common are mechanisms for storing and presenting your data rather than storing it locally or even remotely on another system such as a dedicated database server. That is, you can send the data you collect from your sensors to the cloud for storage and even use additional cloud services to view the data using charts, graphs, or just plain text. The sky is the limit with respect to how you can present your data.

But storing data isn't the only feature you can leverage in the cloud. There are other services that you can use to link to yet other services to form a solution. For example, most paid IoT cloud systems provide features that can "talk" to each other, allowing you to link them together to quickly build a solution. The features are often called components rather than services, but both terms apply.

For example, in Microsoft Azure, you can store your data with one of several components, then link it to others that allow you to modify the data via queries, others to route the data to other places (even to another cloud service vendor), and to one of several components for displaying the data. Yes, it really is a set of building blocks like that.

Now that we've had a general overview of cloud systems, let's look at those that support IoT projects directly.

IoT Cloud Systems

There are a number of IoT cloud vendors that offer all manner of products, capacities, and features to match about anything you can conjure for an IoT project. With so many vendors offering IoT solutions, it can be difficult to choose one. The following is a concise list of the more popular IoT offerings from the top vendors in the cloud industry:

- *Oracle IoT*: www.oracle.com/internet-of-things/

- *Microsoft Azure IoT Hub*: https://azure.microsoft.com/en-us/product-categories/iot/

- *Google IoT Core*: https://cloud.google.com/iot-core

- *IBM IoT*: www.ibm.com/internet-of-things

- *Arduino IoT Cloud*: www.arduino.cc/en/IoT/HomePage

- *Adafruit IO*: https://io.adafruit.com/

- *If This Then That (IFTTT)*: https://ifttt.com/

- *MathWorks ThingSpeak*: https://thingspeak.com/

Most of the vendors offer commercial products, but a few like Google, Azure, Arduino, IFTTT, and ThingSpeak offer limited free accounts. A few are free like Adafruit. IO and Arduino IoT Cloud but may limit you to a particular platform or a smaller set of features. As you may surmise, some of the offerings are complex solutions with steep learning curve, but the IFTTT and ThingSpeak offerings are simple and easy to use. Since we want a solution that is easy to use (and free!), we will then use ThingSpeak in the next chapter to round out our introduction to IoT cloud systems.

Tip   If you want or need to use one of the other vendors, be sure to read all of the tutorials thoroughly before jumping into your code.

Let's look at some of the types of services available in cloud systems that support IoT projects.

IoT Cloud Services Available

IoT projects offer an amazing opportunity to expand our knowledge of the world around us and to observe events from all over the world no matter where we are located. To address these capabilities, IoT Cloud Services provide an array of services that you can leverage in your applications.

There are services for collecting data, managing your devices, performing analytics, and even application and processing extensions for you to exploit. For example, some vendors include complete user management where you can provide user accounts for people to log in and use your cloud solution and see your data.

The following lists a number of the types of services available. Some vendors may not offer all of the services, and a service common among the vendors may work very differently from one vendor to another. However, this should give you an idea of what services are available and a general idea of the feature set:

- *Device management*: Allows you to set up, manage, and track what devices are in your IoT network.

- *Data storage*: Permits storage of your IoT data either on a temporary (typically free for a number of days) or permanent (paid) storage.

- *Data analytics*: Allows you to perform analysis on your data to find trends, outliers, or any form of analytical query.

- *Data query and filters*: You can perform queries or filter your IoT data after it has been sent to the cloud service for detailed presentations or transformations.

- *Big data*: Permits you to store vast amounts of data and perform operations on the data (think data warehousing).

- *Visualization tools*: Various dashboards and graphics you can use to help present your data in meaningful ways (spreadsheet, pie charts, etc.).

- *High availability*: Provides features that allow you to operate even if portions of your cloud servers (or the vendor's) fail or go offline due to network issues.

- *Third-party integration*: Allows you to connect your IoT services to other IoT servers from other vendors, for example, connecting your Adafruit.IO data to IFTTT for triggering an SMS message.

- *Security (data, user)*: Provides support for managing user accounts, security access, and more for your applications.

- *Encryption*: Allows you to encrypt your data either in the cloud or when transmitting the data from one service to another.

- *Deployment*: Similar to device management, but on a grander scale where you build IoT devices using common profiles, operating systems, configurations, etc.

- *Scalability*: The ability to scale from a small number of devices and services to many devices. This is often only available in the larger, paid vendor services.

- *API's (Rest, programming)*: Allows you to write code to communicate directly with the services instead of issuing web requests. Often part of the larger, paid vendor services.

For our beginning IoT projects, we will be focusing on a subset of these services, which can be grouped into several categories. Let's look at a few of the most common services you may want to start using right away.

Data Storage

These services allow you to store your data in the cloud rather than on your local device. Some data such as alerts or notices do not need to be stored, and you should think about whether you will need the data in the future and will be project dependent. For example, if you wanted to create a weather alert project, you may not care what the temperature was a week or even a month ago. However, if you want to do some amateur weather forecasting, you will want to store data for some time (perhaps years). You may consider storing the data locally, which may be possible for some platforms such as the Raspberry Pi, but the Arduino and similar boards have very limited storage capabilities.

Thus, if you need to store your data for some period and storing it locally is not an option, you should consider this when selecting a cloud vendor. Look for how data will be stored, the mechanisms needed to send the data to the service, and how to get the data out of the service.

Data Transformation (Queries)

These services allow you to perform queries on the data as it flows to or through the cloud services. You may want to show only a subset of the data to your users, or you may want to filter the data so that data from certain devices, dates, etc., are shown for one of several views.

The case where you'd want to consider these is for IoT projects that collect data from multiple sensors or multiple devices, and the data is stored for a period of time. For example, if you have devices geographically distributed over a wide area, you may only want to see data from a subset of those devices. Similarly, if you have data from several time periods, hours, days, and weeks, you may only want to see data from a specific time.

Visualization Tools

These services along with routing and messaging are the most commonly used for beginning IoT projects. These are simply services that allow you to see your data on the Internet. It may be nothing more than a simple list of the data, or it may be an elaborate data dashboard complete with controls that users can use to manipulate the display. Fortunately, most cloud vendors provide a robust set of tools (some more than one) that you can use to present your data to yourself or your users.

Routing and Messaging

These services are the heart or the bones of the IoT cloud. They encompass the glue to bind different services together. More specifically, they provide mechanisms for you to connect your devices to services, those services to other services such as queries, filters, and visualization tools, permitting you to build an IoT solution using several cloud services.

What Can Cloud Services Do for Our IoT Projects?

Thus far, we haven't discussed how to use the data generated from our projects other than saving the data in a file on our MicroPython board. Due to the limited size of these options, you will encounter issues you need to resolve such as how much data you want to store and for how long.

While those are things that can be solved, the bigger question is what are you going to do with the data? Would you want to see how the data changes over time, how one sensor data compares to another, how often a value changes, or more basic statistics like min, max, and average values? All of these things require processing power that the Pico doesn't have to spare.

Furthermore, you may want to see the data presented in one or more graphs that you can use for a pictorial representation. The best way to do this is to take advantage of IoT Cloud services. Not only can you store the data easily, but you can also perform analysis on the data and present it in one of several graphics. Let's discuss what is possible with cloud computing and IoT before we dive into several projects.

Getting Started with Cloud Computing

There are many cloud providers offering IoT solutions for developers and more being added every year. The complexity and features of some of the providers are impressive and are typically beyond the needs of the enthusiast and hobbyist. These services are paid services, and the cost can add up over time. Fortunately, several options are available that are inexpensive (some are free with limitations on features) that we can use to get started with IoT projects.

This section introduces three cloud service providers that offer reasonably priced or free services. These include using message queue telemetry transport, which we will use with Adafruit IO, the Arduino IoT Cloud,[2] and ThingSpeak from MathWorks.

---

[2] Not just for Arduino!

Message Queue Telemetry Transport

The first technology we will explore is a mechanism to send "messages" to other computers (services) using a defined protocol (a way to communicate) that is often supported by specialized programming interfaces. One of the easiest to use with microcontrollers defines a protocol with publish and subscribe roles. That is, you can publish data (write), or you can subscribe to data (read) and even be notified when new data is available. One of the easiest-to-use publish/subscribe protocols is called message queue telemetry transport (MQTT).

The publish/subscribe model has been around for some time at least in theory and concept. There are also programming constructs that implement the roles. A publisher publishes data to a location (a server, database, or repository of structured data) that permits subscribers to get the data. Thus, publishers are writers and subscribers are readers.

In the case of IoT projects, we have one or more sensor nodes sending data to the repository using a message queue that records messages that contain the data. When subscribers subscribe to the data, they get the messages in the order that they were received and parse the message for the data. Thus, they do not have to add a data abstraction layer like those we would use with a database server. In this case, the MQTT protocol is all you need.

MQTT is a simple and very lightweight protocol (meaning it doesn't require a huge library with a complex set of steps to use) that you can use with your MicroPython boards. Since MQTT is based on a message queue, the protocol is very tolerant of unreliable delivery of data. And since it doesn't require a lot of memory to use, it can be used on small devices. What this means is MQTT is a way to ensure your small IoT devices can send data to a server (called a broker) with a reasonable assurance of delivery – both for publishers and subscribers. This makes MQTT a perfect tool for use in IoT projects.

Interestingly, MQTT has been around since 1999. It was invented by Dr. Andy Stanford-Clark of IBM and Alren Nipper of Arcom (Eurotech). It has changed very little since then and has been adapted to a growing number of platforms. For more information about MQTT, see http://mqtt.org/faq.

Arduino IoT Cloud

The last service we will look at is the Arduino IoT Cloud, sometimes simply called Arduino Cloud, which is designed for enthusiasts and hobbyists to explore using Arduino boards. However, it also permits you to use your MicroPython board (those that support the RP2040) as well as many other Arduino boards.

The Arduino IoT Cloud is designed to make getting started with IoT in the cloud as easy as possible with a quick setup, simplified APIs, and powerful display options (called dashboards). The Arduino IoT Cloud also permits you to control your IoT devices over the Internet and even provides an interface with Amazon's Alexa API. How cool is that?

The service uses concepts such as things (IoT projects), dashboards (displays), devices (MicroPython board/platform), etc., presented in a simplified setup interface that anyone can use. The following is a brief list of the intriguing features available, some of which are only available through the Arduino programming language, but most are available for MicroPython projects. Oh, and the best part is the service is free to use!

- `Data Monitoring`: Monitor sensor values and display them on a dashboard

- `Variable Synchronization`: Sync your variables across devices

- `Scheduler`: Schedule actions to run at specific times

- `Over-The-Air (OTA) Uploads`: Update devices over the air

- `Webhooks`: Create "hooks" to connect projects to other services

- `Amazon Alexa Support`: Control your project with your voice through Alexa

- `Dashboard Sharing`: Share data with the world

Tip   See `https://docs.arduino.cc/arduino-cloud/getting-started/iot-cloud-getting-started` for more details and how to get started with the Arduino IoT Cloud.

ThingSpeak

Another service similar to MQTT permits you to store your data in the cloud using a popular, easy-to-use, cloud-based IoT data-hosting service from MathWorks called ThingSpeak (www.thingspeak.com).

ThingSpeak offers a free account for noncommercial projects that generate fewer than three million messages (or data elements) per year or around 8,200 messages per day. Free accounts are also limited to four channels (a channel is equivalent to a project and can save up to eight data items). If you need to store or process more data than that, you can purchase a commercial license in one of four categories; each with specific products, features, and limitations: Standard, Academic, Student, and Home. See https://thingspeak.com/prices and click each of the license options to learn more about the features and pricing.

ThingSpeak works by receiving messages from devices that contain the data you want to save or plot. There are libraries available that you can use for certain platforms or programming languages such as Python or the Arduino platform.

However, you can also use a machine-to-machine (M2M) connectivity protocol (called MQTT[3]) or representational state transfer (REST[4]) API designed as a request-response model that communicates over HTTP to send data to or read data from ThingSpeak. Yes, you can even read your data from other devices.

Tip   See www.mathworks.com/help/thingspeak/channels-and-charts-api.html for more details about the ThingSpeak MQTT and REST API.

When you want to read or write from/to a ThingSpeak channel, you can either publish MQTT messages, send requests via HTTP to the REST API, or use one of the platform-specific libraries that encapsulate these mechanisms for you. A channel can have up to eight data fields represented as a string or numeric data. You can also process the numeric data using several sophisticated procedures, such as summing, average, rounding, and more.

---

[3] http://mqtt.org/
[4] https://en.wikipedia.org/wiki/Representational_state_transfer

Summary

In this chapter, we learned more about cloud systems and how they can be used in IoT projects, and we are ready to modify our projects to use them. However, we've only just scratched the surface here. There is so much more that can be done with another simple, free cloud solution.

In the next chapter, we will expand our tour of cloud systems for IoT by looking at the Arduino IoT Cloud – an easy-to-use, cloud-based IoT data-hosting service from `arduino.cc`. You will learn how to send your data to the cloud and display it using nice, easy-to-use graphics.

CHAPTER 13

Arduino IoT Cloud

Now we begin what some would consider the real meat of IoT projects: incorporating cloud services to make IoT projects accessible from the Internet. Thus far, we have seen how to use a simplified web server to display information, but this typically requires making the network on which the MicroPython board connects visible (accessible) from the Internet – a situation few can afford (it costs more money to obtain, host, and manage an Internet subnet), manage, or maintain – hence the usefulness of cloud computing services.

In the last chapter, we took a quick look at what is available for building low-cost IoT solutions hosted in cloud services. Hosting in this sense means we are using one or more services to complete our IoT project. For example, the most common services are presentation services that allow us to build an Internet-enabled user interface.

In this chapter, we will take our project from Chapter 9, the pedestrian stoplight, and demonstrate how you can use cloud services to control your MicroPython board. That's right, we will replace the physical button in our project with a button on the Internet. The cloud service that is uniquely designed for such a feature is Arduino IoT Cloud from arduino.cc.

Overview

Recall from the last chapter that the Arduino IoT Cloud is an easy-to-use service dedicated to IoT projects. As such, it provides everything you need to create and host IoT projects. While the service is designed to work with the Arduino and Arduino-compatible platforms, you can use it with any platform where there is a library (driver) available. Fortunately, for us, there are several Python libraries available.

© Charles Bell 2024
C. Bell, *MicroPython for the Internet of Things*, https://doi.org/10.1007/978-1-4842-9861-9_13

The following section presents a short tutorial on how to get started using the Arduino IoT Cloud. As you will see, there is a bit of setup and complexity working with some of the features and some of the components and code are not as intuitive as some of the other cloud services. Nevertheless, the project we will implement will demonstrate the power of using Arduino IoT Cloud services in your future projects.

Tip If you would like to learn more about Arduino IoT Cloud and how to use it with the Arduino platform of microcontrollers, see the online documentation at `https://docs.arduino.cc/arduino-cloud/getting-started/iot-cloud-getting-started`.

Let's get started using Arduino IoT Cloud.

Getting Started with Arduino IoT Cloud

In this section, we will learn how to start using Arduino IoT Cloud including some of its terminology and tools demonstrated with a simple test program you can use to ensure your connection to Arduino IoT Cloud is working.

START SMALL, BUILD BIG

Resist the temptation to jump directly to a complete solution when encountering innovative technologies. You will find it frustrating debugging code that contains all of your features that have not been tested in advance. The best course of action for any complex project is to start small and test isolated features before incorporating them. This will permit you to build your code from working parts into a whole with bugs sorted in advance.

To get started with Arduino IoT Cloud, you must create an account on arduino.cc. Then, you can start creating IoT projects (called things) that contain devices (your IoT board), variables (where your data is sent/updated), and dashboard for displaying data.

Briefly, we will first create a device that represents our MicroPython board that includes one or more variables where we will send our data, then a thing (project), and add widgets that are linked to variables to configure the user interface. Once again, these concepts are intuitive, but some of the configurations and code aren't as intuitive.

Let's get started by creating an account.

Create Your Arduino Account

To create an account, visit `arduino.cc` and click the *Sign In* button in the upper-right corner.

Note   You may be asked to specify your region to best direct your connection.

When you click the link, you will see a new page that permits you to log in to Arduino if you already have an account, or you can sign in using your Google, GitHub, Facebook, or Apple account.[1] If you do not have an account, you can click Create one as shown in Figure 13-1.

Figure 13-1. *Create a New Account*

---

[1] I do not recommend these options, but it is your choice.

427

Once you create your account, click *Sign In* again and provide the new account and password. You will see a page similar to Figure 13-2. Click Cloud to access the cloud services.

Figure 13-2. *Sign-In Landing Page (arduino.cc)*

The next page displays the landing page for the Arduino IoT Cloud services. The portion we want to access is the IoT services, which we can open by clicking Get Started as shown in Figure 13-3.

Figure 13-3. *Launching Arduino IoT Services*

The next page presents you with a host of information, including access to a treasure trove of documentation (mostly for the Arduino platform) and access to the IoT services. To start using the IoT services, click *IoT Cloud* in the *Cloud apps* section as shown in Figure 13-4.

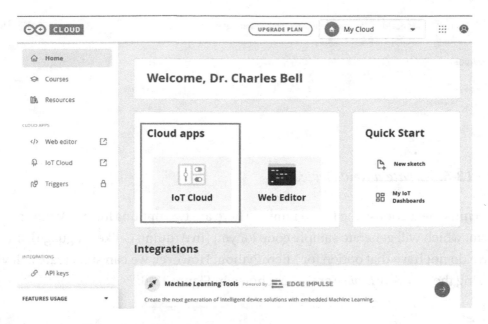

Figure 13-4. *Arduino IoT Cloud Home Page*

The next page is your home page for the Arduino IoT Cloud. If you have projects (called things) created, you will see them listed, but on your first visit, you will need to create them. However, it all begins with creating a device.

Create a New Device

A device in Arduino IoT Cloud is our MicroPython board. You have to create the device so that you can connect to the Arduino IoT Cloud, which on first connection will establish a trust relationship together with your device ID and secret key (more on those later). You must create a new device for each board to send data. While most of the features are Arduino specific, we can create a device that represents our MicroPython boards. To create a new device, click the *Devices* tab on the toolbar, then click *Add* as shown in Figure 13-5.

Figure 13-5. *Create a New Device*

You must next choose the board family. There are two options for the Arduino platform, which will generate sample code for you (in Arduino C-like language), but sadly we do not have that option for MicroPython. However, we can still create a device by clicking the *DIY Any Device* option as shown in Figure 13-6.

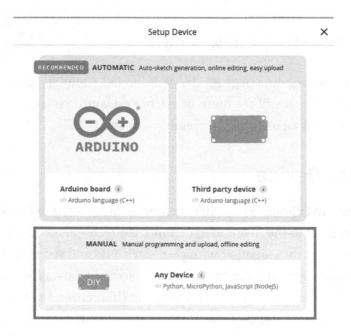

Figure 13-6. *Select the DIY Option*

Click *Continue* on the next screen after reading the limitations of using this option, then enter a name for your device. If you are following along, name it RP2040 or whatever you like. Once you've changed the name, click *Next* as shown in Figure 13-7.

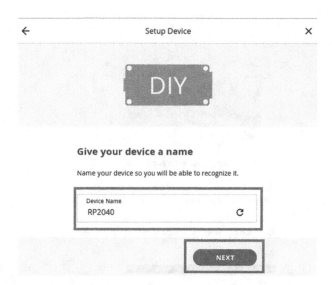

Figure 13-7. *Name the Device*

The next step presents you with your device ID and secret key. It is very important that you copy or download these keys before moving forward. You can download a `.pdf` file with the keys by clicking *download the PDF* and download a file that you can store in a safe place for later use. Whether you copy the keys or download the `.pdf` file, you must acknowledge the warning that your device ID and secret key cannot be recovered. Figure 13-8 shows the dialog with the data masked out. Why? Because if you know the device ID and secret key, you can access the thing associated with the device, which means access to the data. Thus, you should not share your device ID and secret key with anyone.

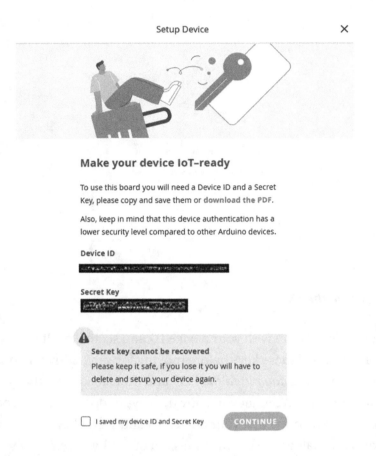

Figure 13-8. *Record Your Device ID and Secret Keys*

Caution   Do not forget to record your device ID and secret key! You will not be able to recover these and must recreate the device if you forget them.

Once you have the data saved, click *Continue* and then *Got It* on the documentation reminder (or click the links to visit the documentation, but it is for the Arduino platform).

Devices are linked to things. So, once you create your device, you will see a link to create a new thing as shown in Figure 13-9.

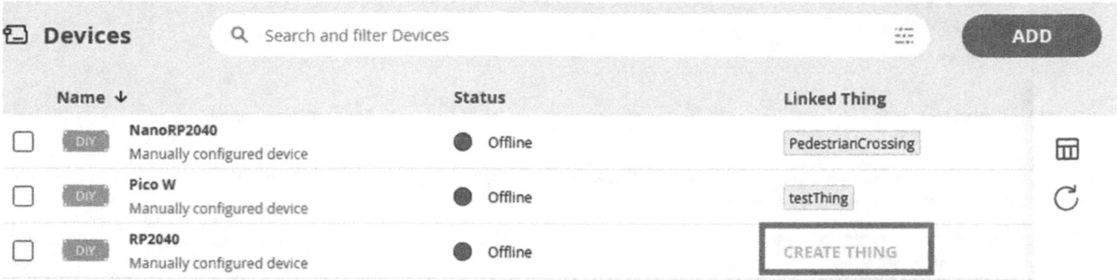

Figure 13-9. *Create a Thing for a Device*

This is the end of the general setup and configuration for Arduino IoT Cloud. The next steps are project specific (again, called a thing). We create a new thing (think project) once we know what variables we will want to send to the cloud. Thus, you should create your new thing once you know what you want to do. Let's look at a simple example to complete our tutorial.

Using Arduino IoT Cloud with MicroPython

The example we will use to explore using Arduino IoT Cloud with MicroPython will turn on and off the onboard LED for our MicroPython board with a virtual (cloud-based) switch. Thus, we need two variables: one for the LED to store its state (on or off) and another for the switch (again, on or off). This also means the hardware for this example is simply the MicroPython board. As you will see, there isn't much code to write, but it can take a moment to understand how it works.

We begin with creating a new thing.

Create a New Thing

When ready, click *CREATE THING* to start creating a new thing. You will see a new screen that allows you to add variables and change the title of the thing as shown in Figure 13-10.

Figure 13-10. *Name a Thing and Add Variables*

To change the name, click the name (currently Untitled) and type your new name. If you want to follow along with this example, name it testArduino.

To add variables, click the *Add Variable* button. We will be creating two Boolean variables (labeled bool): ledSwitch to control the switch and onboardLed for the onboard LED. Once you click the *Add Variable* button, you will see a dialog that permits you to name the variable and choose its type as shown in Figure 13-11 for the ledSwitch variable. Leave the rest of the settings as the default. Once you have set the name and chosen the type as Boolean, click *Add Variable*.

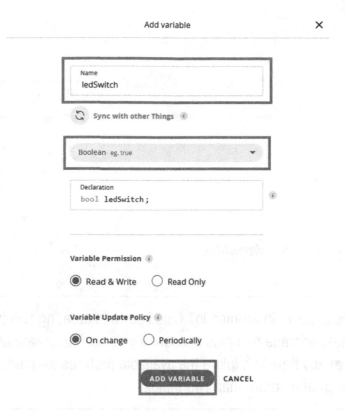

Figure 13-11. *Create the onSwitch Variable*

Once you create the variable, you will see a new dialog for your thing that shows the variables created. To add another, click the *Add* button to repeat the process for the onboardLed variable.

Once the two variables are added, you should see the variables for your thing as shown in Figure 13-12.

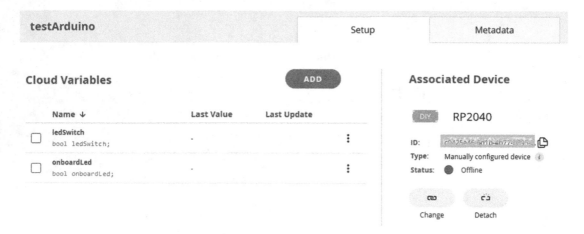

Figure 13-12. *Thing with Variables*

Note   The free account in Arduino IoT Cloud permits creating two projects (things). You must upgrade to a paid account if you need to create additional things. Click Upgrade at any time to explore the available features for paid accounts, which includes creating more than two things.

The next step is to create a dashboard for displaying our user interface controls.

Create a Dashboard

The dashboard is where we will build our interface using widgets (controls and display visualizations). To create a new dashboard, click the *Dashboards* tab, then click the *CREATE* button as shown in Figure 13-13.

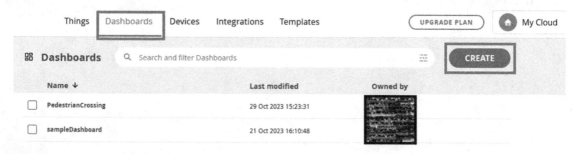

Figure 13-13. *Create a New Dashboard*

When you create a new dashboard, it is an empty slate that we must add widgets. You can also change the name. To change the name, click the current name (Untitled) and change it to SwitchLED as shown in Figure 13-14. To add widgets, click the *Add* button as shown.

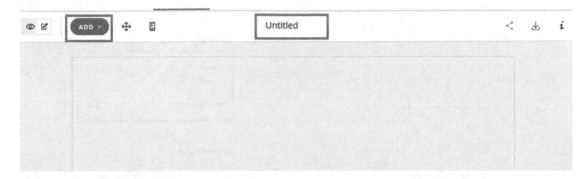

Figure 13-14. *New Dashboard*

When you click *Add* to add new widgets, you will see a lengthy list of widgets that you can use. You will find a switch, pushbutton, slider, LED, and many more widgets. When you add a widget to a dashboard, they are linked to a variable in a thing. That variable will then provide the data for the widget. In the case of a button, the variable type we want to use is Boolean (bool) where the values True and False will control whether the widget is "on" or "off." Figure 13-15 shows a partial list of the widgets available.

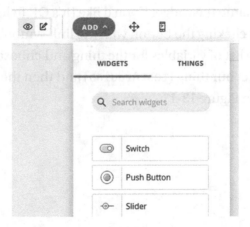

Figure 13-15. *Adding a Widget to the Dashboard*

For this example, we want to add two widgets: a switch and an LED. Let's start with the switch. Click the *Add* button on the dashboard and then choose the Switch in the list. Figure 13-16 shows the dialog you will see to configure the widget. In this case, we want to link the widget to the switchLed variable.

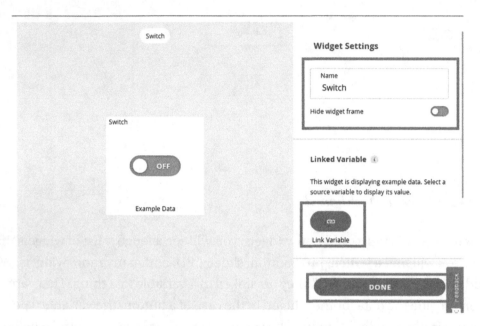

Figure 13-16. *New Widget (Switch)*

Notice that you can name the widget if you'd like (it's OK to leave it as Switch), and you can link variables by clicking the button with the link symbol labeled *Link Variable*. Click the link to open the list of variables for the thing and choose the ledSwitch variable. We need to select our thing (testArduino) and then the variable, then click *Link Variable* as shown in Figure 13-17.

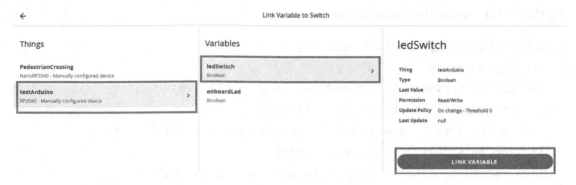

Figure 13-17. *Link Variable to the Widget*

When you are finished linking the variable, click *Done* to add the widget to the dashboard.

We will repeat the process to add an LED widget and link it to the onboardLed variable. Note: You will have to scroll down the list of widgets to find the LED widget. Once the widgets are added, your dashboard should look like Figure 13-18.

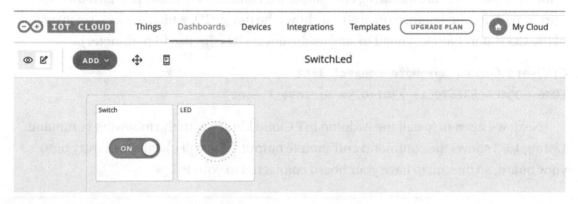

Figure 13-18. *Completed Dashboard (testArduino)*

The next thing we must do is install the correct libraries for our boards.

Install the Arduino IoT Cloud Library

First, you need to install mpremote (MicroPython remote), which is a MicroPython remote installation program that makes installing libraries on your MicroPython board very simple. The command is pip3 install mpremote, which works on any PC with Python 3 installed. You need to run this only once on your PC. Listing 13-1 shows the output of running the command.

Listing 13-1. Installing mpremote

```
C:\Users\Chuck> pip3 install mpremote
Collecting mpremote
  Downloading mpremote-1.21.0-py3-none-any.whl (27 kB)
Collecting importlib-metadata>=1.4 (from mpremote)
  Downloading importlib_metadata-6.8.0-py3-none-any.whl (22 kB)
Collecting pyserial>=3.3 (from mpremote)
  Using cached pyserial-3.5-py2.py3-none-any.whl (90 kB)
Collecting zipp>=0.5 (from importlib-metadata>=1.4->mpremote)
  Downloading zipp-3.17.0-py3-none-any.whl (7.4 kB)
Installing collected packages: pyserial, zipp, importlib-metadata, mpremote
Successfully installed importlib-metadata-6.8.0 mpremote-1.21.0
pyserial-3.5 zipp-3.17.0
```

Begin by closing any applications you have that are connected to your board such as Thonny. Next, enter the following command in a command window to check the COM port or path for the board. Notice also it shows the device ID, which we will use instead of the COM port (you just need to specify the device ID with the `id` parameter).

```
C:\Users\Chuck> mpremote connect list
COM6 5034C60632679C18 2341:025e Microsoft None
```

Next, we need to install the Arduino IoT Cloud library with the following command. Listing 13-2 shows the command and sample output. This will install the library onto your board, so be sure to have your board connected to your PC.

Note   On some platforms, you may need to start mpremote with "`py -m mpremote`."

Listing 13-2. Installing the Arduino IoT Cloud Library

```
C:\Users\Chuck> mpremote connect id:5034C60632679C18 mip install
github:arduino/arduino-iot-cloud-py
github:arduino/arduino-iot-cloud-py
Install github:arduino/arduino-iot-cloud-py
Installing github:arduino/arduino-iot-cloud-py/package.json to /lib
```

```
Installing: /lib/arduino_iot_cloud/__init__.py
Installing: /lib/arduino_iot_cloud/ucloud.py
Installing: /lib/arduino_iot_cloud/umqtt.py
Installing: /lib/arduino_iot_cloud/ussl.py
Installing senml (0.1.0) from https://micropython.org/pi/v2 to /lib
Installing: /lib/cbor2/__init__.mpy
Installing: /lib/cbor2/encoder.mpy
Installing: /lib/cbor2/decoder.mpy
Installing: /lib/senml/senml_pack.mpy
Installing: /lib/senml/__init__.mpy
Installing: /lib/senml/senml_record.mpy
Installing: /lib/senml/senml_base.mpy
Installing: /lib/senml/senml_unit.mpy
Done
```

Notes on Using the Pico

The Pico works well but requires one additional library because the MicroPython image may not include the library. You must install the logging library. You can do this in Thonny by connecting your board, then clicking *Tools* ➤ *Manage packages…*, then typing in logging into the search box, and clicking *Search micropython-lib and PyPI* as shown in Figure 13-19.

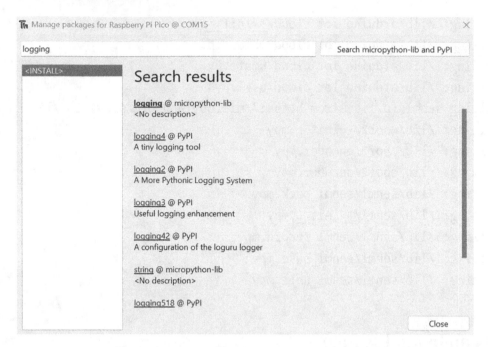

Figure 13-19. Adding a Library (Thonny)

Click the MicroPython logging library and click *Install* to complete the install.

Notes on Using the Nano RP2040 Connect

Unfortunately, the MicroPython image for the Nano RP2040 performs differently than expected from the Pico. Fortunately, the code still works but, with the Arduino IoT Cloud library, needs a small adjustment to work on the Nano RP2040 because the MicroPython image we are using for the Nano RP2040 does not have an `asyncio` library but does have a `uasyncio` library.

Fortunately, we can open the `arduino_iot_cloud` folder on the board, then edit the `ucloud.py` file as shown in the following in bold. These are the only lines of code that need to be changed. Make the change, then save the file.

```
import uasyncio as asyncio
from uasyncio import CancelledError
try:
    from uasyncio import InvalidStateError
except (ImportError, AttributeError):
    # MicroPython doesn't have this exception
```

```
class InvalidStateError(Exception):
    pass
```

Now, we're ready to start writing our code!

Write the Code

The code for this test is very simple, and we will reuse the connect() function from previous projects. The imports section requires only the network, sys, time, and Pin libraries and the variables (constants) from our secrets file.

```
import network, sys, time
from machine import Pin
from project5.secrets import DEVICE_ID, SECRET_KEY, SSID, SSID_PASS
```

The secrets file (secrets.py) has four values as follows. Be sure to update them with the correct values from your device ID and secret keys as well as your SSID and SSID password.

```
# Arduino IoT Cloud Parameters
DEVICE_ID  = "DEVICEID"
SECRET_KEY = "SECRETKEY"
# WiFi values
SSID = "SSIDNAME"
SSID_PASS = "SSIDPASSWORD"
```

However, the rest of the code requires a bit of explanation. We control widgets on the dashboard by updating the value for the variable. We do this via an instance of the client class from the Arduino IoT Cloud library that is passed as a parameter for callback functions. For example, to update the onboardLed variable for the LED widget, we reference the variable by name in the client in the callback function as follows:

```
client["onboardLed"] = value
```

Changes to widgets such as when the switch is toggled require supplying a callback function that is triggered when the switch is toggled. We will need one callback for the switch that not only sets the variable for the LED widget but also sets the value for the onboard LED. The following shows the on_switch() callback function. Notice we update the LED variable, onboardLed, that is linked to the LED widget. Thus, when we set this to True, the LED on the board and the LED widget will turn on.

```
# Control the onboard led
def on_switch(client, value):
    client["onboardLed"] = value
    Pin("LED").value(value)
```

Notice the parameters are the client instance and the value. The value is the value of the switch variable, switchLed, that is set to either True or False depending on which position it is in. The last line is the code that sets the onboard LED for our board (it works on the Pico and Nano RP2040 Connect). You may be thinking, so far, so good. But there's a bit more we need to do.

We also need to initialize the Arduino IoT Cloud library and then register each of the widgets. This registration code uses the register() function to pass in the name of the variable, its initial value, callback function (if needed), and interval for checking its status. This is where things get a little fuzzy as the documentation for the MicroPython Arduino IoT Cloud library is a bit terse.

Tip   You can find the documentation in the GitHub repository for the library at https://github.com/arduino/arduino-iot-cloud-py. You can find a bit more in the examples folder.

Let's look at the code one step at a time. First, we need to initialize the Arduino IoT Cloud class as follows, passing in the device_id, username (same as the device ID), and password, which is our secret key from the Arduino IoT Cloud:

```
# Create a client object to connect to the Arduino IoT cloud
client = ArduinoCloudClient(device_id=DEVICE_ID,
                            username=DEVICE_ID, password=SECRET_KEY)
```

Next, we need to register our variables. We only need the minimal parameters for the onboardLed since it is a passive widget (has no action). However, for the ledSwitch, we need to set a callback for the on_write() function and set the interval to 250 milliseconds. The following are the register statements for these operations:

```
# Register cloud objects
client.register("onboardLed", value=False)
client.register("ledSwitch", value=False, on_write=on_switch,
interval=0.250)
```

Finally, we simply start the client as follows. Once we do that, the client has a loop that runs, and our only link to controlling the code is through our callback function.

```
client.start()
```

That's all the code we need. If you have more complex widgets, the registration code can become a bit complicated, but take your time with the documentation and study the example (in the examples/micrpython.py folder on GitHub at https://github.com/arduino/arduino-iot-cloud-py) for how they do it. You should be able to find a configuration that works for most basic widgets. If you have more complex widgets, you can look at the documentation for the Arduino library for inspiration.

Now, let's look at the completed code. Listing 13-3 shows the code for the test program stored in a file named test_arduino.py. Take a few moments and look through the code to ensure you understand how it works.

Listing 13-3. Test Code for Arduino IoT Cloud Library

```
#
# MicroPython for the IoT Second Edition - Chapter 13
#
# Chapter 13 - Pedestrian Crossing with Arduino IoT Cloud Client
#
# Test the Arduino IoT Cloud Client
#
# Imports for the project
import network, sys, time
from machine import Pin
from arduino_iot_cloud import ArduinoCloudClient
from project5.secrets import DEVICE_ID, SECRET_KEY, SSID, SSID_PASS

# Setup the board to connect to our network.
def connect():
    wlan = network.WLAN(network.STA_IF)
    wlan.active(True)
    wlan.connect(SSID, SSID_PASS)
    while not wlan.isconnected() and wlan.status() >= 0:
        print("Waiting to connect...")
        time.sleep(1)
```

```python
    if not wlan.isconnected():
        print("Cannot find SSID!")
        sys.exit(0)

    print("Connected!")
    print("My IP address is: {0}".format(wlan.ifconfig()[0]))
    return True

# Control the onboard led
def on_switch(client, value):
    client["onboardLed"] = value
    Pin("LED").value(value)

# Main function
def main():
    # Connect to WiFi
    connect()

    # Create a client object to connect to the Arduino IoT cloud
    client = ArduinoCloudClient(device_id=DEVICE_ID, username=DEVICE_ID,
                                password=SECRET_KEY)

    # Register cloud objects
    client.register("onboardLed", value=False)
    client.register("ledSwitch", value=False, on_write=on_switch,
                    interval=0.250)

    print("Starting Arduino IoT Client.")

    # Start the Arduino IoT cloud client.
    client.start()

if __name__ == '__main__':
    try:
        main()
    except (KeyboardInterrupt, SystemExit) as err:
        print("\nbye!\n")
    sys.exit(0)
```

OK, now we're ready to start testing the code. Let's see how to do that.

Execute!

Be sure to copy the secrets.py file to a folder on your MicroPython board named project5. That's all we need for now. When ready, simply run the test_arduino.py code. You should see output similar to the following:

```
Waiting to connect...
Connected!
My IP address is: 10.0.0.14
Starting Arduino IoT Client.
```

Next, click the switch widget on the Arduino IoT Cloud dashboard and observe that the LED on the dashboard and the onboard LED turns on. Try this a few times. You may need to set the switch to "off" before running your code if the control gets out of sync.

Tip   To synchronize the dashboard with your code, you may need to set the switch to "off" before running your code for the first time.

Once you're satisfied it's working, take a victory lap around your desk. You've just written an IoT project that controls your MicroPython board from the Internet. Huzzah!

Now that we have had a tour of getting started with Arduino IoT Cloud, let's take a look at how we can modify our project from Chapter 9 to use the Arduino IoT Cloud as an Internet-based pedestrian crossing application.

Project: IoT Pedestrian Crossing

This project uses some of the same code from Chapter 9 but with modifications. Also, the hardware for this project is the same as Chapter 9 but without the hardware button. We repeat the information from Chapter 9 for convenience.

Required Components

Table 13-1 lists the components you will need in addition to your MicroPython board and USB cable. This is the same as Chapter 9 except there is no button.

Table 13-1. *Required Components for the IoT Pedestrian Crossing*

Component	Qty	Description	Cost	Links
Red LED	2	Pack of 25	$4.00	www.adafruit.com /product/299
		Single	$0.35	www.sparkfun.com /products/9590
Yellow LED	2	Pack of 25	$4.95	www.adafruit.com /product/2700
		Single	$0.35	www.sparkfun.com /products/9594
Green LED	1	Pack of 25	$4.00	www.adafruit.com /product/298
		Single	$0.35	www.sparkfun.com /products/9592
220 or 330 ohm resistors	5	Variety kit	$7.95	www.sparkfun.com /products/10969
		Pack of 25	$0.75	www.adafruit.com /product/2780
Breadboard	1	Prototyping board, full-sized	$5.95	www.sparkfun.com /products/12615
			$5.95	www.adafruit.com /product/239
Jumper wires	11	M/M jumper wires, 7" (set of 30)	$2.25	www.sparkfun.com /products/12615
		M/M jumper wires, 6" (set of 20)	$1.95	www.adafruit.com /product/1950

Be sure to follow the warnings about resistor sizes described in Chapter 9. Now, let's see how to wire the components together.

Set Up the Hardware

Let's see how to make the connections for both the Raspberry Pi Pico and the Arduino Nano RP2040 Connect. Let's begin with the Pico.

Connections for the Raspberry Pi Pico

Table 13-2 shows the connections needed for this project.

Table 13-2. *Connections for the IoT Pedestrian Crossing Simulation (Pico)*

Physical Pin	GPIO Num/Function	Connection
37	GND	Breadboard ground (bottom)
17	GP13	Resistor for red LED (stoplight)
16	GP12	Resistor for yellow LED (stoplight)
15	GP11	Resistor for green LED (stoplight)
11	GP8	Resistor for red LED (walk light)
10	GP7	Resistor for green LED (walk light)
N/A	Breadboard ground	All LED negative side
N/A	Resistor	All LED positive side

Figure 13-20 shows the wiring drawing for the project on the Pico.

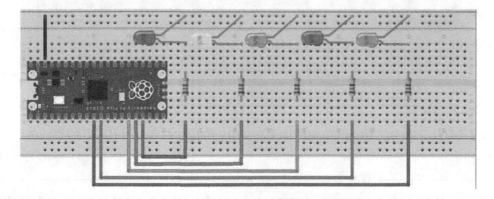

Figure 13-20. *Wiring the IoT Pedestrian Crossing Project (Pico)*

Connections for the Arduino Nano RP2040 Connect

Table 13-3 shows the connections needed for this project.

Table 13-3. *Connections for the IoT Pedestrian Crossing Simulation (Nano RP2040)*

Physical Pin	GPIO Num/Function	Connection
19	GND	Breadboard ground (bottom)
11	GP13	Resistor for red LED (stoplight)
10	GP12	Resistor for yellow LED (stoplight)
9	GP29	Resistor for green LED (stoplight)
7	GP27	Resistor for red LED (walk light)
6	GP27	Resistor for green LED (walk light)
N/A	Breadboard ground	All LED negative side
N/A	Resistor	All LED positive side

Figure 13-21 shows the wiring drawing for the project on the Nano RP2040.

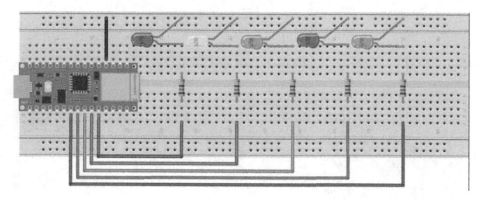

Figure 13-21. *Wiring the Pedestrian Crossing Project (Nano RP2040)*

Caution   Never plug or unplug jumper wires when the project is powered on. You risk damaging your board or the components.

Once again, always make sure to double-check your connections before powering the board on. The next step is to create a new thing and dashboard (we can use the same device but must add additional variables).

Set Up Arduino IoT Cloud

Recall, we must first create our variables, then create widgets linked to them on a new dashboard. We will use the same device. We won't see all of the details of how to create the thing and dashboard, but we will see the finished configurations for each. Refer to the preceding sections if you need to see the details. Let's begin with creating a new thing.

Create a New Thing

Sign in to arduino.cc and navigate to the IoT Cloud dashboard. There, create a new thing named PedestrianCrossing with three Boolean (bool) variables (button, walkGreen, and walkRed). We will use the button widget (a pushbutton) and two LED widgets to represent the red and green pedestrian LEDs. Figure 13-22 shows the new thing with the variables created. Notice I deleted the variables we used in the tutorial, but you do not have to do so.

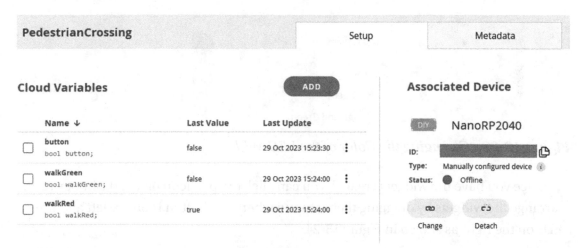

Figure 13-22. New Thing (PedestrianCrossing)

Next, we need to create a new dashboard.

Create a New Dashboard

Create a new dashboard and name it PedestrianCrossing. Add three widgets: a pushbutton linked to the button variable, an LED linked to the walkGreen variable, and an LED linked to the walkRed variable. You can change the color of the LED to either red or green as shown in Figure 13-23.

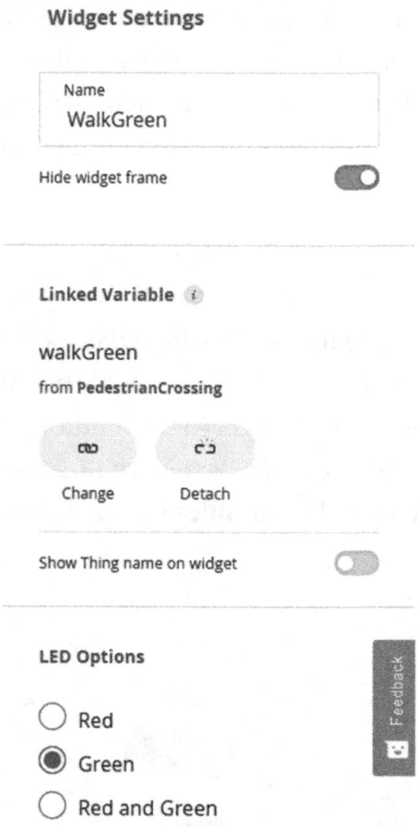

Widget Settings

Name
WalkGreen

Hide widget frame

Linked Variable ⓘ

walkGreen
from **PedestrianCrossing**

Change   Detach

Show Thing name on widget

LED Options

○ Red
◉ Green
○ Red and Green

Figure 13-23. Changing the Color of the LED Widget

Once you have the widgets created, you can click the pen icon on the dashboard and rearrange the widgets by dragging them around where the button is on the left and the LEDs on the right as shown in Figure 13-24.

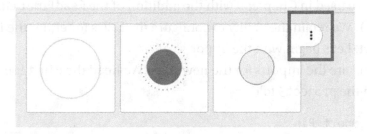

Figure 13-24. *New Dashboard (PedestrianCrossing)*

If you decide to edit the widgets and click the pen icon, you can edit the widgets settings by clicking the ellipse as shown in Figure 13-25. The ellipse appears when you hover your mouse over the widget.

Figure 13-25. *Editing the Settings for a Widget*

OK, that's all for the user interface! Now, let's talk about the code we need to write.

Write the Code

The code for this project is very similar to the code from Chapter 9 but with some changes to the way we control the LEDs. Since we are working with a callback, we must use the callback to initiate the stoplight cycle, but we cannot use the `time.sleep()` function like we did in Chapter 9. Fortunately, we can use the `ReadTimer` from Chapter 10 to control how long the LEDs remain turned on.

We will import the usual libraries from the `project5` folder along with our secrets file that contains the following constants. Be sure to update these with your own data.

```
# Arduino IoT Cloud Parameters
```

```
DEVICE_ID  = "DEVICEID"
SECRET_KEY = "SECRETKEY"
# WiFi values
SSID = "SSIDNAME"
SSID_PASS = "SSIDPASSWORD"
```

Recall from Chapter 9 that our code was in a single module named `pedestrian_crossing.py`. In this project, we will move all of the code for the stoplight simulation to a new class mode. We will name the new code module `stoplight_iot.py` and the new class `StoplightIoT`. Let's look at that code first.

StoplightIoT Class

The code from Chapter 9 is a good start, but we can remove all of the code for the button, and we must rewrite the code for cycling the lights. As you will see, most of the code is similar to what we used in Chapter 9 with the addition of the `ReadTimer` class instead of `time.sleep()`. We retain the ability to configure the LEDs for either the Pico or Nano RP2040 Connect. Let's begin with the imports.

The following are the imports for the new class. We need the `Pin`, `time`, and `ReadTimer` from the `project5` folder:

```
from machine import Pin
import time
from project5.read_timer import ReadTimer
```

The constructor for the class needs to set up the LEDs and the Read Timer. Listing 13-4 shows the code for the constructor. This is largely the same code from Chapter 9. However, we use a class variable named `self.walking` to use as a state variable that is set to `True` when the button is pressed, signaling a pedestrian crossing light cycle. This will become clearer as we move through the code.

Listing 13-4. Constructor (StoplightIoT Class)

```
    def __init__(self, frequency=15000):
        # Pins for the Arduino Nano RP2040 Connect
        #stoplight_red = Pin(13, Pin.OUT)
        #stoplight_yellow = Pin(12, Pin.OUT)
        #stoplight_green = Pin(29, Pin.OUT)
```

```
#pedestrian_red = Pin(27, Pin.OUT)
#pedestrian_green = Pin(26, Pin.OUT)

# Pins for the Pico
stoplight_red = Pin(13, Pin.OUT)
stoplight_yellow = Pin(12, Pin.OUT)
stoplight_green = Pin(11, Pin.OUT)
pedestrian_red = Pin(8, Pin.OUT)
pedestrian_green = Pin(7, Pin.OUT)

# Setup lists for the LEDs
self.stoplight = [stoplight_red, stoplight_yellow, stoplight_green]
self.pedestrian_signal = [pedestrian_red, pedestrian_green]

# Turn off the LEDs
for led in self.stoplight:
    led.off()
for led in self.pedestrian_signal:
    led.off()

# Start with green stoplight and red pedestrian_signal
self.stoplight[2].on()
self.pedestrian_signal[0].on()

# Setup read event handler
self.walk_event = ReadTimer(frequency)
self.walking = False
self.walk_event.reset()
```

Next, we need a function for cycling the lights. This function behaves similar to the code from Chapter 9, but instead we wrap the code in a try block in case something goes wrong. Listing 13-5 shows the code for the function. Notice that we check the ReadTimer and, if we are in a walking state, control the LEDs accordingly.

Listing 13-5. Cycle Lights Function (StoplightIoT Class)

```
# Function to check the status of the LEDs
def cycle_lights(self, client):
    try:
        if self.walking and self.walk_event.time_to_read():
```

455

```
            print("complete.")
            self.walking = False
            self.walk_event.reset()
        if not self.walking:
            # Stop=green, walk=red
            self.pedestrian_signal[1].off()
            self.pedestrian_signal[0].on()
            time.sleep_ms(500)  # Give the pedestrian a chance to see it
            self.stoplight[0].off()
            self.stoplight[2].on()
            client["walkRed"] = True
            client["walkGreen"] = False
            self.walk_event.reset()
        if self.walking:
            # Blink the walk light
            self.pedestrian_signal[1].off()
            time.sleep_ms(500)
            self.pedestrian_signal[1].on()
            time.sleep_ms(500)
    except:
        pass
```

Finally, we need a function that permits us to react when the pushbutton is pressed. This code is part of the cycle lights function that controls the walking LEDs on the board and the LEDs on the Arduino IoT Cloud dashboard. The code isn't difficult, and we leave its explanation as an exercise. Listing 13-6 shows the complete code for the On-Pushbutton callback function.

Listing 13-6. Pushbutton Callback Function

```
# Callback function for when pushbutton is pressed on the dashboard
def on_pushbutton(self, client, value):
    # Ignore any callbacks where button is not pressed
    # (value = True means button was pressed)
    if value and not self.walking:
        # Go yellow.
        self.stoplight[2].off()
```

```
        self.stoplight[1].on()
        # Wait 2 seconds
        time.sleep_ms(2000)
        # Go red and turn on walk light
        self.stoplight[1].off()
        self.stoplight[0].on()
        time.sleep_ms(500)  # Give the pedestrian a chance to see it
        self.pedestrian_signal[0].off()
        self.pedestrian_signal[1].on()
        print("Walk initiated...", end="")
        self.walking = True
        self.walk_event.reset()
        client["walkRed"] = False
        client["walkGreen"] = True
```

Listing 13-7 shows the complete code for the StoplightIoT class. Be sure to read through it until you are comfortable, and you understand how it works. Don't worry that it looks like a lot of code. It doesn't differ much from the code in Chapter 9.

Listing 13-7. New StoplightIoT Class

```
#
# MicroPython for the IoT Second Edition - Chapter 13
#
# Chapter 13 - Pedestrian Crossing with Arduino IoT Cloud
#              Client - Stoplight class
#
# Imports for the project
from machine import Pin
import time
from project5.read_timer import ReadTimer

class StoplightIoT:
    """Stoplight class for pedestrian crossing controlling LEDS and
        toggling LED widgets in Arduino IoT Cloud."""

    # Constructor
    def __init__(self, frequency=15000):
```

```python
        # Pins for the Arduino Nano RP2040 Connect
        #stoplight_red = Pin(13, Pin.OUT)
        #stoplight_yellow = Pin(12, Pin.OUT)
        #stoplight_green = Pin(29, Pin.OUT)
        #pedestrian_red = Pin(27, Pin.OUT)
        #pedestrian_green = Pin(26, Pin.OUT)

        # Pins for the Pico
        stoplight_red = Pin(13, Pin.OUT)
        stoplight_yellow = Pin(12, Pin.OUT)
        stoplight_green = Pin(11, Pin.OUT)
        pedestrian_red = Pin(8, Pin.OUT)
        pedestrian_green = Pin(7, Pin.OUT)

        # Setup lists for the LEDs
        self.stoplight = [stoplight_red, stoplight_yellow, stoplight_green]
        self.pedestrian_signal = [pedestrian_red, pedestrian_green]

        # Turn off the LEDs
        for led in self.stoplight:
            led.off()
        for led in self.pedestrian_signal:
            led.off()

        # Start with green stoplight and red pedestrian_signal
        self.stoplight[2].on()
        self.pedestrian_signal[0].on()

        # Setup read event handler
        self.walk_event = ReadTimer(frequency)
        self.walking = False
        self.walk_event.reset()

    # Function to check the status of the LEDs
    def cycle_lights(self, client):
        try:
            if self.walking and self.walk_event.time_to_read():
                print("complete.")
```

```
                self.walking = False
                self.walk_event.reset()
            if not self.walking:
                # Stop=green, walk=red
                self.pedestrian_signal[1].off()
                self.pedestrian_signal[0].on()
                time.sleep_ms(500)  # Give the pedestrian a chance to see it
                self.stoplight[0].off()
                self.stoplight[2].on()
                client["walkRed"] = True
                client["walkGreen"] = False
                self.walk_event.reset()
            if self.walking:
                # Blink the walk light
                self.pedestrian_signal[1].off()
                time.sleep_ms(500)
                self.pedestrian_signal[1].on()
                time.sleep_ms(500)
        except:
            pass

# Callback function for when pushbutton is pressed on the dashboard
def on_pushbutton(self, client, value):
    # Ignore any callbacks where button is not pressed
    # (value = True means button was pressed)
    if value and not self.walking:
        # Go yellow.
        self.stoplight[2].off()
        self.stoplight[1].on()
        # Wait 2 seconds
        time.sleep_ms(2000)
        # Go red and turn on walk light
        self.stoplight[1].off()
        self.stoplight[0].on()
        time.sleep_ms(500)  # Give the pedestrian a chance to see it
        self.pedestrian_signal[0].off()
```

```
        self.pedestrian_signal[1].on()
        print("Walk initiated...", end="")
        self.walking = True
        self.walk_event.reset()
        client["walkRed"] = False
        client["walkGreen"] = True
```

Now, let's look at the main code.

Main Code

The main code file is named `pedestrian_crossing_iot.py`, and it contains little of the code from Chapter 9. However, the code does not contain anything we have not seen thus far. We need to add the `connect()` function from our previous projects. We also need to set up our new `StoplightIoT` class.

The code for the Arduino IoT Cloud library is similar to our example earlier, but we will be using two callback functions: one for the pushbutton and another for cycling the lights using a task. Both of these are provided for us in the preceding `StoplightIoT` class.

The most unique feature of the code is the use of the `Task` class from the Arduino IoT Cloud library. The `Task` class allows us to set up a task that runs periodically. In this case, we want the code to check to see if the pushbutton was pressed, and if it is, start the cycle to change the LEDs.

The code to register our variables and set up the task is shown as follows:

```
# Register cloud objects.
client.register("walkRed", value=True)
client.register("walkGreen", value=False)
client.register("button", value=None, on_write=stoplight.on_pushbutton,
                interval=0.250)

client.register(Task("user_task", on_run=stoplight.cycle_lights,
                interval=0.500))
```

Listing 13-8 shows the complete code for the main module.

Listing 13-8. Main Code (pedestrian_crossing_iot.py)

```
#
# MicroPython for the IoT Second Edition - Chapter 13
```

```
#
# Chapter 13 - Pedestrian Crossing with Arduino IoT Cloud Client
#
# Imports for the project
import network, sys, time
from arduino_iot_cloud import ArduinoCloudClient, Task
from project5.secrets import DEVICE_ID, SECRET_KEY, SSID, SSID_PASS
from project5.stoplight_iot import StoplightIoT

# Setup the board to connect to our network.
def connect():
    wlan = network.WLAN(network.STA_IF)
    wlan.active(True)
    wlan.connect(SSID, SSID_PASS)
    while not wlan.isconnected() and wlan.status() >= 0:
        print("Waiting to connect...")
        time.sleep(1)
    if not wlan.isconnected():
        print("Cannot find SSID!")
        sys.exit(0)

    print("Connected!")
    print("My IP address is: {0}".format(wlan.ifconfig()[0]))
    return True

# Main function
def main():
    # Connect to WiFi
    connect()

    # Setup the walk timer
    stoplight = StoplightIoT(15000)

    # Create a client object to connect to the Arduino IoT cloud
    client = ArduinoCloudClient(device_id=DEVICE_ID, username=DEVICE_ID,
                                password=SECRET_KEY)

    # Register cloud objects.
```

461

```
    client.register("walkRed", value=True)
    client.register("walkGreen", value=False)
    client.register("button", value=None, on_write=stoplight.on_pushbutton,
                    interval=0.250)

    client.register(Task("user_task", on_run=stoplight.cycle_lights,
                    interval=0.500))

    print("Starting Arduino IoT Client.")

    # Start the Arduino IoT cloud client.
    client.start()

if __name__ == '__main__':
    try:
        main()
    except (KeyboardInterrupt, SystemExit) as err:
        print("\nbye!\n")
    sys.exit(0)
```

Take a few moments and look through the code until you are comfortable you understand how it works.

Now, let's run this project!

Execute!

Now we are ready to run the code and test it out. Be sure to copy all of the files we need to the project5 folder. This includes the secret.py and stoplight_iot.py code modules and the read_timer.py module from Chapter 10.

Running the code should result in the red LED on the dashboard to turn on the green LED off. When you press the pushbutton (click for more than a few microseconds), you will see the lights cycle on your board and the green LED turn on in the dashboard. After about 30 seconds, the red LED turns on and the green LED off.

You should find this works well, but maybe not with the instant feedback of a physical pushbutton. You can improve the reaction time by adjusting the task interval, but it works well as written. Go ahead and try it out for a while. It's fun!

Taking It Further

This project shows excellent prospects for reusing the techniques in other projects. This is especially true since we have now learned how to use analog devices (LEDs). You should now consider taking time to explore some embellishments. Here are a few you may want to consider. Some are easy and some may be a challenge or require more research and more complex coding:

- Use NeoPixels (`www.adafruit.com/category/168`) instead of LEDs. These are RGB LEDs, so you need only two – one for the stoplight and one for the walk light. See `https://github.com/JanBednarik/micropython-ws2812` for more information and examples.

- Add a counter that tracks the number of times the crossing was requested and display it on the dashboard.

- Use OLED from the last project in place of the LEDs for the walk sign to show "WALK" or "DON'T WALK." Add a widget on the dashboard to display this information.

- Add another stoplight to complete the simulation for a pedestrian crossing.

- Add three more stoplights and extend the simulation to include controlling stoplights in two directions. By this point, you will have a lot of wires in your breadboard, so you may need to use a second breadboard to keep all of the wiring tidy.

- Once you have four stoplights working, add a second pedestrian crossing for the other intersection and a new button on the dashboard. Tip: The coding for timing of this solution can be a bit intense, so take your time and work through it one part at a time.

Of course, if you want to press on to the next project, you're welcome to do so, but take some time to explore these potential embellishments – it will be good practice.

Summary

Working with discrete electronic components and controlling them from the Internet is fun and an exciting new skill for us to explore. With cloud services like the Arduino IoT Cloud, controlling our IoT projects remotely becomes easy.

In this chapter, we implemented a simulation of a pedestrian crossing using a remote, Internet-controlled button. We used a series of LEDs to represent the stoplight and walk signal controlled over the Internet.

In the next chapter, we will explore another cloud service–enabled IoT project using weather sensors and the Adafruit IO Cloud Services.

MQTT with Adafruit IO

Building a full-fledged IoT project requires using technologies that permit your MicroPython board to collect and send data to services on the Internet that can store, retrieve, and visualize the data. These Internet services are often cloud-based services. Chances are you've used some of these technologies without knowing. We've already seen an early, simple form of this in Chapters 10 and 11 – using an HTML server to send data to a client over the Internet.

Sending data via HTML may be fine for some projects, but projects where you may need to visualize the data in some other form, or if you want to perform analysis on the data, will require a more advanced mechanism to transmit and store the data. Fortunately, there are many technologies we can use, including those that permit the controlled transmission of data.

Such technologies have a defined protocol (a way to communicate) and often are supported by specialized programming interfaces. One of the easiest to use with microcontrollers defines a protocol with publish and subscribe roles. That is, you can publish data (write) or you can subscribe to data (read) and even be notified when new data is available. One of the easiest-to-use publish/subscribe protocols is called message queue telemetry transport (MQTT).

We will use MQTT in this chapter to see an example of a complete IoT project that reads data from sensors and sends the data to a server, which can then be accessed by clients that use MQTT to subscribe to the data. Best of all, some MQTT services like the one we will use in this chapter also provide visualization tools that allow you to see the data as it is being generated.

We will be using the same hardware and much of the same code from Chapter 11. The complexity in this project comes from using cloud services to host the data and MQTT to publish the data. As you will see, it isn't that difficult to build. Let's begin with an overview of MQTT and Adafruit IO.

© Charles Bell 2024
C. Bell, *MicroPython for the Internet of Things*, https://doi.org/10.1007/978-1-4842-9861-9_14

Overview

Adafruit IO (`io.adafruit.com`) is a cloud-based data visualization system that is easy to use, requiring very little programming knowledge to use. This is accomplished with support for representational state transfer (REST) and MQTT APIs. We will be using the MQTT API for this project.

The goal of Adafruit IO was to cut out all the complexity of the current data loggers and cloud-based data services solutions and make it easy to use, and Adafruit has done so very well. Briefly, we use an MQTT client driver (library), write our code to connect to, and subscribe to data or publish data. The visualization part takes place on the Adafruit IO server itself where we create our own user interface to see the data. There are four steps to getting started with Adafruit IO:

1. Create an account.

2. Set up feeds (message queues) for your data.

3. Set up a dashboard to visualize the data.

4. Connect your devices and start publishing and subscribing.

All you need to get started with Adafruit IO is a user account. To create an account for Adafruit IO, just head over to `https://io.adafruit.com/`. If you already have an account on Adafruit's server, you can use that one and just register for access to Adafruit IO. The process is simple and easy to follow. Once you are logged in, you will see the administrative interface where you can create feeds and dashboards.

A feed is the core component of Adafruit IO. A feed is where you place your data in the form of messages from your devices. Feeds can store data (via publish), and devices (clients) can read the data by subscribing to the feed. You can have more than one feed, and each is defined by its name and referenced via your user ID.

Dashboards are the views of the data in the feeds. Adafruit IO provides a drag-and-drop interface for building simple views of the data very quickly using predefined user interface controls called "blocks." Each dashboard can have one or more blocks, which can be connected to your feeds. Data is then shown in the blocks automatically updated when new data arrives.

Once we have our feeds and dashboard set up, we can write our code to use the MQTT library and send (or receive) data. We can then return to our dashboard and view the data. We will see a detailed walk-through for setting up the feeds and a dashboard for the project in this chapter in a later section.

If you want to learn more about io.adafruit.com, check out these excellent tutorials from Adafruit. You can also find some interesting project ideas for using Adafruit IO at `https://learn.adafruit.com/search?q=io.adafruit.com&`.

- *Adafruit IO*: `https://learn.adafruit.com/adafruit-io/rest-api?view=all`

- *Adafruit IO Basics – Feeds*: `https://learn.adafruit.com/adafruit-io-basics-feeds/resources?view=all`

- *Adafruit IO Basics – Dashboards*: `https://learn.adafruit.com/adafruit-io-basics-dashboards/creating-a-dashboard?view=all`

- *MQTT, Adafruit IO & You*: `https://learn.adafruit.com/mqtt-adafruit-io-and-you/arduino-plus-library-setup?view=all`

There are three components to a basic MQTT service: sensor nodes or publishers that produce messages containing data, clients or subscribers that read the messages, and a broker or server that stores the messages distributing them to subscribers. Figure 14-1 shows a concept of how the three components work.

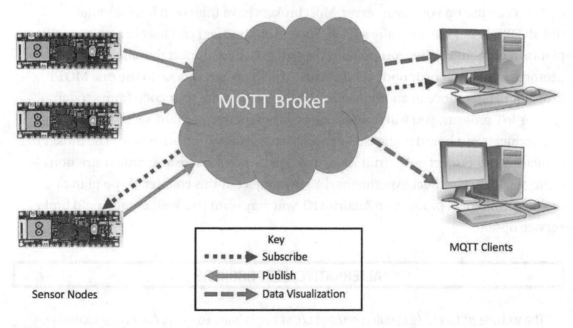

Figure 14-1. MQTT Concept

Notice we have sensor nodes on the left that can publish data (depicted by solid lines), clients on the right that can subscribe to messages (depicted by dotted lines), and a visualization component provided by the broker (depicted as dashed lines). Notice also there are sensor nodes that can publish and subscribe as well as a client that can visualize data and subscribe to messages. In fact, you can have any combination of publish and subscribe. We will see how to both publish and subscribe to messages from our MicroPython project.

Clients

An MQTT client is simply a device (or computer) that has an MQTT library that you can use to program your device to send messages (publish) to or read messages (subscribe) from a broker. Fortunately, the ports of MicroPython include an MQTT library.

Brokers

There are several brokers you can use including those that are cloud based as well as one you can use on your own server. Most brokers have their own implementation of the MQTT client (some require specific drivers or libraries) and may run on a specific platform or require other components. Regardless, they support the same MQTT protocol from the sensor nodes and clients. Thus, you can choose to use one MQTT broker and later move to another without having to rewrite your code from scratch.

For IoT projects, you will want to choose a broker that is cloud based so that you can connect your board to the cloud and access the data from anywhere. The broker of choice for this project is Adafruit IO (`io.adafruit.com`). There are some restrictions – none of which will affect experiments like the project in this chapter. If you plan to base a commercial product on Adafruit IO, you may want to consider their paid broker service option.

ALTERNATIVE MQTT BROKERS

The website `https://github.com/mqtt/mqtt.github.io/wiki/servers` contains a list of MQTT brokers. You will find some that cater to a specific platform or programming language such as Java. You will also find some commercial MQTT services you can use for larger projects or projects you want to monetize.

However, if you want to set up your own MQTT server on your network, you can use Mosquito (http://mosquitto.org/), which is open source and very popular among hobbyists. There is even a public test server you can use. Better still, you won't have to change the code in this project much to use it. You should consider Mosquito as a stepping stone from a free MQTT broker like Adafruit IO to a commercial MQTT broker.

Getting Started with Adafruit IO

Now, let's build a simple project for learning how to use MQTT with Adafruit IO. Rather than build a new project with new components, we will use a test project that simply generates some random data to simulate a sensor. The data isn't the focus here; rather, the focus is learning how to get started with MQTT and how to connect our code to the Arduino IO service.

The first thing we need to do is to create an account.

Create Account on Adafruit IO

Begin by visiting https://accounts.adafruit.com/users/sign_in. If you already have an account with www.adafruit.com, you can use that login for Adafruit IO. Otherwise, you need to create an account by clicking *SIGN UP* and follow the prompts to create your account.

Once you have your account, you can click the IO link at the top of the page as shown in Figure 14-2.

Figure 14-2. *Accessing Adafruit IO from Adafruit Login*

Next, we need to set up our Adafruit IO feeds and dashboard, then write the code before we're ready to test the project.

Configure Adafruit IO

Now we are ready to configure Adafruit IO. We will create only a single feed for our example project. The dashboard will have several blocks to show each of the feeds. Let's see how to create the feeds and dashboard for our project.

Set Up Feeds

To set up a feed, log in to Adafruit IO and select *Feeds* from the list of links on the left of the screen, then click + *New Feed* as shown in Figure 14-3.

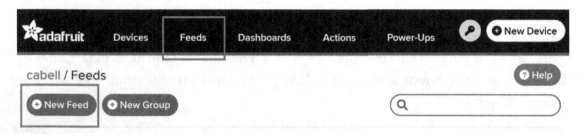

Figure 14-3. *Create a New Feed*

Next, you can provide a name and description (optional) for the feed. Name the first feed Temperature as shown in Figure 14-4. When you're satisfied with the data entered, click *Create* to create the feed.

Create a new Feed   ×

Name

Temperature

Maximum length: 128 characters. Used: 11

Description

Temperature in Celsius

Cancel   Create

Figure 14-4. *Create a New Feed Dialog*

Repeat the process and create feeds for storing humidity (named Humidity) and barometric pressure (named Pressure). When complete, you should see the new feeds as shown in Figure 14-5.

My Feeds				
Feed Name	**Key**	**Last value**	**Recorded**	
☐ Humidity	humidity		less than a min...	🔒
☐ Pressure	pressure		1 minute from n...	🔒
☐ Temperature	temperature		less than a min...	🔒

Figure 14-5. *Feeds for the Weather Project*

Notice at this point there is no data in the feeds. We won't see any data until we've set up and connected our MicroPython board. Now that the feeds are set up, we can create a dashboard to see the data once we publish it.

Set Up a Dashboard

You can create as many dashboards as you want to view the data in your feeds. In fact, you can make one dashboard for each feed or several dashboards that connect to one or more of your feeds. For this project, we will create one dashboard that connects to all four feeds.

To set up a dashboard, select *Dashboards* from the list of links on the left of the screen, then click + *Dashboard* as shown in Figure 14-6.

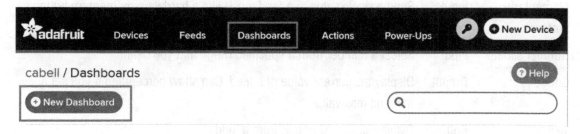

Figure 14-6. *Create a New Dashboard*

Next, you can provide a name and description (optional) for the dashboard. Name the dashboard *WeatherData* and provide a description (optional) as shown in Figure 14-7. When you're satisfied with the data entered, click *Create* to create the dashboard.

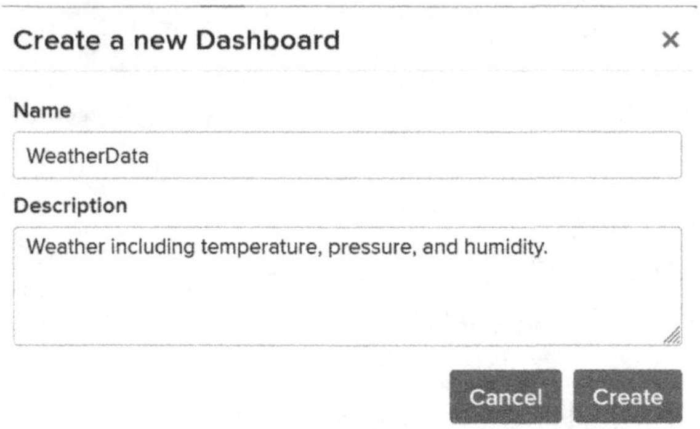

Create a new Dashboard   ×

Name

WeatherData

Description

Weather including temperature, pressure, and humidity.

Cancel   Create

Figure 14-7. *Create a New Dashboard Dialog*

Once you've created the dashboard, we must edit it to add blocks. Click the dashboard to open it for editing. The available blocks and their uses are shown in Table 14-1. Some blocks can be connected to one and only one feed, and other blocks can be connected to multiple feeds.

Table 14-1. *Adafruit IO Blocks*

Name	Type	Description
Toggle button	Input	Choose between two values, either text or numeric. Think of it like a switch
Momentary button	Input	Send a single value to a feed much like a hardware momentary button
Number slider	Input	Select a number from a specified range that you define
Gauge	Output	Display the current value of a feed. Can show percentage if you set a min and max value
Text box	Both	Display static text or text from a feed
Stream	Output	Display messages from one or more feeds
Image	Output	Display images in a feed
Line graph	Output	Display data in a line graph from a feed
Color picker	Input	Select an RGB value and send it to a feed
Map	Output	Track the locations of your feed data (if geo data is available)
Remote control	Input	Mimic the Mini Remote Control sold by Adafruit

For our project, we will add the following blocks:

- *Line graph*: One block each to connect the Temperature, Humidity, and Pressure feeds

- *Stream*: One block to see the raw data from the board

To add a block, click the gear icon/drop-down box in the upper-right area of the dashboard edit screen as shown in Figure 14-8.

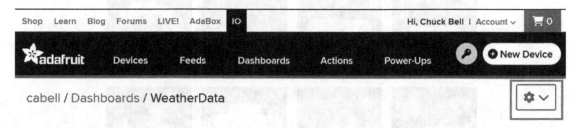

Figure 14-8. Add a Block

Next, click *Create New Block* from the menu as shown in Figure 14-9.

Figure 14-9. Dashboard Settings

When you click *Create New Block*, you will be shown a list of blocks available. The blocks listed in Table 14-1 are shown in Figure 14-10, listed in order from the top left. To add the block of your choice to your dashboard, click the block.

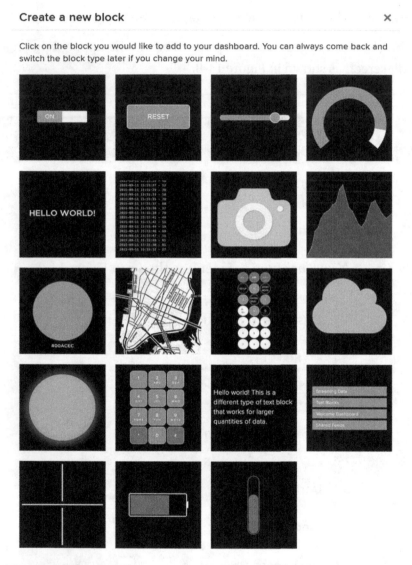

Figure 14-10. Available Blocks

When you select the block, you must select the feed(s) for the block. Figure 14-11 shows an example of selecting the feeds for the line graph for the Temperature feed. As you can see, you could select any number of feeds. However, be sure to consider the scale of each data before using a line graph for multiple feeds. In this project, we have different scales for the three types of data. If we used one line graph, the feed with the lowest range would appear at the bottom of the graph and may obscure data variation over time (it may appear as a flat line).

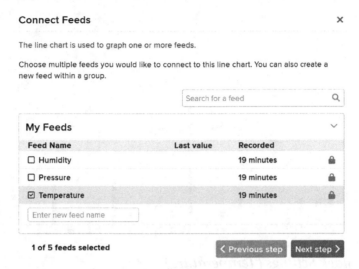

Figure 14-11. Selecting the Feeds for a Block

Once you've selected the feeds by ticking the box next to the feed name, click *Next step* to configure the block. The dialog will look different for each block type. Figure 14-12 shows the settings for the Temperature line graph block.

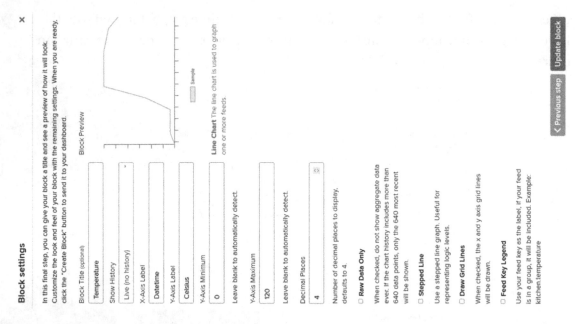

Figure 14-12. *Block Settings (Temperature)*

Notice I chose to set the name for the block to the same name as the feed, and I changed the labels for the X and Y axes. I also set the minimum and maximum values for the Y axis. When you are satisfied with the settings, click *Create block* to add the block to the dashboard.

If you want to only see data that is written while the dashboard is viewed, choose *Live (No history)* for the *Show History* option, or you can choose a range such as one hour to show the data from the last hour. Take some time to consider what you want to see and then change this setting accordingly as noted in the "Execute!" section.

Go ahead and create two more line graphs for the Humidity and Pressure feeds. You can name the blocks in a similar manner but use the range 0,100 for Humidity and range 800,1200 for Pressure. You may want or need to adjust those if the elevation of your geographic location differs, resulting in slightly different ranges.

Finally, we add a block for logging all the data. For this, we will use a stream block. Add the stream block and select all three feeds. You can name it however you want, and the default settings are OK. Figure 14-13 shows the settings I used. This block is a nice block to use when setting up a new dashboard as it lets you see the data as it arrives in each field.

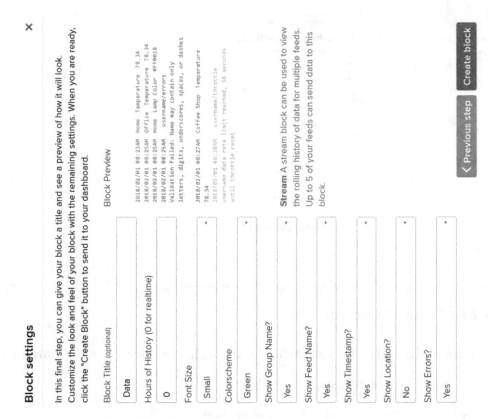

Figure 14-13. *Block Settings (Stream Block)*

There is one more step. Adding blocks to your dashboard places them on the screen in the order they appear and at default sizes. You can edit the layout and move the blocks around by clicking the gear icon and choosing Edit Layout as shown in Figure 14-14. You can also resize the blocks to make them fit your layout.

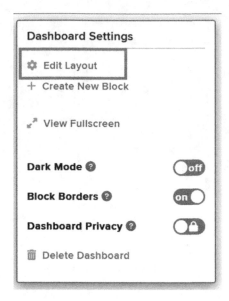

Figure 14-14. *Edit Dashboard Layout*

Go ahead and do this now. You can use a layout like the one shown in Figure 14-15.

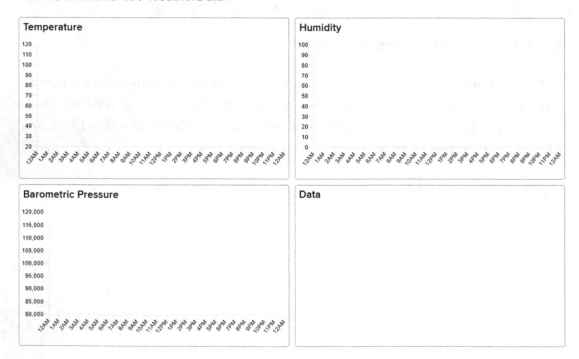

Figure 14-15. *Rearranging Blocks on the Dashboard*

When you are finished editing your dashboard, click *Save Layout*. You can always edit your dashboard later if you want to change scales on one of the blocks or move the blocks around. To edit a block that you've already added, click the small gear icon on the dashboard edit screen for the block you want to edit.

Get Your Credentials

There is one more thing you need to do. Connection to Adafruit IO is done through your user account and a special key generated by the system. We use this data instead of a user ID and password. To retrieve your key, click the yellow key button as shown in Figure 14-16.

Figure 14-16. *Retrieve Keys Button*

You will see a dialog appear like the one shown in Figure 14-16 (data masked to ensure security). Notice I have obscured the data. You should treat this data like you would any other password. Figure 14-17 shows an example of the Adafruit 10 keys. Notice there are examples of how to use the keys in code.

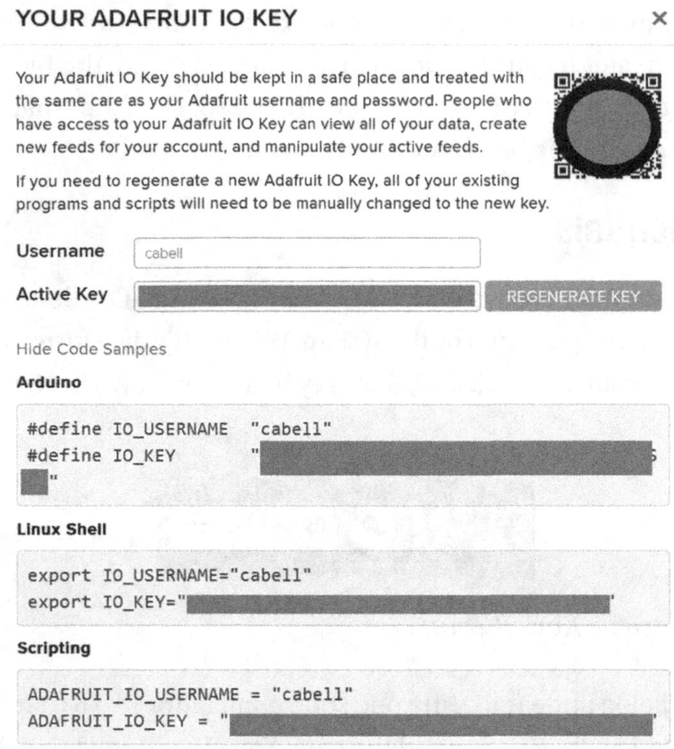

YOUR ADAFRUIT IO KEY   ×

Your Adafruit IO Key should be kept in a safe place and treated with
the same care as your Adafruit username and password. People who
have access to your Adafruit IO Key can view all of your data, create
new feeds for your account, and manipulate your active feeds.

If you need to regenerate a new Adafruit IO Key, all of your existing
programs and scripts will need to be manually changed to the new key.

Username   cabell

Active Key   REGENERATE KEY

Hide Code Samples

Arduino

```
#define IO_USERNAME   "cabell"
#define IO_KEY        "                                    "
```

Linux Shell

```
export IO_USERNAME="cabell"
export IO_KEY="                                         "
```

Scripting

```
ADAFRUIT_IO_USERNAME = "cabell"
ADAFRUIT_IO_KEY = "                                    "
```

Figure 14-17. Adafruit IO Keys

You will need both your username and your IO key in the source code, so it is best
to get these values now and save them some place safe. You can always refer to this
page in the future if you do not want to save these values in a file. Also, if you ever need
to regenerate your key, you can do so by clicking *REGENERATE KEY*, but don't do that
unless you need a new key!

OK, now we're ready to start sending some data. Let's see how to do that.

Project: IoT Weather

This project uses some of the same code from Chapter 11 but with some major
modifications. Also, the hardware for this project is similar to Chapter 11. Thus, we will
see the complete code for this project but omit discussion about code fragments and
hardware that we have seen discussed in Chapter 11.

Now let's see what components are needed for this project, and then we will see how to wire everything together. We repeat the hardware connections for convenience.

Required Components

Table 14-2 lists the components you will need. As you can see, we only need the BME280 sensor. We will not use the RTC because Adafruit IO will record the date and time of each sample uploaded to the feed.

Table 14-2. *Required Components*

Component	Qty	Description	Cost	Links
BME280	1	Weather sensor	$20	www.sparkfun.com/products/ 13676
			$15	www.adafruit.com/ product/2652
Jumper wires	4	M/M jumper wires, 6" (cost is for a set of 10 jumper wires)	$4	www.sparkfun.com/ products/8431

Fortunately, the wiring for this project is less complex than the last two projects. Now, let's see how to wire the components together.

Set Up the Hardware

The hardware setup for this project is easier than those for the last chapter. We have only the BME280 sensor.

We will see how to make the connections for both the Raspberry Pi Pico and the Arduino Nano RP2040 Connect. As you will see, the connections are similar in that you will wire the breakout boards with the same connections and number of wires, but where those wires connect to the board differs. Let's begin with the Pico.

Connections for the Raspberry Pi Pico

Table 14-3 shows the connections needed for this project for the Raspberry Pi Pico.

Table 14-3. *Connections for the Weather Monitoring Project (Pico)*

Physical Pin	GPIO Num/Function	Connection
29	GP21	BME280 – 3.3V
38	GND	BME280 – GND
11	GP8	BME280 – SDA
12	GP9	BME280 – SCL

Figure 14-18 shows the wiring drawing for the project on the Pico.

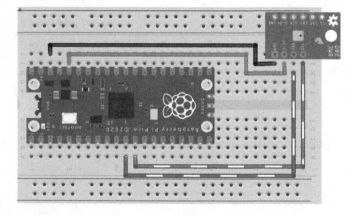

Figure 14-18. *Wiring the Weather IoT Project (Pico)*

Connections for the Arduino Nano RP2040 Connect

Since we are using the same components for the Arduino Nano RP2040 Connect, the connections are going to be similar, but as noted in previous chapters, the Nano RP2040 has a different pin layout. Thus, some of the connections are going to be different. Table 14-4 shows the connections needed for the Nano RP2040.

Table 14-4. *Connections for the Weather Monitoring Project (Nano RP2040)*

Physical Pin	GPIO Num/Function	Connection
2	3.3V	BME280 – 3.3V
19	GND	BME280 – GND
8	SDA	BME280 – SDA
9	SCL	BME280 – SCL

Notice most of the connections are the same. What differs is where the jumper wires connect to the board. Figure 14-19 shows the wiring drawing for the project on the Nano RP2040.

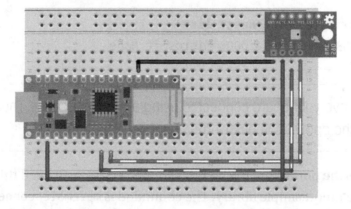

Figure 14-19. *Wiring the Weather IoT Project (Nano RP2040)*

Once again, always make sure to double-check your connections before powering the board on. Now, let's talk about the code we need to write. Don't power on your board just yet – there is a fair amount of discussion needed before we're ready to test the project.

Write the Code

The code for this project is relatively easy to write once you understand the MQTT library. As you will see, it pairs well with Adafruit IO in ease of use. To make this project more interesting and more applicable to how you would write IoT projects for the MicroPython platform, we will place all the code for reading the sensors and publishing the data in a class. We will then use that class in a code module that we can call from our weather_iot.py code module on boot. Since the code doesn't use any constructs that we haven't already seen, the description of the code will be brief and focus only on the new concepts and the MQTT code specifically.

However, we first need to download an MQTT library and the BME280 driver from Chapter 11.

Installing the MQTT Library for MicroPython

Like the last chapter, we need to install the Arduino IoT Cloud library using mpremote. If you have not installed mpremote, see Chapter 13 for how to install mpremote on your PC.

Next, we need to determine where the MicroPython board is connected. Be sure the board is connected to your PC before running the following command shown in bold face:

```
C:\Users\Chuck> mpremote connect list
COM15 E661AC8863913F23 2e8a:0005 Microsoft None
```

Note   If you have your board connected using a code editor like Thonny, you will need to close the application before running this command.

The output is the port where the board is connected. We will need this in the next step to install the umqtt.simple library. The command is mpremote connect COM15 mip install umqtt.simple and is demonstrated as follows. Be sure to use the correct COM port (Windows) or path (Mac and Linux).

```
C:\Users\Chuck> mpremote connect COM15 mip install umqtt.simple
Install umqtt.simple
Installing umqtt.simple (latest) from https://micropython.org/pi/v2 to /lib
Installing: /lib/umqtt/simple.mpy
Done
```

Once this command completes, and you open Thonny again, you should see a new folder on your MicroPython board named lib, which contains the libraries you installed. Cool. Figure 14-20 shows an example of what the file tree will display in Thonny.

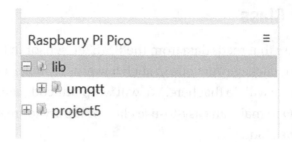

Figure 14-20. *Installed Libraries (mpremote)*

Once the MQTT library is installed, we are ready to write the sensor code and main code. But first, let's discuss a common technique for writing programs that contain sensitive data like passwords and IO keys.

Secrets File

A common practice for projects that contain sensitive variables or constants is to include a secrets file stored in a Python file. For example, it is common practice to save the file with the name secrets.py where we place our WiFi user ID and password along with any other data we want to keep. The following shows an example of the secrets.py file used for this project. Go ahead and create one with your data and save it on your PC. We will copy it to our MicroPython board later.

```
SSID = "yadayada"
SSID_PASS = "yadayadayada"
IO_USER ="yada"
IO_KEY = "yadayadayadayadayadayadayadayadayada"
```

We include these variables (constants) using an import statement such as the following:

```
from project6.secrets import SSID, SSID_PASS, IO_USER, IO_KEY
```

Next, we need to write a class to read the data from the sensor.

Weather Sensor Class

We wrote a similar class that reads data from the BME280 sensor in Chapter 11. There, we learned that we can package our code in such a way as to make a set of operations on data easier to use. We will do that here. We will wrap our code around the BME280 sensor and Adafruit IO to make an easy-to-use class or library for reading weather data and publishing it to the cloud.

If you want to follow along, we will name the class WeatherSensorIoT since it encapsulates the sensor and publishes data. We will name the code module weather_sensor_iot.py.

Rather than go through every detail, we will focus on the highlights of the code and leave the complete explanation for an exercise. Let's begin with a look at the imports section.

The imports section requires several libraries. We need the I2C and MQTT libraries, the BME280 driver, and the time library for delays. The following shows the imports needed for the class:

```
import time
from umqtt.simple import MQTTClient
from project6.bme280 import BME280
```

The constructor needs to accept the Adafruit IO username, AIO key, and frequency (sample rate). The device ID can be any string you want to use, but it is suggested you use a short name for the device. We will also use a parameter for the port of the MQTT server in case you want to change it, but we will use a default value of 1883, which is the port for Adafruit IO. Listing 14-1 shows the constructor for the class. Notice we also set up the BME280 sensor.

Listing 14-1. Constructor (WeatherSensorIoT Class)

```
# Constructor
def __init__(self, i2c, io_user, io_key, frequency, port=1883):
    # Save variables passed for use in other methods
    self.io_user = io_user
    self.io_key = io_key
```

```
self.update_frequency = frequency
self.port = port

# Now, setup the sensor
self.sensor = BME280(i2c=i2c, address=0x77)
time.sleep(0.100)
print("Weather MQTT client is ready.")
```

Notice this function simply initializes several class variables (designated with self.) for storing the connection values and frequency. The constructor also initializes the I2C interface and the BME280 sensor class instance.

The read data function is the same as we used in Chapter 11 but without the writing to the log files.

The next function we need is a function we can use as a callback for the MQTT messages from the feeds. We will name the function message_function(). In this case, we need only the topic and message parameters. The following shows the code for the message_callback() function:

```
# A simple callback to print the message from the server
def message_callback(self, topic, msg):
    print("[{0}]: {1}".format(topic, msg))
```

The last function we need is the one that is going to do all the work for collecting data from the sensor and publishing it on our feeds on Adafruit IO. This is where the core of using the MQTT library occurs, so we will go through this bit a little slower.

The first thing we do is get an instance of the MQTTClient class. We pass in the hostname of the server (in this case, io.adafruit.com), the user ID, AIO key, and port.

Once we have an instance of the client, we can set the callback for getting any messages from our subscribed feeds associated with our device ID; we use the set_callback() function passing in the name of our method to handle the messages. Recall, this is message_callback().

Next, we specify the feed using the topic parameter. Feed names are always formed using the user ID and the feed name. You can think of this like a path. Be sure to check the feed names carefully to ensure you've got the right one. You can always check your Adafruit IO page to double-check.

Next, we write the while loop to read data from the sensors. To make this easy, we will loop indefinitely (but you may want to change that if you plan to make this project more than an experiment). When we read the data using our read_data() function, then publish each data element to the appropriate feed using the client.publish() function. For example, to send data to the temperature feed, we specify the user ID and feed using the topic parameter and send the data via the msg parameter as follows:

```
client.publish(topic="{0}/feeds/temperature".format(self.io_user),
msg=str(data[0]))
```

At the end of the loop, we do several things. We sleep for the number of seconds specified in the frequency parameter. This is how we can avoid sending too much data too frequently and match our data collection to what is a realistic interval. Next, we check for messages using the client.check_msg() function. This function simply checks to see if any new messages have arrived. If there are, since we specified a callback function, the callback function will be called for each new message. See, no polling needed. Listing 14-2 shows the completed code for the weather sensor class.

Listing 14-2. Weather Sensor Class (weather_sensor_iot.py)

```
#
# MicroPython for the IoT Second Edition - Chapter 14
#
# Chapter 14 - BME280 Weather Class with MQTT and Adafruit IoT
#
# Required Components:
# - (1) BME280 Weather Sensor
#
# Imports for the project
import time
from umqtt.simple import MQTTClient
from project6.bme280 import BME280

class WeatherSensorIoT:
    """Sensor node using a BME280 sensor to send temperature, humidity, and
        barometric pressure to io.adafruit.com MQTT broker."""
```

```python
# Constructor
def __init__(self, i2c, io_user, io_key, frequency, port=1883):
    # Save variables passed for use in other methods
    self.io_user = io_user
    self.io_key = io_key
    self.update_frequency = frequency
    self.port = port

    # Now, setup the sensor
    self.sensor = BME280(i2c=i2c, address=0x77)
    time.sleep(0.100)
    print("Weather MQTT client is ready.")

# Reads the sensor. Returns a tuple of (temperature, humidity,
pressure)
def read_data(self):
    time.sleep_ms(50)
    raw_values = self.sensor.raw_values
    temperature = raw_values[0]
    humidity = raw_values[2]
    pressure = raw_values[1]
    print("Data read:", self.sensor.values)
    return (temperature, humidity, pressure)

# A simple callback to print the message from the server
def message_callback(self, topic, msg):
    print("[{0}]: {1}".format(topic, msg))

def run(self):
    # Now we setup our MQTT client
    client = MQTTClient("WeatherIoT", "io.adafruit.com",
                        user=self.io_user,
                        password=self.io_key, port=self.port)
    client.set_callback(self.message_callback)
    client.connect()
```

```
    while True:
        data = self.read_data()
        client.publish(topic="{0}/feeds/temperature".format(
                    self.io_user), msg=str(data[0]))
        client.publish(topic="{0}/feeds/humidity".format(self.io_user),
                    msg=str(data[1]))
        client.publish(topic="{0}/feeds/pressure".format(self.io_user),
                    msg=str(data[2]))
        time.sleep(self.update_frequency)
        client.check_msg()
```

Take a few moments to study the code until you are confident you know how it works.

Now that we have our sensor class, we can write the main code.

Main Code

The main code file is named weather_iot.py. As you will see, it is very short and simple. This is because all the work is being done in our class module! The following sections briefly describe the major parts of the main code starting with the imports.

Since all the work is being done in the WeatherSensorIoT class, we only need to import that code module (weather_sensor_iot) and those libraries we need for connecting our board to our WiFi network as follows:

```
import network, sys, time
from machine import Pin, SoftI2C
from project6.weather_sensor_iot import WeatherSensorIoT
from project6.secrets import SSID, SSID_PASS, IO_USER, IO_KEY
```

We also need one constant for the frequency of updates. We will use a conservative 30 seconds for testing, but you may want to increase it should you put this project into service to avoid uploading too much data too quickly.

```
FREQUENCY = 30 # seconds
```

We will use the same connect() function as we've used in previous chapters, but we change it to use the SSID and SSID_PASS variables from the secrets.py file (see the following complete code).

The main() function is very simple. All we need to do is call the connect() function to connect to our WiFi network, set up the BME280 using the same code from Chapter 11 that permits the use of the Pico or Nano RP2040 Connect, then instantiate the WeatherSensorIoT class, and then call the run() function for the class as follows:

```
# Run the weather MQTT client
weather_mqtt_client = WeatherSensorIoT(i2c, IO_USER, IO_KEY, FREQUENCY)
weather_mqtt_client.run()
```

That's it! Can you see how much easier it makes our code if we use classes to contain the core of our project? Hopefully, you will see the benefits and start constructing your own projects in a similar manner. Listing 14-3 shows the completed code for the Weather main code module (weather_iot.py).

Listing 14-3. Main Code (weather_iot.py)

```
#
# MicroPython for the IoT Second Edition - Chapter 14
#
# Chapter 14 - MicroPython Weather IoT with MQTT and Adafruit IO
#
# Required Components:
# - (1) BME280 Weather Sensor
#
# Imports for the project
import network, sys, time
from machine import Pin, SoftI2C
from project6.weather_sensor_iot import WeatherSensorIoT
from project6.secrets import SSID, SSID_PASS, IO_USER, IO_KEY

FREQUENCY = 30 # seconds

# Setup the board to connect to our network.
def connect():
    wlan = network.WLAN(network.STA_IF)
    wlan.active(True)
    wlan.connect(SSID, SSID_PASS)
    while not wlan.isconnected() and wlan.status() >= 0:
        print("Waiting to connect...")
```

```
        time.sleep(1)
    if not wlan.isconnected():
        print("Cannot find SSID!")
        sys.exit(0)

    print("Connected!")
    print("My IP address is: {0}".format(wlan.ifconfig()[0]))
    return True

# Main function
def main():
    # Setup the socket and respond to HTML requests
    # Connect to the network
    if not connect():
        sys.exit(-1)
    #
    # Arduino Nano RP2040 Connect uses sda=12, scl=13
    #sda = Pin(12)
    #scl = Pin(13)
    #
    # Raspberry Pi Pico uses sda=8, scl=9
    sda = Pin(8)
    scl = Pin(9)
    #
    # Software I2C (bit-banging) for the RTC
    i2c = SoftI2C(sda=sda, scl=scl, freq=100000)

    # Run the weather MQTT client
    weather_mqtt_client = WeatherSensorIoT(i2c, IO_USER, IO_KEY, FREQUENCY)
    weather_mqtt_client.run()

if __name__ == '__main__':
    try:
        main()
    except (KeyboardInterrupt, SystemExit) as err:
        print("\nbye!\n")
    sys.exit(0)
```

Now, let's run this project!

Execute!

Now is the fun part! We've got the code all set up to read weather data from the sensor and publish the data in Adafruit IO.

First, let's copy the files we need to our MicroPython board. You will need to create a folder on the board named project6 and copy the secrets.py and weather_sensor_iot.py files there. You also need to copy the bme280.py library from Chapter 11 to the project6 folder on the board. Finally, you can copy the weather_iot.py file to the / folder on the board.

There is one additional thing to consider when working with data in your feeds concerning the Show History setting. You can change this value to match your expectations for data. Using the Live (no history) option is best to see data as it is being recorded, but if you want to see historical data, you should choose one of the other options to see more data.

For example, you can choose to see the last hour of data. To change the history setting, edit your layout and then click the gear icon for the block you want to change, then click the drop-down box to change the history setting as shown in Figure 14-21. A setting of one hour is best for testing your projects.

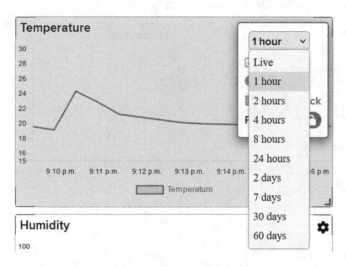

Figure 14-21. *Changing Show History Option for Block*

Once you have the history option changed to one hour, you can execute the code on your MicroPython board. Listing 14-4 shows an example of the output you should see.

Listing 14-4. Sample Output

```
Connected!
My IP address is: 10.0.0.14
Weather MQTT client is ready.
Data read: ('20.3C', '993.96hPa', '63.00%')
Data read: ('20.13C', '994.01hPa', '63.49%')
Data read: ('19.97C', '993.95hPa', '63.92%')
Data read: ('19.92C', '993.97hPa', '64.20%')
Data read: ('19.86C', '993.93hPa', '64.39%')
Data read: ('19.8C', '994.05hPa', '64.52%')
Data read: ('19.76C', '993.88hPa', '64.66%')
Data read: ('19.71C', '993.96hPa', '64.77%')
Data read: ('19.66C', '993.93hPa', '64.86%')
...
```

Since the frequency is set to 30 seconds, you should let the program run for a few minutes before viewing your dashboard. Once you do, you should see data similar to Figure 14-22.

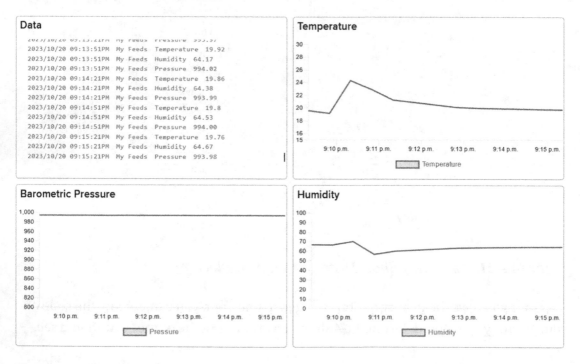

Figure 14-22. *Sample Dashboard with Data*

If you see something similar, huzzah, you've done it! If not, be sure to diagnose any code issues and fix them and let the code run for about 10–15 minutes.

Notice the pressure and humidity lines don't change much. This is expected since this example was run indoors during a very short time. However, you may notice a rise and dip or two in the data for temperature. This was due to artificial changes to the temperature. That is, I moved a heat source close to the sensor to make the area warmer and thus record higher values. Similarly, I used a cool air source to cool the area, causing a dip in the values. When I did so, it caused a slight change in the humidity values. Can you think of why that happened?[1]

You can try this out yourself, but be careful! Don't touch the sensor lest you damage it and don't use any open flame or other heat sources that could cause burns (or worse).

Caution   Resist the temptation to touch the sensor. You could damage the sensor.

If you like this project, you can consider making it run over a longer time span, reducing the sampling frequency to every few hours. You will still see the data, but perhaps if the temperature in your environment changes, you'll see the actual variation in data rather than simulated changes.

At this point, you've completed another real MicroPython IoT project. In this case, we saw an IoT project that collects and displays data in the cloud. How cool is that?

Taking It Further

This project shows excellent prospects for reusing the techniques in other projects. This is especially true now that you know how to use MQTT. If you liked seeing your sensor data over the Internet, you should consider taking time to explore some embellishments. Here are a few you may want to consider. Some are easy and some may be a challenge or require more research:

- Add more sensors to expand your project to more weather observations.

- Modify the dashboard to display the data using different blocks.

---

[1] I used a can of air, which was much drier than the ambient environment.

- Add more sensor nodes to gather data observations from other places, creating new feeds for each.

- Set up your own MQTT broker and attach your sensor nodes.

Summary

Using cloud services is the next step for your IoT projects, providing you with endless possibilities for storing and exchanging your data with others, companies, and other cloud services. With so many possibilities available, you can do almost anything with your IoT project, and I encourage you to explore what is possible.

In this chapter, we demonstrated this by building a weather sensor project that connected our board to the Adafruit IO cloud service and used that service to store and visualize the data. While in retrospect this project seems easier than the previous projects, we gained specialized knowledge in those projects that made this project easier to implement. That is, without the basics of how to build IoT projects, jumping into the deep end of IoT projects would be folly.

Fortunately, with the help of the nice folks at Adafruit, we can now build IoT projects to send data to the cloud and share it with the world. Not only that, but we can also build solutions that allow us to control our projects from the Internet (hint: use the `subscribe()` function) – everything done quickly with very little effort and no need to learn a complicated API. How cool is that?

In the next chapter, we will see one of our previous projects elevated to an IoT project using Arduino IoT Cloud as the cloud service provider. As you will see, it will enable us to control our MicroPython board from the Internet.

CHAPTER 15

ThingSpeak

Now that we've built a good foundation of experience working with several projects, including those that use cloud services, we are ready to create our last IoT project for MicroPython that uses more advanced cloud services.

In this chapter, we will learn how to use the cloud-based IoT data-hosting service from MathWorks called ThingSpeak (`www.thingspeak.com`). We will see how to take our plant monitoring example project and connect it to ThingSpeak. We will be creating a cloud-based monitoring project that you can see at a glance, the soil moisture value over the Internet.

Overview

Recall from Chapter 12 that ThingSpeak is another cloud service similar to MQTT that permits you to store your data in the cloud using a popular, easy-to-use, cloud-based IoT data-hosting service from MathWorks.

ThingSpeak offers a more robust toolbox to build IoT dashboards than most of the other cloud services. As you will see in this chapter, the project we will build will use four dashboard items (called visualizations) that you can configure to show data in an almost endless format.

Perhaps best of all is the ease of which it is to send data to ThingSpeak. As you will see, it requires a simple HTTP message sent to the ThingSpeak server where we specify our API key and a list of fields to update. Thus, ThingSpeak is one of the easiest to incorporate into our IoT projects.

Let's see how to get started with ThingSpeak, including a deeper look into how to build a class for connecting to ThingSpeak that you can reuse for future projects.

© Charles Bell 2024
C. Bell, *MicroPython for the Internet of Things*, https://doi.org/10.1007/978-1-4842-9861-9_15

Getting Started with ThingSpeak

We won't get too far into the details of the protocols needed to communicate with ThingSpeak; rather, we will see how to use ThingSpeak as a quick start guide. MathWorks provides a complete set of tutorials, documentation, and examples. So, if you need more information about how ThingSpeak works, check out the documentation at `www.mathworks.com/help/thingspeak/`.

There are several steps needed to set up your project to use ThingSpeak. The following is a list of the steps:

- Create an account (if you don't already have one).

- Create a channel.

- Retrieve your API keys.

Let's begin by creating an account in ThingSpeak.

Create an Account in ThingSpeak

To use ThingSpeak, you must first sign up for an account. Fortunately, they provide the option for a free account. In fact, you get a free account to start with and add (purchase) a license later. To create a free account, visit `https://thingspeak.com/`, click *Get Started For Free*, then click Create one! as shown in Figure 15-1.

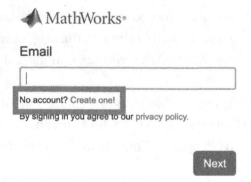

Figure 15-1. *Create a New ThingSpeak/MathLabs Account*

On the next page, type in your email address, location (general geographic), and first and last name, then click *Continue*. You will then be sent a validation email. Open that and follow the instructions to verify your email and complete your free account by choosing a password. You may be asked to complete a short questionnaire. Be sure to log in before continuing.

Next, let's create our first channel.

Create a Channel

Once you log in to ThingSpeak, you can create a channel to hold your data. Recall, each channel can have up to eight data items (fields). From your login home page, click *New Channel* as shown in Figure 15-2.

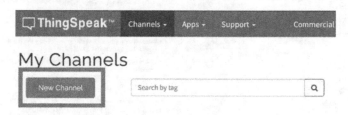

Figure 15-2. *Creating a Channel in ThingSpeak*

You will be presented with a really long form that has a lot of fields that you can fill out. Figure 15-3 shows an example of the form.

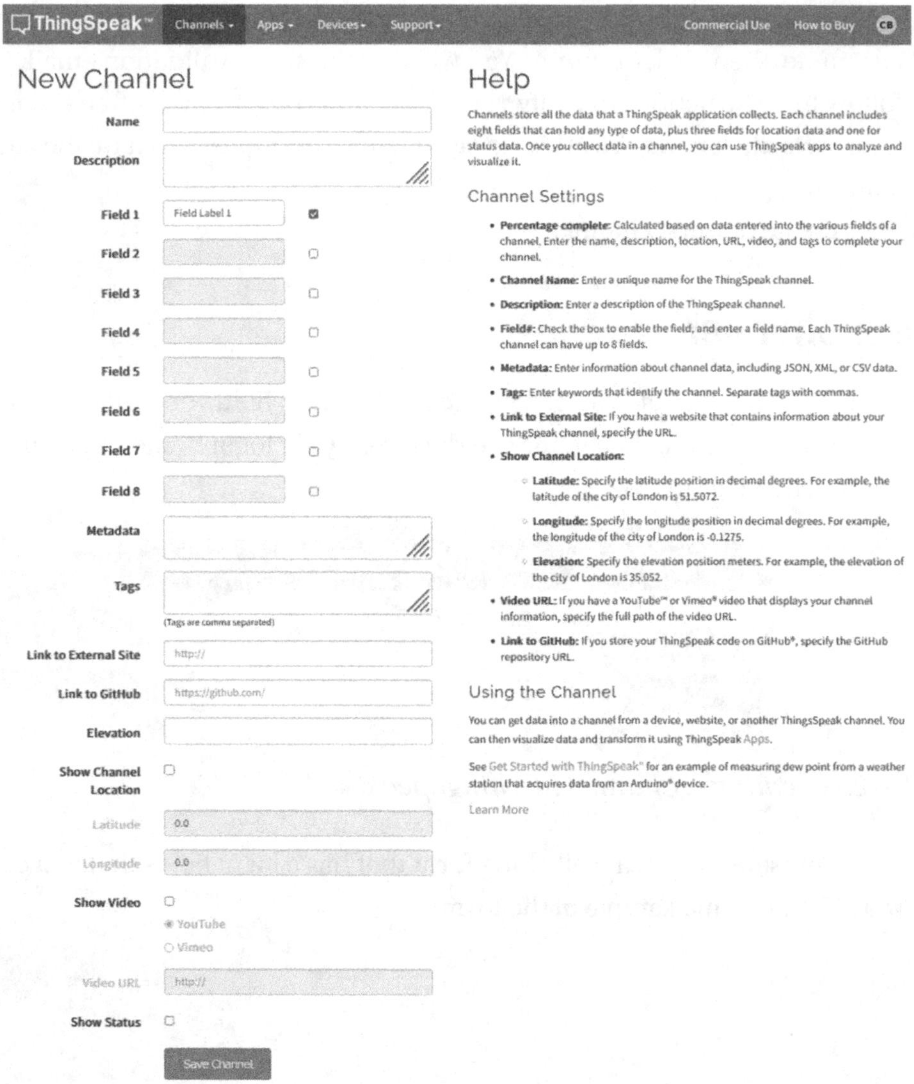

Figure 15-3. *New Channel Form*

At a minimum, you need only name the channel, enter a description (not strictly required but recommended), and then select (tick) one or more fields naming each.

So, what are all those channel settings? The following gives a brief overview of each. As you work with ThingSpeak, you may want to start using some of these fields:

- *Percentage complete*: A calculated field based on the completion of the name, description, location, URL, video, and tags in your channel.

- *Channel Name*: Unique name for the channel.

- *Description*: Description of the channel.

- *Field#*: Tick each box to enable the field.

- *Metadata*: Additional data for the channel in JSON, XML, or CSV format.

- *Tags*: A comma-separated list of keywords for searching.

- *Link to External Site*: If you have a website about your project, you can provide the URL here to publish on the channel.

- *Show Channel Location*: Tick this box to include the following fields.

  - *Latitude*: Latitude of the sensor(s) for the project or source of the data

  - *Longitude*: Longitude of the sensor(s) for the project or source of the data

  - *Elevation*: Elevation in meters for use with projects affected by elevation

- *Video URL*: If you have a video associated with your project, you can provide the URL here to be published on the channel.

- *Link to GitHub*: If your project is hosted in GitHub, you can provide the URL to be published on the channel.

Wow, that's a lot of stuff for free! As you will see, this isn't a simple toy or severely limited product. You can accomplish quite a lot with these settings. Notice there are places to put links to a video, website, and GitHub. This is because channels can be either private (only your login or API key, as we will see, can access) or public. Making a channel public allows you to share the data with anyone, and thus those URL fields may be handy to document your project. Cool.

Now, let's create a practice channel that we will use in the next section to see how to write data (sometimes called upload) to ThingSpeak. Use the following parameters for the fields on the New Channel form:

- *Name*: `practice_channel`

- *Description*: Practice channel for testing MicroPython

- *Field 1 label*: `RandInt`

Note   The field names we enter in the channel setup are for presentation purposes only (they are labels). Fields are referenced by `fieldN` starting with 1 (e.g., `field1`). We will see this as we move forward.

Enter the values as shown, then click *Save Channel* to complete the process. Now we are ready to test writing some data.

Get Your API Keys

Once you create your channel, it is time to write some data. There are two pieces of information you will need for most projects: the API key for the channel and for some libraries the channel number (the integer value shown on the channel page). There are libraries available for many platforms, and on some platforms, there may be several ways (libraries or techniques) to write data to a ThingSpeak channel.

You can find the API key on the channel page by clicking the *API Keys* tab. When you create a new channel, you will have one write and one read API key. You can add more keys if you need them so that you can use one key per device, location, customer, etc.

If you make your channel public, do not share the write key with anyone you don't want to allow to write to your channel. You can create new keys by clicking the *Generate New Write API Key* or *Add New Read API Key* button. You can delete read keys by clicking the *Delete API Key* button. You can also add a note to remind you of any pertinent data you may want to recall later.

Figure 15-4 shows the API Keys tab for the channel created previously.

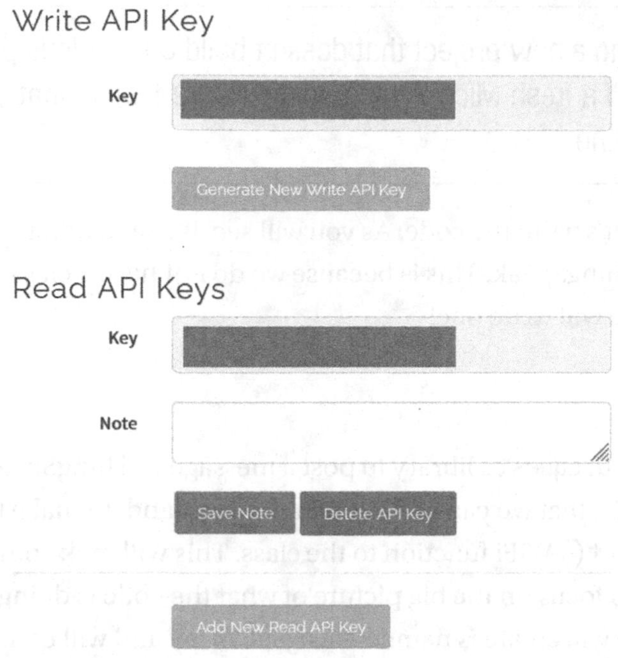

Write API Key

Key

Generate New Write API Key

Read API Keys

Key

Note

Save Note   Delete API Key

Add New Read API Key

Figure 15-4. *API Keys for Practice Channel*

Notice I masked out the keys. We use the key in our code to allow the device to connect to and write data to the channel. So, we typically copy this string from the channel page and paste it into our code as a string.

Now that you understand the basics of writing data to ThingSpeak, let's take a look at a more advanced configuration that will help you reuse much of what is needed to incorporate ThingSpeak into future projects.

Using ThingSpeak with MicroPython

Once again, this project is a very simple sketch to learn how to connect and write data to a ThingSpeak channel. For the data, we will be generating a random integer and send that to the channel.

The hardware we will use is simply our MicroPython board (Pico or Nano RP2040 Connect). No additional hardware is needed. However, you may want to consider installing a fresh image onto your MicroPython board.

Tip   When starting a new project that doesn't build on previous projects, it is a good idea to install a fresh MicroPython image (`.uf2` file) so that you start with a known good baseline.

That's it! Now, let's write the code. As you will see, it uses a different mechanism for uploading data to ThingSpeak. This is because we do not have a class to encapsulate the functionality, but we will write one!

Write the Code

We will be using the `urequests` library to post a message to ThingSpeak over HTTP. We will create a new class that we can use in other projects, and, to make things easier, we will move our `connect()` WiFi function to the class. This will make our main code much shorter and easier to focus on the big picture of what the code is doing.

The class file we will create is named `thingspeak.py` and will contain a class named ThingSpeak. For most of the examples where you will use the class, we need only a constructor, our `connect()` WiFi function, and a function to write (upload) data to ThingSpeak. To make it a bit more tolerant of networking issues, we will also build a retry loop into the upload procedure.

Let's begin with the imports and constants. We need to import the `network`, `time`, and `urequests` libraries as follows. We also need values from a `secrets.py` file like we used in previous projects but with one additional value: our API write key for ThingSpeak. We will use two constants: a value for the maximum number of retries and a string for the HTTP header that we will send to ThingSpeak. The idea is the upload will retry up to `MAX_RETRIES` times before aborting. This will help when the board is connected to a slow or intermittent network.

```
import network, time, urequests
from project7.secrets import SSID, SSID_PASS, THINGSPEAK_WRITE_APIKEY

# Constants
MAX_RETRIES = 10
HTTP_HEADERS = {"Content-Type": "application/json"}
...
```

For the constructor, we will accept the user-customized maximum retries with a default of MAX_RETRIES. We will also set up the WiFi class like we have in previous projects. Once again, we will simply copy in our connect() function from previous projects.

For the upload_data() function, we will require a Python dictionary that includes each of the keys and their values. We have to add the API key, but we can do that easily. In the function, we will create a loop that contains a try...except block for calling the network functions we will use.

Specifically, we open a connection to the ThingSpeak server, issue the POST request, then wait for a status code. Notice that we use the urequests.post() function to send the URL, which is the ThingSpeak URL plus our write API key, the data payload (a dictionary of key-value pairs), and the header that we created as a constant. We then test the status code to ensure the upload worked. A status code of 200 means success, but if we get anything else, we print the response data (headers, reason, and status_code) for later analysis.

If you see a reason, return code, or any fields in the response packet with the value 6, it likely means you have a problem with the way you have formatted the dictionary of data values. ThingSpeak "counts" field keys starting at one (field1, field2, field3, etc.), which correspond to the fields as you defined that, but not the label you assigned them. If you get strange return codes or you do not see any data in your dashboard, check the dictionary keys.

> **Tip** If you do not get a 200 (OK) status code, check the dictionary for your data payload to make sure the keys and values are formatted correctly.

If we encounter a problem with any of the network functions, we sleep for five seconds, then try the command again. We will do this up to MAX_RETRIES or until the operation succeeds.

Listing 15-1 shows the complete code for this class. Take some time to read through it so that you familiarize yourself with how it works.

Listing 15-1. The ThingSpeak Class

```
#
# MicroPython for the IoT Second Edition - Chapter 15
#
```

```python
# MicroPython IoT Plant Monitoring with ThingSpeak
#
# ThingSpeak class with networking
#
# Import libraries
import network, time, urequests
from project7.secrets import SSID, SSID_PASS, THINGSPEAK_WRITE_APIKEY

# Constants
MAX_RETRIES = 10
HTTP_HEADERS = {"Content-Type": "application/json"}

class ThingSpeak:
    """This class permits you to upload data to ThingSpeak
        using your API write key."""

    # Constructor
    def __init__(self, num_retries=MAX_RETRIES):
        self.api_key = THINGSPEAK_WRITE_APIKEY
        self.max_retries = num_retries
        self.wlan = network.WLAN(network.STA_IF)
        self.wlan.active(True)

    # Setup the board to connect to our network.
    def connect(self):
        self.wlan.connect(SSID, SSID_PASS)
        while not self.wlan.isconnected() and self.wlan.status() >= 0:
            print("Waiting to connect...")
            time.sleep(1)
        if not self.wlan.isconnected():
            print("Cannot find SSID!")
            sys.exit(0)

        print("Connected!")
        print("My IP address is: {0}".format(self.wlan.ifconfig()[0]))
        return True

    # Upload the data in the form of a dictionary of key,
```

```python
# values to ThingSpeak.
def upload_data(self, param_dict, timeout=5000):
    # Make sure we're connected to the WiFi
    if not self.wlan.isconnected():
        if not connect():
            return False

    # Attempt to retry if the timeout fails
    retry = 0
    while retry <= self.max_retries:
        try:
            print("Sending data...", end="")
            response = urequests.post(
                "http://api.thingspeak.com/update?api_key=" +
                self.api_key, json=param_dict,
                headers=HTTP_HEADERS,
            )
            break
        except Exception as err:
            print("\nWARNING: Update failed: {0}".format(err))
            if retry <= self.max_retries:
                print("Retrying in 5 seconds. [{}]".format(retry+1))
                time.sleep(5)
                retry = retry + 1
            else:
                retry = self.max_retries + 1
                print("WARNING: Cannot upload to ThingSpeak. "
                    "Exceeded number of retries. Abort.")
                response.close()
                return False
    # Check header for correct status.
    if response.status_code == 200:
        print("done.")
    else:
        print("\nWARNING: data not acknowledged.")
```

```
        print("Header: {0}\nStatus: {1}\nReason: {2}"
              "\n".format(response.headers,
                          response.status_code,
                          response.reason.decode('ascii')))
    response.close()
    return True
```

Next is the code for the main script. We will use the new class to upload the random number we generate. We will name the main script test_thingspeak.py. If you are following along, open a new file now with that name.

Like our previous projects, we will create a project folder on our MicroPython board (project7) and copy our libraries there. Be sure to place the thingspeak.py module in the python7 directory before running the test code.

Listing 15-2 shows the complete code for the script for this project. It follows a now familiar pattern where we create a main() function and call it from a try…except block to catch a *CTRL+C* key sequence. The code is very simple. All you need to do is put your API key in the constant and run it.

Listing 15-2.   Complete Code for the test_thingspeak.py Script

```
#
# MicroPython for the IoT Second Edition - Chapter 15
#
# Chapter 15 - IoT Plant Monitoring with ThingSpeak
#
# Test ThingSpeak
#
# Import libraries
import random, sys, time
from project7.thingspeak import ThingSpeak

# Run the program to upload random data to ThingSpeak
def main():
    print("Welcome to the ThingSpeak using MicroPython demonstration!")
    print("Press CTRL+C to stop.")
    thing_speak = ThingSpeak()
    thing_speak.connect()
```

```
    while True:
        # Generate a random integer
        rand_int = random.randint(1, 20)
        print("Random number generated: {}".format(rand_int))
        thing_speak.upload_data({'field1': rand_int})
        # Sleep for 30 seconds
        time.sleep(10)

if __name__ == '__main__':
    try:
        main()
    except (KeyboardInterrupt, SystemExit) as err:
        print("\nbye!\n")
    sys.exit(0)
```

Notice the dictionary we used to pass the data to the upload() function. Here, we used field1 as the key for the channel field. As it turns out, we must use field1, field2, etc., for the field key names regardless of how we may name them in the channel. While this may be a little strange, you should get in the habit of listing the fields in the dictionary in the order they appear in the channel setup.

Note   Be sure to substitute your API key in the location marked. Failure to do so will result in runtime errors.

Now that you have all the code entered, let's test the code and see if it works.

Execute!

Recall that we can start your code from Thonny, or you can connect to your MicroPython board via REPL and execute the code from the REPL console. Listing 15-3 shows an example of the output you should see. You may want to allow the code to run for a few minutes to generate several values. Let it run so that you generate about 20 values before checking your ThingSpeak channel for data.

Listing 15-3. Sample Output for the Example (Python)

```
Welcome to the ThingSpeak using MicroPython demonstration!
Press CTRL+C to stop.
Connected!
My IP address is: 10.0.0.14
Random number generated: 15
Sending data...done.
Random number generated: 18
Sending data...done.
Random number generated: 13
Sending data...done.
Random number generated: 17
Sending data...done.
Random number generated: 19
Sending data...done.
Random number generated: 16
Sending data...done.
Random number generated: 4
Sending data...done.
Random number generated: 16
Sending data...done.
...
Sending data...done.

bye!
```

Let the sketch run for about three minutes before you visit ThingSpeak. Once the sketch has run for some time, navigate to ThingSpeak, log in, and click your channel page, then click the *Private View* tab. We use the private view because channels are private by default. You should see results similar to those shown in Figure 15-5.

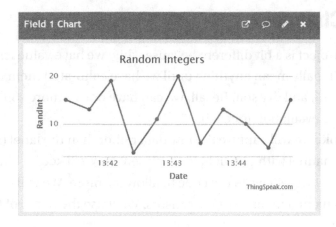

Figure 15-5. *Practice Channel Data*

If you do not see similar data, go back and check the return codes as discussed in the last project. You should see return codes of 200 (success). Check and correct any errors in network connectivity or syntax or logic errors in your script until it runs successfully for several iterations (all samples stored return code 200).

If you see similar data, congratulations! You now know how to generate data and save it to the cloud using two different platforms.

Now, let's turn our attention to one of our previous example projects, retooling them to upload their data to ThingSpeak.

Note   ThingSpeak free accounts are limited to four channels. If you plan to implement all of the example projects in this chapter, you may need to delete one or more channels or upgrade your account to a paid subscription. To delete a channel, from your home page you can click the *Settings* tab to the channel settings, scroll down to the bottom, and click *Delete Channel*.

Now, let's look at an IoT project that improves our plant monitoring solution.

Project: IoT Plant Monitor

Let's take the project from Chapter 10 and make it a true IoT project. We will add the ThingSpeak code we saw in the previous section to send our data to the cloud. Let's begin with creating a new ThingSpeak channel.

Create the Channel

The data for this project is a bit different because while we have values from our soil sensors, they don't really mean anything until we have calibrated them to determine the range for wet, OK, and dry soil. Recall, we can have one or more soil sensors, and we generate a moisture evaluation for each.

For this example, we will capture the raw data rather than the label (category). Thus, we will need one channel with one field for each sensor. We'll keep it simple and use only two sensors, but we will write the code to allow for more. We will create a channel that has two fields named for each of the sensors. We'll use the name of the plant(s) they monitor for clarity.

Log in to your ThingSpeak account and click *New Channel*. We will name the channel *Plants IoT* or *IoT Plants* (or whatever you'd like). Use the information shown in Figure 15-6 to complete the form, then click *Save Channel* at the bottom of the form. Or, you can press *Enter*, which will save the channel for you. Note that you will need to tick the checkbox for fields 1 and 2 to get them to accept input.

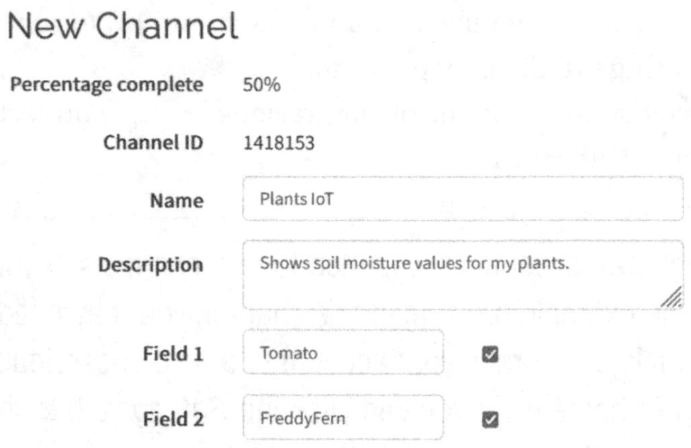

New Channel

Percentage complete	50%
Channel ID	1418153
Name	Plants IoT
Description	Shows soil moisture values for my plants.
Field 1	Tomato ☑
Field 2	FreddyFern ☑

Figure 15-6. *Plants IoT Channel Settings*

Recall, we need to remember the order of the fields. Here, we have defined *Tomato* and *FreddyFern* where they will be referenced as field1 and field2, respectively, in our code.

Configure ThingSpeak

The next step in configuring our ThingSpeak channel is to create visualizations and widgets to present the data. Recall, we have sensors that produce integers that are not very helpful in determining the soil moisture (more precisely, whether the plant needs more or less water). We will create visualizations for the sensor raw data, but what is more interesting is a visualization that shows us, at a glance, whether the plant needs watering. Thus, we will need two visualizations for the raw data and two widgets that depict our wet, OK, and dry ranges.

Create the Visualizations

On your channel page, click the *Private View* tab. You should see a single visualization (chart) that is the default view. Click the pencil icon as shown in Figure 15-7 to edit the chart.

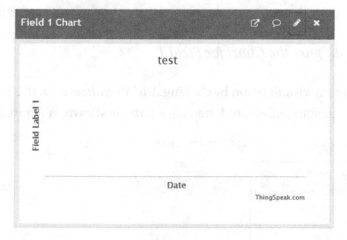

Figure 15-7. *Edit Visualization*

Next, we will need to change the configuration for the visualization as shown in Figure 15-8, then click *Save*.

Field 1 Chart Options

? ×

Title:	Tomato Plant (outside)	Timescale:	⌄
X-Axis:		Average:	⌄
Y-Axis:		Median:	⌄
Color:	#d62020	Sum:	⌄
Background:	#ffffff	Rounding:	
Type:	line ⌄	Data Min:	
Dynamic?:	true ⌄	Data Max:	
Days:		Y-Axis Min:	
Results:	60	Y-Axis Max:	

Save   Cancel

Figure 15-8. *Configure the Chart for Field 1*

Next, create a new visualization by clicking *Add Visualizations*, then choose the chart named "Custom (no start code)," and then click *Save* as shown in Figure 15-9.

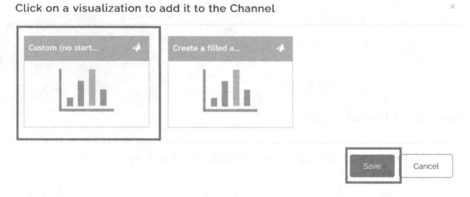

Figure 15-9. *Choose a Chart for Field 2*

Next, edit the new visualization and change its configuration as shown in Figure 15-10, then click *Save*.

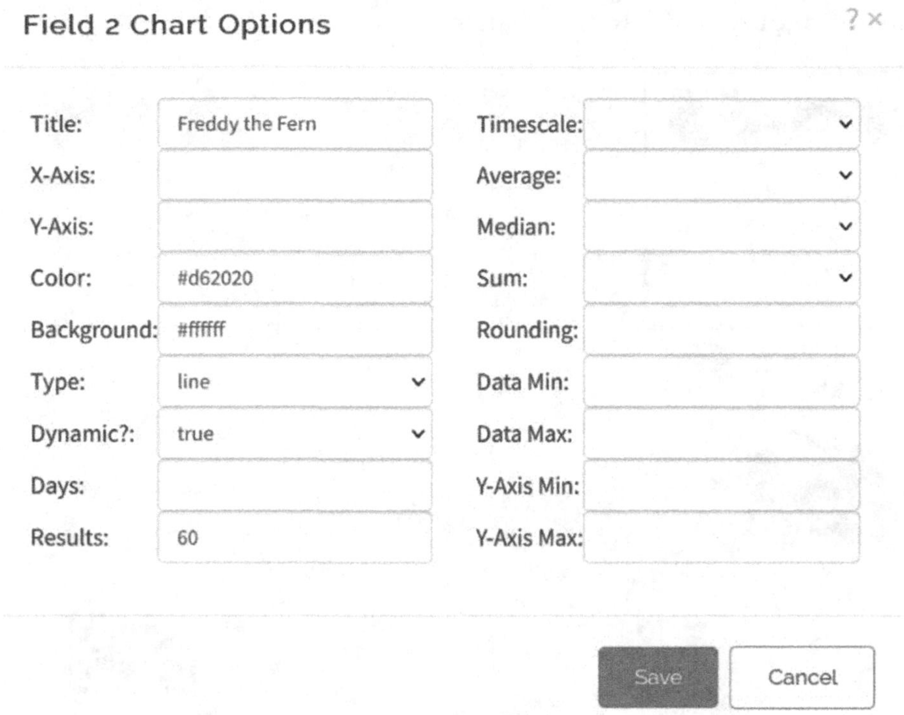

Field 2 Chart Options   ? ×

Title:	Freddy the Fern	Timescale:	⌄
X-Axis:		Average:	⌄
Y-Axis:		Median:	⌄
Color:	#d62020	Sum:	⌄
Background:	#ffffff	Rounding:	
Type:	line ⌄	Data Min:	
Dynamic?:	true ⌄	Data Max:	
Days:		Y-Axis Min:	
Results:	60	Y-Axis Max:	

Save   Cancel

Figure 15-10. *Configure the Chart for Field 2*

Next, we want to create our widgets.

Create the Widgets

We need some way to visualize the data from our sensors that shows us the wet, OK, and dry ranges. The best widget to do that is a gauge because the gauge allows us to create ranges that are color coded. Thus, we can create a range for dry (low values), the OK range, and another for wet. Cool. We will create two gauges, one for each field.

To create a widget, click the *Add Widgets* button, then choose the gauge widget, and click *Next* as shown in Figure 15-11.

Click on a widget to add it to the Channel

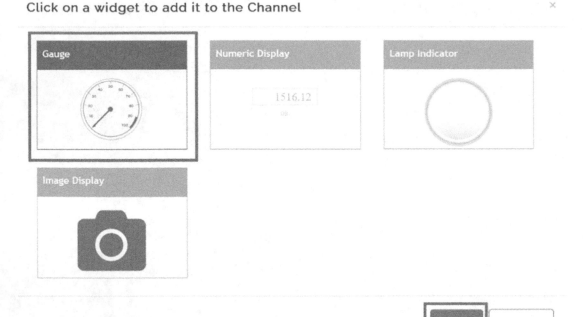

Figure 15-11. Add a Widget (Gauge)

Next, we will configure the parameters (settings) for the widget. Here, we will want to set the data range for the gauge using the values we discovered when we calibrated the sensors. Refer to Chapter 10 on how to do that if you have not done so already.

We can set up the tick marks, labels, and much more! Finally, we also need to set up the colored ranges for our gauge. We will create three ranges. The dry range from my calibration run was 0–700. The OK range was 701–2500 and the wet anything over 2500. You can add ranges at the bottom of the dialog by clicking the + button. I choose colors of red, green, and orange for dry, OK, and wet.

Figure 15-12 shows the setup for the gauge for the first sensor (field 1). Make the changes and click *Save*.

Soil Moisture - Tomato Options   ? ×

Name	Soil Moisture - Tomato
Field	Field 1 ⌄
Min	0
Max	3000
Display Value	☐
Units	Enter Measurement Units
Tick Interval	500
Update Interval	15 second(s)

Range	0	700		×
	701	2500		×
	2501	3000		×

+

Save   Cancel

Figure 15-12. *Configure a Gauge for Field 1*

The gauge for the next field is very similar except for the labels. Add a new gauge and then configure it as shown in Figure 15-13.

517

Soil Moisture - Fern Options   ? ×

Name	Soil Moisture - Fern
Field	Field 2 ⌄
Min	0
Max	3000
Display Value	☐
Units	Enter Measurement Units
Tick Interval	500
Update Interval	15 second(s)

Range	0	700	⬛ ×
	701	2500	⬜ ×
	2501	3000	⬛ ×

+

[Save] [Cancel]

Figure 15-13. *Configure a Gauge for Field 2*

Once you have the two visualizations and two widgets created, you can move them around on your dashboard. I placed the gauge for Field 1 under the chart for Field 1 and the same for Field 2. You may want the gauges above the raw data, or after you have used the project, you may want to delete the charts to make the interface tidier. After all, you really only need the gauges.

Once you have the dashboard arranged, you should see the two charts and two gauges in a layout similar to Figure 15-14. Note that there is no data in the channel yet, so the gauges won't appear normal. In fact, you may see an error message that the field is unavailable. You can ignore that for now.

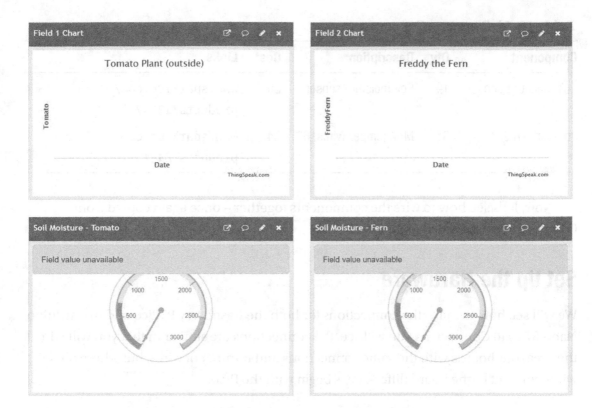

Figure 15-14. *Layout of Plants IoT Dashboard (No Data)*

Now that we have the channel created and have our visualizations and widgets configured, we can go to the *API Keys* tab and copy and then record the API key in our secrets.py file or just store it somewhere for later use. You will need this information in the next step. Now we are ready to modify our code.

Required Components

Table 15-1 is a copy of the table from Chapter 10 and lists the components you will need in addition to your MicroPython board and USB cable minus the RTC because ThingSpeak will add the time the value was written as a reference.

Table 15-1. *Required Components*

Component	Qty	Description	Cost	Links
Soil moisture sensor	1+	Soil moisture sensor	$6	www.sparkfun.com/products/13637
Jumper wires	3*	M/M jumper wires, 6"	$4	www.sparkfun.com/products/8431

Now, let's see how to wire the components together – once again copied from Chapter 10 and included for clarity.

Set Up the Hardware

We will see how to make the connections for both the Raspberry Pi Pico and the Arduino Nano RP2040 Connect. As you will see, the connections are similar in that you will wire the breakout boards with the same connections and number of wires, but where those wires connect to the board differs. Let's begin with the Pico.

Connections for the Raspberry Pi Pico

Table 15-2 shows the connections needed for this project for the Raspberry Pi Pico. Since the Pico has multiple GND pins, we will use those for our sensors.

Table 15-2. *Connections for the Plant Monitoring Project (Pico)*

Physical Pin	GPIO Num/Function	Connection
27	GP20	Sensor 1 – SIG
32	GP27	Sensor 1 – VCC
28	GND	Sensor 1 – GND
29	GP21	Sensor 2 – SIG
34	GP28	Sensor 2 – VCC
38	GND	Sensor 2 – GND

Figure 15-15 shows the wiring drawing for the project on the Pico.

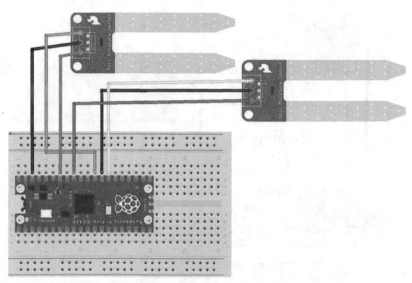

Figure 15-15. *Wiring the IoT Plant Monitoring Project (Pico)*

Connections for the Arduino Nano RP2040 Connect

Table 15-3 shows the connections needed for the Nano RP2040.

Table 15-3. *Connections for the IoT Plant Monitoring Project (Nano RP2040)*

Physical Pin	GPIO Num/Function	Connection
5	GP20	Sensor 1 – SIG
27	GP27	Sensor 1 – VCC
N/A	Breadboard GND	Sensor 1 – GND
6	GP21	Sensor 2 – SIG
26	GP28	Sensor 2 – VCC
N/A	Breadboard GND	Sensor 2 – GND
28	GND	Breadboard ground (top)

Figure 15-16 shows the wiring drawing for the project on the Nano RP2040.

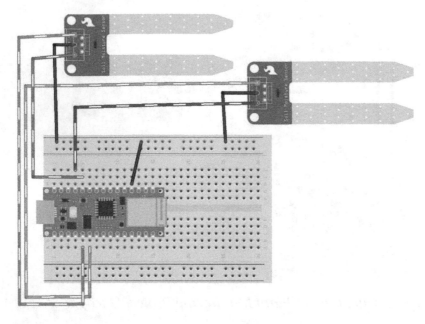

Figure 15-16. *Wiring the Plant Monitoring Project (Nano RP2040)*

Once again, always make sure to double-check your connections before powering the board on. Now, let's talk about the code we need to write. Don't power on your board just yet – there is a fair amount of discussion needed before we're ready to test the project.

Write the Code

In this section, we will modify the project from Chapter 10 to work with ThingSpeak. We will need our `thingspeak.py` module we created previously and a `secrets.py` file that we will use to store our SSID, SSID_PASS, and ThingSpeak API Write key. We will also be using the same `read_timer.py` file we created in Chapter 10. Be sure to set the delay to something reasonable.

The `secrets.py` file should be created with the following content and saved in the project7 directory on your MicroPython board:

```
# WiFi Parameters
SSID = "MY_SSID"
```

```
SSID_PASS = "MY_SSID_PASSWORD"
# API KEY
THINGSPEAK_WRITE_APIKEY = "MY_API_WRITE_KEY"
```

There are only two more code files we need to discuss: modifications to our SoilMoisture class from Chapter 10 and a new main code file. Let's look at those next.

SoilMoisture Class for IoT

Recall from Chapter 10, our SoilMoisture class was designed to read the sensors and then write the data to a log file. We must modify the code to simply return a dictionary of values with one key-value pair for each sensor. We will format the dictionary to make it easy to send to ThingSpeak. Like previous chapters, we will rename this code soil_moisture_iot.py and the class SoilMoistureIoT.

However, we cannot use the code as it is written. We must strip out all of the code for writing to the log file as well as the date and time functions. All that we need is the constructor, the _get_values() private function (with some modifications), and heavy modifications to the read_values() function. Let's look at the read_values() function, then leave the rest of the changes as an exercise.

The read_values() function from Chapter 10 needed code to handle writing to a log file, but all we need is to simply read the sensors and return a dictionary. It is building the dictionary that contains the majority of the changes.

The dictionary is built to create a dictionary of fieldN:valueN entries starting with field1 for the first sensor and field2 for the second and so on. We then get the value for the sensor read and store it as the value in the dictionary under that key. This helps us considerably because now the main code need only call this function and then send the data to ThingSpeak without further modification. Cool! Listing 15-4 shows the code for the modified read_values() function.

Listing 15-4. Modified read_values() Function

```
# Monitor the sensors, read the values, and save them
def read_sensors(self):
    values_read = {} # Create a new dictionary for the values
    for i in range(0,self.num_sensors):
        field_name = "field{0}".format(i+1)
        # Read the data from the sensor and convert the value
```

```
            sensor = self.sensors[i]
            value = self._get_value(sensor['sensor'], sensor['power'])
            values_read.update({field_name:value})
            print("Value read: {0}".format(value))
        return values_read
```

Take some time to study the code until you are certain you know how it works.

Listing 15-5 shows the completed SoilMoistureIoT class code file. As you will notice, there are other changes in the code, and the code file is much smaller than what we used in Chapter 10. Most of the extra code removed was for the log file and capturing the date and time from the RTC, which is no longer needed. This illustrates how much simpler code can be when working with cloud systems. Nice.

Listing 15-5. SoilMoistureIoT Class

```
#
# MicroPython for the IoT Second Edition - Chapter 15
#
# MicroPython IoT Plant Monitoring with ThingSpeak
#
# Soil Moisture class
#
import os
import time
from machine import ADC, Pin

# Thresholds for the sensors
LOWER_THRESHOLD = 500
UPPER_THRESHOLD = 2500
UPDATE_FREQ = 120    # seconds

class SoilMoistureIoT:
    """

    This class reads soil moisture from one or more sensors and writes the
    data to a comma-separated value (csv) file as specified in the
    constructor.
```

It also requires a list (array) or sensor dictionaries in the following form.

```
sensor = {
  'pin': sensor_pin,
  'power': power_pin,
  'location': location or description
  'nick': nickname for the sensor
}
```

Sensors are numbered in the order they appear in the list.

Note: Intermediate calls to get_values() will return the last value(s) read or None if no sensors have been read.
```
"""
```

```
# Initialization for the class (the constructor)
def __init__(self, sensor_list):
    # Loop through the sensors specified and setup a new dictionary
    # for each sensor that includes the power and ADC pins defined.
    self.sensors = []
    for sensor in sensor_list:
        # Setup the dictionary for each soil moisture sensor
        soil_moisture = {
            'sensor': ADC(Pin(sensor['pin'])),
            'power': Pin(sensor['power'], Pin.OUT),
            'location': sensor['location'],
            'nick': sensor['nick']
        }
        self.sensors.append(soil_moisture)
    self.num_sensors = len(self.sensors)
    print("Soil moisture sensors are ready...")

# Read the sensor 10 times and average the values read
def _get_value(self, adc, power):
    total = 0
    # Turn power on
    power.high()
```

```
    # Wait for sensor to power on and settle
    time.sleep(5)
    for i in range (0,10):
        time.sleep(1)
        # Read the value
        value = adc.read_u16()
        total += value
    # Turn sensor off
    power.low()
    return int(total/10)

# Monitor the sensors, read the values, and save them
def read_sensors(self):
    values_read = {} # Create a new dictionary for the values
    for i in range(0,self.num_sensors):
        field_name = "field{0}".format(i+1)
        # Read the data from the sensor and convert the value
        sensor = self.sensors[i]
        value = self._get_value(sensor['sensor'], sensor['power'])
        values_read.update({field_name:value})
        print("Value read: {0}".format(value))
    return values_read
```

Now, let's look at the main code.

Main Code

The main code for this project can be named plants_iot.py, and, like the
SoilMoistureIoT class, it is much simpler due to the use of the thingspeak.py module
we created earlier. All we need in the main code is a loop that uses the ReadTimer class
to read the sensors every sampling interval and send the data to ThingSpeak. Since our
secret values are tucked into a secrets.py file, we don't need to pollute our main code
with a bunch of constants. Nice, neat, and tidy.

Rather than offer a detailed walk-through of the main code, we present it as complete, leaving the walk-through as an exercise. Listing 15-6 shows the completed main code file. As you will see, it is very similar to what we saw in Chapter 10 only simplified for use with ThingSpeak, but it is indicative of the typical code one would find building similar read-update-view cloud-based IoT solutions.

Listing 15-6. Main Code (plants_iot.py)

```
#
# MicroPython for the IoT Second Edition - Chapter 15
#
# Chapter 15 - IoT Plant Monitoring with ThingSpeak
#
# Required Components:
# - (N) Soil moisture sensors (one for each plant)
#
# Imports for the project
import network, sys, time
from project7.read_timer import ReadTimer
from project7.soil_moisture_iot import SoilMoistureIoT
from project7.thingspeak import ThingSpeak

# Main function
def main():
    # Setup ThingSpeak and connect to the network
    thingspeak = ThingSpeak()
    if not thingspeak.connect():
        sys.exit(-1)

    # Setup the sensors
    sensor_list = [
        {
            # Arduino Nano RP2040 Connect and Pico uses pin=27, power=20
            'pin': 27,
            'power': 20,
            'location': 'Green ceramic pot on top shelf',
            'nick': 'Ivy',
```

```
        },
        {
            # Arduino Nano RP2040 Connect and Pico uses pin=28, power=21
            'pin': 28,
            'power': 21,
            'location': 'Fern on bottom shelf',
            'nick': 'Fern',
        }
    ]

    # Setup the soil moisture object instance from the
    SoilMoistureIoT class
    plants = SoilMoistureIoT(sensor_list)
    # Setup read event handler
    data_read_event = ReadTimer(120000)
    print("Ready for connections...")
    while True:
        if data_read_event.time_to_read():
            data_read_event.reset()
            print("Reading data...")
            data = plants.read_sensors()
            # Send data to ThingSpeak channel
            thingspeak.upload_data(data)
        time.sleep(1)

if __name__ == '__main__':
    try:
        main()
    except (KeyboardInterrupt, SystemExit) as err:
        print("\nbye!\n")
    sys.exit(0)
```

Take some time to review this code until you're comfortable how it works.

Before you run the project, be sure that the project7 folder on your MicroPython board has the read_timer.py, secrets.py, thingspeak.py, and soil_moisture_iot.py files downloaded.

That's it; we're ready to execute the project. We will need to let it run for a few minutes, so we can get some data. If you're running the project in a controlled environment where the values do not change, you may not notice much variation. As an exercise, consider altering the environment to stimulate changes in the data. Don't use flame or touch the electronics in any way while they are running.

Execute!

At this point, you can set up the hardware and run the project. Let it run for about 20 minutes, then visit your ThingSpeak channel page. You may not see a lot of variances in the data if you run it in a controlled environment. For better results in a controlled environment, you should consider changing the sample rate from 30 seconds to every 4–6 hours. This should help show how the data changes over the course of a day. When you're done, and ThingSpeak refreshes the view, you should see four widgets like those in Figure 15-17.

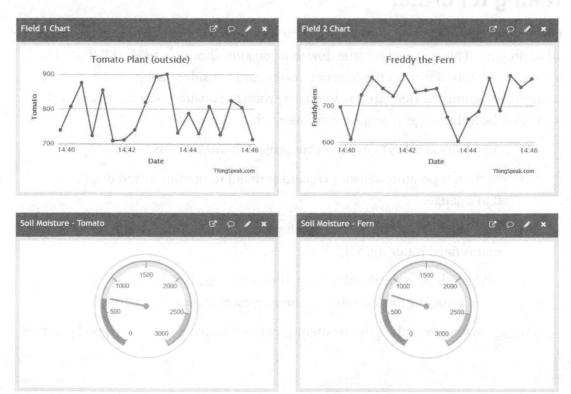

Figure 15-17. *Example Results with Gauges (IoT Plants)*

Notice we can now see the data changes over time as well as the current soil moisture status for each plant. Cool!

Also, notice the difference in the chart and gauge for the fern. Here, the line graph doesn't tell the whole story, but looking at the gauge tells us that the soil for one is nearly dry and needs watering. Go ahead and try leaving this project run for several days or try it with other plants. You will find this simple project can help you keep track of your plants even while you are away. Best of all, it's a nice, practical project that you can show your friends and encourage them to pick up their own MicroPython board.

Note   Recall, we can delete the channel data by clicking *Settings* for the channel on your home page and clicking *Clear Channel* at the bottom.

Taking It Further

This project, like the last one, shows excellent prospects for reusing the techniques in other projects. This is especially true now that you know how to use MQTT. If you liked seeing your sensor data over the Internet, you should consider taking time to explore some embellishments. Here are a few you may want to consider. Some are easy and some may be a challenge or require more research:

- Add more sensors to expand your project to more plants.

- Add a temperature sensor to record ambient temperature and display it in a gauge.

- Add LEDs to your board and the dashboard to illuminate when the plants need watering.

- Add a button to the dashboard to force a data read of the sensors to permit reading the soil moisture on request rather than passively.

Take some time to explore these potential embellishments – it will be good practice.

Summary

Taking a small board like the Pico or Nano RP2040 Connect, adding sensors, and writing relatively short MicroPython code to connect to the Internet and produce data that you can view from anywhere in the world demonstrate the concepts of the Internet of Things in a working project. We have now learned how we can leverage our new knowledge of MicroPython and the small MicroPython boards to achieve true IoT solutions.

In this chapter, we demonstrated this by building a plant monitoring project that connected our board to the ThingSpeak cloud service and used that service to store and visualize the data. While in retrospect this project seems easier than the previous projects, we gained specialized knowledge in those projects that made this project easier to implement.

Fortunately, we can now build IoT projects to send data to the cloud and share it with the world. Not only that, but we can also build solutions that allow us to control our projects from the Internet – everything done quickly with very little effort and no need to learn a complicated API. How cool is that?

With the experience gained in this book, you are now ready to build sophisticated IoT solutions from simple projects that you run for fun to full cloud-based solutions. Now it's time for you to engage your own imagination and put the tools and techniques you learned in this book toward building your own MicroPython IoT solutions.

In the next chapter, we will see how you can take what you've learned in this book further as you plan more MicroPython projects and join the growing community of MicroPython hobbyists and enthusiasts.

CHAPTER 16

Where to Go from Here

Now that you have had a thorough introduction to MicroPython, breakout boards and assorted electronics hardware, the Internet of Things, and the types of projects you can create and tutorials as well as examples, it is time to consider what you can do beyond the pages of this book.

In this chapter, we will explore what you can do to continue your craft of building IoT solutions. Most people will want to simply continue to develop projects for themselves either for fun or to solve problems around the home or office. However, some will want to take their skills to the next level.

Whichever the case, there are a few things that you should consider. In the following sections, we will look at sources for more example projects, how to join the community of IoT enthusiasts through social media and other Internet resources, and finally how to become a contributing member of the growing throng of makers.

More Projects to Explore

If you want to work on more MicroPython IoT projects, you will be happy to learn that there are many examples that you can explore. Most of the examples are either in the various documentation sites or are contributions from the community, ranging from a high-level overview to detailed instructions on how to complete the project. Sadly, most of the examples are presented with little or no instruction. However, now that you have had detailed instructions[1] on working with MicroPython IoT projects and the various MicroPython boards, you should be able to complete the examples with little or no documentation (but documentation always helps).

There are several repositories for MicroPython IoT example projects. Most are either in forums dedicated to MicroPython or the MicroPython board (e.g., the Raspberry

---

[1] This is one of my major motivations for writing this book.

© Charles Bell 2024
C. Bell, *MicroPython for the Internet of Things*, https://doi.org/10.1007/978-1-4842-9861-9_16

Pi Pico), but there is also a cool site named Hackster.io, which is a general hardware community forum (`www.hackster.io`). We will see how to navigate that site in a moment. First, let's look at a couple of resources for MicroPython sample projects.

MicroPython Project Samples

There are several websites that host MicroPython examples. There are three basic types of websites: forums that have categories where people can post their projects, documentation sites that have example projects, and repositories where people can upload their projects. Let's look at each of these.

Tip   The best way to find MicroPython examples is to google for "MicroPython Example" or "MicroPython Sample." You'll find lots of hits including those resources listed in this chapter.

Forums

The first type, forums, offers a list of categories ranging from announcements, questions and answers, frequently asked questions, technical support, and more. Fortunately, several also have a category for projects. Sometimes, the category includes many entries (topics) with most being questions about how to implement a certain project. The MicroPython forum has such a category (`https://forum.micropython.org/viewforum.php?f=5`). And while there are over 100 topics and most are questions, there are a few gems in there you can explore.

Using a forum to find example projects or samples can take a little work because they are intended to be used by a community and thus contain a lot of questions and commentary, but I feel they are still one of the best resources. However, keep in mind they are intended for a specific board. The best way to use them is to navigate to the forum and either scroll through the topics or search for a key phrase.

Documentation

The MicroPython documentation is also a good resource for finding example code (but not entire projects). They're typically better than the forums because they are much better organized and sometimes better written. However, like the forums, the MicroPython documentation sites, especially the samples, are hardware specific.

However, there are some example projects buried in the documentation. Unfortunately, some are not as well documented or may be partially documented. Regardless, the code in these samples is generally far superior to what you may find in the forums (generally).

The best way to use the documentation sites is to simply navigate to them and browse through the table of contents (that alone makes them better than forums). For example, Figure 16-1 shows an example project from the Arduino Nano RP2040 Connect MicroPython documentation for using the BLE feature (`https://docs.arduino.cc/tutorials/nano-rp2040-connect/rp2040-python-api#bluetooth-low-energy`).

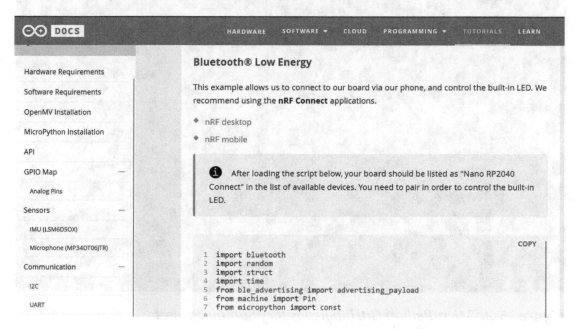

Figure 16-1. *BLE Sample MicroPython Project (Courtesy of arduino.cc)*

Repositories

The best websites for MicroPython projects are repositories. These are typically hosted in a source control service such as GitHub. What makes these sites most useful is that you can navigate directly to the source files and see the code in your browser, skipping the documentation or demonstration page. This makes it nice if you just want to see how to implement some feature rather than walk through a long page of text. Of course, the best way to use the samples is to download the entire set of samples. Simply visit the GitHub main site and download the sample projects. How cool is that?

The main MicroPython site (`https://github.com/micropython/micropython`) is one of the best examples of MicroPython sample project repositories. This repository has a lot of samples, and while some are geared to a specific MicroPython board, you can use them as templates for how to write code for a wide variety of projects. Just be sure to research whether the hardware used is compatible with your board. Figure 16-2 shows an excerpt of the repository example page.

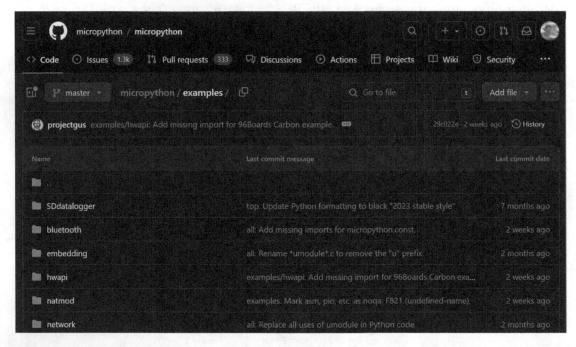

Figure 16-2. *MicroPython GitHub Repository Sample Projects*

Most (if not all – I haven't checked all) of the samples are licensed under an open source license such as the MIT license, which makes it very convenient for everyone since the MIT license permits you to use and even publish the code. (See `https://opensource.org/licenses/MIT` for a sample of the MIT license.) This is great because I have many times wanted to use a sample or demonstration of a project, only to discover the license doesn't permit it.

Community Project Sites: Hackster.io

The Hackster site is a community dedicated to learning hardware. You can find all manner of hardware sample projects, including many of those for MicroPython, Python, Raspberry Pi, Arduino, and more! There is a small but growing list of MicroPython projects. When you visit the parent site (`www.hackster.io`), you can search for projects by typing "MicroPython" in the search box. Once you enter the search criteria, the search results page, you see all the projects you can explore. Each is marked with a relative level of difficultly, ranging from easy to advanced. You also see a count of the number of times the sample project was viewed and the number of thumbs-up ratings the project received from others in the community (you must join Hackster.io to rate a project). Best of all, there is a comment section that you can use to encourage the designer or ask the designer for help with the project.

Tip   Use the golden rule when posting comments or questions in online forums. Resist the temptation to post opinions, fan the flames of dissent or ridicule, and stick only to the facts.

What I like most about the Hackster site is that the samples are generally well documented and often include several photos of the project. Due to the unique structure of the site, the samples are organized in parts that make it easy to follow. For example, the web page for "Character LCD over I2C" (`www.hackster.io/dzerycz/character-lcd-over-i2c-ba8ee9`) contains an overview section that presents a short description of the project, associated tags, difficulty rating, publication date, and even the license. This makes reviewing the project very easy.

For example, there is an excellent example of an intermediate-level project that is not only well documented but also well written. It is the "MicroPython Leak Detector with Adafruit and Home Assistant" by Robin Cole. Figure 16-3 shows an excerpt from the project overview. If you want to see another excellent project, visit `www.hackster.io/robin-cole/micropython-leak-detector-with-adafruit-and-home-assistant-a2fa9e`.

Robin Cole
Published April 17, 2017 © GPL3+

MicroPython Leak Detector with Adafruit and Home Assistant

Detect water leaks using a MicroPython sensor node and receive mobile notifications via Home Assistant.

⟨ Intermediate   📄 Full instructions provided   ⏱ 1 hour   👁 7,664

Figure 16-3. Hackster.io Sample Project

If you scroll down from the overview, you find sections that demonstrate how to connect the hardware (like how I introduce the projects in this book), a short walk-through of the code, and descriptions and demonstrations on how to use the project.

Some samples include short videos to demonstrate or explain the project. At the end of the page, you find the comment section, which you can use to read what others have said about the project, as well as the questions that others have had regarding the project. If you get stuck on a sample, be sure to read all the comments – there is a good chance that someone has already asked the question or solved the problem.

WHAT ABOUT HACKADAY.IO?

Another site that is like Hackster.io that is gaining a folvlowing is Hackaday.io. It is very like the Hackster.io site in that you can search for MicroPython projects. However, I don't like it as much as Hackster.io, but don't let that stop you from exploring it – try it!

Knowledge Repositories: learn.adafruit.com

Another excellent source of information about MicroPython is learn.adafruit.com. This site contains articles, blogs, and tutorials on a wide range of topics. Much like the user forums, content is added to this site frequently. So, you should visit the site periodically and search for your topic. For example, to find the MicroPython content, simply search for MicroPython. Or you can use this link: `https://learn.adafruit.com/search?q=micropython`.

Figure 16-4 shows an excerpt from `learn.adafruit.com` showing some of the interesting content for MicroPython. Be sure to check the site for recent additions.

Figure 16-4. *MicroPython Content on learn.adafruit.com*

Notice there are a lot of different categories you can explore. Feel free to explore these categories to see the wide coverage this site offers. I've often used this site to find ideas for projects. Even if the article, blog, or tutorial isn't exactly what you want or it may not match your hardware, it is often worth reading for tips. For example, if you're planning to build a project using a Charlieplex LED (`www.adafruit.com/?q=charlie`), you can find a tutorial at `https://learn.adafruit.com/micropython-hardware-charlieplex-led-matrix/software?view=all`.

While this tutorial features the Feather and ESP8266 board, you can still learn quite a bit about using the Charlieplex LED including a driver (that you can modify), hints, and insights in how to make it work with other MicroPython boards.

Now that you have seen a couple of resources for more sample projects, let's discuss how you can join the community and contribute to the growing repository of all things MicroPython for the IoT.

Join the Community

Once you have mastered the sample projects in this book as well as a few from other resources, it is time to take your hobby a bit further by joining the community of IoT developers and enthusiasts.

In this section, I discuss some of the reasons you may want to share your knowledge, etiquette for sharing and contributing, and a few example communities you may want to join or at least monitor. As you will see, most are not devoted to MicroPython, but can be an excellent source for ideas. Let's begin with why we would want to share.

Why Contribute?

As more and more free thinkers drive hobbies like MicroPython and the IoT, the more prevalent the concept of sharing becomes. This is no accident. Many of the founders and pioneers of the Python, MicroPython, and IoT are open hardware and open source advocates. This applies not only to hardware and software, but it also applies to other intellectual products such as the source code and documentation for published projects.

Many feel their code should be free for anyone to use and modify with reciprocal expectations. For example, if you modify someone else's design or code, you should share not only the improved design but also credit the originator. In some cases, this is as simple as listing the original author, but other times it may mean giving the original author your modifications. So long as you follow the guidelines of the license, all is fair and well in sharing.

However, depending on how the sample code was written (licensed), there may be some limitation to what can be shared. For example, it may not be possible to share code from a proprietary library. While you may be the creator of the code that uses the library, you do not own the library and cannot share it. You most likely can share your code with others, but publication may be restricted.

Sharing your projects also means placing them someplace where others can find them. You may want to make them freely available to anyone, or you may want to limit what people can do with your project. Fortunately, there are websites that can handle things quite well.

So, why contribute your project? There are many reasons including the fact that it can be a good feeling to see one of your projects being liked, used, and made by others. Perhaps the most important reason for contributing is to help others learn what you have or, better, learn how to avoid pitfalls or problems. In this way, we all benefit by learning best practices or simply better ways to implement our ideas. Finally, your own project and experiences, when shared, will inspire others to create other projects or perhaps improve yours.

I've had this happen with my own projects. People have taken what I have made and improved it. Since they, in turn, shared their project, I could incorporate a lot of their improvements in my projects, making them even better than I envisioned.

Which License, Where?

So, how do you know which license is in play? Every website that hosts any form of source code, documentation, examples, etc., will have a clearly marked license. It may appear on the screen at the bottom or some other discrete location or even only on a special page marked "license" or similar label.

For example, the license on the micropython.org website is located under the heading "Completely free, open source software" and cites the MIT license for the MicroPython core and paraphrases that license as follows:

> *You can freely use and adapt MicroPython for personal use, in education, and in commercial products.*

Similarly, the github.com website has a section for specifying the license whenever someone uploads a project. Figure 16-5 shows an example of a typical license you will find, GNU Public License version 3 (GPLv3), which can be found at `https://opensource.org/license/gpl-3-0/`. Most projects provide either a file that contains the license or a link that you can click to read the license. Fortunately, most projects on Hackster.io and other sites are open source, and you should be safe to use them in your projects (but check anyway).

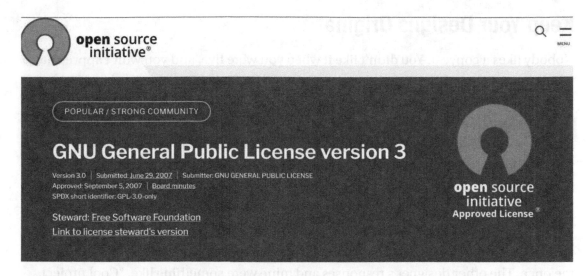

Figure 16-5. *Example License: GPLv3*

Tip   Always check the license of any example you use before you publish it to ensure you are conforming to not only the originator's wishes but also the legal restrictions of the license assigned.

Now, let's focus on how to go about sharing your projects.

How We Share

You may be wondering why anyone would want to give something they have worked on for hours away for free. While it is true that the expectation is that you should share your cool projects with others, it isn't a hard and fast rule. In fact, there are some who have made their projects available for a fee as a precursor to selling the IoT solution in a commercial avenue. However, the clear majority of enthusiasts share their ideas and projects for free.

There are several communities where you can share your projects, and we will see some of these in the next section. But first, there are some things you must understand about sharing objects. Believe it or not, there is a set of rules – some written, some not – that you are expected to follow should you decide to embrace the community of the IoT or any similar community. The following lists some guidelines (rules) you would do well to heed when sharing your ideas, projects, and commentary with the community.

Keep Your Designs Original

Nobody likes a copycat. You didn't like it when you were five, and you won't appreciate it when you see something you designed and shared for free being presented as "design of the month" credited to someone else.

Thus, you must do your homework to make sure your design is unique. You don't have to purposefully alter your design so that it doesn't resemble someone else's, but you should do due diligence and at least search for similar projects. Remember, it is OK if you develop a similar project, but it generally is bad form (or perhaps a violation of the license) to simply reproduce something someone else has published.

In the rare case when it so happens your project is nearly identical to another, so long as your work is your own, there shouldn't be a problem. In fact, this happened to me once. The other designer's responses and mine were something like, "Cool project. Like minds, eh?" Once again, there is nothing wrong with that, provided you both acknowledge the resemblance and there are no licensing issues.

If the other project like yours is truly the same design but was licensed differently, you may have to negotiate with the other designer. This can happen when projects are licensed for ownership (e.g., commercial property), but it is rare given most IoT sample repositories are sites where people share their projects for free.

Let's look at another, non-source code example. What is the likelihood that a dozen different cases for a Raspberry Pi will be similar in size, have the same openings for ports, and perhaps even assemble the same way (snap together)? Very likely, yes? Does this mean there is one original and 11 copies? No, certainly not. This is not what I am talking about.

What I mean by unique is of those 12 cases, you should be able to identify some differences among them – be that how they print (e.g., orientation on the build platform), if they are made from several parts, whether they have designed with ventilation, etc. Even if all 12 designers started at the same time, there would be some minor differences. More importantly, each is its own work. That is, no one used the design of another to pass off as their own.

In the case of a software project, the source code is most likely going to be a little different from the examples. While how much difference qualifies source code to be deemed different is something for lawyers to sort out, suffice to say if your code and another's are nearly identical, but created without knowledge of the other, it is OK to share your code provided there are no licensing conflicts.

Finally, when you share your project that is based on the work of another, you must annotate your code, documentation, and project website, giving credit to the original designer. That is, you state unequivocally that your project is a derivation of the original. It is also good form to include a link to the original design along with a list of your modifications. Once again, this assumes the license permits it.

Check the License

I have mentioned licensing under the aspect of downloading and using sample projects. Recall that most repositories will require you to specify a license for your project. This permits the repository to host your project and communicate to everyone what your intentions are regarding ownership, permissions to use, etc.

As I stated previously, you need to check the license before using any design. If you plan to modify it, you need to pay close attention to the license. The clear majority of licenses will allow you to use the design, and most will allow you to modify it.

However, where some licenses differ concerns the ownership of the modifications. Some open source licenses, like GPL, permit modifications but require you to surrender those modifications to the original owner (the person or organization that created and licensed it) if you plan to distribute those changes. That is, you can modify it at will for personal use, but once you distribute those changes, you must give them to the owner of the license.

I have only run into this a couple of times, but in those cases, the designer was prototyping designs for a commercial product. The license and indeed the text of the project made it clear they were looking for help with the design but that the design would not be made public. Watch out for this and tread lightly. Any work you do could be for the benefit of the owner and not yours to keep or profit.

Tip   When in doubt about a license, contact the originator and ask them directly.

Since most sample IoT projects are licensed for sharing and free modification, you normally don't have to worry too much. However, I recommend you check the license before using any project, especially if you intend to share or publish your derivation.

Keep It Appropriate

Believe it or not, there are hobbyists and enthusiasts with impressively vivid imaginations who have come up with IoT projects that some may consider inappropriate or even obscene. No matter what your own views are, you should strive to tolerate the views of others. That doesn't mean you must compromise your own views; just be aware yours may offend and strive to minimize the offense.

More specifically, don't upload projects with inappropriate themes to sites that are viewable by everyone. It's (maybe) fine to upload some project that promotes a theme, ideal, etc. (provided there are no copyright violations); just don't upload projects or commentary that are clearly offensive or intended to cause harm.

For example, if you consider the fact that IoT projects are being used in schools to teach children the technology and techniques of working with hardware and designing software, you shouldn't upload projects with themes that parents may deem as inappropriate. The most obvious of course are offensive language, adult themes, and slanderous images.

You should check the usage and user agreement for the site that hosts your chosen repository as part of the post-no-post decision. Make sure you read the section about what is and is not appropriate and adhere to that.

There is another angle to consider. You should avoid uploading sample projects that are or could potentially be illegal or unlawful. This may be difficult to discern considering the IoT community includes the entire globe. However, most sites will have language to suggest what is and is not permitted. And some have language in the agreement that gives them (the site) the right to remove things they deem inappropriate.

For example, I once saw a project for a radio frequency identification (RFID) reader that could be used to read RFIDs from a distance. This sounds harmless, but consider the number of things that use RFID such as security badges, identification, and even credit cards. Clearly, reading RFID from things you own is fine (indeed, that's what the project demonstrated), but the project could be (and most likely has been) used for evil. Fortunately, others noticed this, and the project site has been removed (URL results in a 401 error).

So, before you upload a design or sample project, make sure you understand and agree to the terms of the user agreement as to what is and is not appropriate. Most times, a misunderstanding is not something that will get you into trouble, but if you do it more than once, chances are someone at the site will want to speak with you or restrict your access, which brings me back to the opening of this section – be sure to respect the views of others and especially the intended audience of the site. If you disagree, find another site.

Annotate Your Work

One of the ways I can tell if a sample IoT project is good or of high quality is how it is annotated and documented, that is, how well the designer described the project on its site. If I encounter a project that looks appealing only to discover the designer didn't bother to describe how to connect the hardware or explain the code with more than seven words (or less), didn't provide any instructions, or worse didn't present any photos of the actual implementation, I won't use it.

Thus, you should strive to provide as full a description as possible. You don't have to write a novel, novella, or a dissertation, but you should provide enough information to describe the intended use, what problem it solves, as well as a set of instructions for how to write the source code, compile, and deploy it.

The only exception is a case where you are still working on a project, or you plan to make changes before finalizing it. In this case, you should mark (annotate) the project with some verbiage about a work in progress, being experimental, etc. If your repository has a feature to mark the project as such, use that. This way, others will know your project isn't quite ready for general adoption. One reason for doing this may be to get feedback from others. I've done this myself with mixed results. Mostly people are happy to comment that they like it, but don't comment, or if they do, however encouraging, don't suggest any changes or improvements.

I would also suggest you provide some level of contact information so that others who have questions can contact you. Most sites make it easy for viewers to contact you through the site, but you may want to provide other forms of contact (e.g., email). You may not want to provide your home address and phone number (don't do that), but an email address is a nice way to make yourself open to the community.

For example, I have seen blogs, sample projects, and even tutorials where people have posted their IRC handle, email address, and even in one case their business phone number. While I may not go quite that far, I suggest providing an email address so that you can communicate with people who like the project. Plus, it's nice to connect 1:1 with someone to discuss your work!

Be a Good Citizen

Suppose you run across a sample project that not only isn't high quality but is also (in your opinion) designed or implemented incorrectly. Should you immediately comment and crush the designer's ego with a flippant remark about how dumb their code is? No, certainly not!

What I would do (most likely) is ignore the project altogether. I mean, why make things worse by pointing out the defects? I have found the community at large (there are some exceptions) will likely do the same and not comment. Recall one of the keys to determining whether a project is well designed (good) is how many people use it. Typically, there is a counter you can check for this. If no one has liked it or even downloaded it, you can be sure it won't make it to the top of any search lists or sample project of the month.

On the other hand, if you feel compelled to comment, be sure to either contact the designer privately or be as constructive as you possibly can. The goal should be to help the designer improve their projects, not challenge their intellect (or pride).

When I do comment on projects that I find strange and perhaps flawed (and it is rare), I generally phrase my comments in the form of a question. A question normally doesn't put someone on the defensive and if worded properly should also not offend.

For example, I may ask, "Have you found the code may hang if the user presses the button more than once?" This is a nice way of asking if the designer has tested their project under the conditions you expect it to fail. This is good, constructive criticism in a most intellectual form. I am certain if you think about what you are about to say, you can find other and perhaps more elegant ways of helping people improve their projects.

Now that we've seen why we share and how to share in a responsible manner, let's discover some of the communities you may want to join or at least monitor.

Suggested Communities

There are quite a few general Python and MicroPython websites and online communities you can visit and even join. Most online communities have repositories that you can search for examples, tips, techniques, and even complete projects that you can explore. Most also have one or more areas where members can comment, ask questions, or generally communicate with others on the forum. You typically must join to be able to post a reply or ask a question, but viewing is typically permitted by anyone.

The best way to use these resources is to visit them periodically. More specifically, you should read the articles (that interest you) and forum posts regularly. This allows you to keep up to date on current events, new techniques, and even new solutions to challenging problems.

For example, I try to connect to the Raspberry Pi sites to keep tabs on what is going on there. I can often get ideas for IoT projects or simply ideas for features by seeing projects implemented for the Raspberry Pi and its native operating system. I find it is often the case that while the source code can be quite different, most of the hardware (connections, etc.) apply without modification, which makes sense since the hardware is not tied to the operating system running on the device (but the libraries that drive the hardware does).

Also, don't discount the power of a keyword search using your favorite online search tool. I have often found obscure gems of information that aren't posted on the more popular sites. In most cases, they are well-written blogs. I often start with a keyword search before I visit the sites listed earlier. If nothing else, it confirms whether what I am researching is unique or ubiquitous. You should also consider using key phrases from error messages as search terms to get help for specific errors.

There are also a few excellent periodicals that you should consider obtaining. I exclude the typical Windows, PC, and general programming periodicals not because they aren't helpful but because they are far too general for IoT-related research. Rather, the following are periodicals that I've found to be very helpful in my IoT research or any electronics or hobby project:

- *The MagPi Magazine*: A monthly magazine devoted to all things Raspberry Pi. It includes many articles on sample projects, news about the Raspberry Pi, peripherals, and general hardware reviews (`raspberrypi.org/magpi`).

- *Make:* A magazine devoted to the broad realm of the maker community presenting sample projects, tutorials, hardware, tools, drones, robots, and more! It truly is a one-stop periodical for all things hacking, tweaking, and general DIY hobbyist, enthusiast, and professional alike (`http://makezine.com/`).

Now that we've seen several online communities (but not in a complete list as more are being added seemingly weekly) as well as a couple of periodicals you can buy, let's discuss the next step you can take once you have become a productive contributing member of IoT and IoT-related online communities – becoming a maker.

Become a Maker

The next progression in your growth from novice to enthusiast (and even professional) is to practice your craft regularly and share your knowledge with the world. One excellent outlet for this desire is to become a maker. Makers are widely regarded as experts in their areas of interest. The best part is a maker's interests can vary greatly from one to another. That is, becoming a maker isn't about learning a specific set of techniques (academic or otherwise). It is about practicing a craft.

What's a Maker?

Sadly, there is no single definition of what a maker is or should be. This is because a maker is someone with highly creative skills who desires to tinker and work on projects that can range from mechanical sculptures that spit fire to electronic gizmos to new ways to recycle materials to build things on the cheap.

Indeed, a maker is simply an artisan, craftsman, hobbyist, or enthusiast who desires to create things – hence maker. Thus, there are many kinds of makers. However, what unites them is the willingness to share their techniques and skills with others. Thus, to truly become a maker, you must participate in the community of makers.

Share Your Ideas

You can become a maker and not contribute at all to the online communities, and while that's perfectly fine, if you want to help make the community stronger, you should become more involved. The best way to do this is to join one or more of the online forums and start contributing.

That doesn't mean you must start off by posting some fantastically cool and successful MicroPython or IoT project complete with award-winning documentation and bulletproof code that computer science professors will use someday to teach young minds to mimic your brilliance. Sure, you may scoff (or even laugh) at that, but I have encountered people who are afraid of posting anything lest they be wrong or ridiculed for inaccuracies. Don't worry about that – the best contributors are those that help you grow, and you grow by learning better techniques!

The best way to avoid that is to start out slow by first asking questions of your own. You can also start by throwing out a few positive comments for those ideas and projects you like. As you become more involved with the topics and techniques, your knowledge will expand to the point where you can start answering questions of others.

I encourage you to consider this level of involvement if you want to become more involved with MicroPython. I believe interacting with the community and gaining a reputation for being helpful and sharing ideas is one of the things that separates a hobbyist from an enthusiast.

Thus, if you want to become a maker, you should share your ideas with others.

Attend an Event

Another way you can become more involved with the maker community is to attend a Maker Faire (makerfaire.com/). These events are held all over the world. The events allow makers to showcase their creations, teach others, and generally celebrate all things maker. See the Maker Faire site for events in your area near you.

If you live in or near a larger city, you may find there are local user groups for Python, Raspberry Pi, MySQL, Arduino, and even maker user groups. Try searching for events and groups in your area and find out where and when they meet. Most groups have an open-door policy and invite one and all to attend their meetings. Some, however, do have dues for charter members, but this often comes with additional perks such as access to tools, labs, and discounts on bulk purchases.

You may be wondering how a maker event could possibly help you with MicroPython or IoT projects. I am happy to report there are a very strong attendance and many attendees who are interested in IoT and even Python! As we learned from other chapters in this book, a lot of what we can learn to do in Python transfers to MicroPython. The same is true with hardware and IoT. Sure, you may only see demonstrations of IoT projects using other boards like a Raspberry Pi or Arduino, but much of the hardware can be used in MicroPython. If nothing else, you will gain knowledge of what is possible, which you can leverage in your next project idea.

Once you have attended an event – even one that has nothing to do with MicroPython such as a Raspberry Pi meetup – you'll be hooked. You can learn quite a lot from others this way, and, who knows, perhaps one day you will be presenting at an event. Speaking from experience, it can be very satisfying sharing your knowledge with others in an open forum like a conference, user group, meetup, or Maker Faire. That's when you know you've obtained the reputation, skills, and knowledge that a typical maker possesses.

Tip Many users of the Raspberry Pi use Python in their projects. Don't hesitate to seek out a Raspberry Pi meetup as you can learn quite a lot from Raspberry Pi Python developers.

That doesn't mean that by the time you read this chapter, you're an expert at all things IoT or even profess to be an expert, but you should be well on your way all the same.

Summary

Taking your IoT skills to the next level is what most people will ultimately be inspired to achieve. However, even if you do not want to become a traveling maker teaching the world, you can learn quite a lot by simply joining the online communities that serve Python, IoT, and open hardware.

In this chapter, I have presented suggestions on how best to interact with online communities, where to look to join an online community, and even how to take your skills to the highest level of enthusiasm and become a maker. This chapter therefore rounds out our journey down the road of MicroPython for the IoT that I hope inspires you to continue practicing your skills and ultimately join the community of like-minded enthusiasts.

I sincerely hope that this book has opened many doors for you concerning Python, MicroPython, IoT, and anything open hardware. May your IoT projects all be successful, and if they aren't, may you learn something in the process. Just remember to share your experiences – good or bad – with the world and give back a little of what you can take from the efforts of others.

Index

A

© Charles Bell 2024
C. Bell, *MicroPython for the Internet of Things*, https://doi.org/10.1007/978-1-4842-9861-9

Printed in the United States
by Baker & Taylor Publisher Services